JOHN LEE

VANCOUVER
C I T Y   G U I D E

INTRODUCING VANCOUVER

Cameras at the ready for great sea-and-skyscraper city vistas

RYAN F

Cyclists zip around the seawall, glancing at snow-frosted peaks across the water. A floatplane buzzes overhead, shimmying toward its glassy landing strip. A chattery hubbub bounces off the mirrored towers that forest downtown like latter-day totems.

When the Olympic and Paralympic Winter Games took over Vancouver in early 2010, there was no shortage of jaw-dropping visuals to accompany global TV coverage. But for anyone living here, these glossy highlights are just the most obvious aspects of the city's charms. In fact, beyond the breathtaking setting lies a comparatively young metropolis that's still trying to discover its true identity – just 150 years after a 'gassy' Englishman kicked it all off with a makeshift pub.

Covering the main attractions will certainly give you an introduction. After that it's highly advisable to dig beneath the surface to find out what makes this laid-back lotusland tick. You'll uncover the 'real Vancouver' in the lively Commercial Dr coffee shops, the hipster haunts of South Main (SoMa), the gay-friendly streets of the West End, the kaleidoscopic thoroughfares of old Chinatown and the historic, reinvigorated Gastown district, where that original pub once stood.

With the Olympics now a distant memory – and the flag-waving multitudes dissolved from Vancouver's streets – there's never been a better time to come and explore this urban, nature-backed metropolis for yourself. Hit those highly individual neighborhoods for a different flavor on every day of your trip. And save plenty of time to jump into the waiting realm of outdoor attractions calling your name from the edge of the city.

CONTENTS

THE AUTHOR

John Lee

Originally from the near-London UK city of St Albans, John first checked out Canada during Vancouver's Expo '86 world's fair, a sunny summer of dancing girls, live music and levitating Japanese trains. Swayed by all this exotica, he returned home to plot a permanent move. While most BC colleges turned him down flat, the University of Victoria eventually allowed him to study utopian political theory, although it turned out to be not quite as vocational as an MBA. After teaching English in Japan and hopping on the Trans-Siberian Railway for a laugh, he suddenly jumped into a full-time travel-writing career. Moving permanently to Vancouver in 1999, John has since worked on 18 Lonely Planet books. His award-winning journalism, appearing online at www.johnleewriter.com, has also run in more than 150 publications around the world, including the *Guardian*, *Los Angeles Times*, *Chicago Tribune*, *Globe and Mail* and *National Geographic Traveler*.

JOHN'S TOP VANCOUVER DAY

Despite being a tea-dependent Brit, no day really gets rolling until a late-morning java, so I walk to the bustling patio café at the Vancouver Art Gallery (p56) and chat with a buddy over a large latte. Catching the number 10 bus nearby, I'm soon at Granville Island (p88), where I nose around the back-alley galleries before ducking into the cavernous Public Market. Lunch quickly becomes a wandering smorgasbord of deli treats as I snack from the bakeries and fruit stands – Okanagan cherries are in season. Feeling drowsy, I hop onboard a miniferry (p227) just outside the market and take a bobbling, sun-dappled cruise along False Creek to Science World (p78). But rather than heading inside the shiny geodesic dome, I jump on the nearby number 3 bus that's heading south up Main St. Within 20 minutes, I'm strolling the cool indie shops of SoMa (p119), picking up a hand-printed greeting card at the Regional Assembly of Text (p119). Checking my watch, I dash for the next bus and head back the way I came along Main, eventually rolling into the Gastown neighborhood for a long-arranged beer with some friends. We meet at the Alibi Room (p155), where the communal tables are already crowded with hipsters supping on the city's best menu of BC microbrews. I go for the taster selection of four beers, asking the smiling server to surprise me with what's on offer. As a dedicated imbiber, I can tell one of them is my favorite Old Yale Pale Ale. After a barbecued pork belly sandwich, it's time to call a taxi. A couple of us are taking in one of Vancouver's signature spectacles: a Shakespeare play performed on a tented stage at the annual Bard on the Beach festival (p178). It's the best way to spend any summer evening.

WHEN TO GO

Vancouver is an all-season city but specific times of year are best suited to certain interests and pursuits. If you're determined to brush up on your snow sports, December to March is the ideal time to strap on your skis. If you want to bask on the beaches and stroll in shorts through the forests, you should bring your sunscreen to town in July or August. And if you're an arts buff and you just can't wait to get your next culture fix, the theater season kicks off in October and usually stretches to April. Summer is the hot season for festivals – especially outdoor ones – but the city stages large and small events throughout the year.

You can expect pleasant temperatures most of the time. In winter, it rarely drops below 0°C in the city and summer sees long, languid days with 20°C a common marker. It can rain here at any time, but the October to February period is the rainiest – remember that when it's raining here, it's often snowing in the hills. Peak season for hotels is midsummer, but there's good weather in late spring and early fall, and these near-shoulder periods can offer great deals for budget-minded travelers.

FESTIVALS & EVENTS

While summer remains the peak time for several of Vancouver's biggest festivals, the city has a year-round roster of events that should give most visitors a couple of options whatever time of year they roll in. Tourism Vancouver's website (www.tourismvancouver.com) gives you a heads-up on many happenings, but check free listings newspapers like the *Georgia Straight* and *Westender* for up-to-date info on smaller events around the city.

January

POLAR BEAR SWIM   Jan 1
www.vancouver.ca/parks/events/polarbear
This chilly New Year's Day affair has been taking place annually in English Bay since 1920, and it might just be the ultimate cure for a hangover. At around 2.30pm more than a thousand people charge into

the ocean…and most usually leap out shivering a few seconds later.

DINE OUT VANCOUVER   2nd week of Jan
www.tourismvancouver.com
The city's top restaurants offer two weeks of three-course tasting menus for $18, $28 or $38, plus a selection of British Columbia wines. Check the list of participating restaurants on Tourism Vancouver's website and book ahead – top spots always sell out. See the boxed text on p138 for other local food fests.

PUSH INTERNATIONAL PERFORMING ARTS FESTIVAL   3rd week of Jan
www.pushfestival.ca
A three-week season of innovative new theater, music, opera and dance from around the world or around the corner. Adventurous performance-art fans will love this unusual showcase, staged at venues around the city.

February
CHINESE NEW YEAR
www.vancouver-chinatown.com
Depending on the calendar, this multiday celebration in and around Chinatown can take place in January or February, but it always includes plenty of color, dancing and great food. The highlights are the Dragon Parade and firecrackers.

WINTERRUPTION   3rd week of Feb
www.winterruption.com
Granville Island chases away the winter blues with a warming roster of live music,

top picks

QUIRKY FESTIVALS

- Bare Buns Fun Run (p15)
- Polar Bear Swim (left)
- Vancouver Craft Beer Week (opposite)
- Eastside Culture Crawl (p16)
- Parade of the Lost Souls (p16)

theater and family-friendly events. Dress warmly – many of the events are outside, you'll enjoy the hot chocolate more.

March

VANCOUVER INTERNATIONAL DANCE FESTIVAL
2nd week of Mar

www.vidf.ca

Local, national and international contemporary artists come together for this calf-stretching spree of workshops and performances, showcasing the city's credentials as a major dance center.

CELTICFEST VANCOUVER
3rd week of Mar

www.celticfestvancouver.com

Downtown's annual St Patrick's Day parade and multi day Irish cultural fiesta attracts those who like their beer to be green-hued at least once a year. Expect some shamrock-tinged shenanigans and a chance to mix with local and visiting Irish folk.

VANCOUVER PLAYHOUSE INTERNATIONAL WINE FESTIVAL
4th week of Mar

www.playhousewinefest.com

The city's fave excuse for a drink – and one of North America's oldest wine fests – the week-long schedule includes tastings, seminars and galas. Book ahead, since many events quickly sell out. The core of the festival is the giant tasting room at Canada Place.

April

VANCOUVER FASHION WEEK
early Apr

www.vancouverfashionweek.com

If you feel like hitting the catwalk – or at least watching others do so – check out this annual event. A series of shows, galas and educational events highlighting the work of regional and international designers, it's the top draw of the West Coast industry calendar.

SUN RUN
4th week of Apr

www.sunrun.com

One of North America's largest street races lures 50,000 runners, speed walkers and wheezing wannabes for a spirited spring jaunt around the city. There's a family-friendly atmosphere as the route twists via Stanley Park, the waterfront and Burrard

Bridge to BC Place Stadium, where you can collapse with a big smile on your face. See the boxed text on p186 for more information.

May

VANCOUVER INTERNATIONAL MARATHON
1st week of May

www.bmovanmarathon.ca

Smaller than the Sun Run (left), this one's for serious hoofers. Strap on your running shoes and race through the streets, along with hundreds of local fitness fans and athletes from around the world.

VANCOUVER CRAFT BEER WEEK
1st week of May

www.vancouvercraftbeerweek.com

Reflecting a frothy surge in regional microbrewing, this popular event lures beer-loving locals to tastings, pairing dinners and tipple-fueled gatherings across the city. Expect to rub shoulders with brew-meisters from the likes of Driftwood Brewing, Salt Spring Brewing, Yaletown Brewing and dozens more.

VANCOUVER INTERNATIONAL CHILDREN'S FESTIVAL
3rd week of May

www.childrensfestival.ca

Bristling with kid-friendly storytelling, performances and activities in a charming tented Vanier Park site, this eight-day Kitsilano event is highly popular. Expect to be lured by face-painters or balloon-twisters while your kids run riot, giddy with ice-cream-smeared excitement.

June

PORTUGUESE HERITAGE MONTH
Jun

www.portuguesemonth.com

This showcase of all things Portuguese brings the local expat community together for a month-long roster of cultural happenings, including film, theater, dance, sport and culinary celebrations. Staged at venues around the city and in the surrounding suburbs.

BARD ON THE BEACH
1st week of Jun

www.bardonthebeach.org

Shakespeare performed the way it should be: in striped tents with the North Shore mountains peeking peacefully from behind the stage. A local legend for more than two decades, the four-show roster runs to late September. See p178 for details and book ahead.

VANCOUVER INTERNATIONAL STORYTELLING FESTIVAL 2nd week of Jun
www.vancouverstorytelling.org
A three-day celebration of the art of storytelling, usually with a different theme each year – expect creative workshops and public readings. An ideal way to meet local writerly types, check its website for additional events including monthly story-swaps.

CAR-FREE VANCOUVER DAY 3rd week of Jun
www.carfreevancouver.org
An increasingly popular day-long event where the main streets of several neighborhoods – in Kitsilano, Commercial Dr, the West End, Main St and North Vancouver – close to traffic and surrender to music, vendors, performers and food. Family-friendly, it's a great way to pretend you're a local.

DRAGON BOAT FESTIVAL 3rd week of Jun
www.dragonboatbc.ca
An epic weekend splashathon for around 180 teams from Metro Vancouver and beyond, this colorful event churns the normally placid waters of False Creek. Around 100,000 landlubbers turn up (for free) to cheer them on from the banks…and partake of the accompanying mini-festival of music, theater and food.

FESTIVAL D'ÉTÉ FRANCOPHONE DE VANCOUVER 3rd week of Jun
www.lecentreculturel.com
Connect with your inner Francophone at this multiday celebration of music and performance from French Canada and around the world. There are performances at venues throughout the city, plus a weekend outdoor show on Granville Island.

GREEK DAY 4th week of Jun
www.greekday.com
The local Hellenic community comes together for this rip-roaring showcase of

top picks

COMMUNITY FESTIVALS

- Powell Street Festival (opposite)
- Chinatown Festival (opposite)
- Greek Day (left)
- Portuguese Heritage Month (p13)
- Caribbean Days Festival (opposite)

Greek culture. The one-day Kitsilano event (on W Broadway, between MacDonald and Blenheim Sts) features two performance stages, wandering street entertainers and a belt-challenging array of great food.

VANCOUVER INTERNATIONAL JAZZ FESTIVAL 4th week of Jun
www.coastaljazz.com
Now more than 25 years old, this giant, nine-day music party is second only to Montréal in the gargantuan jazz fest stakes. It combines superstar performances (Oscar Peterson and Diana Krall are past masters) with smile-triggering free outdoor shows in Gastown and Yaletown, and on Granville Island.

July

CANADA DAY CELEBRATIONS Jul 1
www.canadaday.canadaplace.ca
Canada Place is the main location for celebrations marking the country's July 1 birthday. Expect music, food and fireworks from 10am onwards, plus an early-evening street parade along W Georgia St. Maple-leaf face painting and impromptu renditions of 'O Canada' are the order of the day. There's also a smaller Granville Island event.

DANCING ON THE EDGE 2nd week of Jul
www.dancingontheedge.org
Top companies and performers from across Canada gather for 10 days of world-leading contemporary dance at venues around the city. Expect some challenging but expertly executed performances. Wear your leotard and they might let you join in (or maybe not).

VANCOUVER FOLK MUSIC FESTIVAL
2nd week of Jul

www.thefestival.bc.ca

Kitsilano's Jericho Beach is the venue for this sunny, weekend-long festival of alfresco shows, covering folk, world music and beyond. Wear your sun block and join the 30,000 hippies and hipsters at one of Vancouver's oldest and most popular live music events.

CARIBBEAN DAYS FESTIVAL
3rd week of Jul

www.caribbeandaysfestival.com

Great music, dancing and food highlight these two days of fun held at Waterfront Park near Lonsdale Quay in North Vancouver. One of the North Shore's most popular community events, it draws around 15,000 party-loving locals.

EARLY MUSIC FESTIVAL
3rd week of Jul

www.earlymusic.bc.ca

This celebration of medieval to baroque music stretches intermittently over three weeks, as lute and harpsichord players roll into town to celebrate some of the world's most beautiful but lesser-known compositions. Expect plenty of chin-stroking musos listening intently to highly authentic performances, mostly held at the University of British Columbia (UBC).

POWELL STREET FESTIVAL
4th week of Jul

www.powellstreetfestival.com

This annual celebration of Japanese Canadian culture is one of the city's most popular and enduring community festivals. Staged in East Vancouver's Oppenheimer Park, it's a fascinating and colorful day of food, music, dance and theater.

CELEBRATION OF LIGHT
4th week of Jul

www.celebration-of-light.com

One of the world's largest musical fireworks competitions takes place in English Bay over four nights in late July and early August. Three competing countries (which change each year) put on their most spectacular displays, then come together for a dazzling finale on the fourth night, when the winning country – chosen by popular vote – is announced. Funding has been an issue in previous years, so check ahead to make sure it's still on.

August

PRIDE WEEK
1st week of Aug

www.vancouverpride.ca

A week-long kaleidoscope of gay-, lesbian- and bisexual-friendly fashion shows, gala parties and concerts culminating in western Canada's largest pride parade. Typically held on the first Sunday of August, this saucy mardi gras–style street party draws up to 500,000 people to its West End route: expect bands, disco-beat floats and plenty of gyrating, scantily-clad locals.

ABBOTSFORD INTERNATIONAL AIR SHOW
2nd week of Aug

www.abbotsfordairshow.com

You'll need a car to get to this three-day event – Abbotsford is 56km southeast of the city – but it will be worth it for what has become 'Canada's national air show.' The displays from world-leading aeronautical teams are thrilling and, if you're in Vancouver during the event, you'll likely see the Canadian Snowbirds noisily buzzing over the city before flying on to their show.

CHINATOWN FESTIVAL
2nd week of Aug

www.vancouver-chinatown.com

Celebrating the color, traditions and modern-day vibrancy of one of North America's oldest and largest Chinatown communities, this weekend event takes over Keefer and Columbia Sts with performances, hawker stalls, great food and lots of family-friendly fun.

MUSICFEST VANCOUVER
2nd week of Aug

www.musicfestvancouver.com

Formerly Festival Vancouver, this 10-day grab bag of live music covers every genre, often including orchestral, choral, operatic, jazz, world and chamber music. Venues vary but there's usually a free outdoor stage on the W Georgia St side of the Vancouver Art Gallery.

BARE BUNS FUN RUN
2nd week of Aug

www.wreckbeach.org

The clothing-free Buns Run takes place – where else? – on Wreck Beach. Among the prizes are those for 'best-decorated buns' and 'wackiest hat.' Apply lots of sunscreen to those hard-to-reach areas and check the website for further pants-free frolics throughout the year.

PACIFIC NATIONAL EXHIBITION
3rd week of Aug

www.pne.bc.ca
This smashing country fair has evolved way beyond its original 1910 farm focus. Locals now come every year for music shows, family-friendly performers (check out those Superdogs), retail halls of oddball products (its ShamWow time!) and an artery-clogging menu of food stands: miss the mini-donuts at your peril. Don't forget the fairground, with its kick-ass wooden rollercoaster.

September

DAVIE DAY
2nd week of Sep

www.westendbia.com
The West End community along Davie St, between Broughton and Burrard Sts, invites the city (and visitors) to drop by for a day of live music, food and fun. This is the center of the city's gay community, so you might notice a few drag queens teetering past.

VANCOUVER INTERNATIONAL FRINGE FESTIVAL
2nd week of Sep

www.vancouverfringe.com
One of the city's biggest arts events, this lively 11-day roster of wild and wacky theatrics draws thousands to large, small and unconventional Granville Island venues. Expect short plays, stand-up routines and satiric comedy revues from local, regional and international performers. The shows usually cost around the $10 mark, so you can afford to be adventurous.

VANCOUVER COMEDY FEST
3rd week of Sep

www.vancouvercomedyfest.com
Ten days of rib-tickling mirth, with Canadian and international acts raising the roof at various venues around town. Improv events feature heavily but there are tons of stand-up comedians doing their thing, too. Book ahead for headline acts, which have previously included Steve Martin and Flight of the Conchords.

VANCOUVER INTERNATIONAL FILM FESTIVAL
4th week of Sep

www.viff.org
Lacking the star-studded glamour of its Toronto rival, this giant, highly popular film fest celebrates smaller, artsy movies. Its 17-day roster covers hundreds of screenings of local, national and international films, plus gala events and industry schmoozes. Book ahead. For other local film fests, see the boxed text on p175.

October

VANCOUVER INTERNATIONAL WRITERS AND READERS FESTIVAL
3rd week of Oct

www.writersfest.bc.ca
Despite the mouthful of a name – with all those writers around, can't they think of something catchier? – this five-day literary event is highly popular. Local and international scribblers turn up for seminars, galas and public forums; past guests have included Salman Rushdie, Irvine Welsh and Douglas Coupland. It's held at venues around Granville Island.

NEW MUSIC FESTIVAL
3rd week of Oct

www.newmusic.org
Staged at downtown's Dance Centre, this fascinating four-night event showcases a highly eclectic array of contemporary, often challenging music performances that can range from indie guitar and free jazz to hip-hop and jungle mash-ups. There are workshops for visiting muso types and several pre-show artist chats.

PARADE OF THE LOST SOULS
4th week of Oct

www.publicdreams.org
A spectral Day of the Dead celebration in which a torch-lit procession of spookily dressed performers moves through the streets around Grandview Park, on Commercial Dr. Highly atmospheric, it's a Vancouver Halloween tradition with artsy locals making their own festively macabre torches.

November

EASTSIDE CULTURE CRAWL
4th week of Nov

www.eastsideculturecrawl.com

Dozens of local artists from Vancouver's Eastside open their studios to visitors at this excellent and ever-growing three-day showcase. Expect to come across a wild and wacky array of works, from found art installations to woodblock portraits of iconic Canadians. Perfect for picking up a memorable souvenir.

BRIGHT NIGHTS IN STANLEY PARK
4th week of Nov

www.vancouver.ca/parks/events/brightnights
Vancouver's biggest urban park kicks off Christmas with this month-long fairy-lighted wonderland. Wander the forested pathways of Yuletide scenes and elfish dioramas then hop on the miniature train for a fun trundle through Christmas scenes, many with animatronic moving parts. It's the city's most popular seasonal attraction, so book ahead.

December

CAROL SHIPS PARADE OF LIGHTS
from early Dec

www.carolships.org
An enduring Vancouver Yuletide tradition, around 50 boats lit up like Christmas trees pootle around the area's waterfront for 20 nights. You can join some of them on board (for a fee) or just enjoy them from the shoreline as they sail past. Check the website so you know where they'll be on a given night and bring your singing voice for a few rounds of 'O Come All Ye Faithful' et al.

SANTA CLAUS PARADE
1st week of Dec

www.rogerssantaclausparade.com
Rivaling the summertime Pride Parade for spectator numbers, this giant, smile-triggering Christmas procession is a family favorite. Wrap up warm and find a spot on downtown's W Georgia or Howe Sts and watch the pageant roll past: expect marching bands, youth orchestras, cartoon characters, carol-singing floats and, right at the end, the great man himself. And, yes, he's the real one.

FESTIVAL OF LIGHTS
2nd week of Dec

www.vandusengarden.org
VanDusen's Yuletide tradition – and a clever way to keep the money coming in during the off-season – sees the botanical garden

magically illuminated with thousands of fairy lights. Popular with families, who bring their kids to meet the jolly old elf himself, look out for additional treats like Gingerbread wood and the Candy Cane Express model train. Wrap up and be sure to down a hot choc or two.

WINTER SOLSTICE LANTERN FESTIVAL
3rd week of Dec

www.secretlantern.org
Five Vancouver neighborhoods continue the age-old Winter Solstice tradition by staging mini-lantern parades at the same time (6pm) throughout the city. Expect to see the flickering lights in Yaletown, Granville Island, Chinatown, Strathcona and the Eastside. Music and festivities ensue at indoor venues in each neighborhood.

COSTS & MONEY

With the Canadian dollar rising in value in recent years, a visit to Vancouver is not the out-and-out bargain it was a few years ago. Even for Canadians, the city is often regarded as one of the country's most expensive vacation spots (although Toronto probably takes the prize for being the priciest Canadian destination).

Wherever you're visiting from, though, there are some creative ways to keep your costs down. Families can take advantage of discounted admission at museums and attractions, and there are passes available that can save a considerable amount for those planning to see many attractions (see Discount Cards on p232). For an even better deal, check the free attractions in the boxed text on p60.

HOW MUCH?

1L of gasoline $1.10

1L of bottled water $1.50

Pint of microbrew beer $6

Souvenir T-shirt $20

Vancouver Sun newspaper $1.12-2.24

Movie ticket $12

Tim Hortons medium coffee $1.28

Transit fare (one zone) $2.50

Food-court lunch $6-8

Overseas postcard stamp $1.70

ADVANCE PLANNING

If you'd like your Vancouver vacation to be as eco-friendly as possible, plan your trip using some of the tips offered in the Green Vancouver section (p47).

Most regional sights and outdoor activities don't require much advance booking, but during the summer peak it's a good idea to book specialized guided tours (p236) before you arrive. The Vancouver Art Gallery (p56) occasionally runs blockbuster exhibitions that require timed-entry tickets – book ahead on its website.

The city's main cultural festivals (p12) – especially the Film Festival, Jazz Festival and Fringe Festival – often require advance booking for many events. Visit their websites before you arrive for purchasing information.

The same is true of many theaters (p178), especially if you are on a tight schedule and want to be sure of getting tickets for a specific day. The hottest ticket in town, where booking ahead is essential, is the annual summertime Bard on the Beach festival (p178).

Many sporting events are easy to get into, but catching a Vancouver Canucks hockey game (p191) is a different story: book as far in advance as possible or you'll be relying on the predatory scalpers outside the stadium.

To see what's on in the city before you arrive, visit the *Georgia Straight* (www.straight.com) website for comprehensive listings. Also check *Tickets Tonight* (www.ticketstonight.ca) for ticket booking and late-breaking discount seats to theatrical and sporting events. And if you're determined to eat in one of the city's top restaurants, check the recommendations in the Eating chapter (p127) and book ahead.

It's also worth remembering that kids stay free at many Vancouver hotels. Some of these have kitchenettes which can help to keep your dining budget down. See p193 for hotel reviews. If you're eating out, many restaurants will prepare half-orders for children, if they don't already have a dedicated kids menu.

The most expensive item in anyone's budget is likely to be their plane ticket and, after that, accommodations. Sleeping at mid-priced hotels or B&Bs, eating at neighborhood restaurants or shopping-mall food courts, and stretching your attractions budget with a few freebies will mean that two people traveling together should be able to keep costs down to $100 or so each per day.

INTERNET RESOURCES

Beyond Robson (www.beyondrobson.com) Multi-author blogger site covering diverse aspects of the scene.

City of Vancouver (www.vancouver.ca) Resource-packed official city site with downloadable maps.

Inside Vancouver (www.insidevancouver.ca) Stories on what to do in and around the city.

Lonely Planet (www.lonelyplanet.com) Includes info on Vancouver and travelers trading information on the Thorn Tree.

Miss 604 (www.miss604.com) Vancouver's favorite blogger.

Scout Magazine (www.scoutmagazine.ca) Food and culture zine, with good restaurant listings.

Tourism Vancouver (www.tourismvancouver.com) Official tourism site, stuffed with trip-planning resources.

Urban Diner (www.urbandiner.ca) Up-to-the-minute listings and reviews of area restaurants.

Vancity Buzz (www.vancitybuzz.com) Popular locals-focused blog on the city vibe.

Vancouver is Awesome (www.vancouverisawesome.com) Vibrant, artsy-focused online magazine.

Visitors Choice Vancouver (www.visitorschoice.com) Good maps and an overview of attractions and accommodations.

BACKGROUND

HISTORY
LIVING OFF THE LAND

The ancestors of Vancouver's First Nations people began arriving in British Columbia (BC) at least 10,000 years ago, crossing via a land bridge at the Bering Strait near Alaska. They trickled southwards from here, with many setting up camp in coastal areas that are still regarded as important First Nations lands to this day. Those who traveled furthest eventually arrived at the warmer waters of what is now known as the Lower Mainland.

These first Vancouverites lived in villages comprising wood-plank houses arranged in rows, often surrounded by a stockade. Totem poles were set up nearby as an emblem of family or clan. It's not surprising that these groups were attracted to this area – the local beaches and rivers teamed with seafood, the forests bristled with tasty wildlife, including deer and elk, and fat silvery salmon were abundantly available to anyone who fancied outsmarting the odd bear for the privilege.

Several distinct communities formed. The Musqueam populated Burrard Inlet, English Bay and the mouth of the Fraser River, although they shared some of this area with the Squamish, who were largely based at the head of Howe Sound, but also had villages in North and West Vancouver, Kitsilano Point, Stanley Park and Jericho Beach. The Kwantlen controlled the area around New Westminster, while Delta and Richmond were home to the Tsawwassen. The Tsleil-Waututh occupied much of North Vancouver, while Coast Salish tribes, such as the Cowichan, Nanaimo and Saanich, set up seasonal camps along the Fraser River when the salmon were running.

Art and creativity were key features of everyday life at this time. Many homes were adorned with exterior carvings and totem poles – later examples of which are displayed at the Museum of Anthropology (p101). These exemplified a reverential regard for nature, suggesting that early First Nations people enjoyed a symbiotic relationship with their surroundings. In many ways, they were Vancouver's 'green' founding fathers.

Scant evidence exists about this intriguing period in Vancouver's history: most settlements have crumbled to dust and few have been rediscovered by archaeologists. In addition, these early settlers generally maintained oral records – they told each other (often in song) the stories of their ancestors, rather than writing things down for posterity. This method would have been highly successful until the disruptive arrival of the Europeans.

CAPTAIN VAN HITS TOWN

After centuries of unhindered First Nations occupation, Europeans began arriving in the late 18th century. The Spanish sent three expeditions between 1774 and 1779 in search of the fabled Northwest Passage. They ended up by the entrance to Nootka Sound on Vancouver Island but didn't initially venture into the Strait of Georgia. British explorer Captain James Cook elbowed into the area from the South Pacific in 1779. He had a similar Northwest Passage motive, and a similar result: he hit the west coast of Vancouver Island and believed it to be the mainland. It wasn't until 1791 that the mainland-lined

TIMELINE

8000 BC	1774	1791
The region's first inhabitants begin arriving from Asia, via the Bering Strait. Rather than head back after a quick look around, they decide to stay and enjoy the abundant food and temperate climate.	A little later than the First Nations settlers, the Spanish arrive in the area in search of the fabled Northwest Passage. They don't bother to venture any further than Nootka Sound on Vancouver Island.	A little more adventurous than his colleagues, Spanish explorer José María Narváez edges into the Strait of Georgia, perhaps looking for a Tim Hortons donut shop.

NEW SPAIN?

Despite the name 'Vancouver' eventually sticking to the area, it's worth remembering that the Spanish stepped on shore here a few months before their British seafaring rivals. On the Point Grey coastline, not far from the University of British Columbia campus, you'll find a concrete, anchor-shaped public art installation facing a forested coastline that hasn't changed much since those early expeditions. Captain José María Narváez named this stretch of what's now called Spanish Banks Islas de Langara and his country's early influence can still be found in city street names and around the British Columbia coastline, where islands sport names like Saturna, Galiano and Texada.

Strait of Georgia was properly explored. Spanish navigator José María Narváez did the honors, sailing all the way into Burrard Inlet.

Next up was Captain George Vancouver, a British navigator who had previously sailed with Cook. In 1792 he glided into the inner harbor and spent one day here – a lucky day, as it turned out, though it didn't seem so at first. When he arrived, he discovered that the Spanish, in ships under the command of captains Valdez and Galiano, had already claimed the area. Meeting at what is today known as Spanish Banks, the men shared area navigational information. Vancouver made a note of the deep natural port, which he named Burrard after one of his crew. Then he sailed away, not thinking twice about a place that would eventually be named after him.

As Spanish influence in the area waned over the next few years in favor of the more persistent British, explorers such as Simon Fraser and Alexander Mackenzie began mapping the region's interior, opening it up for overland travelers, the arrival of the legendary Hudson's Bay Company, and the eventual full entry of the region into the British Empire.

GOLD, FUR & TIMBER

The region's abundant natural resources spurred creeping development throughout the first half of the 19th century. In 1824 the Hudson's Bay Company, under James McMillan's leadership, launched a network of fur-trading posts. McMillan noted a particularly good location about 50km from the mouth of the Fraser River, building Fort Langley (p109) there in 1827. The region's first permanent European settlement, the fur-trading fort shipped more than 2000 beaver pelts in 1832. Today the Hudson's Bay Company has developed into the Bay, a cross-Canada chain of department stores. Its flagship downtown location is at the corner of Granville and Georgia Sts.

In 1858 an interesting tidbit of news began percolating around the region: gold had been discovered on the banks of the Fraser River. More than 25,000 American prospectors rapidly swept in with picks, pans and get-rich-quick dreams. Concerned that the influx might inspire a US northern push, the mainland – following the lead of Vancouver Island, which had declared its colony status in 1849 – announced it was officially becoming part of the British Empire. James Douglas was sworn in as the governor of the expanded region – officially named British Columbia – although BC and the island remained separate protectorates at this time. The proclamation was made at Fort Langley on November 19, 1858.

Douglas requested British support and the Royal Engineers, under the command of Colonel Richard Moody, arrived at the end of 1858. Alarmed by Fort Langley's poor strategic location,

1792	1827	1858
The Brits decide to join the party when the Royal Navy's Captain George Vancouver sails into Burrard Inlet. He stays 24 hours then turns tail and heads out, just like many latter-day cruise-ship passengers.	The Hudson's Bay Company builds Fort Langley, the first European settlement to grace the region. It would be several more decades before the Bay launches its first department-store sale.	Gold is discovered on the banks of the Fraser River, prompting more than 25,000 prospectors to arrive with picks and pans.

top picks

HISTORY BOOKS

- **At Home with History: the Secrets of Greater Vancouver's Heritage Houses**, Eve Lazarus (2007) – fascinating and colorful tales of ghosts, murderers and secret rooms in the region's old clapboard homes.
- **Immigrants: Stories of Vancouver's Peoples**, Lisa Smedman (2009) – evocative, photo-packed tales of those from the US and beyond who came to Vancouver to start new lives.
- **Saltwater City**, Paul Yee (2006) – illuminating and well-illustrated retelling of the often tumultuous history of Vancouver's Chinese community.
- **Wreck Beach**, Carellin Brooks (2007) – revealing history of Vancouver's famed naturist beach.
- **City of Love and Revolution: Vancouver in the Sixties**, Lawrence Aronsen (2010) – tracing the hippie-dippy days of psychedelic Vancouver, when Kitsilano was the center of the diamond-studded universe.

Moody selected another site on the Fraser River – closer to its mouth – and built New Westminster, which was declared BC's first capital. In 1859 Moody forged a trail (now called North Rd) from New Westminster to Burrard Inlet, providing the colony with an ice-free winter harbor. In 1860 he built another trail, more or less where Kingsway is today, linking New Westminster to False Creek. These trails were the foundation for moving the settlement to its present downtown location – although at this point it was a dense area of rainforest.

The sawmills soon changed all that. The first mills were set up along the Fraser River in 1860, and their logging operations cleared the land for farms across the region. It wasn't long before the companies began chewing northward through the trees toward Burrard Inlet. In 1867 Edward Stamp's British-financed Hastings Mill, on the south shore of the inlet, established the starting point of a town that would eventually become Vancouver.

In 1866 the protectorates of Vancouver Island and BC officially merged under the title of British Columbia. With the creation of a new country called Canada out east in 1867, the colony became concerned about its future, fearing US annexation. With the promise of access to a new national railway network, BC joined the Canadian Confederation in 1871. It would be another 16 years before the railway actually rolled into the region.

THE CITY'S BOOZY START

True, Hastings Mill was there first, but it was the demon drink that really launched Vancouver. In 1867 Englishman 'Gassy' Jack Deighton rowed into Burrard Inlet with his First Nations wife, a yellow dog and a barrel of whiskey. He knew the nearest drink for thirsty mill workers was 20km away in New Westminster so he announced to the workers that, if they helped him build a tavern, drinks were on him. Within 24 hours the Globe Saloon was in business, and when a village sprang up around the establishment it was dubbed 'Gastown.' In 1870, in an attempt to formalize the ramshackle township, the colonial administration renamed it 'Granville,' although almost everyone continued to call it Gastown.

Another town thriving around a sawmill was Port Moody, at the eastern end of Burrard Inlet, which had been chosen as the western terminus of the Canadian Pacific Railway (CPR). However, a CPR official – who also happened to be an influential Granville landowner – 'discovered' that

1867	1871	1886
'Gassy' Jack Deighton rows in with a barrel full of whiskey and a head full of big ideas. He opens a saloon, and a small, thirsty settlement – called Gastown – soon springs up near the entrance.	With the promise of access to a new national railway network, British Columbia joins the Canadian Confederation. Sixteen years later, the railway rolls into the region.	The fledgling town is incorporated as the City of Vancouver, silencing those who wanted to bid for the 2010 Gastown Olympics. Within weeks, the new city burns to the ground in just 45 minutes.

VISITING OLD-TOWN VANCOUVER

There are several still-existing reminders of early days Vancouver that are well worth a visit. While the Hastings Mill is long gone, its original workers' store was relocated by barge to Kitsilano in the 1930s. Used as a makeshift morgue on the day of the Great Fire, it's now the city's oldest structure and houses a small museum (p98).

Gastown – designated a national historic site in 2010 – is a lively reminder of the past, with its heritage buildings now housing some of the city's best bars, restaurants and independent shops. Doff your hat to the Gassy Jack statue in Maple Tree Sq – jauntily standing atop a whiskey barrel – then check out the recently restored Byrnes Block a couple of steps away. On the site of Deighton's second bar, this handsome edifice is the oldest Vancouver building still in its original location. Like the other preserved structures lining adjacent Carrall St, it's a reminder of the city's early reconstruction immediately after the 1886 fire.

the eastern end of Burrard Inlet wasn't a practical harbor for large ships. Granville was suddenly selected as the new railway terminus location, much to the disgust of Port Moody residents.

The CPR negotiated with the provincial government for 24 sq km in the area, making it Granville's largest property holder. The story goes that in 1884, while workers rowed the railway company's general manager, William Van Horne, around what would later be Stanley Park, he commented that the new city needed a name to live up to its future as a great metropolis. Van Horne reasoned that since Granville was an unknown name, the city should be called 'Vancouver' after the man whom everyone knew was responsible for literally putting the area on the map. In April 1886 the town of Granville was incorporated as the City of Vancouver – which makes 2011 the city's 125th birthday.

The first piece of business for the city's new council was to lease a 400-hectare military reserve from the federal government and establish it as the city's first park – and so Stanley Park was born. But the city faced a less enjoyable task at the tender age of two months: on June 13, 1886, CPR workers lit a fire to clear brush that rapidly spread out of control. The 'Great Fire,' as it came to be known, took 45 minutes to destroy Vancouver's 1000 wooden structures, kill as many as 28 people (the number remains disputed) and leave 3000 homeless.

Within hours, reconstruction was underway. But this time the buildings were constructed from stone and brick. By 1887, when the first transcontinental CPR passenger train pulled into the city, Vancouver was back in business. You can visit this proudly preserved locomotive today at the Roundhouse Community Arts & Recreation Centre (p71). Within four years the city grew to a population of 13,000, and between 1891 and 1901 the population skyrocketed to more than double that.

GROWING PAINS

The railway was responsible for shaping much of the city as it exists today. The CPR built Granville St from Burrard Inlet to False Creek, cleared and paved Pender and Hastings Sts, and developed the land around False Creek for railway yards and housing. The company also developed residential areas like the West End, Kitsilano, Shaughnessy Heights and Fairview. Shaughnessy Heights, once known as 'CPR Heaven,' was the home of Vancouver's new upper classes – just so long as they weren't Jewish or Asian, since both groups were forbidden from owning in the area.

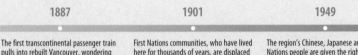

1887	1901	1949
The first transcontinental passenger train pulls into rebuilt Vancouver, wondering exactly where it is. The residents of Port Moody, the originally proposed terminus for the major new service, decide never to speak to Vancouverites again.	First Nations communities, who have lived here for thousands of years, are displaced from their settlements in the Vanier Park area, as rapacious colonials sweep them and the forests away.	The region's Chinese, Japanese and First Nations people are given the right to vote in provincial elections; a poor swap for losing their ancestral lands or their lives while building the railroad network.

STROLLING CHINATOWN'S PAST

One of North America's largest and most historic Chinatowns, the colorful, commerce-busy streets next to Gastown are a great spot for history-huggers. Take your time and wander on foot here and you'll come across many preserved, flare-topped buildings from the early days of the city's Chinese 'ghetto.' A few steps from the Chinatown Millennium Gate, nip down Shanghai Alley. A quiet backstreet today, it was once home to hundreds of men, domiciled in cheap lodgings and crammed into every available space. With its own shops, hole-in-the-wall eateries and 500-seat Sing Kew Theatre, the bustling alley was designed as a one-way street that could be barricaded and defended in the event of attack from locals. On the next block, you'll find the entrance to the excellent Dr Sun Yat-Sen Classical Chinese Garden (p78). Enter the adjoining courtyard from Pender St and you'll spot a wall-mounted bronze frieze recognizing the thousands of 'Chinese pioneers' who helped build Canada in the early days of the railroad.

Anti-Asian feeling was not new to Vancouver. Between 1881 and 1885 more than 11,000 Chinese arrived by ship to work on the construction of the railroad. In many respects they were treated as second-class citizens. They were paid $1 per day, half of what white workers were paid (but almost 20 times what they were paid at home). Government legislation denied all Asians the right to vote in federal elections, and did not allow Chinese women to immigrate unless they were married to a white man. In 1887 a white mob destroyed a Chinese camp in False Creek, and in 1907 an anti-Asian riot ripped through Chinatown and Japantown.

It was an issue the city would have to remedy, because by 1911 the census showed that Vancouver was a city of immigrants, with most people born outside of Canada. Indigenous rights were also taking a beating during this time. In 1901 the local government displaced a First Nations community from Vanier Park, sending some families to the Capilano Indian Reserve on the North Shore and others to Squamish.

During the first 30 years of the 20th century, all the suburbs around the city grew substantially. By 1928 the population outside the city was about 150,000. When Point Grey and South Vancouver amalgamated with the city in 1929, bringing in a combined population of more than 80,000, Vancouver became Canada's third-largest city – the ranking it retains today.

While the 1930s Great Depression saw the construction of several public works – the Marine Building, Vancouver City Hall, the third and present Hotel Vancouver, and Lions Gate Bridge, to name a few – many people were unemployed, as was the case throughout Canada. This marked a time of large demonstrations, violent riots and public discontent.

WWII helped to pull Vancouver out of the Depression by creating instant jobs at shipyards, aircraft-parts factories and canneries, and in construction with the building of rental units for the increased workforce. Japanese Canadians didn't fare so well, however. In 1942, following the bombing of Pearl Harbor, they were shipped to internment camps in the province's interior and had to endure the confiscation of all their land and property, much of which was never returned. Chinese, Japanese and First Nations people were finally given the provincial vote in 1949.

EXPO-SING THE CITY

By the start of the 1950s, Vancouver's population was 345,000 and the area was thriving. The high-rise craze hit in the middle of the decade, mostly in the West End. During the next 13 years 220 apartment buildings went up – and up – in this area alone.

1956	1964	1977
The West End is rezoned for greater population density. The high-rise boom begins as hundreds of wooden homes are bulldozed to make way for apartment blocks and the annual Pride Parade that's due to kick off any decade now.	Canada's gay-rights movement begins when a group of feminists and academics create the Association for Social Knowledge, the country's first gay and lesbian discussion group.	The SeaBus passenger ferry service launches between downtown Vancouver and the North Shore, sparking an immediate rush for the best seats at the front of the boat.

In the 1960s and '70s, Vancouver was known for its counterculture community, centered on Kitsilano. Canada's gay-rights movement began here in 1964 when a group of feminists and academics started the Association for Social Knowledge, the country's first gay and lesbian discussion group. In 1969 the Don't Make a Wave Committee formed to stop US nuclear testing in Alaska, sending a protest vessel to the region in 1971. A few years later, the group morphed into the environmental organization Greenpeace. If you take the seawall walkway west from Granville Island towards Vanier Park, you'll find a discreet plaque marking the launch of the ship and the resulting international movement.

As the years passed, the city's revolutionary fervor dissipated and economic development became the region's main pastime. Nothing was more important to Vancouver in the 1980s than Expo '86, the world's fair that many regard as the city's coming of age. The six-month event, coinciding with Vancouver's 100th birthday, brought millions to the city and kick-started a rash of regeneration in several tired neighborhoods. New facilities built for Expo included the 60,000-seat BC Place Stadium (p71), which – during research for this book and on the eve of the city's 125th birthday in 2011 – was being spruced up with a new, multimillion-dollar retractable roof after playing a starring role in the opening and closing ceremonies of the 2010 Olympic and Paralympic Winter Games.

MULTICULTURAL MILESTONES

The brewing issue of First Nations land rights spilled over in the late 1980s, with a growing number of rallies, road blockades and court actions in the region. Aside from a few treaties covering a tiny portion of the province, land-claim agreements had not been signed and no clear definition of the scope and nature of First Nations rights existed. Until 1990 the provincial government refused to participate in treaty negotiations. That changed in December, when the BC Claims Task Force was formed among the governments of Canada, BC and the First Nations Summit with a mission to figure out how the three parties could solve land-rights matters. It's a slow-moving, ongoing process that in Vancouver's case involves the Tsawwassen, Tsleil-Waututh, Katzie, Squamish and Musqueam nations.

Prior to the British handover of Hong Kong to China in 1997, tens of thousands of wealthy Hong Kong Chinese migrated to BC's Lower Mainland area, boosting the area's permanent Asian population by about 85% and creating the largest Asian population in any North American city. Real-estate prices rose, with Vancouver's cost-of-living figures suddenly rivaling those of London, Paris and Tokyo. Many of the new arrivals shunned the city proper in favor of the suburbs, especially Richmond. By 1998 immigration had tapered off but the city's transformation into a modern, multicultural mecca was already complete. By then, about 40% of Vancouver residents were foreign-born, and an ethnic smorgasbord of restaurants, stores and cultural activities had emerged, solidifying the worldly reputation the city earned by hosting Expo '86.

DOWNTOWN EASTSIDE UPSWING

An ever-present forest of cranes – plus the attendant soundscape of construction noise – shows that development continues apace across latter-day Vancouver. Downtown is where much of the action is, but as space becomes scarce, new Coal Harbour, Gastown and South Main (SoMa) developments are enticing the moneyed young to once bleak or nondescript neighborhoods. One area that's traditionally been a tougher nut for developers to crack has also finally become part of the plan.

1979	1983	1985
Granville Island is developed from a grungy industrial wasteland, where tracking down artisan cheese was always a challenge, into one of the city's most popular hangouts. A cement factory stays behind to keep the faith.	BC Place Stadium inflates its Teflon roof and opens for business. Non-sports fans instead head to the old courthouse building, now transformed into the new Vancouver Art Gallery.	The first SkyTrain line opens, linking the communities of New Westminster and Vancouver. New Westminsterites flood into town and wonder what all the fuss was about.

top picks

LIVE WEBCAMS

- Downtown Vancouver (www.vancouver.com/webcam/south-east)
- English Bay & Burrard Bridge (www.katkam.ca)
- Vancouver Aquarium otter (www.vanaqua.org/ottercam)
- Jericho Beach (www.jericho.ca/webcam/webcam)
- Port of Vancouver (www.portmetrovancouver.com)

Long-blighted by drugs, prostitution and a high concentration of mentally ill residents, the Downtown Eastside – centered on Main and Hastings Sts – has long been a no-go skid row for locals. But this wasn't always the case. In fact, while nearby Gastown was the historic genesis of the city, the key streets of the Downtown Eastside were originally lined with the banks, shops and bustling commercial enterprises of the region's main business district. When new development shifted the city centre across to the Robson and Granville Sts area of downtown in the 1940s, though, this old 'hood began a graceless decline. City and provincial policies to concentrate services for the poor and homeless in the area didn't help, with squalid rooming houses and dodgy pubs soon becoming standard fixtures.

While local politicians have made regular pronouncements about solving the area's problems since the 1990s – current mayor Gregor Robinson recently claimed he would end homelessness across the city by 2015 – the most effective strategy in dealing with the Eastside appears to be gentrification. The opening of a massive new housing, shops and university-campus complex on the old Woodwards department-store site in 2009 has become the catalyst for change in the Downtown Eastside, with new businesses recolonizing the area's paint-peeled storefronts for the first time in decades.

The gentrification drive is not without controversy, though. While city hipsters move into their pricey loft apartments and sip their macchiatos at exposed-brick coffee shops, the residents who have called this area home for the last few decades are feeling threatened and increasingly marginalized. Finding the right balance between rampant development and support for the people who already live in the Eastside will continue to be the city's biggest challenge over the coming years.

GOING FOR GOLD

In the opening decade of the new millennium, Vancouver became a regular on those global surveys that designate the best places in the world to live. Seizing the initiative and recalling the success of Expo '86, the region again looked to the future, winning the bid to host the 2010 Olympic and Paralympic Winter Games.

With events staged in and around the city, and also at Whistler (p214), a global TV audience of more than two billion gazed admiringly at picture-perfect snow-and-blue-sky vistas, while athletes from 80 countries competed for gold. And while many locals had grumbled about the cost of the Games, the entire city exploded in a 17-day mardi gras of support that surprised even the organizers.

Upwards of 200,000 Maple Leaf–waving partiers hit the streets around Robson and Granville Sts every night to hang out with overseas visitors, catch LiveSite music shows and break into impromptu renditions of the national anthem. This all-enveloping Canadian pride hit fever pitch during the men's gold medal hockey game when the host nation beat the US with a dream-like last-gasp goal. For many Vancouverites, this moment was the best thing that's ever happened in the city's short modern history.

1986	1996	2010
The international spotlight shines on Vancouver as the Expo '86 world's fair dominates the summer, bringing Sheena Easton and Depeche Mode to local stages – although sadly not on the same bill.	With the Hong Kong handover to China imminent, Vancouver sees a massive influx of Asian immigrants into the city. Richmond is transformed from a farming backwater into the region's new Chinatown.	Locals break into street-party mode as Vancouver hosts the Olympic and Paralympic Winter Games. Flags are waved, national anthems sung and a seismic group cheer erupts when Canada wins gold in the men's hockey.

ARTS

Ask around and many locals will tell you that Vancouver doesn't even have an arts scene. It's the knee-jerk reaction from those who think that art only means blockbuster gallery shows, stadium-sized music concerts or visiting Broadway musicals that have absolutely nothing to do with the city. These are usually the kind of people who wouldn't know an artist from a hole in the ground (otherwise known as an installation).

In fact, Vancouver is crammed with galleries, authors, musical groups, film auteurs, theater companies and dance troupes. But reflecting a kind of citywide parochialism, these creative types often operate in isolation – rarely is Vancouver's true abundance of artists and activities counted together and regarded as a 'scene.' An even bigger challenge facing the scene is that, due to a province-wide cut in public arts funding announced in 2010, many smaller groups are currently facing challenging economic straits.

For visitors, if you want to tap into Vancouver's artistic side, you'll have to go looking for it. In the same way that exploring the separate, distinctive neighborhoods here reveals the city's true nature, so Vancouver's artistic soul is uncovered only if you scratch beneath the surface. If you're prepared to make the effort, you'll be rewarded with an artsy output that's authentically West Coast.

Luckily, you'll be spoilt for choice. Visual art – particularly photography – is a local specialty that attracts international recognition. The city's live-music scene is bursting with activity and ranges from hot local rock bands to an astonishing array of classical recital companies. Literature is another key area, with some world-renowned authors calling the city home (and often using it as a 'character' in their novels). Long regarded as 'Hollywood North,' Vancouver is also a major movie production site as well as a center for independent filmmaking. In performance arts – especially dance and theater – Vancouver has a depth and diversity that rivals much bigger cities.

And if you time your trip well, you can dip into festivals (p12) that cover film, music, fringe performance and just about everything in between. Check out the queues snaking around venues at these fests and then make up your own mind about whether Vancouver has an arts scene.

Flick to the Arts chapter (p169) for suggestions on what to see while you're here.

VISUAL ARTS

The region's artistic bent was sparked thousands of years ago when the First Nations arrived in the area and began adorning their homes with artsy reflections of the natural world. Later

---

AN OLYMPIAN TRANSFORMATION

Vancouverites were neatly divided into two camps when the city won the bid to host the 2010 Olympic and Paralympic Winter Games. Many were deliriously happy to be staging the planet's biggest party while at least as many others felt the vast budget could be spent on far more important region-wide improvements. But while the death of Georgian luge athlete Nodar Kumaritashvili on day one and the massive challenges of staging alpine events in what came to be the city's hottest winter for a century threatened to turn the Games into a huge Canadian embarrassment, a sudden transformation happened a couple of days after the flame was lit that changed the event dramatically.

Often regarded as a city that doesn't really know how to party, the first two nights of the Olympics were tame affairs here, but on day three – perhaps spurred by negative media coverage – the locals took to the downtown streets en masse…and never really left. Maple Leaf flags and painted faces became the norm as Vancouverites transformed Robson and Granville Sts into a wandering carnival of family-friendly bonhomie. And while national pride is something few Canadians are used to exhibiting in public, the nighttime shenanigans changed all that with rampant flag-waving and regular, heartfelt sing-alongs of 'O Canada'. As a record haul of Canadian medals fueled the crowds, the streets soon became the best place to hang out and catch the Olympic spirit – along with 200,000 of your new closest friends.

When the flame was extinguished at the closing ceremony on February 28, the locals wiped off the red face paint and trudged back to their regular lives. But there was a widely held feeling that the city had grown up a little, coupled with talk of reigniting the mass community spirit with many more giant events like this one.

For a reminder of the Games, and a chance to choose your fave mascot (it's probably Quatchi the cuddly sasquatch), check www.vancouver2010.com.

---

settlers continued to use nature as their muse, often adding images of the mysterious First Nations themselves to their canvases. In recent decades, the city's visual artists have moved successfully into provocative abstract painting and photography. A visit to the Vancouver Art Gallery (VAG; p56) will reveal some leading lights, while dropping by the Emily Carr University of Art + Design (p90) will point you to the rising stars. Visit www.art-bc.com for listings of regional galleries and events.

Photography

Vancouver has an international, cutting-edge reputation for contemporary photography and is associated with a certain brand of photo-conceptual art now called the 'Vancouver School.' Stan Douglas, Roy Arden, Chris Gergley and Jeff Wall are among its most celebrated exponents and have exhibited at major galleries around the world. Rodney Graham, who also came from this photo-conceptual group, has moved on to installations, music and video expression. While Wall has become the most famous exponent of the Vancouver School, Douglas has created some of the most evocative images of the city. These include the giant new public artwork *Abbott & Cordova, 7 August 1971* (see the boxed text, p28) and the celebrated *Every Building on 100 West Hastings,* a 3m-long panorama of mostly derelict but once-handsome buildings in the Downtown Eastside. The image is now part of the permanent collection at the VAG. It's also worth dropping by the Contemporary Art Gallery (p60), which often exhibits works by local photographers.

Painting & Sculpture

The natural beauty of Greater Vancouver, with its varied landscapes, colors, textures and ever-changing light, has long been an inspiration to painters and sculptors. In addition to the VAG and Emily Carr University, you can dip into the scene at the many private and artist-run galleries in South Granville, Gastown and Yaletown.

Among the famous regional artists to look out for are Emily Carr and EJ Hughes. Regarded as Canada's first major female artist, Carr painted swirling nature-themed canvases that are moving tributes to the West Coast landscape. The VAG has a large permanent collection, as does the Art Gallery of Greater Victoria (p212) on Vancouver Island. In contrast, Hughes was rediscovered in the years before his death in 2007. His stylized, often whimsical canvases of BC life – coastal communities feature heavily – now command million-dollar price tags. The VAG has the largest permanent collection of Hughes' work.

Other famed artists in the region include sculptors Gathie Falk and Alan Storey, whose brushed steel *Pendulum* is the permanent centerpiece of the Pendulum Gallery (p60), as well as Group of Seven painters Lawren Harris and Frederick Horsman Varley. Abstract painter Jack Shadbolt has an international reputation, while other celebrated contemporary artists include Chris Woods, Jim Cummins and Mark Atomos Pilon.

Public Art

Vancouver has a vigorous public-art program and you'll likely spot challenging installations, decorative apartment-building adornments and sometimes puzzling sculptures dotted throughout the city. Check www.vancouver.ca/publicart for an online registry of works and some handy maps, or pick up the excellent book *Public Art in Vancouver: Angels Among Lions,* by John Steil and Aileen Stalker. It has photos and information on more than 500 works around the city, divided into neighborhoods. Also, check the website of the Vancouver Biennale (www.vancouver biennale.com), a massive public-art showcase, staged in two-year chunks, that brings monumental, often challenging installations to the city's streets from artists around the world.

Among Vancouver's most popular permanent artworks are *Monument for East Vancouver,* a towering neon cross by Ken Lum at Clark Dr and E 6th Ave; *Lightshed,* a handsome silver replica of a freight shed on piles by Liz Magor, on the Coal Harbour seawall; *Knife Edge Two Piece,* a large Henry Moore bronze in Queen Elizabeth Park; and the hulking granite inukshuk (Inuit sculpture) by Alvin Kanak on the beach at the foot of Bidwell St in the West End – originally created for Expo '86, it's a great spot for a perfect Vancouver photo.

BACKGROUND ARTS

RIOTOUS ARTWORK

Look for the large London Drugs shop in the Woodward's building on W Hastings St and enter the building's new courtyard, carved from what was originally the interior of one of the city's largest department stores. The space is now dominated by Vancouver's most evocative public artwork.

Measuring 15m by 9m and created by Stan Douglas, *Abbott & Cordova, 7 August 1971* is a mammoth black-and-white photo montage depicting a key moment in the history of local social protest: the night when police in full riot gear broke up a pro-marijuana smoke-in being staged in the Downtown Eastside.

The action – the image shows mounted police pushing against unarmed locals and miscreants being stuffed into police wagons – soon spiraled out of control, with pitched battles and general chaos triggering a siege-like atmosphere on the area's streets. Later, the event became known as the 'Gastown Riot' and 'The Battle of Maple Tree Square.'

Entering into the spirit, the Vancouver International Airport has lined its public spaces with gallery-quality artworks – check out the magnificent bronze *Spirit of Haida Gwaii* by Bill Reid, and its ocean-themed *Great Wave Wall* backdrop by Lutz Hauschild. Both are in the atrium space between the US and international check-in areas.

First Nations Art

First Nations artists have contributed mightily to Vancouver's visual-arts scene, primarily through carving. Two carvers who preserved the past while fostering a new generation of First Nations artists were Charles Edenshaw, the first professional Haida artist, who worked in argillite, gold and silver; and Mungo Martin, a Kwakiutl master carver of totem poles. Martin passed on his skills to Bill Reid, the outstanding Haida artist of his generation and the first Haida artist to have a retrospective exhibition at the VAG. His work is permanently displayed at the Museum of Anthropology (p101) and also at downtown's new Bill Reid Gallery of Northwest Coast Art (p56), where works from many other First Nations artists are also on display.

Lawrence Paul Yuxweluptun is a well-known contemporary First Nations artist. He graduated from the Emily Carr University with a painting degree, and uses Coast Salish mythological images to comment on political, environmental and indigenous issues. Look out also for Roy Henry Vickers of Tofino, who expresses traditional themes through wildlife paintings, and Susan Point, a Coast Salish artist whose traditional themes show up in a variety of media.

One of the world's hottest First Nations artists, Brian Jungen disassembles well-known objects and recreates them in challenging new forms, usually fusing them with traditional arts-and-crafts visuals. His most famous works are the First Nations masks made from resewn sections of Nike running shoes, and his detailed whalebone sculptures created from humdrum plastic chairs.

MUSIC

Vancouver has a strong and diverse musical tradition founded on decades of home-grown talent. Sarah McLachlan, Nickelback, The New Pornographers and even Michael Bublé are based here, while jazz diva Diana Krall hails from across the water on Vancouver Island.

If you miss your favorite performer, it's worth delving into one of Vancouver's pitch-perfect music festivals (p12), which cover genres from jazz to folk and from classical to new music.

Arch Vancouver group The New Pornographers electrifies stages here and abroad courtesy of its guitar-and-keyboard power pop and the vocals of Neko Case. When in town, the band is likely to turn up at the Commodore (p167). If you can't catch the band itself, Pornographers members have side projects

BLOG IT

Before you hit town, jump into the indie scene via these eclectic local music blogs:
Indie Files (www.theindiefiles.com)
Ronatron (www.ronatron.net)
Van Music (www.vanmusic.ca)
Backstage Rider (www.backstagerider.com)
Winnie Cooper (www.winniecooper.net)

that play locally on occasion: Carl Newman heads Zumpano and Neko Case solos as a Patsy Cline–like country singer.

The city was also a prime – if cultish – player on the late-1970s punk scene, with acts like The Black Halos, Dayglo Abortions (from Victoria) and Joey 'Shithead' Keithley's DOA spitting up a storm at venues across town. A more mellow tone had developed by the 1990s, though, when local gal Sarah McLachlan burst onto the scene, eventually racking up sales of more than 40 million albums worldwide. Following her smash 1997 album *Surfacing,* she organized the women-only Lilith Fair tours before putting out the accomplished *Afterglow* in 2003. After a long recording hiatus, she was back on the scene with new album *Laws of Illusion* in 2010, when she also kick-started the Lilith live extravaganza.

From Nanaimo, jazz pianist and vocalist Diana Krall – who lives in BC with hubby Elvis Costello – is often considered a Vancouver local: the couple turned on the city's Christmas tree lights in 2009. For more hard-core jazzsters, there's also François Houle, a clarinetist who likes to mix it with a little classical music. Many jazz aficionados spend their time in the city mooching at the subterranean Cellar Restaurant & Jazz Club (p166), where owner and saxophonist Cory Weeds releases celebrated CDs of the venue's most spine-tingling performances. Alternatively, blues fans will appreciate Jim Byrnes, who frequently holds court at the Yale (p166).

But the city's music scene is at its liveliest at the grassroots level, where local indie acts hit stages small (and slightly larger) every night of the week. Do some sound research online before you arrive – check the blogs in the boxed text, opposite, and time your visit for some great shows at the Commodore, Biltmore, Rickshaw, Railway Club or beyond. If the choice looks bewildering, tap local stores like Zulu Records (p120) and Red Cat Records (p120) for recommendations and a chance to rub shoulders with muso Vancouverites. Alternatively, pick up a free copy of local music magazine *Discorder* (www.discorder.ca), produced by the University of British Columbia's Student Radio Society.

Of course, it's not all about kicking it here. Vancouver has one of North America's most vital classical music scenes, with chamber and choral groups particularly well represented. Favorites include the Vancouver Bach Choir (p176), whose Messiah sing-along is a Christmastime legend; the internationally renowned Vancouver Chamber Choir (p176), which covers everything from jazz to avant-garde; and the Vancouver Symphony Orchestra (p172), which effortlessly draws serious music fans and first-timers with a stirring mix of classics and 'pops'.

For further information on plugging into Vancouver's music scene, see p165, p170 and p176.

LITERATURE

With an estimated 1500 professional authors living in the BC region, Vancouver is a center of Canadian literature. It's also home to a bulging bookcase of small and mid-sized publishers, including Heritage House, which offers intriguing historic and locally-focused non-fiction titles, and Arsenal Pulp Press, which produces a roster of colorful, often quirky tomes.

The region is also said to boast the highest number of book readers anywhere in the country, which might explain the wild success of the Vancouver Public Library's One Book, One Vancouver campaign. Like a giant book club, the annual drive promotes books either with a local tie or an iconic following, sparking mass reading, heated discussions and literary events at the library and beyond.

Bookstores, from general to specialist, abound in the city, while regular literary events range from poetry slams to script readings (see p177). The city also hosts a couple of literary festivals that are among Vancouver's most popular events. These include Word on the Street (p177) and the Vancouver International Writers and Readers Festival (p16).

For more insight into local authors, read *The Essentials: 100 Great BC Books, 100 Great BC Authors* (2010) by Alan Twigg, who also publishes the free tabloid-format *BC Bookworld*, available at bookstores. The Saturday edition of the *Vancouver Sun* has a book section covering regional authors and bookish events, while the website of the Association of Book Publishers of BC (www.books.bc.ca) provides an insightful introduction to the area for traveling bookworms. If your time is limited, drop into the Vancouver Public Library central branch near the corner of W Georgia and Hamilton Sts: it stages regular free readings by local authors.

Fiction

While Vancouver has spurred the creative juices of thousands of novelists, many of its writers have focused on troubled times of their own. Hard-drinking Malcolm Lowry wrote his masterpiece *Under the Volcano* (about a day in the life of an alcoholic consul in central Mexico) when he lived in a cheap hovel in North Vancouver. Local author Michael Turner illuminated his teenage years in the city in *The Pornographer's Poem*, while the Chinese immigrant experience is explored in Wayson Choy's award-winning book *The Jade Peony*. Evelyn Lau shot to prominence at the age of 18 with *Runaway: Diary of a Street Kid*, which details her life as a prostitute on Vancouver's streets after she left her traditional Chinese home.

In fact, the darker side of Vancouver is often never far from the minds of city authors. In *Stanley Park* Timothy Taylor exposes the soft underbelly of the local foodie scene and the city's famed green space, while crime novelist Laurence Gough is one of Vancouver's most prolific writers, best known for his Willows and Parker crime novels about a detective duo on the Vancouver police force. The city always plays a prominent role in Gough's storylines: a body shows up in the Vancouver Aquarium whale tank in *Killers;* another is fished from Coal Harbour in *Karaoke Rap*.

Perhaps the city's most celebrated living novelist, Douglas Coupland reputedly coined the term 'Generation X' in his novel of the same name. His books frequently explore the slacker-flavored ennui of modern-day life and can give travelers a fascinating insight into the city's psyche before they arrive. Recommended Coupland tomes include *J-Pod*, *Eleanor Rigby* and *Girlfriend in a Coma*. Coupland is also an artist (although not many of his works have been displayed in recent years) and he sometimes appears at the Vancouver International Writers and Readers Festival, where he once co-presented a fascinating Q&A with visiting writer Chuck Palahniuk.

Nonfiction

There's a celebrated creative nonfiction edge to much of Vancouver's best bookish output. In fact, two of the city's leading authors produced recent back-to-back wins in the Charles Taylor Prize for Literary Nonfiction, arguably Canada's most prestigious book

top picks

BEST OF VANCOUVER AUTHORS

- **Vancouver Special**, Charles Demers (2009) – a grittier antidote to Coupland's quirky *City of Glass*, this black-and-white graphic tome offers Demers' witty personal reflections on the city.
- **Stanley Park**, Timothy Taylor (2002) – illuminating modern-day Vancouver through a story fusing the life of a local chef with the park's dark secrets.
- **Runaway: Diary of a Street Kid**, Evelyn Lau (2001) – a 14-year-old honor student when she ran away from home, Lau makes her personal experience the basis for this novel about a dangerous life on the streets.
- **The Jade Peony**, Wayson Choy (1995) – a searing portrayal of growing up in a Vancouver Chinese immigrant family in the 1930s.
- **J-Pod**, Douglas Coupland (2006) – one of a string of novels by local lad Coupland exploring slacker-flavored modern-day life.
- **Vancouver Stories** (2005) – an evocative series of shorts about the city by writers such as Douglas Coupland, Alice Munro, Ethel Wilson, Malcolm Lowry, William Gibson and Timothy Taylor.
- **The Shark God**, Charles Montgomery (2006) – a highly evocative re-tracing of an 1892 missionary trip by the Bishop of Tasmania through the islands of Melanesia by his insightful great-grandson.
- **Dead Man in Paradise**, James Mackinnon (2007) – with a reporter's nose for facts and a detective novelist's eye for a great tale, Mackinnon uncovers the truth about the 1960s murder of his relative in the Dominican Republic.

accolade. Charles Montgomery won in 2005 for his book *The Last Heathen: Encounters with Ghosts and Ancestors in Melanesia,* later published around the world as *The Shark God,* while a year later his buddy James Mackinnon scooped the $25,000 pot with *Dead Man in Paradise.* Mackinnon, with his partner Alisa Smith, also produced *100-Mile Diet: A Year of Local Eating* to great acclaim. All three authors are members of the FCC, a small band of literary Vancouver journalists dedicated to narrative nonfiction.

There are also some fascinating nonfiction tomes covering the city itself, including *Vancouver: Representing the Postmodern City,* edited by Paul Delany; *Greenpeace: The Inside Story,* by Rex Wexler, which relates the development of the international movement from its early Vancouver days; and *Hope in Shadows,* by Brad Cran and Gillian Jerome, an evocative, photo-heavy reflection of the Downtown Eastside with personal stories from its residents. One of the most popular nonfiction books about Vancouver is Douglas Coupland's *City of Glass,* a quirky, picture-packed alternative guidebook of musings and observations on contemporary life here.

For a listing of great history books on the city, see the boxed text on p21; cooking fans should check out the boxed text on p135 for some recommended books by famed local chefs.

Science Fiction

Science-fiction author William Gibson, who was born in North Carolina but moved to Vancouver several years ago, is the godfather of 'cyberpunk.' His 1984 novel *Neuromancer* launched the genre of bleak, high-tech neo-reality, which showed up in the mainstream in popular movies like *The Matrix. Neuromancer* won the sci-fi triple crown of Hugo, Nebula and Philip K Dick awards, an unheard-of feat. Gibson's subsequent novels include *Idoru, Mona Lisa Overdrive* and *Virtual Light.*

Speaking of Philip K Dick, how's this for a tenuous Vancouver tidbit: Dick, who wrote the story that eventually became *Blade Runner,* spent a few months in the city's Downtown Eastside in 1972, including time in a heroin rehab home. Some theorize that *Blade Runner's* vision of non-stop rain and urban decay germinated there. Another well-known sci-fi writer who now calls Vancouver home is Spider Robinson, the author of *Stardance* and *Callahan's Crosstime Saloon.*

Poetry

Historically, E Pauline Johnson is Vancouver's most famous woman of poetic words. The daughter of a Mohawk chief and a middle-class Englishwoman, Johnson wrote poetry and recited it in public performances where she dressed in buckskin, rabbit pelts and metal jewelry, and carried a hunting knife and Huron scalp given to her by her great-grandfather. The 'Mohawk Princess' didn't come to Vancouver until later in her life, but she loved the city dearly and was quite prolific during her time here, which included the writing of *Legends of Vancouver,* a collection of Squamish myths.

Many area novelists also dabble in the dark arts of poetry. In 1992 Evelyn Lau became the youngest poet ever to be nominated for the Governor General's Award (one of Canada's most prestigious literary prizes) for her collection *Oedipal Dreams.* Canadian literary icon George Woodcock, the author of 150 books, was also a poet *(Tolstoy at Yasnaya Polyana* and *The Cherry Tree on Cherry Street)* – when he wasn't busy penning history, biography and travel tomes plus his seminal *Anarchism* text. *The Gentle Anarchist* is an excellent biography of this prolific author by Vancouverite George Fetherling, who's been known to pen a poem or two himself. The city also created its own Poet Laureate position in 2006: at the time of writing, the incumbent scribe was Brad Cran.

CINEMA & TELEVISION

The film industry has a starring role in Vancouver's 'Hollywood North' economy, and the city ranks third in North American movie and TV production (behind the obvious hot spots, Los Angeles and New York). True, not many stories are set in Vancouver, and not many mainstream filmmakers are based here, but the industry was home to more than 239 productions

BE PART OF THE ACTION

The website of the BC Film Commission (www .bcfilmcommission.com) should be the first stop for anyone interested in working in the industry. It gives the weekly lowdown on what's filming and who's in the cast and crew, and provides contact information for productions seeking extras.

in 2009, pumping more than $1.3 billion into the local economy and greasing the palms of 30,000 local workers. Home of the influential Vancouver Film School – which counts director/actor/screenwriter Kevin Smith (of *Clerks* fame) as its most famed alumnus – actors who have moved on to global acclaim from the city include Seth Rogen, Ryan Reynolds and Michael J Fox.

You can mix with the local auteurs at screenings and industry events at the 17-day Vancouver International Film Festival (p16), held annually from late September. It's even more grassroots at the many smaller movie showcases scheduled throughout the year – see the boxed text, p175.

But it's as a TV and movie-set location that Vancouver has earned most of its screen time. While the locally shot *X-Files* TV series and resulting 2008 movie used Vancouver visuals in its supposedly US locations – watch for the SkyTrain sliding blithely past in some shots – recent shows such as *Smallville* and *Stargate* have made more of an effort to disguise their Vancouver backdrops.

As for movies, with its mountain, ocean, forest and urban settings, the city is a vast and adaptable set for directors. It has stood in for everything from the North Pole in Will Ferrell's *Elf* to Tibet in director Martin Scorsese's *Kundun* and back-alley New York in Jackie Chan's *Rumble in the Bronx*. The area's mild climate allows for year-round filming, and with an army of skilled industry professionals and facilities, it's easy to see how the city slides so easily onto the screen.

Recent and upcoming Hollywood titles shot in the area that you may have heard of (for better or worse) include *X-Men 2*, *Catwoman*, *Tron 2*, *The A-Team*, *Scooby-Doo 2* and *Fantastic Four*. The city was also the site for much of the *Twilight* saga filming, when legions of fang-loving teenage girls descended for a glimpse of their favorite heartthrobs at work. Big-budget movies are more the exception than the rule, however. What are most commonly filmed here are Movies of the Week and B flicks that go straight to DVD. Keep your eyes peeled: wherever you wander in the city, it's common to come across lines of white trailers marking the latest shoot.

The city is also a hotbed of animation and special-effects shenanigans, with postproduction work on recent titles including *Avatar*, *Zombieland*, *District 9* and *Angels & Demons*.

To catch the end rsults, check the section for Vancouver's movie theaters and events on p173.

THEATER

Vancouver is home to one of Canada's most energetic independent theater scenes, with more than 30 professional performance groups. The Arts Club Theatre Company (p178) and the Playhouse Theatre Company (p179) hog the main spotlights. Both companies were formed

top picks

VANCOUVER INDIE FLICKS

- **On the Corner**, directed by Nathaniel Geary (2003) – this gritty look at life in Vancouver's heroin-plagued Downtown Eastside follows a young man drawn into the worlds of addiction and prostitution after he comes to live with his sister.
- **Double Happiness**, directed by Mina Shum (1994) – a comedy about 20-something Jade (Sandra Oh), who is trying to keep secret her modern career choice (actress) and boyfriend (he's Caucasian) from her traditional Chinese parents in the Vancouver suburbs.
- **That Cold Day in the Park**, directed by Robert Altman (1969) – a lonely spinster (Sandy Dennis) invites a young hippie in from the Vancouver rain and then goes to drastic measures to make him stay; a bit dated, and odd, in retrospect.
- **The Delicate Art of Parking**, directed by Trent Carlson (2003) – a mockumentary about a Vancouver parking officer and the hassles he encounters as he tickets irate motorists.
- **Mount Pleasant**, directed by Ross Weber (2007) – three couples from Vancouver's Mt Pleasant (otherwise known as SoMa) find their lives fusing into a tangled mess of obsession and tragedy when a child finds a discarded needle in her garden; it's intense and disturbing.

in the 1960s, making them the city's oldest, and both stage classics and new works by Canadian playwrights, often starring a recognizable name or two from the national theater scene.

The real excitement lies in emerging companies and their creation of new works. A shortage of mid-sized venues (those in the 100- to 250-seat range) means groups have to be creative. The Firehall Arts Centre (p179) is in a former fire station, Performance Works (p171) occupies an old machine shop on Granville Island, and the Fei & Milton Wong Experimental Theatre (p171) is an exciting new space on the SFU campus at the recently completed Woodwards development. Smaller companies without permanent homes often use these spaces.

Veteran leading lights of the Vancouver theater scene include actors such as Christopher Gaze and Bernard Cuffling. You can also catch the up-and-coming next generation of thesps at several local colleges (see the boxed text, p180); each produces a full (and highly professional) season of stage productions every year.

One of the city's most popular annual events, the Vancouver International Fringe Festival (p16) attracts more than 100 smaller companies to the region each fall, many performing site-specific works everywhere from garages to dance clubs to a moving miniferry. This event is Canada's third-largest fringe fest, after Edmonton and Winnipeg.

Outdoor theater is also a hit in Vancouver, which is no wonder given the environs. Bard on the Beach (p178) is Shakespeare performed in a waterfront park against a backdrop of mountains and ocean. Also, the outdoor Malkin Bowl in Stanley Park has been around since 1940 and is home to the summer-performing Theatre Under the Stars (p180) troupe.

Amateur community-theater groups, which come under the umbrella organization Theatre BC (☎ 250-591-0018; www.theatrebc.org), stage productions at venues around the region. In addition, the

ALL THE WORLD'S A STAGE

Which plays have been most popular with audiences over the years? *A Midsummer Night's Dream* has always been a big hit. There is something magical about the setting of the play against the backdrop of our natural Vancouver skyline. *The Taming of the Shrew* is also hugely popular and we've had great success with *The Comedy of Errors, Twelfth Night, The Tempest* and *As You Like It*.

What do you think is the appeal of the tented setting for audiences? It is simply a splendid way to spend a summer day or evening; it's the quintessential Vancouver experience. Our tented theaters are a modern interpretation of Shakespeare's Globe: they are festive, elegant and they protect against the vicissitudes of the seasons.

What have been some of the big challenges of making the festival a success? Our funding and infrastructure has built slowly and steadily, and the caliber of our work has become more profound as our resources have continued to grow. Perhaps one of the most challenging aspects is responding to the demand and continuing to grow in a manner that will allow us to accommodate a larger audience while still maintaining the intimate experience of our festival.

Regular faces reappear on stage at Bard every year. What's the appeal for actors? I believe that one of the greatest aspects of our festival is the camaraderie amongst the actors, as well as a six-month contract at a prestigious theater company. When you work on Shakespeare you work on the greatest plays and the greatest parts.

What's the difference between shows chosen for the main stage or the studio stage? Generally speaking, because the studio stage is smaller, we put on productions of the lesser-known works and therefore risk less. However, it is intriguing to sometimes put well-known plays in the extremely intimate studio stage – it's very appealing to be within 3ft of Hamlet, Falstaff and Henry V.

What are your favorite Shakespeare roles to play? I loved playing Bottom in *A Midsummer Night's Dream*, Shylock in *The Merchant of Venice* and the title roles in *Lear* and *Richard III*.

What do you think Shakespeare would make of the festival? I hope most sincerely that he would be delighted. We strive to honor his words and provide audiences with an accessible interpretation of his work. The ultimate fantasy would be to have old Bill come down, grab a beer and some popcorn and take in a wonderful show. He would then realize that his plays were not of an age but for all time.

An interview with Christopher Gaze, actor and founding artistic director of Bard on the Beach (p178), Vancouver's massively popular Shakespeare festival, staged in tents every year in Vanier Park.

Playwrights Theatre Centre (☎ 604-685-6228; www.playwrightstheatre.com) annually chooses from more than 100 scripts submitted by aspiring playwrights, rigorously workshops around 30, and eventually performs several at its May New Play Festival on Granville Island.

For more information on Vancouver's theater scene, see p178.

DANCE

Vancouver is second only to Montréal as a Canadian dance center. The city's dance scene is as eclectic as its cultural makeup, and ranges from traditional Japanese and Chinese dance to classical ballet and edgy contemporary. There are dozens of professional dance companies and many more independent choreographers in the Vancouver area. The Dance Centre (p172) is the main resource in the province and its range of activities is unparalleled in Canada, including support for professional artists, operation of Western Canada's flagship dance facility and presentation of programs and events for the public.

Until the 1960s, Vancouver's dance scene was represented by those who trained in the city before leaving for greater things. The creation of the Pacific Ballet Theatre by Maria Lewis in 1969 saw the first permanent ballet company take hold in Vancouver and, now renamed Ballet BC (p172), it has become one of the country's top ballet companies – despite a funding crisis that saw it almost spinning its last pirouette in 2009.

One of the first modern dance companies to emerge was the Western Dance Theatre in 1970. It inspired a generation of Vancouver dancers to form companies, including Karen Jamieson (p173). In contrast, Experimental Dance and Music, founded in 1982, is an internationally respected company taking a multimedia-meets-improvisational approach. It inspired key dance companies such as Mascall Dance and Lola Dance.

Many of Vancouver's top dance companies converge at annual dance festivals, which help foster the city's reputation as a dance stronghold. The three-week Vancouver International Dance Festival (p13) is held during spring, and the highly anticipated 10-day Dancing on the Edge (p14) event is in July.

For more information on Vancouver's dance scene, see p172.

ARCHITECTURE
BUILT TO LAST

When the first version of Vancouver burned to the ground in just 45 minutes during the Great Fire of 1886, it seemed prudent to consider brick and stone for the new town that would emerge from the smoldering ashes. Some of the buildings from this era still survive and have been preserved as a reminder of a time when Vancouver's skyline was not just about glass towers.

While responsible for only a few of the Vancouver buildings created during this period, controversial turn-of-the-20th-century colonial Francis Rattenbury set the tone for the city's monumental rebuilding. Arriving from the UK in his early 20s with a modest background in architecture, he pumped up his credentials and impressed the locals with his grandiose ideas for city halls and courthouses across the province, at a time when BC was attempting to lay its foundations for the future. Those towns that didn't choose one of his turreted, multicolumned edifices usually chose designs that copied his grand confections.

Victoria was Rattenbury's main muse – the Parliament Buildings (p209) and the Fairmont Empress Hotel (p214) were both his, and both have design quirks that show his architectural deficiencies – but he also won a couple of commissions in Vancouver. He designed

ARTWORK POWER STATION

While next door's blue-tiled Electra apartment building, former headquarters of BC Electric, is a preserved reminder of 1950s Vancouver modernism, the anonymous-looking Dal Grauer Substation at 950 Burrard St is easily ignored. Which is a shame, since it was originally one of the most exciting public art installations in Vancouver. Fronting the machinery of a large substation, local artist BC Binning added a vast exterior of colored glass panels, giving the impression of a giant Mondrian painting that revealed the staircases and industrial workings of the interior. Following a 1980s fire, the panels were replaced with utilitarian plastic sheets. Plans to restore the site to its original look have, so far, failed to materialize.

Roedde House (p66) in 1893, oversaw the facelift of the original Hotel Vancouver in 1901 and created the handsome Vancouver Courthouse (now the Vancouver Art Gallery, p56) in 1912.

Despite his role in shaping the look of early Vancouver and the wider province, Rattenbury is remembered today in rather less auspicious terms. As work dried up in the 1920s – there are only so many grand courthouses and city halls required in any given area – he was forced to return home to the UK, where he found his colonial designs were largely out of fashion. In March 1935 he was killed by his wife's young lover (the couple's chauffer), leading to a tawdry court case that gripped the nation's tabloid newspapers.

But Rattenbury's ideas had already become passé on the West Coast by the time of his demise. The buildings being fashioned in Vancouver in the 1920s and 1930s reflected influential international movements like art deco and art nouveau: sinuous streamlined designs that seemed far superior to the chunky monuments of the city's early days. The few elegant edifices that remain from this era are today among the city's favorite buildings, although their chequered histories make their existence almost miraculous.

These include the copper-colored Dominion Building at the corner of Hastings and Cambie Sts, built by the Dominion Trust Company in 1910. The company went bankrupt four years later and its manager committed suicide. The beloved Sylvia Hotel (p200) overlooking English Bay was built in 1912 but its owner had to sell up during WWI as a depression hit the city. When the green-domed World Tower (100 W Pender St) opened its doors in 1913, it claimed to be the tallest building in the British Empire – a claim already made by the Dominion two years earlier. Later renamed as the Sun Tower, it was home to the *Vancouver Sun* for decades. Take a look at the waterfront concrete monstrosity *Sun* staffers now work in – it's the one blighting your view from the towering Vancouver Lookout (p57).

The city's most beloved building from this era also has a colorful past. The Marine Building (p57) was started in 1929, just before the Great Depression. When the financial tsunami hit town, the builders decided to soldier on but couldn't find any tenants. When finished, they offered their $2.5 million tower to the city for $1 million. The city declined – a mistake, since it would have made an ideal city hall – and it was sold on to local developers at a massive loss. The no-expense-spared creation remains arguably the most attractive building in the city, complete with exterior aquatic friezes, interiors resembling a Mayan temple and elevators inlaid with 12 types of rare hardwood.

Of course, not all architecture of the time was quite so grandiose. In the early decades of the 20th century, Craftsman-style bungalows and large family homes sprouted up around the city, primarily in neighborhoods such as Kitsilano, Kerrisdale and Shaughnessy. Many of these were built for managers and senior workers in the burgeoning rail and port sectors and were the first wholesale attempts to colonize areas of the city that had previously been forest or traditional First Nations land.

These woodsy residences were distinguished by their brick chimneys, shingle exteriors, stained-glass flourishes and interior woodwork, often featuring built-in cupboards and shelves. While many of these oak-floored structures were cleared to make way for concrete towers and 'more efficient' developments from the 1950s onwards, the remaining homes are today the most sought-after in Vancouver, frequently fetching million-dollar price tags.

CONTEMPORARY CONSTRUCTIONS

By the late 1950s the city's architecture had lost its flair. Nondescript but functional high-rises began foresting the West End and creeping across other parts of the city, often replacing cute housing developments and handsome business towers that seemed suddenly old-fashioned.

HERE COMES THE BIG ONE

Supposedly ever-ready with their 'emergency earthquake kits,' Vancouverites reside in one of North America's most active quake zones. Of the 300 or so tremors that hit every year, most go unnoticed by all except seismologists. The rest of the region is reminded of the danger every 20 to 50 years, when a larger quake strikes the area – such as the one that hit north of Courtenay on Vancouver Island in 1946 and measured 7.3 on the Richter scale.

Every 300 to 600 years, the region has been hit by a major quake measuring 8.5 – that's the 'big one' that may be due any day now, since the last one of this magnitude was in 1700. In the worst-case scenario, an 8.5+ quake would result in landslides and tsunamis along the coast, and damage up to 30% of Greater Vancouver's homes and 15% of its high-rises.

About $300 million has been spent to reinforce bridges, tunnels, buildings and other structures in the region, while an emergency operations center has been built at Rupert and Hastings Sts. Three saltwater pumping stations with earthquake-resistant piping have been built around town to act as backups in case the main water supply fails or is shut down, and other waterlines are gradually being upgraded.

The idea of heritage preservation was yet to take hold in Vancouver. By the time it eventually did, in the 1970s, huge swathes of architectural and social history had been lost and now only small pockets of it remain. The Architectural Institute of British Columbia (p236) offers highly recommended walking tours exploring this colorful heritage.

But the city's golden age of building design was not just a flash in the pan. By the 1960s a new movement emerged that put the city back on the architectural map. Jumping on the modernist bandwagon that was sweeping the world at the time, Vancouver developed its own timber-framed version – called 'post and beam' – where horizontal lintels are supported by posts at either end. Attributes of this approach (considered novel at the time) included a flat roof and large windows to capitalize on scenery and natural light. The premier proponent was local architect and landscape designer Arthur Erickson. He took the idea to the next level, creating a look so specific to the city that it became known as 'Vancouver architecture.'

Erickson positioned his first project, Simon Fraser University, along the ridge of nearby Burnaby Mountain, using Douglas fir beams and steel tie-rods to support a glazed roof. The setup around a central mall encouraged student interaction, so much so that the design was blamed for prompting student unrest in the late 1960s. His most important contribution to the downtown core is Robson Sq and the adjoining Provincial Law Courts – just across the street from the Vancouver Art Gallery building, Vancouver's original court.

The giant Provincial Law Courts building, envisaged like a structure encased in a cool glass wrapper, was opened back in 1979 but Erickson remained active and prolific in the city – despite being revered as one of Canada's greatest living architects – right up until his death in 2009. His work can be seen in diverse projects around Vancouver, including the Museum of Anthropology (p101), the Sikh Temple and the Dance Centre (p172). Among his most striking – and controversial – downtown blocks is the MacMillan Bloedel Building (1075 W Georgia St), perhaps the epitome of 'Vancouver architecture.' Coloquially known as the 'waffle building,' it combines a flared base (like tapering tree trunks) with a multifloored tower of uniform concrete squares, each a deeply recessed window.

Expo '86 delivered more new forms to the local cityscape. Canada Place (p57), with its five great sails of fiberglass fabric, rose on the site of an old cargo pier. Credited to designers Eberhard Zeidler (architect of Toronto's Eaton Centre), Musson Cattell Mackey Partnership and Archambault Architects, the building was intended to rival Australia's Sydney Opera House. Reflecting a newer 'West Coast' approach in regional design that often includes dramatic stone walls and glossy golden wood ceilings, a giant convention center extension with a quite different look was added next door in 2010. Its signature feature is a shaggy grass-covered roof.

Appearing on almost as many postcards as Canada Place, Science World (p78) is visually renowned for its silver, golf ball–like geodesic dome. Local boy and UBC grad Bruno Freschi created it from 766 vinyl-covered aluminum triangles yielding a volume of 36,790 cu meters. The best part? It lights up at night. During the 2010 Winter Olympics, the striking building was used to showcase Sochi, site of the 2014 games in Russia.

International architect Moshe Safdie has said there's no connection between his $100 million Vancouver Public Library (p60) built in 1995 and Rome's Colosseum, but everyone else disagrees. The library drew criticism from the design community as an out-of-place eyesore, but its shop-filled piazza and bright spaces for reading, studying and hanging are firm favorites among the locals. In fact, its glass-enclosed atrium is a reflection of latter-day Vancouver's main architectural moniker, 'City of Glass' – a label that continues to apply to the latest construction projects here.

Completed in 2001, the sleek One Wall Centre on Burrard St was the tallest tower in the city for almost a decade until the Shangri-La, at the corner of W Georgia and Thurlow Sts, opened in 2009. Dominating its surroundings, the neck-cracking 201m glass block houses a luxury hotel on its lower floors and pricey condominiums on its upper floors – including a penthouse estate that sold for a rumored $15 million. Not bad for a city where small wooden houses were the only option just a century or so before.

ENVIRONMENT & PLANNING

THE LAND

Greater Vancouver straddles the lowlands of the Fraser River and the Coast Mountains of southwest BC. The Coast range, at only 20 million years of age, is one of North America's youngest mountain groups. The Coast's North Shore Range stretches from the Black Mountain in the west to Mt Seymour in the east. It is separated by Burrard Inlet's Indian Arm fjord from the Golden Ears mountain group, which dominates the Fraser Valley.

The Fraser River, which cuts through the center of the Lower Mainland, has its source in the Rocky Mountains and travels 1375km to its delta on the Strait of Georgia. The Fraser's tributaries include the Coquitlam, Chilcotin, Nechako, Pitt and Thompson Rivers. Not only is this Canada's third-largest river, it is also the country's fifth-largest river system and the richest salmon river in North America. The many bays, inlets and river branches that lap the coastline are distinctive features.

The region's original First Nations inhabitants occupied many of the best waterfront stretches here, favoring areas that offered inlet shelter, access to hunting grounds and proximity to rivers. The later colonials also stayed close to the shoreline in their first few years, gradually clearing the dense forests and moving into the interior as far as the baseline of local mountains. Latter-day Vancouverites are lucky if they can afford to live on the waterfront, although mountain views are a cheaper and more ubiquitous substitute.

URBAN PLANNING & DEVELOPMENT

Much of the city's recent urban planning was driven by the 2010 Olympic and Paralympic Winter Games. The chichi Olympic Village built on the southeast corner of False Creek aimed to be a model for sustainable development, mixing market and social housing with eco-friendly construction approaches. It didn't quite turn out like that: due to escalating costs, the City of Vancouver was forced to underwrite the project to the tune of almost $1 billion and the social-housing element was reduced after the Games so that costs could be more effectively recouped. The third leg of the SkyTrain system (known as the Canada Line) was also opened just in time for the Olympics and is now the only transit option for traveling from the airport to downtown. Finally, the winding Sea-to-Sky Hwy (Hwy 99) between Vancou-

THE PERFECT STORM

The day after an epic windstorm lashed Stanley Park (p62) in late 2006, city employees gingerly entered to assess the damage. At least 45 hectares – an estimated 10,000 trees – had been leveled, mostly on the exposed western side. Stretches of the seawall were blocked by debris and some of the upturned old trees were suddenly exposing root systems several meters high – one uprooted tree remains near the W Georgia St entrance as a reminder of the tempest. After extensive clearing and renovation, the park was fully reopened almost a year later. It's worth remembering that 1962's Hurricane Frieda was the last storm to hit the park with such ferocity: the area it flattened was used to lay tracks for the Miniature Railway (p62), now one of the city's top kid-friendly attractions.

ver and Whistler underwent a $600 million upgrade to make it a wider and comparatively safer drive.

The grungy Downtown Eastside area around Main and Hastings Sts has been the subject of gentrification dreams for decades. But it wasn't until the landmark Woodwards department-store building was finally redeveloped into housing, shops and a university campus that change began effectively blowing into the area. Complete with its reproduction 'W' neon sign on the roof, the new Woodwards should finally become the catalyst that sparks the area's long-overdue recovery.

Tower blocks continue to sprout across the downtown area and beyond while older apartment blocks – especially in the West End – are being snapped up, renovated and put back on the market at much higher rents by developers with little regard for the occupants who have called the area home for decades. It's an issue that will continue to define – and redefine – the neighborhood for years to come.

GOVERNMENT & POLITICS

Under the terms of its Vancouver Charter, the city (www.vancouver.ca) has a mayor – its chief administrative official – plus nine city councilors. Each is elected every three years and serves at the imposing City Hall, located at the intersection of W 12th Ave and Cambie St. The officials all represent the entire city, although this has been the subject of ongoing debate, with some locals believing the city should be split into wards again, as it was until the mid-1900s.

Provincial party politics do not have a direct bearing on city government, although there are affiliations. When it comes time for elections, there are civic political parties, including Vision Vancouver and the Non-Partisan Association (NPA), which put forward candidates, although many individuals run and have been elected as independents. However, these political parties don't seem to have much bearing on the actual policies implemented by the mayor or councilors during their tenure.

For several years Vancouver maintained a fairly conservative-leaning city council, but the new millennium brought a more progressive group to office, including Mayor Larry Campbell and his NPA successor Sam Sullivan. While Campbell was known for championing safe drug injection sites (see the boxed text, below), Sullivan will always be remembered for the image that flashed around the world from the 2008 Beijing Summer Olympics, where he waved a giant five-rings flag from his wheelchair and accepted the next Games for Vancouver.

It wasn't enough to win him the next election, though, and a new fella was already in the hot seat by the time the Winter Olympics kicked off in the city in February 2010. After making his fortune with an organic juice company, Gregor Robertson took on the city's thorny issues, most notably the Downtown Eastside. Perhaps rashly, he has promised to end homelessness in the area and across the city by 2015. The locals wait with bated breath.

SAFE INJECTION SITES

In September 2003 Vancouver opened North America's first safe injection site (also called a supervised injection site), a 12-seat room where users come in to inject drugs under the supervision of trained health-care staff, who issue clean needles, spoons, tourniquets and water.

The site is located in the Downtown Eastside, which has one of the largest concentrations of injection drug users on the continent. With AIDS and hepatitis beginning to reach epidemic proportions, the controversial program is part of a 'four pillars' approach (harm reduction, prevention, treatment and enforcement) pioneered in Switzerland and Germany. The idea is to reduce disease, infections, overdose deaths and drug-related crime.

After injecting, clients move to a 'chill-out' room, where staff can connect them with on-site services, such as medical care and counseling, or off-site services such as withdrawal management. In the site's first year, an average of 588 injections took place daily, 107 overdose incidents were successfully prevented and two to four clients per day were referred to addiction treatment.

The experimental facility has remained controversial since it opened – locals are divided on whether they want it in their city and the conservative federal government has threatened to pull the plug several times, noting that its pioneering approach has yet to prove itself fully effective in 'solving' the problem of drug use.

HAPPILY EVER AFTER

Following the kind of ugly, multiyear tussle usually associated with the end of a marriage rather than the beginning, Canada's Equal Marriage Act finally became law throughout the country in July 2005, two years after BC had passed its own legislation officially recognizing same-sex unions. Anyone over the age of 19 can now marry in BC, once a marriage license has been issued by the province. With a simple one-page application form, and costing $100, the required license is valid for three months. After pioneering the idea of gay marriage, BC – and particularly Vancouver, with its large gay population – has since become a destination of choice for travelers who want to tie the knot on their West Coast visit: don't be surprised to find beaming same-sex couples having their wedding photos taken in summertime Stanley Park. For handy information and resources on gay (or straight) marriage, visit www.vs.gov .bc.ca/marriage.

Including the city, Greater Vancouver – officially renamed Metro Vancouver (www.metro vancouver.org) in 2009 – consists of 21 Lower Mainland municipalities, each with its own elected mayor and councilors. Metro Vancouver oversees the joint interests of these municipalities and is a voluntary federation designed to deliver essential services more economically and equitably. In addition, the Government of BC (www.gov.bc.ca) has jurisdiction over Vancouver and the rest of the province from its Victoria base, while the Government of Canada (www.canada.gc.ca), located across the country in Ottawa, is responsible for federal political issues.

Although the provincial capital is Victoria, Vancouver is the center of the region's economy, with head offices and financial institutions crowding the downtown area. While the tourism and film industries are among the most important here, the older resource sectors continue to dominate. Forestry and mining are major industries in BC, which is one of the main reasons why environmental organizations are so strong here. Logging has particularly drawn the ire of local environmentalists over the years, sparking protests against clear-cutting and nonsustainable forestry practices by locals across the region. These protests have clearly affected the way logging companies operate in BC – and not only the amount of money they now spend on public relations.

As logging and mining slowly diminish, newer industries are taking hold in Vancouver's economy. These include high-tech and biotech: the city is home to dozens of upstart biotech companies, many clustered around UBC, and has also become a key international player in computer animation and game development – both offshoots of the city's veteran film-industry role. Finally, with its geographical role as a gateway to Asia, the city's port is the biggest and busiest in Canada, hence the continual movement of freight containers at the bustling waterfront east of town.

MEDIA

Vancouverites like to read, which explains the presence of two daily newspapers – the *Vancouver Sun* and the *Province* – plus Canada's largest alternative weekly, the *Georgia Straight*. There are also dozens of freebie community titles, a pair of competing weekday commuter rags and many specialty publications, including glossies ranging from society-focused *Vancouver Magazine* to literary quarterly *Vancouver Review*.

Some locals will tell you that quantity does not always equal quality, however, and they point to the city's two dailies as evidence of this. Vancouver's two main newspapers were originally owned by media behemoth Canwest, which was forced to sell them in 2010 due to a massive raft of accrued debt. At the time of writing, it remained to be seen whether the new owners will up the quality or look for further cost savings.

HOT BLOG

While the *Georgia Straight* (www.straight.com) and *The Tyee* (www.thetyee.ca) each do a great job of covering local political issues that the mainstream dailies seem to miss, the local reporter who has her finger on every important pulse in the city is Frances Bula. A veteran journo who writes for *Globe and Mail*, *Vancouver Magazine* and *BC Business* magazine, Bula often breaks stories on local hot topics that no-one else comes close to finding. Her blog, State of Vancouver (www.francesbula.com), is well worth a read if you want to have something to talk about with the locals when you roll into town.

Not everyone is taking a wait-and-see approach, though. Former *Sun* editor David Beers established *The Tyee* (www.thetyee.ca) in 2004. Named after a 'feisty fish,' it features the work of some of the city's best journalists. While it breaks stories missed by the mainstream media, its key strength is its in-depth analysis of pertinent local issues, which can range from street racing in Richmond to the green building claims of local developers. Predominantly a listings paper, the *Georgia Straight* often fulfills a similar investigative role in its feature stories, although its news beat has been reduced in recent years.

For a comprehensive listing of the city's media publications, see p235.

VANCOUVER LIFE

Inspired by their stunning surroundings, Vancouverites have discovered more ways to interact with the outdoors than almost anyone. But the locals are not just a bunch of Lycra-clad, rice cake-noshing fitness freaks. This is one of Canada's top dining towns and it's undergone a seismic shift in great new restaurants in recent years, triggered by an inspiring fusion of international influences and ingredients from across the province. Imbibing has undergone a similar revolution: bars here now proudly showcase distinctive, lip-smacking wines and beers produced right on the city's doorstep. Vancouverites, it seems, have become dedicated and informed 'locavores.' The arts and nightlife scenes are similarly tasty – although you'll have to get creative to discover their sometimes well-hidden highlights.

'This really is a city where you can ski in the morning and hit the beach in the afternoon'

Wherever you end up rubbing shoulders with the residents, it won't be long before you've told them how much you love their city and they've replied that it's not all perfect. For every Vancouverite who enjoyed the Olympics, you'll find another with a mental shopping list of what else the money could have been spent on. House prices have also been shooting skywards here in recent years, triggering angst among residents who want to stay but can't afford to buy. And that's before you get onto the thorny topic of the Downtown Eastside, the destitute neighborhood that's been a blot on the city's 'best place in the world to live' reputation for decades.

But while the serious side of life is always bubbling beneath the surface, Vancouverites also know how to let their hair down. With its giant free fireworks displays, jazz, fringe and film festivals and dozens of year-round annual events, the 'city of glass' can be great fun for in-the-know visitors. You'll come to Vancouver for the picture-postcard views but you'll stick around for the lively but always laid-back vibe.

Stanley Park (p62) – postcard-perfect in the fall – is a sea, sand and forest spectacular dear to the city's heart

HIGHLIGHTS

DINING, DRINKING & DISTRICTS

The lifeblood of the city is its distinctive neighborhoods, many worth a day of exploring. A rolling smorgasbord of great nosh will keep you fueled. While seafood is a good starting point, make sure you dip in to some finger-licking ethnic eateries and taste-trip at a night market.

❶ Vij's
Fusion is a Vancouver dining trait, pioneered at this contemporary Indian restaurant (p143)

❷ Gastown
Vancouver's once-grungy original 'hood is now alive with great bars (p154)

❸ SoMa
South Main's eclectic designer shops are dripping with hipster fashions (p119)

❹ Commercial Drive
The Drive's coffee-fueled counterculture vibe keeps this area lively (p85)

❺ Chinatown Night Market
Paper lanterns light up the alfresco market (p79)

LAWRENCE WORCESTER

LAWRENCE WORCESTER

LAWRENCE WORCEST

④

⑤

ACTIVE VANCOUVER

Vancouverites are born wearing Lycra, so you can expect to see plenty of muscle-stretching locals sweating their way around the city. Visitors can mix with the heavy-breathing fraternity on jogging and cycling trails, or at local ski, beach and kayaking hot spots.

1 Stanley Park
Seawall cycling, jogging or blading are ideal scenery-ogling activities (p182)

2 Kayaking
Hop in a kayak and admire the cityscape from the water (p185)

3 Grouse Mountain
Cafe diners look down at Vancouver's top winter playground and the city below (p187)

LEE FOSTER

DOUG MCKINLAY

CHRISTOPHER HERWIG

MICHELE FALZONE/JAI/CORBIS

LAWRENCE WORCESTER

CITY STYLE

Set amid mountains, sea and forest, Vancouver is a visual treat for camera-wielding visitors. But it's not just about the natural surroundings here: the city is stuffed with non-natural sights that complement the appeal of those well-known outdoorsy vistas.

① Public Art
The city challenges with some wild and wacky public art displays (p27)

② Totem Poles
The handsome Stanley Park totems (p63) are stirring reminders of the region's first residents

③ City of Glass
Downtown's shimmering glass towers (p35) are Vancouver's modern-day forests

MANFRED GOTTSCHALK

ANDREW BAIN

RYAN FO...

① Granville Island
Spend an afternoon soaking up waterfront shops and galleries (p88)

② False Creek
The city's colorful miniferries (p227) are the best way to hit the water

③ Second Beach
By day a sunbathing hot spot, but come dusk it's a sunset-viewing favorite (p64)

WATER, WATER EVERYWHERE!

Surrounded by water on three sides, Vancouver is a port city that will always have a little sea salt running through its veins. For visitors, there are plenty of ways to enjoy this coastal undercurrent.

RICHARD CUMMI...

GREEN VANCOUVER

Enjoy the rich fall colors of Stanley Park (p62), the lungs of the city

LAWRENCE WORCESTER

GREEN VANCOUVER

Temperate rainforest, North Vancouver (p105)

LAWRENCE WORCESTER

It's hard to see Vancouver as anything but a green city. Its dense, majestic forests and verdant, rain-fed plant life make nature an ever-present fact of life here. But beyond the breathtaking visuals, how does the city measure up to its environmental responsibilities? And – just as importantly – what can visitors do to reduce their eco-footprints in the region without turning their vacations into monastic, fun-free zones?

Wandering the city, you'll notice an active, outdoorsy populace that likes to celebrate the natural surroundings on foot, blade or bike whenever possible (and in all weathers). Many of these grinning, superfit locals are members of one of Vancouver's dozens of eco-active lobby groups. Their widespread concern for the environment means that large developments – whether improvements to Hwy 99 or new housing blocks at the University of British Columbia – are usually accompanied by plenty of hand-wringing and, more often than not, some determined protests.

As environmental issues become more pressing, Vancouver is rising to prominence as an important think tank for ideas such as livability, sustainability and urban density. City and provincial governments have gradually accepted that the area's green agenda has moved from the periphery to the political mainstream. In 2003 Vancouver's city council instituted a Climate Change Action Plan designed to reduce greenhouse-gas emissions in its operations by 20% before 2010. That target was met but the next ones include making all operations carbon neutral by 2012 and reducing emissions across the community by 33% by 2020. The birthplace of Greenpeace and the home of David Suzuki may finally be ready for its long-touted green leadership role on the world stage.

top picks
VANCOUVER'S GREEN BOOKS

The Legacy, David Suzuki (2010) – distilling Suzuki's wisdom on the environment into a single tome, complete with a vision for the future.

Greater Vancouver Green Guide, UBC Design Centre for Sustainability (2009) – a showcase of green buildings, projects and initiatives around the city.

Guerilla Gardening: A Manualfesto, David Tracey (2009) – tips for greening your urban space, including where to find cheap or free plants and how to plant them without permission.

100-Mile Diet: A Year of Local Eating, Alisa Smith and James Mackinnon (2007) – fascinating autobiographical story of what happened to a local couple when they tried to source their entire diet from their Vancouver doorstep.

The Greenpeace to Amchitka, Robert Hunter (2004) – firsthand account of the inaugural protest voyage from Vancouver that kick-started Greenpeace.

PAINTING THE TOWN GREEN

Vancouver has an international reputation for being a green city, but that doesn't mean everyone here wears biodegradable socks and eats only elderly vegetables that have died of natural causes. In fact, if you stroll the Robson St boutiques or dip into a take-out coffee shop, it's easy to think that 'green Vancouver' doesn't exist at all. As with many of the city's best features – think arts and neighborhoods – you have to do a little digging to find the meat (or at least the tofu) of the issue.

VanDusen Botanical Garden (p92)

Given the city's breathtaking natural surroundings, it was just a matter of time before Vancouver's residents were inspired to protect the planet, which explains why a few of them began gathering in a Kitsilano basement in 1969 to plan the fledgling Don't Make a Wave Committee's first protest against nuclear testing in Alaska. By the time their campaign boat entered the Gulf of Alaska in 1971, they had renamed themselves Greenpeace and sailed into environmental history.

Greenpeace set the tone and the city has since become a headquarters for environmental groups (see p47), from the Wilderness Committee to Farm Folk City Folk and the David Suzuki Foundation – the eponymous organization headed by Canada's most celebrated environmental scientist (see p48).

Actions speak louder than words, though, and Vancouver's green scene is not just about protest and discussion. The city is home to dozens of large and small eco-initiatives, enabling many locals to color their lives as green as they choose. Vancouver has one of the largest hybrid-vehicle taxi fleets in North America and has a commitment to mass public transport, including electric trolley buses and a light-rail train system that was recently expanded to the airport. Carpooling is also big in the city, with the Jack Bell Foundation's rideshare scheme (www.ride-share.com) matching travelers with shared vehicle trips throughout the region.

A blader cruises along the seawall promenade in Stanley Park (p62)

top picks

GREAT GREEN ATTRACTIONS

Stanley Park (p62) – a sea, sand and forest spectacular just minutes from downtown

Mt Seymour Provincial Park (p105) – trails, trees and wintertime snow: a great nature-hugger's day out

Lost Lagoon Nature House (p64) – illuminating Stanley Park's flora and fauna, including nature walks

UBC Botanical Garden (p101) – fascinating, educational and evocative landscaped gardens

Lynn Canyon Park & Ecology Centre (p106) – exploring the region's ecosystem, with a free suspension bridge

Plants for sale in UBC's Botanical Garden (p101)

LAWRENCE WORCESTER

In construction, the green potential of any design project is always part of the plan here. And while developers often tout their green credentials as if they're saving the planet single-handedly, few of the new towers currently reforesting the city were built without key environmental considerations – this includes the 2010 Olympic athletes village, built on the southeast edge of False Creek, that was converted into a condominium development after the Games.

Vancouver is also a leader in 'green roofs' – planted rooftops that curb wasted energy through natural evaporation in summer and natural insulation in winter. The Shangri-La Hotel complex (p198) and the Vancouver Public Library (p60) have these, while the giant new extension to the convention centre at Canada Place (p57) also has one: it's a shaggy grass covering that looks like it could use a hungry goat or two to keep it in shape.

Inspired by a surging demand for locally sourced food and the popular 100-Mile Diet movement (www.100milediet.org) established by two local writers (see the boxed text, p42), many city restaurants and food stores are now bringing BC seafood, meat, vegetables and even beer to the tables and kitchens of city diners from just a few kilometers away – rather than the thousands of 'food miles' that used to be attached to them in many city eateries.

MEGAPRESS/ALAMY

A leafy backyard bonanza

Locals celebrate their pedal power through Critical Mass Ride and Roll

TRAVELING GREEN

You're gnawing on a rubbery sandwich at 35,000ft, marveling that your flight to Vancouver is taking just a few hours, when a wave of regret hits you like a burst of unexpected turbulence. It's not that your meal tastes like an old beach sandal, or that the legroom on the plane seems designed for a height-challenged five-year-old. What really raises your hackles is the question of just how green your trip is.

Luckily, there are lots of ways to make your Vancouver vacation a little more enviro-friendly. Travelers from North America can ditch the plane completely and take options that reduce their greenhouse-gas footprint. Trains (p229) from across Canada and south of the border arrive throughout the day, while buses (p227) – still a better option than flying – trundle in from similar locales. If you have to fly, consider a carbon-offsetting scheme (see the boxed text, p226).

Vancouver has an extensive transit network (p229) as well as more than 300km of designated bike lanes (p226), so you can get around the city without burning up the planet. Bike rentals are easy to come by here and there are many operators that can get you on two wheels for a citywide pedal (p182). If you're a die-hard driver and you're here for more than a few days, consider joining the Zipcar (www.zipcar.com) rental network of smaller, often hybrid cars as an alternative to traditional car hire. Alternatively, try an escorted tour with the friendly folk at Vancouver Eco Tours (p236). They operate regional sightseeing excursions in vehicles that run on vegetable oil collected from local restaurants.

ECO SAVINGS

Green-minded travelers who want to save the planet *and* save a few bucks should consider picking up a Green Zebra Guide (www.greenzebraguide.ca). The bulging coupon book – available online or via the businesses listed on its website – costs $20 and offers hundreds of deals and discounts at eco-minded shops, spas, restaurants and attractions throughout Metro Vancouver.

Fall pumpkins, fresh for Halloween

EOIN CLARKE

A-maze-ing VanDusen Botanical Garden (p92)

RICHARD CUMMI

ISLEMOUNT IMAGES/ALA

BACKYARD FARMS TAKE ROOT

Taking the burgeoning local-food movement one step further, Vancouver's City Farm Boy (www.cityfarm boy.com) is colonizing the area's tiny, often forgotten green spaces to grow fruit and vegetables right on people's doorsteps. Founded by Saskatchewan transplant Ward Teulon, City Farm Boy works by turning urban residents' unloved and unused garden plots into mini produce-growing areas for everything from carrots, lettuce and beans to chard, rhubarb and garlic. Usually the owners of the plots, happy to see their unkempt garden corners being put to good use, ask only for a few kilos of produce in payment. Teulon, who deploys pesticide-free organic growing methods, harvests the produce and sells it at local farmers markets the day after it's picked – the produce travels less than 5km from garden to shopping bag. Dedicated to urban agriculture as a way of improving the city landscape and enhancing local lifestyles, the fledgling operation started with four plots and aims to have a network of 20 more within a couple of years.

But Teulon's isn't the city's only backyard-farming initiative in town. In 2010, the city legislated that urban Vancouverites could begin keeping their own chickens, which could transform the 100-Mile Diet idea in a two-step. Check out the new initiative at www .chickensinvancouver.com.

Zipcars – Vancouver's car-sharing scheme (p45)

ON THE GROUND

Once you're in Vancouver (or before you arrive), consider selecting accommodation that has some kind of environmental program. Opus Hotel (p201), for example, has a water and energy conservation scheme, while the Fairmont Hotel Vancouver (p195) deploys energy-efficient lighting and purchases green power for its property.

Dining is also firmly on the green vacation agenda here. Spearheaded by the Vancouver Aquarium and a growing menu of city restaurants, Ocean Wise (www.oceanwise.ca) encourages sustainable fish and shellfish supplies that minimize environmental impact. Visit its website for a list of participating restaurants and check local menus for symbols indicating Ocean Wise dishes. A similar, smaller movement called the Green Table Network (www.greentable.net) can help you identify area restaurants that try to source all their supplies – not just seafood – from sustainable, mostly local sources.

Sustainability also has a social side with Green Drinks (www.greendrinks.org), a monthly drop-in gathering for anyone interested in environmental issues. The meetings take place at Steamworks Brewing Company (p155) and usually attract more than 100 regulars for beer-fueled discussions on alternative energy, global warming and the sky-high price of tickets to Al Gore events.

For more ways to green your visit, head online to Vancouver's sustainable web magazine, Granville (www.granvilleonline.ca). It's bristling with tips, resources and lively forums. And check the GreenDex on p255. It refers you to businesses in this book that demonstrate sustainable approaches to tourism.

HELPFUL ORGANIZATIONS

Local green organizations in Vancouver include the following:

David Suzuki Foundation (☎ 604-732-4228, 800-453-1533; www.davidsuzuki.org) Working with individuals, industry and government stakeholders, this 40,000-member organization researches the root scientific causes of environmental destruction and searches for sustainable alternatives.

Farm Folk City Folk (☎ 604-730-0450; www.ffcf.bc.ca) Creating and encouraging sustainable links between producers and consumers across the region, FFCF is active in building community gardens in Vancouver.

Vancouver Electric Vehicle Association (www.veva.bc.ca) Promoting and encouraging the use of battery-powered electric cars throughout the region, this group meets monthly.

Vancouver Farmers Markets (☎ 604-879-3276; www.eatlocal.org) Listings, maps and information covering farmers markets and producers around the city.

Wilderness Committee (☎ 604-683-8220, 800-661-9453; www.wildernesscommittee.org) One of Canada's largest wilderness preservation organizations, the 30,000-member group has successfully campaigned to save millions of hectares of natural lands across the country, much of it from logging practices.

KEVIN OKE/ALL CANADA PHOTOS/CORBIS

Eat your greens at one of Vancouver's farmers markets

DAVID SUZUKI'S GREEN TRAVEL TIPS

What are some of the biggest issues facing the environment today? Global warming is clearly the number-one issue, since it affects the entire planet. It is also the one that has galvanized public opinion because the evidence that it is happening is now obvious. But looking deeper, I think the problem lies in the beliefs and values that we cling to. We have forgotten that we are biological beings as dependent on nature's services – clean air, clean water, clean food and soil, clean energy, biodiversity – as any other creature. So we 'exploit' the very life-support systems of the planet while failing to recognize it jeopardizes the quality of our own lives.

What can readers of this book do to participate in solutions? They can get involved at every level of their lives. They can start making sustainable decisions by eating locally grown organic food, reducing emissions by using public transit, and making decisions at work that reflect their environmental values. Most importantly, they need to get involved politically and tell their elected leaders to make the environment a priority so that it's easier for us all to make better environmental choices and punish those who do not, like industrial polluters.

How 'green' is Vancouver? While there are some groundbreaking ideas about sustainability taking place here, Vancouver could be doing much more to make itself greener. For example, free public transportation would reduce air pollution and greenhouse-gas emissions and make it easier for people to get around. And considering that it is such a young city, more buildings and developments could be built with better energy efficiency in mind.

What can travelers to Vancouver do to make their vacations as green as possible? They can use public transit instead of renting a car. Most travelers find it a fascinating way to see the city. Vancouver also has lots of natural beauty that is best seen on foot, such as Stanley Park and the beaches around the city. They can also reduce their impact by staying in green hotels, purchase carbon-neutral credits to offset the emissions that come from traveling, and avoid buying things they don't need, like tacky souvenirs for their friends back home.

Are you optimistic about our environmental future? Rationally, I can see we are headed down a very dangerous road, undermining the life-support systems in the name of economic growth. But I have grandchildren and I have hope that we can turn the corner and move to a truly sustainable way of living. The need for change is urgent and I don't see the alarm being sounded in the political or corporate sphere. But I plug away because I have hope and I am inspired by Nelson Mandela, who in 27 years of prison must have despaired but never wavered. I just want to be able to look my grandchildren in the eye and tell them 'Grandpa did the best he could for you.'

An interview with David Suzuki, co-founder of the Vancouver-based David Suzuki Foundation and an award-winning scientist, environmentalist and broadcaster.

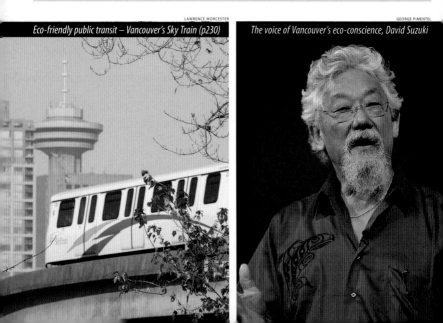

LAWRENCE WORCESTER
Eco-friendly public transit – Vancouver's Sky Train (p230)

GEORGE PIMENTEL
The voice of Vancouver's eco-conscience, David Suzuki

NEIGHBORHOODS

top picks

NEIGHBORHOODS

While 'outsiders' frequently label Vancouver as one of the planet's best places to live, hand-wringing locals often ask themselves whether or not this really is a world-class city. The answer lies not in making futile comparisons with older, larger and denser metropolises like London or New York but in searching for what really makes this area tick.

That's where Vancouver's varied neighborhoods come in. Unlike some cities, there's more than one heart here – no one calls the downtown area the 'city center' – and travelers can have a distinctively different day out depending on where they head. Luckily, with the city's on-foot suitability and user-friendly transit system, these neighborhoods are ideal for a spot of urban exploration.

> 'Unlike some cities, there's more than one heart here…and travelers can have a distinctively different day out depending on where they head'

Since it's where most of the hotels are, many visitors start among the towers and shops of downtown. The gridlike road system makes it easy to find your way around here, and you'll get frequent glimpses of snowcapped mountains grinning at you between the buildings. If you like to mix a little greenery with your concrete, head west along the seawall from Canada Place and you'll arrive at Stanley Park, where you can circumnavigate the forest and drink in the sea-to-sky vistas. In contrast, the adjoining West End is a densely packed residential district with plenty of life, lots of restaurants and some enticing historic enclaves. It's a gay-friendly neighborhood with a buzzing nightlife scene too.

There's also history to the east in Yaletown, a former industrial area reinvented as a 'little SoHo' stretch of yuppie apartments, lounge bars and excellent restaurants. You can stroll north from here to historic Gastown, the city's founding area. Another district reclaimed from a grungy past, it's Vancouver's main old-town neighborhood and has some great bars and characterful brick buildings. There's even more character in the adjoining Chinatown, where brightly painted, clammy-windowed restaurants lure visitors with aromas both sweet and savory.

A different crowd haunts the streets of South Main (SoMa), an edgy, student-chic district where the shabby hovels and mom-and-pop shops have been refreshed with cool coffee shops, unusual new restaurants and stores hawking hipster duds from bright local designers. Coffee is even more important on Commercial Dr, where generations of Italian immigrants serve the city's best java. It's not only about caffeine, though: this bohemian neighborhood is lined with convivial bars and restaurants.

The city's favorite half-day hangout for visitors, Granville Island is a strollable smorgasbord of artisan studios, galleries and the Granville Island Public Market. You can continue exploring in the nearby Fairview area, then take in the window-shopping delights of South Granville.

To the west of South Granville, Kitsilano enjoys some of the province's best urban beaches plus three of the city's main museums – bookstores are an additional shopping specialty here. The bookish might also enjoy the University of British Columbia (UBC). Western Canada's largest uni, it combines a city-best museum, landscaped gardens and rugged parkland.

Exploring Metro Vancouver, many visitors will be lured by North Van's mountainous charms and the coastal promise of West Vancouver. Both are located across Burrard Inlet – this is your excuse to cross the stunning Lions Gate Bridge. In contrast, a trip south of the city will bring you to Richmond, the region's latter-day 'Asia town' that still has a pocket of old fishing-village charm.

Now that you know where to go, it's time to hit the road. There are some handy walking tours in this chapter, but don't be afraid to wander off the beaten path to see what's just around the corner.

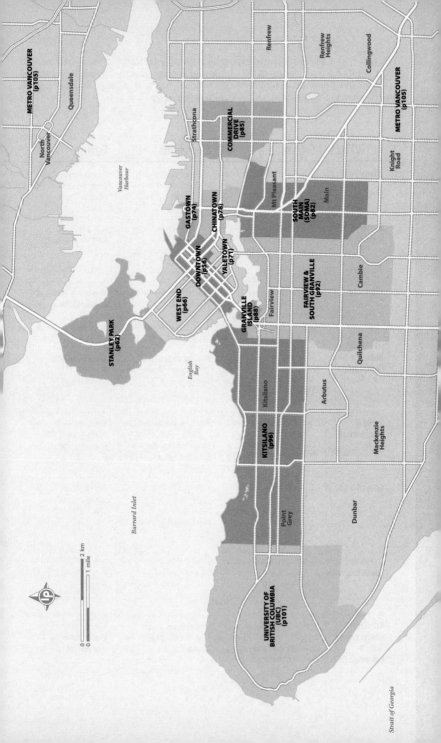

ITINERARY BUILDER

Vancouver's not a difficult city to explore, but to really get under its skin you'll need to check out its distinctive districts, the lifeblood of the city. This tool should help you find a range of treats in all of the featured neighborhoods, from the galleries and bookshops of downtown to the coffee shops and bars of Commercial Dr.

AREA	ACTIVITIES	Sights	Shopping	Eating
	Downtown	Vancouver Art Gallery (p56) Canada Place (p57) Bill Reid Gallery of Northwest Coast Art (p56)	MacLeod's Books (p113) Mink Chocolates (p114) Holt Renfrew (p113)	C Restaurant (p130) Templeton (p130) Chambar (p130)
	Stanley Park & West End	Vancouver Aquarium (p62) Stanley Park Seawall (p62) Roedde House Museum (p66)	Konbiniya Japan Centre (p115) Lululemon Athletica (p114) Little Sister's Book & Art Emporium (p114)	Guu with Garlic (p134) Raincity Grill (p133) Lolita's (p133)
	Yaletown	BC Place Stadium (p71) David Lam Park (p72) Roundhouse Community Arts & Recreation Centre (p71)	Coastal Peoples Fine Arts Gallery (p115) Lola Home & Apparel (p116) Brooklyn Clothing (p116)	Blue Water Café (p135) Regional Tasting Lounge (p136) Glowbal Grill Steak & Satay (p135)
	Gastown & Chinatown	Vancouver Police Museum (p74) Science World (p78) Chinatown Night Market (p79)	Erin Templeton (p118) John Fluevog Shoes (p117) Deluxe Junk (p116)	Judas Goat (p137) Bao Bei (p137) Acme Cafe (p137)
	SoMa & Commercial Drive	South False Creek Seawall (p82) Portobello West (p82) Punjabi Market (p82)	Regional Assembly of Text (p119) Dutch Girl Chocolates (p122) Mountain Equipment Co-op (p120)	Habit Lounge (p139) Chutney Villa (p139) Havana (p140)
	Granville Island	Granville Island Public Market (p88) Granville Island Brewing (p88) Emily Carr University of Art + Design (p90)	Gallery of BC Ceramics (p123) Paper-Ya (p123) Edie Hats (p122)	Go Fish (p142) Sandbar (p141) Agro Café (p142)
	Fairview & South Granville	VanDusen Botanical Garden (p92) Bloedel Floral Conservatory (p94) City Hall (p94)	Bacci's (p124) Oliver + Lilly's (p124) Meinhardt Fine Foods (p124)	Tojo's (p142) Vij's (p143) West (p142)
	Kitsilano & University of British Columbia (UBC)	Museum of Anthropology (p101) Museum of Vancouver (p98) Botanical Garden (p101)	Gravity Pope (p126) Zulu Records (p120) Stepback (p126)	Bishop's (p144) Bistrot Bistro (p144) Maenam (p144)

HOW TO USE THIS TABLE

The table below allows you to plan a day's worth of activities in any area of the city. Simply select which area you wish to explore, and then mix and match from the corresponding listings to build your day. The first item in each cell represents a well-known highlight of the area, while the other items are more off-the-beaten-track gems.

Drinking	Nightlife	Sports & Activities
UVA (p150) Bacchus (p150) Doolins (p151)	Railway Club (p168) Commodore (p167) Yale (p166)	Hockey: Vancouver Canucks (p191) Spa Utopia (p190) YWCA Health & Wellness Centre (p188)
Sylvia's Lounge (p152) Cardero's (p153) O'Doul's (p152)	O'Doul's (p166)	Second Beach Pool (p189) Spokes Bicycle Rentals (p183) Vancouver Aquatic Centre (p189)
Yaletown Brewing Company (p154) Opus Bar (p154) Atlantic Trap & Gill (p154)	Bar None (p163) Capones Restaurant & Live Jazz Club (p166)	Skoah (p190)
Alibi Room (p155) Six Acres (p155) Diamond (p154)	Fortune Sound Club (p164) Shine (p165) Rickshaw Theatre (p168)	
Cascade Room (p156) Narrow Lounge (p156) Three Lions Café (p156)	Biltmore Cabaret (p167) Café deux Soleils (p165) Libra Room (p166)	Cliffhanger Vancouver (p185)
Granville Island Brewing Taproom (p159) Backstage Lounge (p158) Dockside Brewing Company (p158)	Vancouver Theatresports League (p163) Backstage Lounge (p167)	Reckless Bike Stores (p183) Ecomarine Ocean Kayak Centre (p185)
		Baseball: Vancouver Canadians (p191)
Wolf & Hound (p159) Fringe Café (p159) Nevermind (p159)	Cellar Restaurant & Jazz Club (p166) Jericho Folk Club (p165)	UBC Aquatic Centre (p189) Windsure Adventure Watersports (p186) University Golf Club (p184)

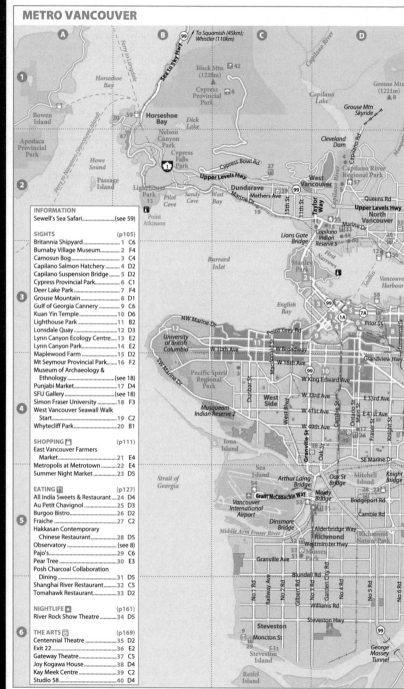

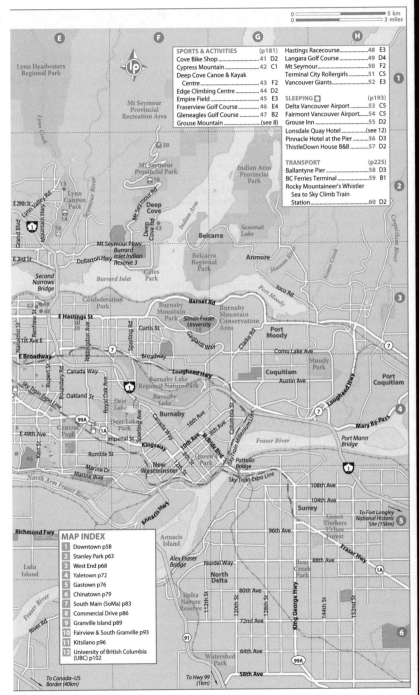

SPORTS & ACTIVITIES	(p181)
Cove Bike Shop	41 D2
Cypress Mountain	42 C1
Deep Cove Canoe & Kayak	
Centre	43 F2
Edge Climbing Centre	44 D2
Empire Field	45 E3
Fraserview Golf Course	46 E4
Gleneagles Golf Course	47 B2
Grouse Mountain	(see 8)

Hastings Racecourse	48 E3
Langara Golf Course	49 D4
Mt Seymour	50 F2
Terminal City Rollergirls	51 C5
Vancouver Giants	52 E3

SLEEPING	(p193)
Delta Vancouver Airport	53 C5
Fairmont Vancouver Airport	54 C5
Grouse Inn	55 D2
Lonsdale Quay Hotel	(see 12)
Pinnacle Hotel at the Pier	56 D3
ThistleDown House B&B	57 D2

TRANSPORT	(p225)
Ballantyne Pier	58 D3
BC Ferries Terminal	59 B1
Rocky Mountaineer's Whistler	
Sea to Sky Climb Train	
Station	60 D2

NEIGHBORHOODS METRO VANCOUVER

DOWNTOWN

Drinking p150; Eating p129; Shopping p112; Sleeping p195

Fringed by shimmering waterfront and the busy but diverse neighborhoods of Yaletown, Gastown and the West End, downtown Vancouver is the hub of the metropolis – which explains why the new Canada Line SkyTrain station at the intersection of Granville and W Georgia Sts is named Vancouver City Centre. Most visitors spend plenty of wandering time here – you can see them on every street corner clutching their maps, facing in opposite directions and looking puzzled. But while you'll soon get your bearings – the streets are on a grid system – there are several key areas that encourage a little additional on-foot exploration.

The waterfront stretch west of Canada Place has been revamped as a pedestrian hangout in recent years, with the new convention centre expansion creating a plaza that enjoys smashing views over the mountain-fringed inlet. Unpack your camera and try to catch a floatplane landing here. For a taste of the city's urban buzz, recline in the sun on the W Georgia St side of the Vancouver Art Gallery: the fountain here will keep you cool while you close your eyes and absorb the sounds (and hotdog aromas) of the downtown core. On the opposite Robson St side of the building, you'll find a large flight of steps that make for another great people-watching perch.

At night, the downtown action is centered on Granville St. This has been Vancouver's neon-lit entertainment strip for decades, although nightclubs and bars have mostly replaced the cinemas and music halls that lined the area in the 1950s. Check the sidewalk near the Orpheum Theatre: it's studded with plaques recalling the famous (and not-so-famous) entertainers who have played the strip over the years.

Main transit access to downtown includes the Granville, Burrard and Vancouver City Centre SkyTrain stations, plus Burrard St's buses 2, 22 and 44. Canada Line construction temporarily moved Granville St buses (including 4, 10 and 50) to nearby Howe St but, at the time of writing, they were poised to return to their original routes.

VANCOUVER ART GALLERY Map pp58-9

VAG; www.vanartgallery.bc.ca; 750 Hornby St; adult/child/senior/student $22.50/7.50/16/17, by donation 5-9pm Tue; ☺ 10am-5pm Wed-Mon, 10am-9pm Tue, reduced in winter; ☐ 5

Once a disappointing regional gallery with nothing more than a clutch of Emily Carr canvases, the VAG – housed in an old court-house but aiming for a new-built venue near the main public library in the coming years – has dramatically transformed since 2000, becoming a vital part of the city's cultural scene. Contemporary exhibitions, often showcasing Vancouver's wealth of renowned photoconceptualists, are combined with blockbuster traveling shows from leading galleries. The top ticket is the quarterly late-night party called FUSE (admission $19.50), where you can hang out with the city's hot young arty types over wine and live music. While entry is slightly reduced in winter, there's a Tuesday by-donation night where you can pay what you want (most pay $5 to $10). Check the website for curator tours and additional special events, and in summer hit the mezzanine-level café (p131), downtown's best patio. Also check out the gallery's new

Offsite, a free outdoor installation space next to the Shangri-La Hotel (p198).

BILL REID GALLERY OF NORTHWEST COAST ART Map pp58-9

www.billreidgallery.ca; 639 Hornby St; adult/child/senior $10/5/7; ☺ 11am-5pm Wed-Sun; Ⓜ Burrard

Downtown's newest art space showcases carvings, paintings and jewelry from Canada's most revered Haida artist. Lined with fascinating artifacts and exquisite works –

HIDDEN ARTWORK

Enter the lobby of the Royal Bank building at the corner of W Georgia and Burrard Sts, then hit the up escalator that's right in front of you. At the top you'll find one of the largest First Nations artworks in western Canada. Measuring 30m long and 2.5m high, the nine carved and painted red cedar panels of the spectacular 'Ksan Mural dramatically cover an entire wall of the building. It took four carvers three months to create in 1972 and it tells the story of Weget (or Man-Raven) and his often-mischievous exploits. Well worth a look, the artwork seems a world away from the bustling streets outside.

plus handy touch-screens to tell you all about them – this is a comprehensive intro to the creative vision of Reid and his Haida co-artists. Check out the Great Hall, where there's often a carver at work, then hit the mezzanine level: you'll be face-to-face with an 8.5m-long bronze of intertwined magical creatures, complete with some impressively long tongues.

CANADA PLACE Map pp58-9
www.canadaplace.ca; 999 Canada Place Way;
M Waterfront

Vancouver's version of the Sydney Opera House – at least judging by the number of postcards it appears on – this iconic landmark is shaped like a series of sails jutting into the sky over the harbor. Now a cruise-ship terminal and convention center (the large, grass-roofed convention center expansion opened next door in 2010), it's also a pier where you can stroll out from the waterfront for some camera-triggering views of the North Shore mountains and the busy floatplanes splashing into the water. If it's raining and you have kids in tow, duck inside to the Port Authority Interpretation Centre (☎ 604-665-9179; www .portvancouver.com; admission free; ⓒ 8am-5pm Mon-Fri), a hands-on showcase illuminating the city's maritime trade. Hit the convention center extension next door: its plaza houses dramatic public artworks, more great views and the tripod-like Olympic Cauldron, a permanent reminder of the 2010 Games.

CHRIST CHURCH CATHEDRAL
Map pp58-9
www.cathedral.vancouver.bc.ca; 690 Burrard St;
admission free; ⓒ 10am-4pm; M Burrard

Completed in 1895 and designated as a cathedral in 1929, the city's most attractive Gothic-style church is nestled incongruously among looming glass towers. Undergoing extensive renovations in recent years, it's a busy site and is home to a wide range of cultural events, including regular choir and chamber music recitals and the occasional Shakespeare reading. Self-guided tours of the 32 stained-glass windows are available, but if you're short of time just head down to the basement for the high-light: a colorful Edward Burne-Jones beauty created by the William Morris

Company. Also check out the church's dramatic hammerbeam ceiling as well as its newest window: the stunning *Tree of Life* by Susan A Point.

VANCOUVER LOOKOUT Map pp58-9
www.vancouverlookout.com; 555 W Hastings St;
adult/child/youth $15/7/10; ⓒ 8:30am-10:30pm
mid-May–mid-Sep, 9am-9pm mid-Sep–mid-May;
M Waterfront

Expect your lurching stomach to make a bid for freedom as one of the two glass elevators here whisks you 169m to the apex of this needle-like viewing tower. Once up top, there's not much to do but wander around and check out the truly awesome 360-degree vistas of city, sea and mountains unfurling around you. If you want to know what you're looking at, join one of the free tours or just peruse the historic photo panels showing just how much the landscape around here has changed. Tickets are pricey but are valid all day – return for a soaring sunset view of the city to get your money's worth.

ROGERS ARENA (GM PLACE)
Map pp58-9
www.rogersarena.ca; 800 Griffiths Way;
M Stadium-Chinatown

With a new corporate sponsor officially renaming what everyone still calls GM Place in 2010, you'll likely hear both names bandied around. Whatever the moniker, the newer of Vancouver's two downtown stadiums hosts the Vancouver Canucks of the National Hockey League (see p191). Game nights, when the 20,000-capacity venue heaves with fervent fans, are the city's most exciting sporting events – you'll enjoy the atmosphere even if the rules are a mystery. The main hockey venue during the 2010 Winter Olympics and the home of a large Canucks team shop, this is also a favored arena for money-spinning stadium rock acts. Behind-the-scenes tours (☎ 604-899-7440; Gate 6; adult/child/student & senior $10/5/7; ⓒ 10:30am, noon & 1:30pm Wed & Fri) take you into the hospitality suites and the nosebleed press box up in the rafters.

MARINE BUILDING Map pp58-9
355 Burrard St; ⓒ 9am-5pm Mon-Fri;
M Waterfront

Vancouver's most romantic old-school tower block and also its best art deco

DOWNTOWN

INFORMATION

Academie Duello Centre for Swordplay	1	G3
Australian Consulate	2	E2
Berlitz	3	F2
Canada Post Main Outlet	4	F4
Care Point Medical Centre	5	F2
Dirty Apron Cooking School	6	G4
Dutch Consulate	7	E2
German Consulate	(see 20)	
Howe St Postal Outlet	8	C5
Indian Consulate	9	F2
Italian Consulate	10	G3
New Zealand Consulate	11	E2
Pharmasave	12	F2
St Paul's Hospital	13	C4
Stein Medical Clinic	14	E2
Tourism Vancouver Visitor Centre	15	F1
Ultima Medicentre	16	E2
Vancouver Bullion & Currency Exchange	17	F2
Vancouver Convention & Exhibition Centre	18	G1
Vancouver Public Library	(see 28)	

SIGHTS (p56)

Bill Reid Gallery of Northwest Coast Art	19	E3
Canada Place	20	G1
Christ Church Cathedral	21	E3
Contemporary Art Gallery	22	E5
Marine Building	23	F2
Pendulum Gallery	24	E3
Port Authority Interpretation Centre	(see 20)	
Rogers Arena (GM Place)	25	G5
Vancouver Art Gallery	26	E3
Vancouver Lookout	27	G2
Vancouver Public Library	28	F4

SHOPPING (p111)

Birks	29	F2
Cherry Bomb	30	E4
Golden Age Collectables	31	F3
Holt Renfrew	32	F3
John Fluevog Shoes	33	E4

MacLeod's Books	34	G3
Mink Chocolates	35	F2
Pacific Centre	36	E3
Roots	37	D3
Scratch Records	38	F4
Sikora's Classical Records	39	G3
True Value Vintage Clothing	40	E3

EATING (p127)

Bin 941	41	C4
C Restaurant	42	B6
Chambar	43	G4
Finch's	44	G3
Gallery Café	(see 26)	
Gorilla Food	45	G3
Japadog	46	E4
La Bodega	47	C5
La Taqueria	48	G3
Le Crocodile	49	D3
Nu	50	B6
Templeton	51	D4

DRINKING (p149)

Bacchus	(see 99)	
Caffè Artigiano	52	E3
Doolins	53	D4
Fountainhead Pub	54	C4
Lennox Pub	55	E4
Mario's	56	E2
Railway Club	57	F3
UVA	(see 92)	

NIGHTLIFE (p161)

AuBar	58	F3
Caprice	59	D4
Celebrities	60	C4
Comedy Mix	(see 85)	
Commodore	61	E4
Media Club	62	F4
Odyssey	63	C5
Persian Tea House	64	D5
Railway Club	(see 57)	
Republic	65	D4
Roxy	66	D4
St Andrew's Wesley United Church	67	C4
Venue	68	E4
Yale	69	C5

See West End Map p68

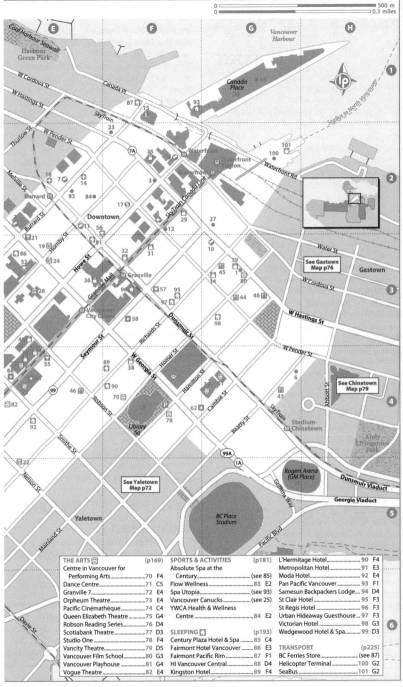

top picks

IT'S FREE

- Lost Lagoon Nature House (p64)
- Dr Sun Yat-Sen Park (p78)
- Vancouver Tour Guys (p237)
- Lynn Canyon Park Suspension Bridge (p106)
- Christ Church Cathedral (p57)
- Stanley Park Totem Poles (p63)
- Contemporary Art Gallery (right)
- Capilano Salmon Hatchery (p107)
- Pendulum Gallery (below)
- Port Authority Interpretation Centre (p57)

building, the graceful, 22-story Marine Building is a tribute to the city's maritime past. Check out the elaborate exterior of seahorses, lobsters and streamlined ships, then nip into the lobby where it's like a walk-through artwork. Stained-glass panels and a polished floor inlaid with signs of the zodiac await; you should also peruse the inlaid wood interiors of the brass-doored elevators. The tallest building in the British Empire when completed in 1930, it now houses offices. If you're a fan of art deco, the elegant City Hall building (p94) is worth a visit.

PENDULUM GALLERY Map pp58-9

www.pendulumgallery.bc.ca; HSBC Bank Bldg, 885 W Georgia St; admission free; ☺ **9am-6pm Mon-Wed, 9am-9pm Thu-Fri, 9am-5pm Sat;** Ⓜ **Burrard**

A creative use for the cavernous atrium of the city's main HSBC Bank Building – you'll be overlooking the cash machines and smiling bank tellers – this gallery offers an ever-changing roster of temporary exhibitions. It's mostly new art, and can range from striking paintings to challenging photographs and quirky arts and crafts. The space also houses one permanent exhibit: a gargantuan 27m-long buffed aluminum pendulum that will be swinging over your head throughout your visit. Designed by Alan Storey, it weighs 1600kg and moves about 6m (the swing is assisted by a hydraulic mechanical system at the top). There's also a coffee shop here if you need to rest your trek-weary feet.

VANCOUVER PUBLIC LIBRARY

Map pp58-9

www.vpl.ca; 350 W Georgia St; ☺ **10am-9pm Mon-Thu, 10am-6pm Fri & Sat, noon-5pm Sun;** Ⓜ **Stadium-Chinatown;** 🛜

This dramatic, Colosseum-like building must be a temple to the great god of libraries. If not, it's certainly one of the world's most magnificent book-lending facilities. Designed by Moshe Safdie and opened in 1995, it contains 1.2 million books and other items spread out over seven levels, all of them seemingly populated by language students silently learning English from textbooks (and messaging each other under the tables). There's free wi-fi available on-site (plus terminals if you don't have your laptop) and the library hosts a lively roster of book readings and literary events. If you're traveling with kids, the downstairs children's section is an ideal hangout.

CONTEMPORARY ART GALLERY

Map pp58-9

www.contemporaryartgallery.ca; 555 Nelson St; admission free, suggested donation $5; ☺ **noon-6pm Wed-Sun;** 🚌 **4**

Originally the Greater Vancouver Artists' Gallery, this small, off-the-beaten-path art space transformed itself into an independent gallery in 1996, moving to a crisp, purpose-built facility a few years later. Focusing on a wide range of modern art, photography is particularly well represented here. Exhibitions are ever-changing and include local and international artists – check the gallery's website for events and openings.

DOWNTOWN GRAND TOUR
Walking Tour

This looping stroll will take you around the main streets and give you a handy overview of the downtown core.

1 Canada Place

Start your stroll at one of Vancouver's most photographed landmarks (p57), giving your camera trigger finger free rein and allowing yourself time to walk along the outer promenade so you can watch the floatplanes diving onto the water. There's often a giant cruise ship or two parked alongside.

WALK FACTS

Start Canada Place
End Canada Place
Distance 3km
Time 1 hour
Exertion Easy
Fuel stop Vancouver Public Library

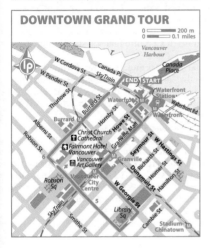

commercial streets. You'll pass coffee shops, clothing stores and the Pacific Centre (p113), downtown's biggest mall.

3 Granville & W Georgia Sts

Get your bearings at this busy street corner, the center of the downtown core. You can check out the department stores here or nip across one block to the Vancouver Art Gallery (p56) for a culture fix.

4 Vancouver Public Library

Stroll southeast a couple of blocks to the magnificent, Colosseum-like library (opposite). Here, the glass-enclosed atrium is a perfect place to grab a coffee, or you can nip inside and check your email for free.

5 Robson St

Head northwest along Robson St, the city's mainstream shopping promenade, where you can wander to your credit card's content at boutiques, bookstores and shoe shops. There are restaurants (p129) here too if it's time to eat.

6 Robson & Burrard Sts

Take a breather at this clamorous intersection, then turn right and head along Burrard St toward the mountain vista glinting ahead of you. You can duck into the Fairmont Hotel Vancouver (p195) for a stroll through the elegant lobby or continue downhill to Christ Church Cathedral (p57). Within minutes, you'll be back at the waterfront Canada Place.

2 Granville St

Head southwest along Howe St, turn left on W Hastings St and then right on Granville St. Follow this uphill thoroughfare; it's one of the city's most important

STANLEY PARK

Eating p132

Adjoining the West End, Vancouver's magnificent Stanley Park (admission free) is one of North America's largest urban green spaces and enjoys one of the world's most breathtaking settings: it's surrounded on three sides by rippling ocean and is watched over by the looming North Shore mountains standing sentinel across the water. The park's 8.8km seawall stroll is one of the best ways to spend your time in the city: a kind of visual spa treatment fringed by a 150,000-tree temperate rainforest. It's a sigh-triggering introduction to 'Beautiful BC.'

Originally home to the Musqueam and Squamish First Nations, Canada's governor general Lord Stanley (who also generously gave his name to hockey's Stanley Cup) opened Vancouver's first park in 1888. His inaugural speech announced that the park was for 'the use and enjoyment of people of all colors, creeds and customs for all time.' It's a motto that still stands: more than eight million visitors are drawn here every year.

Within its 404 hectares you'll find forests of cedar, hemlock and fir, mingled with meadows, lakes and cricket pitches. On a sunny day it seems that all of Vancouver (plus more than a few raccoons and blue herons) is here hiking, cycling and jogging along the seawall or through the woods. There are also a couple of excellent beaches – ideal spots to perch on a driftwood log with a picnic and catch a kaleidoscopic sunset over the water.

But Stanley Park isn't just for dewy-eyed nature lovers; other highlights include the Vancouver Aquarium and the Second Beach Swimming Pool. Not surprisingly, there's also plenty for kids to do here, and there are several good eateries if it's time for lunch.

For more details on the park, check out www.vancouverparks.ca. The park's information center is 500m from the W Georgia St entrance, along the seawall. Tickets for the summertime-only Stanley Park Shuttle (www.vancouvertrolley.com; adult/child $10/5; 11am-6:30pm mid-Jun–mid-Sep) are valid all day so you can hop on and off at 15 stops around the park as much as you like; alternatively, you can board a plodding horse-drawn carriage for a more leisurely tour (see p237). Transit access to the park is via bus 19: you can pick up the shuttle near its main stop.

VANCOUVER AQUARIUM Map opposite

☎ 604-659-3474; www.vanaqua.org; adult/child/youth $27/17/21, reduced in winter;
9:30am-7pm Jul & Aug, 9:30am-5pm Sep-Jun;
19

Stanley Park's biggest draw, the aquarium is home to 9000 water-loving critters – including sharks, wolf eels, beluga whales and a somewhat shy octopus. There's also a small, walk-through rainforest area of birds, turtles and a statue-still sloth. Check out the mesmerizing iridescent jellyfish tanks and the portly sea otter who eats the way everyone should: lying on its back using its chest as a plate (trust us: it's not as easy as it looks). Check the schedule for feeding times and consider booking an Animal Encounter tour (from $24), where you'll learn how to be a trainer. The attraction's newest draw is its 4-D Experience: a 3-D movie theater with added wind, mist and aromas.

MINIATURE RAILWAY & CHILDREN'S FARMYARD Map opposite

☎ 604-257-8531; railway adult/child/youth $6.19/3.10/4.52, farmyard $6.19/3.10/4.52;
11am-4pm mid-May–Jun, 10am-6pm Jul-early Sep, reduced hr rest of year (call ahead);
19

A short walk from the aquarium, these twin, kid-friendly attractions are a big summer draw. The farmyard allows youngsters to interact with llamas, sheep, goats, cows, hens and other small animals in a way that will make you wonder why you bother spending money on much pricier zoos back home. In contrast, the railway offers a 15-minute forest train ride that kids of all ages can enjoy. At Halloween the railway rises from the dead of the off-season to become a ghost train, while at Christmastime its carriages and route are adorned with fairy lights. The farmyard was under threat of a funding-related closure at the time of research – call ahead before you set out with the kids.

STANLEY PARK SEAWALL Map opposite

19

Built between 1917 and 1980, the 8.8km seawall trail is Vancouver's favorite outdoor hangout. Encircling the entire

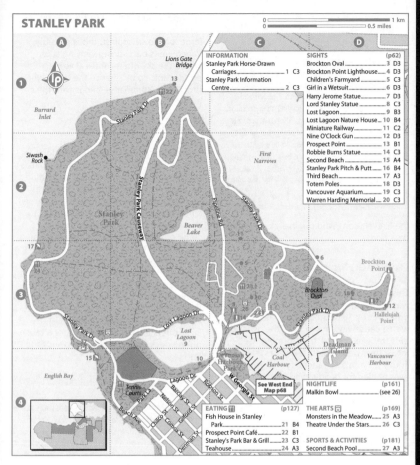

lonelyplanet.com

STANLEY PARK

0 ———————————— 1 km
0 ———————————— 0.5 miles

Lions Gate
Bridge

Burrard
Inlet

Siwash
Rock

First
Narrows

Stanley Park Dr

Stanley Park Causeway

Stanley
Park

Pipeline Rd

Beaver
Lake

Stanley Park Dr

Stanley Park Dr

Brockton
Point

Brockton
Oval

Hallelujah
Point

Lost Lagoon Dr

Lost
Lagoon

Deadman's
Island

Stanley Park Dr

Devonian
Harbour
Park

Coal
Harbour

Vancouver
Harbour

English Bay

Lagoon Dr

W Georgia St

Robson St

Barclay St

Tennis
Courts

Beach Ave

Park La

Nelson St

Gilford St

Comox St

Chilco St

Denman St

See West End
Map p68

NEIGHBORHOODS STANLEY PARK

park, it offers spectacular waterfront mountain-fringed vistas on one side and dense, forest canopy on the other. You can walk the whole thing in two or three blister-triggering hours. Alternatively, consider renting a bike from Spokes (p183) near the park entrance; once on two wheels you'll be able to cover the route in about an hour. Keep in mind that cyclists and rollerbladers must travel counterclockwise on the seawall, so there's no going back once you start rolling. If you enjoy yourself, consider dipping into the 24km of trails that crisscross the park's interior, including Siwash Rock Trail, Rawlings Trail and the popular Beaver Lake Trail (some trails are for jogging only).

BROCKTON POINT Map above
🚍 19

The park's eastern peninsula, this picturesque kneecap of land contains Brockton Oval cricket pitch (both Don Bradman and Freddie Trueman have played here), the squat Brockton Point Lighthouse (where Arnold Schwarzenegger handed the Olympic torch to Sebastian Coe before the 2010 Winter Olympics) and the electrically fired Nine O'Clock Gun (see the boxed text, p64). But the highlight is the clutch of eight colorful totem poles. A favorite tour-bus lure, these are actually photogenic replicas of the originals that were moved here from Alert Bay. In 2008 they were joined by three n-shaped carved 'gateways' created to welcome visitors by

BOOM TIME

Brockton Point's Nine O'Clock Gun is a '12-pounder' naval canon from England that's been a park fixture since 1894, when it was introduced to help local ships synchronize their chronometers. Now a quirky historic hangover, it's loaded with a pound-and-a-half of gunpowder every day, fuelling an electrically charged trigger that booms across the city at precisely 9pm each evening. The blast can be heard as far away as Burnaby Mountain. Now housed in a protective cage, the canon was stolen and held to ransom by naughty UBC students in 1969. Another group, allegedly from the same school, daubed the gun with red paint in 2008.

the First Nations who originally called the park home.

LOST LAGOON Map p63

🚌 19

This rustic area near the park's entrance was originally an extension of Coal Harbour, but by 1916 the bridge was replaced with a causeway, and in 1922 the new body of water was named, transforming itself into a freshwater lake a few years later. Today it's a nature sanctuary – keep your eyes peeled for beady-eyed blue herons – and its perimeter pathway makes for a wonderful stroll. The excellent Lost Lagoon Nature House (☎ 604-257-8544; www.stanleyparkecology.ca; admission free; ⏰ 10am-7pm Tue-Sun May-Sep) provides exhibits and illumination on the park's wildlife, history and ecology. Ask about its fascinating park walks (adult/child $10/5), covering everything from bird-watching strolls to artsy ambles.

SECOND BEACH & THIRD BEACH Map p63

🚌 19

Second Beach is an ever-busy, family-friendly area on the park's western side, with a large, grassy playground, a greasy-spoon snack bar that also serves ice cream, and the Stanley Park Pitch & Putt golf course. It's also close to Creperly Meadows, where free outdoor movie screenings often take place in summer (see the boxed text on p174). Its main attraction, though, is the seasonal outdoor swimming pool (p189) that sits on the waterfront overlooking the gently rippling waves. But if you're craving a more

relaxing hangout, head to Third Beach. A lovely sandy expanse with plenty of large logs to sit against, this is possibly Vancouver's best sunset-viewing spot, where the sky often comes alive with pyrotechnic color – hence the locals who drop by on summer evenings with their picnic baskets.

PROSPECT POINT Map p63

🚌 19

One of Vancouver's most glorious lookouts, this lofty spot is located at the park's northern tip. In summer you'll be jostling for elbow room with the tour groups as you angle for a view of the passing cruise ships – heading down the steep stairs to the viewing platform usually shakes some of them off. Look out for scavenging raccoons here and remember that it's never a good idea to pet these semi-tame, rabies-carrying critters. The cairn here commemorates the 1888 wreck of the SS Beaver, a Hudson's Bay Company steamship that was the first to travel the entire west coast of North America. Prospect Point Café (p132) offers refreshments – aim for a table on the deck and a view of the Lions Gate Bridge.

STATUE SPOTTING

Vancouver's favorite playground is studded with statues, all of which come to life at night (okay, just kidding). On your leisurely amble around the tree-lined idyll, look out for the following and award yourself 10 points for each one you find. If you locate them all, partake of a rewarding beer at Stanley's Park Bar & Grill (p132). If you're on the seawall, it shouldn't be hard to spot Girl in a Wetsuit, a 1972 bronze by Elek Imredy that sits in the water. But how about the Robbie Burns statue unveiled by British Prime Minister Ramsay MacDonald in 1928 or the dramatic bronze of Canadian sprint legend Harry Jerome, who held six world records and won a bronze at the 1964 Summer Olympics? Here's a clue for the next one: it's near the Malkin Bowl. Marking the first official visit to Canada by a US president, this elegant statue depicting the youth of each country is actually a memorial: after visiting in 1923, Warren Harding died a week later in San Francisco. Finally, don't miss the park's main man. Not far from the entrance – but hidden enough that most visitors miss him – a cheery likeness of Lord Stanley stands with his arms outstretched to welcome you.

STANLEY PARK OUTDOOR EXPLORER
Walking Tour

This invigorating walk (or bike ride) will take you right around the park, passing the famed totem poles, inviting stretches of beach and towering trees.

1 Coal Harbour

Start your stroll at the park's W Georgia St entrance, heading north around the curving seawall toward the Tudoresque boat-club building. Continue on to the park's information center, where you can pick up a route map and maybe an ice cream for the trek.

2 Totem Poles

Follow the route until you reach the totems (p63), a highly colorful array of carvings that attract plenty of camera-wielding visitors. There's a gift shop here if you want to grab a postcard and write an evocative line or two about the scenery.

3 Brockton Point

There's an uphill incline from here – grab onto a passing bike for extra help – but you'll be rewarded at the point (p63) with a view across the water from the little lighthouse. Cruise ships pass this way as they head toward the Lions Gate Bridge, which you'll pass under as you continue.

4 Third Beach

After rounding Prospect Point (opposite) you'll find that the trail gets a bit wilder: fewer people make it this far and the walkway is usually buffeted by fresh winds whipping in off the water. It's a nature-lover's delight, however, and a reminder of the city's coastal location. Continue on to Third Beach (opposite), where you can rest on a log and enjoy the view.

STANLEY PARK OUTDOOR EXPLORER

WALK FACTS

Start Coal Harbour
End English Bay
Distance 9.4km
Time 3 hours
Exertion Moderate
Fuel stop Bring a picnic and stop anywhere you like

5 Second Beach

Head on to Second Beach (opposite) and, suitably informed, decide which sandy expanse is your favorite. You can grab a drink at the concession stand here if you're feeling parched after your long trek.

6 English Bay

You'll start to see a lot more people as you reach the end of your nature-hugger's marathon at English Bay (p66). The beach here is often teeming with sun-worshipping locals and buskers and street artists keep things interesting. If it's time to dine, there are dozens of restaurants in this area (see p132).

WEST END

Drinking p152; Eating p132; Shopping p114; Sleeping p198

With its main Denman St and Davie St thoroughfares, the lively West End area borders downtown and Stanley Park and stretches languidly from Coal Harbour to English Bay. Characterized by tree-lined boulevards, streets of neighborhood shops and a cornucopia of midrange dining options (including an excellent Japanese *izakaya* (neighborhood pub) scene), it serves a population of young people and seniors in a largely adult-focused area of the city. It's also home to western Canada's largest gay population – which explains why the mammoth, carnivalesque Pride Week (p15) takes over the streets here every August, attracting up to 500,000 visitors with its parade of oil-covered Speedo-wearers.

But despite the pink bus shelters and rainbow-flagged businesses, the West End isn't just one big 'gayborhood.' In fact, it's among Vancouver's oldest residential districts and still has pockets of highly attractive heritage buildings for visitors of a historic bent. Although many were cleared in a mid-1950s housing boom that saw more than 200 apartment blocks added to the area (some are now heritage buildings in their own right), you can still peek at how the rich locals used to live in Barclay Heritage Sq. Lined with handsome wooden mansions, its highlight is the fascinating Roedde House Museum, complete with antique-lined rooms and a small English country garden.

Of course the waterfront is also a major West End lure. It's hard to beat an afternoon with the locals on the often packed English Bay beach and, if you want to stretch your legs, the Coal Harbour seawall stroll between Canada Place and Stanley Park is one of the prettiest in the city.

The West End's main transit routes are bus 5, which travels along Robson and Denman Sts, and bus 6, running along Davie St.

ENGLISH BAY BEACH Map pp68-9

cnr of Denman St & Beach Ave; 🚌 6

Wandering south on Denman St, you'll suddenly spot a rustle of palm trees ahead of you announcing your arrival at one of Canada's best urban beaches. There's a party atmosphere here in summer as West Enders catch the rays, crowd the busker shows, check out the artwork vendors…or just ogle the volleyballers prancing around on the sand. Be sure to snap a few photos of the beach's towering inukshuk (Inuit sculpture) or just continue along the seawall into neighboring Stanley Park (p62). This is also a popular (but crowded) spot to catch the annual Celebration of Light (p15) fireworks festival.

ROBSON STREET Map pp68-9

east from the Denman St intersection; 🚌 5

Locals, international tourists and recent immigrants – count the number of accents you catch as you stroll along here – throng the hotels, eateries and shops of Robson St, Vancouver's de facto urban promenade. While most shops are of the ubiquitous chain-store variety, it's also worth heading to the Stanley Park end of the strip, where you'll find a modern 'mini-Asia' of internet cafés, authentic *izakayas* (Japanese neighborhood pubs) and discreet karaoke bars

populated by homesick Japanese and Korean language students. It's a great area for a cheap-and-cheerful, authentically south Asian lunch (see p132).

ROEDDE HOUSE MUSEUM Map pp68-9

www.roeddehouse.org; 1415 Barclay St; admission $5; 🕙 10am-5pm Tue-Sat, 2-4pm Sun; 🚌 5

For a glimpse of what the West End looked like before the apartment blocks arrived, drop by this handsome 1893 Queen Anne–style mansion, now a lovingly preserved museum. Designed by infamous BC architect Francis Rattenbury, the house is packed with antiques and the surrounding gardens are planted in period style. Sunday entry – including tour, tea and cookies – costs $1 extra. The abode is the showpiece of Barclay Heritage Sq, a one-block site containing nine historic West End houses dating from 1890 to 1908. If you don your top hat, monocle and twirly waxed moustache, you'll fit right in. Pick up a free map covering the square's history highlights from Roedde House.

COAL HARBOUR SEAWALL Map pp68-9

Canada Place to Stanley Park; Ⓜ Waterfront

An idyllic waterfront stroll from Canada Place to Stanley Park (it's about 2km),

VANCOUVER'S FORGOTTEN LITTLE GERMANY

While today's Robson St is increasingly a hot spot of Asian eateries and businesses, older locals still remember it as 'Robsonstrasse,' an area studded with tempting German bakeries, grocery stores and schnitzel restaurants. European immigrants called this area home for much of the 19th century, when businesses like Mozart Konditorei and European News gave the strip a colorful continental air.

this is a perfect way to spend a sunny afternoon. You'll pass the new convention center expansion, a gaggle of bobbling floatplanes and the grassy nook of Harbour Green Park, where you can stop for a bistro bite at Mill Marine (p153) and catch a breathtaking mountain-framed vista. Continue past the handsome *Light Shed* artwork – a replica of one of the many marine sheds that once lined this area – then look out for the cozy houseboats in the marina and the Westin Bayshore hotel, where Howard Hughes holed up for three months in 1972. You'll soon be on the doorstep of Stanley Park.

SUNSET BEACH Map pp68-9

along Beach Ave, west of Burrard Bridge; 🚍 6
A chain of small, sandy beaches running along the north side of False Creek, this is a quieter alternative to the bustling English Bay spot. The walking, cycling and blading trail here – it links to the Stanley Park seawall trail if you want to extend your trek – is ever-popular in summer, especially with members of the local gay community checking each other out. Swimmers will enjoy the indoor Vancouver Aquatic Centre (p189), and you can also catch a miniferry (p227) from here to Granville Island: a must-do, kid-friendly voyage for any visitor.

WEST END 'HOOD & HERITAGE STROLL
Walking Tour

This urban walk will take you through an attractive residential area, combining old-school clapboard houses with art deco apartment buildings and café-lined streets.

1 Denman St
Start your walk at the corner of W Georgia and Denman Sts and head south along Denman. You'll pass dozens of midpriced restaurants here – choose one to come back to for dinner (see p132) – plus plenty of enticing little shops to attract your wallet.

2 Barclay St
Turn left on Barclay St and stroll through the residential heart of Vancouver's vibrant gay community. This area has some lovely old heritage apartment buildings and wooden Craftsman homes.

3 Barclay Heritage Square
Continue on until you reach this well-preserved plaza of heritage houses, a reminder of how yesteryear Vancouverites used to live. Duck into the antique-lined Roedde House Museum (opposite) and you'll have an even better idea.

4 Firehall No 6
Head southwest along Nicola St and you'll come across this lovely brick-built 1907

WALK FACTS

Start Corner of W Georgia and Denman Sts
End Sunset Beach
Distance 2km
Time 1 hour
Exertion Easy
Fuel stop Melriche's

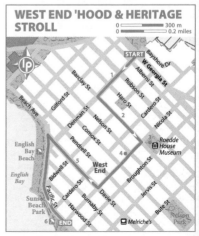

WEST END 'HOOD & HERITAGE STROLL

NEIGHBORHOODS WEST END

WEST END

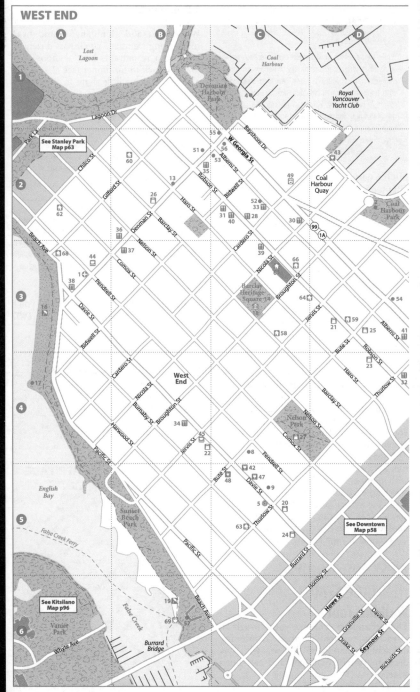

A B C D

1 Lost Lagoon

Coal Harbour

Devonian Harbour Park

Royal Vancouver Yacht Club

Lagoon Dr

Park La

See Stanley Park Map p63

55

Bayshore Dr

W Georgia St

Coal Harbour Quay

43

2 Chilco St

60

51

56

Alberni St

53

35

Robson St

49

Coal Harbour Park

Gilford St

13

26

Haro St

Bidwell St

52

33

31 40 28

Cardero St

30

99

1A

62

36

Denman St

Barclay St

Nelson St

39

Nicola St

66

3 Beach Ave

68

44

37

Comox St

Broughton St

64

54

1

38

Pendrell St

Barclay Heritage Square 14

18

Jervis St

21

59

25

41

Bidwell St

Davie St

58

Burrard St

23

32

16

Cardero St

West End

Butte St

Haro St

Barclay St

Thurlow St

4 17

Nicola St

Burnaby St

Broughton St

Nelson St

Nelson Park

27

English Bay

34

Harwood St

Jervis St

45

22

8

Pendrell St

Comox St

Pacific St

Bute St

42

47

48

Davie St

9

See Downtown Map p58

5 False Creek Ferry

Sunset Beach Park

5

20

63

Thurlow St

24

Pacific St

Beach Ave

Burrard St

Hornby St

Howe St

Davie St

See Kitsilano Map p96

19

69 67

Granville St

Seymour St

6 Vanier Park

Whyte Ave

Burrard Bridge

False Creek

Drake St

Richards St

0 ———————————— 500 m
0 ———————————— 0.3 miles

Deadman's Island

HMCS Discovery Naval Training Station

Vancouver Harbour

Harbour Green Park

W Cordova St
W Hastings St
W Pender St
Canada Pt
Canada Place

SkyTrain
Waterfront Station
W Cordova St
Burrard
W Hastings St

Downtown
W Pender St
Granville
Dunsmuir St
Richards St

W Georgia St

Vancouver City Centre

Robson Sq

Provincial Law Courts

Robson St

Yaletown

Smithe St
Nelson St
Helmcken St
Homer St
Mainland St

Yaletown-Roundhouse

SHOPPING 🛍 (p111)
Book Warehouse	20	C5
Konbiniya Japan Centre	21	D3
Little Sister's Book & Art Emporium	22	B4
Lululemon Athletica	23	D4
Marquis Wine Cellars	24	C5
Signature BC Liquor Store	25	D3
Ten Thousand Villages	26	B2
West End Farmers Market	27	C4

EATING 🍴 (p127)
Capers	28	C2
Coast	29	E4
Grind Cafe	30	C2
Guu with Garlic	31	C2
Il Nido	32	D4
Le Gavroche	33	C2
Lolita's	34	B4
Motomachi Shokudo	35	B2
Mr Pickwick's	36	B2
No Frills	37	B3
Raincity Grill	38	A3
Sura Korean Cuisine	39	C3
Sushi Mart	40	C2
Urban Fare	41	D3

DRINKING 🍷 🍺 (p149)
1181	42	C5
Cardero's	43	D2
Delany's	44	A3
Melriche's	45	B4
Mill Marine	46	E2
O'Doul's	(see 64)	
Pumpjack Pub	47	C5
Sylvia's Lounge	(see 68)	

NIGHTLIFE 🎶 (p161)
Comedy Mondays	(see 48)	
J Lounge	48	C5
O'Doul's	(see 64)	

THE ARTS 🎭 (p169)
Performing Arts Lodge Theatre	49	C2

SPORTS & ACTIVITIES (p181)
Axis	50	E3
Bayshore Rentals	51	B2
Bikram's Yoga Vancouver	52	C2
Denman Bike Shop	53	C2
Fitness World	54	D3
Running Room	55	C2
Spokes Bicycle Rentals	56	C2
Vancouver Aquatic Centre	57	B6
West End Community Centre	(see 13)	

SLEEPING 🛏 (p193)
Barclay House B&B	58	C3
Blue Horizon Hotel	59	D3
Buchan Hotel	60	B2
Empire Landmark Hotel	61	C3
English Bay Inn	62	A2
HI Vancouver Downtown	63	C5
Listel Vancouver	64	C3
Loden Vancouver	65	E3
Riviera Hotel	66	C3
Shangri-La Hotel	67	E3
Sylvia Hotel	68	A3

TRANSPORT (p225)
Ferry Stop	69	B6
Floatplane Terminal	70	F2

INFORMATION
Care Point Medical Centre	1	A3
Coal Harbour Community Centre	2	D2
French Consulate	3	E3
Harbour Cruises	4	C1
Internet Coffee	5	C5
Japanese Consulate	6	E3
Korean Consulate	7	E3
Mexican Consulate	(see 6)	
Qmunity	8	C4
Shoppers Drug Mart	9	C5
Travel Medicine & Vaccination Centre	10	E4
UK Consulate	11	E3
USA Consulate	12	E3
West End Community Centre	13	B2

SIGHTS (p66)
Barclay Heritage Square	14	C3
Coal Harbour Seawall	15	E2
English Bay Beach	16	A3
Inukshuk Sculpture	17	A4
Roedde House Museum	18	C3
Sunset Beach	19	B6

firehall. It's still in use but has the feel (and look) of a museum.

5 Davie St

Continue on Nicola St and turn right into Davie St, a teeming shop and café area that's also the commercial hub of the gay community. It's a popular place at night with plenty of bars and clubs. If you need a coffee break, Melriche's (p153) is nearby.

6 Sunset Beach

When you reach the end of Davie St at English Bay Beach (p66), turn left and stroll along Beach Ave. After a few minutes this becomes the main promenade for Sunset Beach (p67), where you can sit on a grassy bank and watch the locals jog and blade by or catch a miniferry to Granville Island (p88).

Drinking p153; Eating p134; Shopping p115; Sleeping p200

Vancouver's 'little SoHo,' pedestrian-friendly Yaletown was a derelict former rail terminal and warehouse district until being transformed in the early 1990s into swanky condo towers and chichi boutiques and restaurants. Roughly bounded by False Creek, Homer St and Robson St, this modern-day yuppie enclave has a hip and inviting atmosphere – especially at night, when its swanky drink and dine spots are packed to the rafters with the city's beautiful people checking each other (and each other's bank balances) out.

The area has certainly come a long way since Canadian Pacific Railway workers settled here in the late 19th century to be close to the rail yards that merged at nearby False Creek. Many of them had worked at the CPR yards in Yale, about 180km northeast of Vancouver, hence the neighborhood's new moniker. Yaletown thrived as the city's industrial core until the 1940s, when highways replaced rail for goods transport. By the 1970s it was a dodgy 'hood known more for its rough bars and derelict warehouses, where getting beaten up was part of a regular night out.

Vancouver's Expo '86 world's fair changed all that, as planners designated the district a historic area. The first new settlers to arrive were artists seeking studio space, then came bohemian coffee shops and a smattering of stores and galleries. The transformation was complete when high-tech paper millionaires moved in during the 1990s.

Yaletown has since developed into an increasingly attractive area for visitors. It has plenty of pricey boutiques to window shop and lots of places to stop for lunch, coffee or a splurge-worthy dinner. You'll still see plenty of shiny Hummers parked on the streets here, while your fellow shoppers will likely have handbag-dwelling Chihuahuas as fashion accessories. If you're curious about the area's almost-forgotten, rough-and-ready past, follow the old rail lines still embedded in many of the streets and amble over to the Roundhouse Community Arts & Recreation Centre. You'll find a famous mothballed steam train that recalls the area's original raison d'être – it's also one of Vancouver's most important historic artifacts.

Transit access to Yaletown is via buses C21 and C23, and the nearby Cambie St bus 15. The Yaletown-Roundhouse Canada Line SkyTrain station also stops in the heart of the action.

BC PLACE STADIUM Map p72
www.bcplacestadium.com; 777 Pacific Blvd;
Ⓜ Stadium-Chinatown

Site of the 2010 Winter Olympic opening and closing ceremonies, the city's main sports arena was having its dodgy old Teflon roof replaced with a new retractable lid during research for this book, at a cost of around $500 million. On completion (scheduled for summer 2011), it will be the home of both the BC Lions Canadian Football League team (p191) and the Vancouver Whitecaps soccer team (p192). Also used for major rock shows, the stadium was expected to resume its popular behind-the-scenes tours once its shiny new hat is in place. Also keep your eyes peeled for the re-opening of the BC Sports Hall of Fame & Museum (☎ 604-687-5520; www.bcsportshalloffame.com). Closed during the refurb, it's a family-friendly celebration of the province's sporting achievements, with plenty of hands-on exhibits.

ROUNDHOUSE COMMUNITY ARTS & RECREATION CENTRE Map p72
www.roundhouse.ca; 181 Roundhouse Mews, cnr Davie St & Pacific Blvd; ⓨ 9am-10pm Mon-Fri, 9am-5pm Sat & Sun;
Ⓜ Yaletown-Roundhouse

Those interested in Canadian Pacific Railway heritage should visit the Roundhouse, formerly a CPR repair shed. It now houses the handsome and highly historic Engine No 374, which trundled the first passenger train into the city in 1887. Parked in a smashing little volunteer-run museum (www.wcra.org/engine374; admission free), it's a great trainspotter's pit stop. On special occasions, the engine is pulled outside onto the antique turntable. The complex's main building is a busy community center and performance space, with a wide array of shows and cultural events on offer – check the website for listings.

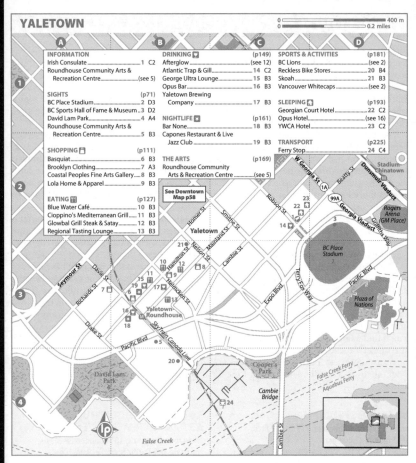

YALETOWN

0 ————— 400 m
0 ————— 0.2 miles

INFORMATION	
Irish Consulate	1 C2
Roundhouse Community Arts &	
Recreation Centre	(see 5)

SIGHTS	(p71)
BC Place Stadium	2 D3
BC Sports Hall of Fame & Museum	3 D2
David Lam Park	4 A4
Roundhouse Community Arts &	
Recreation Centre	5 B3

SHOPPING	(p111)
Basquiat	6 B3
Brooklyn Clothing	7 A3
Coastal Peoples Fine Arts Gallery	8 B3
Lola Home & Apparel	9 B3

EATING	(p127)
Blue Water Café	10 B3
Cioppino's Mediterranean Grill	11 B3
Glowbal Grill Steak & Satay	12 B3
Regional Tasting Lounge	13 B3

DRINKING	(p149)
Afterglow	(see 12)
Atlantic Trap & Gill	14 C2
George Ultra Lounge	15 B3
Opus Bar	16 B3
Yaletown Brewing	
Company	17 B3

NIGHTLIFE	(p161)
Bar None	18 B3
Capones Restaurant & Live	
Jazz Club	19 B3

THE ARTS	(p169)
Roundhouse Community	
Arts & Recreation Centre	(see 5)

SPORTS & ACTIVITIES	(p181)
BC Lions	(see 2)
Reckless Bike Stores	20 B4
Skoah	21 B3
Vancouver Whitecaps	(see 2)

SLEEPING	(p193)
Georgian Court Hotel	22 C2
Opus Hotel	(see 16)
YWCA Hotel	23 C2

TRANSPORT	(p225)
Ferry Stop	24 C4

See Downtown
Map p58

DAVID LAM PARK Map above

www.vancouverparks.ca; cnr Drake St & Pacific Blvd; ⏰ 24hr; Ⓜ Yaletown-Roundhouse
A crooked elbow of landscaped waterfront at the neck of False Creek, this 15-year-old park is Yaletown's main green space. A popular spot for free shows at the Vancouver International Jazz Festival (p14) and also sometimes used for free alfresco summer movie screenings (see the boxed text on p174), this is the perfect launch point for a 2km seawall walk along the north bank of False Creek to Science World. You'll pass intriguing public artworks, glass condo towers foresting the old Expo '86 site and the stadium where the Vancouver Canucks NHL hockey team plays. Look out for birdlife along the route and ask the locals about the unexpected 2010 visit from a grey whale in these waters.

YALETOWN INDULGENCE
Walking Tour

This short stroll – rounded off with a culture stop – is a good way to see what's on offer before you commit to a place for dinner.

1 Hamilton St

One of the city's favorite eat streets, Hamilton St is lined with excellent restaurants (see p134), and high-end seafood eateries are a particular specialty here. One of the city's best is Blue Water Café (p135).

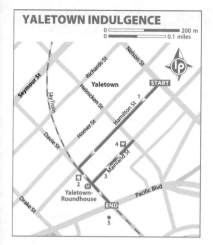

YALETOWN INDULGENCE

WALK FACTS

Start Hamilton St
End Roundhouse Community Arts & Recreation Centre
Distance 1km
Time 45 minutes
Exertion Easy
Fuel stop Yaletown Brewing Company

the excellent Regional Tasting Lounge (p136). Keep this in mind as a dinner option.

4 Yaletown Brewing Company

Continue along Mainland St until you reach this popular brewpub (p154). It's a great place to grab an afternoon beer and decamp to the patio to watch the city go by.

5 Roundhouse Community Arts & Recreation Centre

Double back a couple of blocks along Mainland St and turn left onto Davie St. Check to see if there are any shows or events at the community center (p71) or just content yourself with a view of the preserved steam engine – it brought the first passenger train to the city in 1887.

2 Opus Hotel

Turn left and head down Davie St and you'll hit Opus (p201), a popular boutique hotel. You can nip in here for a coffee or a beer at Opus Bar (p154) – remember to keep an eye open for visiting celebs.

3 Mainland St

Turn left onto Mainland St and you'll find another selection of swish eateries, including

GASTOWN

Drinking p154; Eating p136; Shopping p116

Centered on brick-paved Maple Tree Sq where Powell, Water, Carrall and Alexander Sts meet, Gastown was designated a national historic site in 2010. The recognition was a long time coming but it marks the fact that this is Vancouver's most important old neighborhood – and when you look at the jaunty statue in the heart of the action, you'll realize why. 'Gassy' Jack Deighton, a talkative Yorkshire-born colonial, opened a bar for sawmill workers here in 1867. The ram-shackle development that sprang up around it was the start of modern-day Vancouver (see p21). While an enormous fire wiped out most of the fledgling settlement in 1886, it was soon back in business thanks to the arrival of the transcontinental CPR, which rumbled into town along the nearby waterfront. Eventually the center of Vancouver moved westward to its current location and Gastown hit hard times, becoming a troubled skid-row area by the 1970s.

Just as the city was preparing to bulldoze its problems and start over, a group of history-loving locals successfully lobbied for heritage protection. Thus began a concerted effort to restore the district, pushing its seedier characters further east toward Main and Hastings Sts. The culmination of their efforts was 2010's national historic site award. But the neighborhood isn't resting on its heritage laurels. Its handsome brick and stone buildings have been colonized by some of the city's best bars, restaurants and independent shops in recent years, making this the best area in the city for an old-town afternoon wander as well as a night out.

Most visitors stick to Water St for that all-important Steam Clock photo opportunity, but consider one of the excellent $5 summertime Architectural Institute of British Columbia walking tours (p237), which give you a real flavor of the area's rich past. For an even more arresting tour, consider the colorful Sins of the City walk run by the fascinating Vancouver Police Museum.

For resources and information on Gastown, visit www.gastown.org. Transit access to the area is via Waterfront SkyTrain station and buses 4, 7 and 50.

VANCOUVER POLICE MUSEUM Map p76

☎ 604-665-3346; www.vancouverpolicemuseum.ca; 240 E Cordova St; adult/student/senior $7/5/5; ◷ 9am-5pm; 🚌 7

Contextualizing the history of the crime-and-vice-addled Downtown Eastside streets surrounding it, this quirky museum is lined with confiscated weapons, counterfeit currency and a grizzly former mortuary room where the walls are studded with preserved slivers of human tissue – spot the bullet-damaged brain slices. If your interest in crime is triggered, take the excellent Sins of the City walking tour (adult/student $15/12, includes museum admission), which weaves through Gastown and Chinatown in search of former brothels, opium dens and gambling houses. Also book ahead for an after-hours Forensics for Adults (tickets $12) workshop where you'll learn all about ballistics, blood splatter and beyond.

WOODWARD'S Map p76

149 W Hastings St; 🚌 7

The development that aims to revitalize the long-troubled Downtown Eastside, this former department-store building was a derelict, paint-peeled shell after closing in the early 1990s. Successive plans to renovate and transform it failed until, in 2010, it was finally reopened as a new hub for the community and a trigger for neighborhood gentrification. Combining new condos, shops and a university campus (plus a shiny new reproduction of the iconic neon 'W' that sat on the roof for decades), duck inside the atrium and check out the giant 'Gastown Riot' artwork (p28). And consider coming back for a performance at the Fei & Milton Wong Experimental Theatre (p171).

STEAM CLOCK Map p76

cnr Water & Cambie Sts; Ⓜ Waterfront

Halfway along Water St, this oddly popular tourist magnet lures the cameras with its tooting steam whistle displays. Built in 1977, the clock's mechanism is actually driven by electricity while only the pipes on top are fueled by steam (this might cause a riot if you reveal it to the patiently-waiting tourists). It sounds off every 15 minutes but marks each hour with a little whistling symphony. Once you have the required photo, spend time exploring the rest of cobbled Water St. One of Vancouver's most historic thoroughfares,

AN ARRESTING EXPERIENCE

Who is the Vancouver Police Museum aimed at? Originally, it was mostly a clubhouse for retired cops. We've been working hard in the last few years to expand our activities and exhibits to appeal to a broader range of people, from kids to families and seniors. Some of the most popular parts of the museum will always be adults-only though.

The museum is housed in an historic building. What did it used to be? Built in 1932, the museum building was once the home to the VPD 'Bureau of Science' as well as the city coroner's offices, courtroom and morgue. Almost 15,000 autopsies were performed and countless pieces of evidence were analyzed in this space.

Is it true that Errol Flynn's autopsy was conducted here? Why? With Errol's career as a cinematic sex symbol coming to an end, funds were getting tight. He came to Vancouver to sell his yacht and hit a few parties. On his way to the airport, he complained of pain and was taken to a doctor's apartment, dying shortly thereafter of a heart attack. His autopsy, in our building, is filled with myth and legend and remains one of the wilder nights in this building's history.

Describe some of the confiscated homemade weapons you have on display? In one of our galleries, we have a display nicknamed 'Arsenault's Arsenal,' a collection of weapons seized by the Vancouver Police through the years. From brass knuckles and switchblades to nunchucks and a baseball bat with nails driven through it, this collection goes to show that a police officer must be ready for everything.

Tell me about the tissue samples on the walls of the mortuary room? In the early 1970s, when still an operating morgue, the coroner's staff prepared a traveling exhibit called McDonalds Traveling Wax Museum and Candycane Show made up of various organs subject to different kinds of injury and disease. The exhibit traveled around to high schools to show kids the consequences of unhealthy lifestyles. When it was retired from service, a portion of the exhibit was donated to the museum, where it sits on the wall in our former autopsy suite.

What do you cover in your forensics workshops for adults and children? Our forensics workshops cover a wide range of topics, from fingerprints to bloodstain pattern analysis, although the adult versions are much more graphic and authentic than the kids' versions. There's something deeply fascinating to both youth and adults about the idea of using clues to solve a mystery.

What is your Sins of the City tour all about? Our 'naughty little walking tour' looks at Vancouver's rich history of vice, from brothels and gambling houses to bootlegging joints and opium dens. Although locals sometimes refer to Vancouver as the 'No-Fun City,' our history definitely suggests otherwise.

Do vacationing police officers visit the museum? What do they make of it? Many police museums abroad focus on the 'badges and uniforms' and the institutional history of police departments, so many visiting officers are surprised and pleased to see that we're about so much more, from historical crime to the forensic sciences. Most request that we send information back to their hometown's police museums, which is a real compliment!

An interview with Chris Mathieson, executive director of the Vancouver Police Museum (opposite).

its well-preserved heritage buildings house shops, galleries and resto-bars: cast your gaze above entrance level and check out some cool old-school architectural features.

MAPLE TREE SQUARE Map p76
cnr Alexander, Water, Powell & Carrall Sts; 🚌 7
Vancouver's historic heart, this brick-cobbled area is now lined with convivial bars (see p154) and restaurants (see p136) but it's also still full of heritage charm. Check out the flatiron-style Hotel Europe and peer along Blood Alley (reputedly named for the butcher shops that once were here). The jaunty Gassy Jack statue, perched atop a whiskey barrel, dominates the square. It sits near the spot of his first saloon and the

development that kick-started the modern-day city. Nearby is the red-painted Byrnes Block. One of the first structures built after the 1886 Great Fire, it's the oldest Vancouver building still in its original location. For some context on the area, see p21.

GASTOWN BAR CRAWL
Walking Tour
This short walk will take you to Gastown's best bars and nightclubs.

1 Alibi Room
The city's best bar for regional microbrews, the buzzing Alibi (p155) is convivial enough to make you want to stay all night. The food is

NEIGHBORHOODS GASTOWN

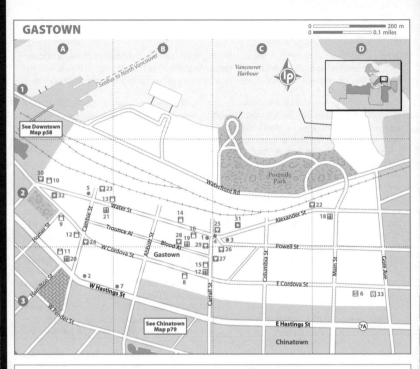

GASTOWN

also good if you want to line your stomach for the debauchery ahead.

2 Chill Winston
Turn right along Alexander St and within five minutes you'll be in Maple Tree Sq. Doff your hat to the Gassy Jack statue, then – if it's sunny – hit the expansive patio of Chill Winston (p154).

3 Diamond
Raise a glass to Old Gassy's spirit across the street (and up the stairs) at the lovely

Diamond (p154), one of the city's coziest and most convivial cocktail bars.

4 Irish Heather
Nip around the corner onto Carrall St and thread yourself through the doorway of the Heather (p156), Vancouver's favorite Irish gastropub. If you haven't eaten yet, this is a great place to start.

5 Six Acres
Duck across the square toward the Gassy Jack statue and head into Six Acres (p155). If it's time

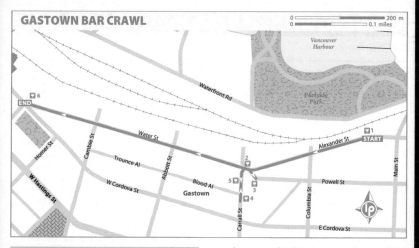

GASTOWN BAR CRAWL

WALK FACTS

Start **Alibi Room**
End **Steamworks Brewing Company**
Distance **1 km**
Time **Depends how fast you drink…**
Exertion **Easy**
Fuel stop **Anywhere you like**

to slow your drinking pace, grab one of the board games to keep you occupied.

6 Steamworks Brewing Company

It's time for a longer, sobering walk – this one's about five minutes. Turn left as you leave Six Acres and left again along Water St. At the top of the street, nip into Steamworks (p155) for a nightcap. Waterfront SkyTrain station is right next door if you need a ride to your bed.

CHINATOWN

Eating p137; Shopping p118

Exotic sights, sounds and scents pervade North America's third-largest Chinatown, predominantly occupying the East Vancouver thoroughfares around Main, Pender and Keefer Sts. You'll find families bargaining over durian fruit in a flurry of Cantonese; shops suffused with the aromas of salted fish and jasmine tea; and vendors hawking silk, jade and Hello Kitty T-shirts. The steamy-windowed wonton restaurants, butchers with splayed barbecued pigs, and ubiquitous firecracker-red awnings will make you think for a moment that you're in Hong Kong.

Chinatown has been around since before the City of Vancouver was incorporated in 1886. At that time, Shanghai Alley (close to what is now the intersection of Carrall and Pender Sts) housed a small Chinese settlement. Ironically, it was the Great Fire that helped Chinatown develop further. In an attempt to rebuild the city, 60 hectares of forested land were leased to Chinese immigrants, who were given a 10-year rent-free agreement on the condition they clear and farm the land. By the end of 1886, almost 90 Chinese lived in the area on farms yielding pigs and produce.

It wasn't long before brightly painted, two-story wooden buildings sprang up along Pender and Carrall Sts, which became a gathering place for socializing and banking (to wire money home). Many Chinese were enticed by the opportunity to earn hard cash working in sawmills, lumber camps and on railroad construction gangs. In 1883 alone, of the nearly 2000 gold miners in BC, 1500 were Chinese, and during the period from 1881 to 1885 more than 11,000 Chinese arrived by ship to work on the construction of the CPR. They were paid $1 a day – half of what white workers were paid.

Some locals will tell you that Chinatown isn't what it used to be, and that the 'real' Chinatown is now located in Richmond (p108), where many of BC's new Asian immigrants have landed in the last 10 years. But this evocative old area has now joined the gentrification renaissance creeping across the Eastside and pockets of new shops and eateries are suddenly jostling for attention with the old family-run haunts. If you only have time for one visit, drop by for the summertime weekend night market (opposite). You might even run into the new panda mascot that now represents the area.

For more information on this neighborhood and its regular special events, visit www .vancouver-chinatown.com. Transit access to Chinatown is via the Stadium-Chinatown and Main St-Science World SkyTrain stations and buses 3, 8 and 19.

SCIENCE WORLD Map opposite

www.scienceworld.ca; 1455 Quebec St; adult/child/youth $21/14.25/17.25; ☉ 10am-5pm Mon-Fri, 10am-6pm Sat & Sun; Ⓜ Main St-Science World

Nestled under the city's favorite geodesic dome (OK, it's only one), the two levels of hands-on science and natural history exhibits here bring out the kid in almost everyone. It's an ideal place to entertain the family – the gallery exploring sustainability issues is especially recommended, along with the water course of ball cannons and bridges. Expect to spend a half-day here as your sprogs run themselves ragged. Level three holds the 400-seat Omnimax Theatre (p174), screening large-format documentary movies to those who need a sit down. If you fancy exploring without the kids, check out the adults-only After Dark events (entry $19.75). During research, a revamp of the site was underway that will include an outdoor science park.

DR SUN YAT-SEN CLASSICAL CHINESE GARDEN & PARK Map opposite

www.vancouverchinesegarden.com; 578 Carrall St; garden adult/student/senior $14/10/11, park free; ☉ 9:30am-7pm mid-Jun–Aug, 10am-6pm Sep & May–mid-Jun, 10am-4:30pm Oct-Apr; Ⓜ Stadium-Chinatown

A tranquility break from clamorous Chinatown, this intimate 'garden of ease' illustrates the Taoist symbolism behind the placing of gnarled pine trees, winding covered pathways and ancient limestone formations. Entry includes a fascinating 45-minute guided tour – look out for the lazy turtles bobbing in the jade-colored water – where you'll learn that everything in the garden reflects balance and harmony. Check the garden's website for its summer schedule of Friday-evening concerts. Adjacent is the free-entry Dr Sun Yat-Sen Park. Not quite as elaborate as

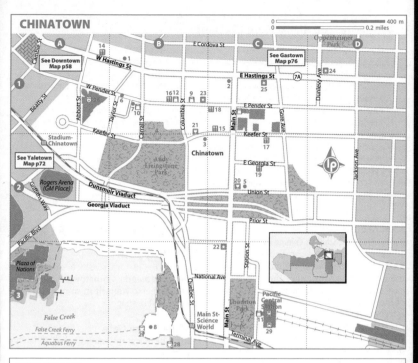

CHINATOWN

its sister, it's still a pleasant oasis of whispering grasses, a large fishpond and a small pagoda.

CHINATOWN NIGHT MARKET Map above
www.vcma.shawbiz.ca; Keefer St, btwn Columbia & Main Sts; 🕑 **6:30-11pm Fri-Sun mid-May–early Sep;** Ⓜ **Stadium-Chinatown**
Smaller and less frenetic than its clamorous Richmond brother (see the boxed text, p118), this colorful downtown

evening bazaar lures with its sensory combination of cheap trinkets, knock-off designer goods and aromatic hawker food – it's like a walk-through buffet of noodles, fish balls and bubble tea. There's live music on stage most nights and, once the sun sets and all you can hear are Chinese voices, it's not hard to imagine yourself in Hong Kong. Order a fresh coconut (plus a straw) and you'll fit right in.

RETURN OF THE DOWNTOWN EASTSIDE?

Vancouver's one-time commercial district, the Downtown Eastside – radiating from the few blocks around the Main and Hastings Sts intersection – became a depressing ghetto of lives blighted by drugs and prostitution in recent decades. But, triggered by the massive new Woodward's redevelopment that opened in early 2010, the neighborhood that time forgot is finally on the rise, encouraging adventurous visitors with street smarts to check it out. (Street smarts means exploring in daylight hours and avoiding the back alleyways).

What you'll find is a clutch of historic buildings that survived the era when similar structures in other neighborhoods were demolished. Now ripe for renovation, many are finally being reclaimed and restored, hence the sudden emergence of cranes in an area that developers have long-avoided. Check out the preserved, copper-colored Dominion Building (Map p76; 205 W Hastings St) and the beautifully upgraded monumental Flack Block (Map p76; 163 W Hastings St), then nip into Woodward's (p74). Don't stay too long outside the Carnegie Centre (Map p79; 401 Main St), but look out for its stained-glass window of Shakespeare, Spenser and Milton. End your short stroll at the Vancouver Police Museum (p74) or take in nearby Chinatown (p78), where you'll be just a few steps from an unlikely shrine to Jimi Hendrix.

SAM KEE BUILDING Map p79

8 W Pender St; Ⓜ Stadium-Chinatown

This structure near the corner of Carrall St made it into the *Guinness World Records* as the world's narrowest office building. It's easy to miss because it looks like the front of the larger building behind, to which it is attached. A businessman's vendetta against city hall led to the structure's anorexic shape. Chang Toy, the Sam Kee Co owner, bought land at this site in 1906, but in 1926 all but a 1.8m-wide strip was expropriated by the city to widen Pender St. Toy's way of thumbing his nose at city officials was to build anyway, and up sprang the unusual 'Slender on Pender' dwelling. It's almost in the shadow of the towering Millennium Gate, inaugurated by Prime Minister Jean Chretien in 2002.

CHINATOWN CULTURE CRAWL
Walking Tour

Dip into the historic streets of one of North America's biggest Chinatown districts and you'll immerse yourself in some fascinating culture and heritage.

1 Millennium Gate

Start your trek at this magnificent Chinatown landmark, dominating the intersection of W Pender and Taylor Sts. Built in 2000, it's a fitting reminder that the area is still a vibrant community.

2 Dr Sun Yat-Sen Classical Chinese Garden

Head under the gate and turn right onto Carrall St. The entrance to this lovely landscaped garden (p78) is on your left. Check out the tranquil pools, intriguing limestone formations and gnarly pine trees.

3 Everything Café

Exit the garden and turn right onto Pender. On the left-hand side of the street, nip into the cool Everything Café (p138) for a coffee break.

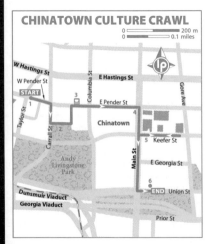

CHINATOWN CULTURE CRAWL

0 — 200 m
0 — 0.1 miles

WALK FACTS

Start **Millennium Gate**
End **Jimi Hendrix shrine**
Distance **1.5km**
Time **1 hour**
Exertion **Easy**
Fuel stop **Everything Café**

4 Main St

Keep walking east on Pender until you reach the intersection with Main St. You're right in the heart of Chinatown here – check out the dragon-covered lampposts and red phone booths.

5 Keefer St

Turn right onto Main St and then left onto Keefer St. Duck in and out of the traditional Chinatown grocery stores here – it's a true sensory immersion.

6 Jimi Hendrix shrine

Return to Main, turn left and continue south along this street for two blocks. Turn left onto Union St and look for the red-painted little shack. On or near the site where Hendrix used to visit his grandmother, it's now a shrine to his time in the city.

SOUTH MAIN (SOMA)

Drinking p156; Eating p138; Shopping p119

Known as Mt Pleasant to anyone over 40 and SoMa, South Main or just Main St to everyone else, this neighborhood starts from the incline around Southeast False Creek, not far from Science World, and then darts up Main St for dozens of blocks. From the 1880s, it was one of the region's most important districts, with monumental buildings flanking grand, tram-lined streets with names like Kingsway, Broadway and Main. The managers from the many factories lining the False Creek shoreline lived in this area. But as the city's industrial fervor declined, Mt Pleasant's fortunes fell. By the 1970s, the area almost matched the Downtown Eastside for dereliction and sketchy skid-row ambience.

But it was this sense of abandonment that eventually saved the area. Artists and bohemians began colonizing the cheap accommodation here in the 1990s, and by 2000 the newly designated SoMa had become the city's hipster 'hood of choice. Now the kind of place where almost every young woman wears vintage-clothing-store chic and every young man sports a trim beard, plaid shirt and skinny jeans, the common pastime here seems to be hanging out in independent coffee shops to complain about how high the rents have become…while checking email on your top-end Apple laptop.

It's not all about appearances, though. SoMa houses many of the city's best indie bars and restaurants, especially radiating from the Main and Broadway intersection – don't miss the excellent Biltmore Cabaret (p167) if you're here for a night out – while past 20th Ave you'll suddenly hit one of the best strips of one-off clothing stores in the city. Further south, starting at 49th Ave, is the Punjabi Market district. Also known as 'Little India,' it's a colorful strip stuffed with tempting all-you-can-eat curry restaurants.

Transit access to the entire stretch of South Main is via bus 3, while buses 9 and 99B-Line will drop you off at the busy Main and Broadway intersection.

SOUTH FALSE CREEK SEAWALL

Map opposite

Foot of Terminal Ave; Ⓜ Main St-Science World
Starting from Science World (p78), this waterfront stroll along the south side of False Creek is around 3km and it's one of the newest stretches of seawall in the city, only opened in 2009. Heading westwards, you'll first pass the giant Olympic Village.

Created for the 2010 Olympic and Paralympic Winter Games and now a snazzy condo development, it's intended to be a new Vancouver neighborhood.

Check out the sci-fi pedestrian bridge over the water here and, further along, you'll also spot nautical-themed public artworks and then Habitat Island, a mini-sanctuary for passing cormorants and herons to perch. Continuing on to Stamps Landing and the superbly named Leg-in-Boot Sq – centerpiece of a 1980s waterfront development – you'll eventually roll up at the back entrance to Granville Island (p88), a perfect spot to rest your legs and grab lunch. Combine this with the stroll around north False Creek (p72) for a great urban waterfront hike.

PORTOBELLO WEST Map opposite

www.portobellowest.com; Rocky Mountaineer Station, 1755 Cottrell St; admission $2 (under 12yr free); Ⓨ noon-6pm last Sun of month Mar-Dec; Ⓜ Main St-Science World
This monthly indoor market enables more than 100 local artists and designers to display and sell their work. Prices are reasonable and you'll find an amazing selection that can include hand-painted boots, striking original paintings, unique ceramics

---

WORTH THE TRIP: PUNJABI MARKET

You won't find cows wandering the streets or bicycle rickshaws weaving between the traffic, but some of the sounds, smells and colors of the subcontinent are condensed into this short Main St market strip (Map p54; Main St btwn 48th & 51st Aves; Ⓜ Main St-Science World, then bus 3). The enclave of sari stores, Bangra music shops, jewelry emporiums and some of the region's best-value curry restaurants has seen better days – as in Chinatown, the younger people have dispersed around the region – but it's still a good spot for a spicy all-you-can-eat lunch followed by a restorative walkabout. Locals are planning to erect an Indian version of a Chinatown gate here, so watch this space.

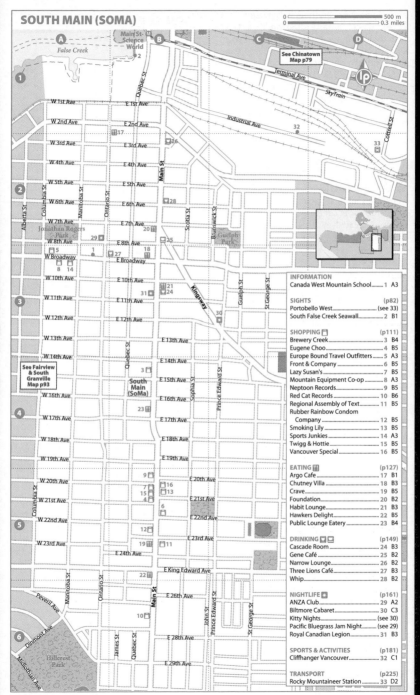

SOUTH MAIN (SOMA)

INFORMATION
Canada West Mountain School........ 1 A3

SIGHTS   (p82)
Portobello West.............................(see 33)
South False Creek Seawall................ 2 B1

SHOPPING 🛍
Brewery Creek.............................(p111)
Brewery Creek.................................... 3 B4
Eugene Choo....................................... 4 B5
Europe Bound Travel Outfitters........ 5 A3
Front & Company................................ 6 B5
Lazy Susan's....................................... 7 B5
Mountain Equipment Co-op............... 8 A3
Neptoon Records................................ 9 B5
Red Cat Records............................... 10 B6
Regional Assembly of Text............... 11 B5
Rubber Rainbow Condom
    Company...................................... 12 B5
Smoking Lily..................................... 13 B5
Sports Junkies.................................. 14 A3
Twigg & Hottie.................................. 15 B5
Vancouver Special............................ 16 B5

EATING 🍴   (p127)
Argo Cafe.. 17 B1
Chutney Villa.................................... 18 B3
Crave... 19 B5
Foundation....................................... 20 B2
Habit Lounge.................................... 21 B3
Hawkers Delight................................ 22 B5
Public Lounge Eatery........................ 23 B4

DRINKING 🍷🍺   (p149)
Cascade Room................................... 24 B3
Gene Café.. 25 B2
Narrow Lounge.................................. 26 B2
Three Lions Café............................... 27 B3
Whip... 28 B2

NIGHTLIFE 🎭   (p161)
ANZA Club.. 29 A2
Biltmore Cabaret............................... 30 C3
Kitty Nights...................................(see 30)
Pacific Bluegrass Jam Night..........(see 29)
Royal Canadian Legion...................... 31 B3

SPORTS & ACTIVITIES   (p181)
Cliffhanger Vancouver....................... 32 C1

TRANSPORT   (p225)
Rocky Mountaineer Station................ 33 D2

and just about everything in between. There's usually a party atmosphere, as DJs spin their stuff and food vendors give you something to munch on while you peruse the goods. To get here from the Main St-Science World SkyTrain station, walk east along Terminal Ave to Cottrell St. Turn right and the station building is just ahead of you. Admission is free in some summer months when the weather is good enough to hold the event outside.

SOMA HIPSTER STROLL
Walking Tour

Vancouver's hip strip is ideal for those who like to browse in cool indie stores stocked with fashions created by the city's bright young designers.

1 Smoking Lily

Start your Main St trek by hopping on bus 3 at the Main St-Science World SkyTrain station, then hopping off at the Main St intersection with 20th Ave. Nip into this smashing little designer shop (p119) that's aimed at intellectual clotheshorses.

2 Lazy Susan's

Cross the street and dip into the cool gifts and accessories at this friendly little store (p119). Anyone for Scrabble-tile cufflinks?

3 Front & Company

Cross over again and increase your coolness quotient in the vintage clothes area of this three-part shop (p119). If you've always wanted a 1950s crushed-velvet smoking jacket to wear with your jeans, this is the place to find it.

4 Crave

Re-cross to the right-hand side of the street and, if it's time to eat, join the local throng at this popular neighborhood resto-bar (p139). Consider a seat on the hidden patio out back.

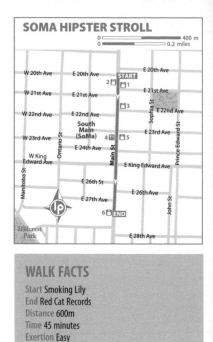

WALK FACTS

Start **Smoking Lily**
End **Red Cat Records**
Distance **600m**
Time **45 minutes**
Exertion **Easy**
Fuel stop **Crave**

5 Regional Assembly of Text

Across the street you'll find one of the city's most eclectic stores. The Assembly (p119) is where you can indulge your fetish for sumptuous writing paper, old-fashioned typewriters and all manner of naughty stationery items. Pick the right day for your visit and join the local hipsters at the monthly letter-writing social club.

6 Red Cat Records

Zigzag back across Main and continue south to one of the city's favorite indie record shops (see the boxed text, p120). Peruse the CDs and vinyl and ask the staff for tips on who to see in town – tickets are available here for area shows.

COMMERCIAL DRIVE

Drinking p157; Eating p140; Shopping p121

Commercial Dr is like Robson St's far more interesting evil twin. Old-world bakery aromas mingle with the smell of patchouli and wafting pot. Skateboarders glide down the sidewalk alongside dainty girls with monstrous tattoos. And this may be the only place in town where you can shop for soy wax candles, belly-dancing supplies and a Che Guevara backpack in one fell swoop.

The centerpiece of the sprawling East Vancouver district, Commercial Dr (everyone calls it 'the Drive' here) is a microcosm of the city's diversity. Focused mainly on the 17-block strip between Broadway and Venables St, it's traditionally melded Italian, Portuguese, Latin American, Caribbean and Southeast Asian immigrant communities, most of whom began arriving here in the 1950s. Stir the pot some more by adding the artist, student and lesbian communities who also call this area home and you've easily got the city's most diverse cultural quarter.

But the Drive's history goes quite a lot further back than most locals realise. The street was named in the early 1900s, when it was the first road built along the interurban rail line from New Westminster to Vancouver (constructed in 1891), triggering a wave of development that transformed it into a major shopping thoroughfare. From the 1950s to the 1970s the Italian community settled here and it became known as 'Little Italy.' You'll still find plenty of family-owned coffee shops from this era, many lined with chatty old Italian men enthusiastically debating the fortunes of their favorite soccer teams 'back home.' (If you're here during a World Cup, this is the best place in town to watch a game).

For visitors there's no better street to hang out with the locals and enjoy some excellent and highly convivial dining – make sure you wander along the strip for a few blocks before you settle on a place that truly whets your appetite. The same goes for the chatty bars here, where you'll meet everyone from pixie-chick bohemians to chin-stroking poets and old-school dope smokers. The Drive is also 'patio central,' making it the best place in Vancouver to drink and dine alfresco on languid summer evenings.

For more information on Commercial Dr, visit www.thedrive.ca. Transit access is via the Commercial-Broadway SkyTrain station and bus 20. Buses 9 and 99B-Line can also drop you off at the intersection of Commercial and Broadway.

GRANDVIEW PARK Map p86

Commercial Dr, btwn Charles & William Sts; admission free; 🕐 **24hr;** 🚌 **20**

Commercial's alfresco neighborhood hub is named after its smashing views: to the north are the looming mountains of the North Shore, while to the west you'll have a great cityscape vista of twinkling towers.

Grandview isn't just about good looks, however. Undergoing a refurb on our visit, this narrow band of sun-baked grass and busy playgrounds has a surprising amount of history. It originally housed the drill hall of the local Irish Fusiliers and is now home to a slender granite war memorial. Wreaths are still laid here on Remembrance Day. The rest of the year, you'll find buskers, impromptu garage sales and a waft or two of illicit substances.

COMMERCIAL DRIVE DRINK & DINE
Walking Tour

You don't have to hit all these recommended drink and dine spots, but it's a good idea to see what's on offer before you make a decision.

1 St Augustine's

From the Commercial-Broadway SkyTrain station, walk north for one block to St Aug's (p157), a large local bar. You'll find the city's biggest array of draft, mostly BC microbrews.

2 Prado Café

If you've haven't indulged too much, continue north on Commercial and sober up with a coffee at Prado (p157). If you're packing your laptop, it has free wi-fi here.

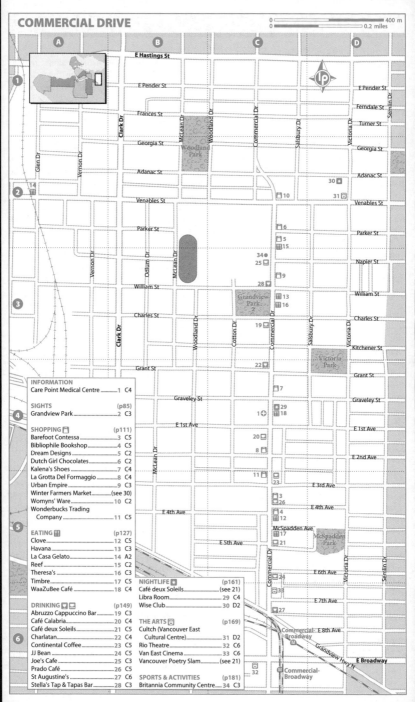

E Hastings St

E Pender St

E Pender St

Frances St

Ferndale Dr

Turner St

Clark Dr

Vernon Dr

Glen Dr

McLean Dr

Woodland Dr

Commercial Dr

Salsbury Dr

Victoria Dr

Semlin Dr

Georgia St

Woodland Park

Georgia St

Adanac St

Adanac St

30

31

Venables St

Venables St

Parker St

6

5

15

Parker St

Vernon Dr

Odlum Dr

McLean Dr

34

25

Napier St

28

9

William St

Grandview Park 2

13

16

William St

Charles St

Clark Dr

Woodland Dr

Cotton Dr

Commercial Dr

Salsbury Dr

Victoria Dr

Charles St

19

Kitchener St

22

Victoria Park

Grant St

7

Grant St

Graveley St

Graveley St

E 1st Ave

29

18

1

E 1st Ave

McLean Dr

20

E 2nd Ave

8

11

23

E 3rd Ave

3

26

E 4th Ave

E 4th Ave

4

12

McSpadden Ave

17

McSpadden Park

21

Commercial Dr

E 5th Ave

Victoria Dr

Semlin Dr

24

E 6th Ave

33

27

E 7th Ave

Commercial-Broadway

E 8th Ave

Grandview Hwy N

E Broadway

32

Commercial-Broadway

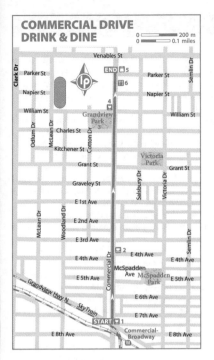

COMMERCIAL DRIVE DRINK & DINE

WALK FACTS

Start St Augustine's
End Reef
Distance 1km
Time How fast can you drink?
Exertion Easy
Fuel stop Pick one!

3 Grandview Park

If it feels like time for a rest, continue north on Commercial and lay back on the grass in this park (p85) – but not before you've checked out the handsome vistas to the north and west.

4 Stella's Tap & Tapas Bar

Peel yourself from the park and nip next door to this Euro-style bistro (p157). Play it safe with a whiskey or work your way down the amazing menu of imported Belgian microbrews. Even better, forsake the booze and try a bowl of Belgian-style mussels.

5 Dutch Girl Chocolates

If it's not too late in the day and it's still open, stroll to the end of the next block and cross the road to salivate over this eclectic little chocolate shop (p122). Aside from the handmade chocs, it imports an array of sweet treats from the Netherlands.

6 Reef

If you didn't eat at Stella's (and you haven't stuffed yourself with chocolate), drop into this cheery Caribbean restaurant (p140) a couple of doors away. The hearty soul food here is nicely spicy. And if you've had too much to drink, the tropical cocktails also come in handy non-alcoholic versions.

GRANVILLE ISLAND

Drinking p158; Eating p141; Shopping p122; Sleeping p201

Vancouver's favorite urban hangout should be the first port of call for anyone with an afternoon to spare and a penchant for wandering around waterfront shops and galleries, cool craft studios and a foodie-loving indoor market. If you're more in the mood for an evening of theater, dining and a little imbibing, this is also a great spot. But it wasn't always thus. In fact, you'd have been crazy to spend more than five minutes here 50 years ago.

A peninsula (it's not actually an island) created from natural sandbanks topped up with landfill, the original 'Mud Island' and 'Industrial Island' (two names that didn't quite stick) was a bustling hotbed of small factories for much of the last century. But as with all the other industries originally lining False Creek, decline was swift after WWII and the 'island' became a derelict slum of rotting sheds and grubby back alleys.

In the 1970s, interest in reclaiming the area as a people-friendly new neighborhood emerged and, after major federal government investment, the Granville Island Public Market opened for business in 1979. Successful from day one, it kick-started a renaissance that saw the crumbling factory buildings patched up and given a new lease of life as artisan studios and gallery-style arts and crafts shops. Granville Island was reborn, becoming one of North America's most successful urban redevelopment projects.

Once you've exhausted the shopping, save plenty of time to simply wander around and get a little lost (if you fall into the water, you've probably walked too far). Weaving along the labyrinthine alleys, look out for the old rail lines embedded in the sidewalks, check out the flotilla of lovely houseboats at the island's hotel end, and take the lip-smacking tour of Granville Island Brewing – Canada's oldest microbrewery. And save time to peruse the large cement factory: an incongruous still-working reminder of the island's industrial past; it hosts annual behind-the-scenes open days.

For more information on Granville Island – including a handy downloadable map – visit www.granvilleisland.com. Aside from transit bus 50, which stops near the island's Anderson St entrance, there are a couple of other fun ways to get here. You can take a kid-friendly miniferry (p227) across False Creek, which lands you in the heart of the action. Alternatively, in summer, you can hop the Canada Line SkyTrain service from downtown to the Olympic Village stop, then clamber aboard the antique Downtown Historic Railway (see the boxed text, p229) for a fun trundle to the island's main entrance.

GRANVILLE ISLAND PUBLIC MARKET
Map opposite

www.granvilleisland.com; Johnston St, near cnr of Duranleau St; ⊙ 9am-7pm; 🚌 50

A multisensory deli specializing in gourmet cheese, fruit and bakery treats, the 51-vendor covered market is a chatty, visceral place to mix with the locals. It's a great spot to pick up picnic fixings (Vanier Park is a short seawall stroll away if you're looking for a seat) and buskers are a regular fixture in and around the building. There's a small but tasty international food court here (eat off-peak to avoid the rush) as well as a regular clutch of arts and crafts stalls. Traveling foodies should consider a guided market tour ($49) or a market dinner ($90) organized by Edible BC (☎ 604-812-9660; www.edible-britishcolumbia.com). See the boxed text on p123 for more info on the market, including details of specific stalls.

GRANVILLE ISLAND BREWING
Map opposite

☎ 604-687-2739; www.gib.ca; 1441 Cartwright St; tours $9.75; ⊙ tours noon, 2pm & 4pm; 🚌 50

Canada's oldest microbrewery offers half-hour tours where the smiling guides will walk you through the tiny brewing nook (production has mostly shifted to larger premises) before depositing you in the

top picks

RAINY-DAY ACTIVITIES

- Umbrella Shop (p122)
- Bloedel Floral Conservatory (94)
- Granville Island Brewing tour (above)
- Bill Reid Gallery of Northwest Coast Art (p56)
- Vancity Theatre (p175)

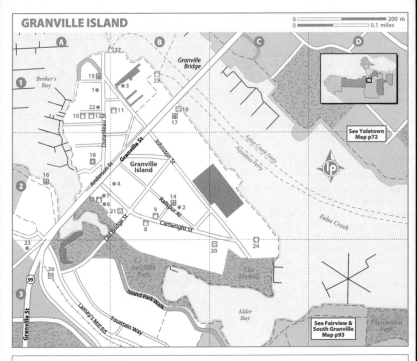

GRANVILLE ISLAND

Taproom for four generous samples, often including the summer-favorite Hefeweizen, mildly-hopped Brockton IPA or the recommended Kitsilano Maple Cream Ale. You'll spot many of these brews in bars and restaurants around the city. You can also buy some takeout in the adjoining store – look out for any seasonal or special-batch

tipples that might be worth a try (the Ginger Ale is a winner).

RAILSPUR ALLEY Map above
btwn Old Bridge & Cartwright Sts; 🚌 **50**
Seemingly far from the madding crowds of the public market – at least on summer days when every tourist in town seems to

be there – this somewhat hidden back-alley strip is a relaxing alternative. You'll find a string of unique artisan stores, including a painter, fiber artist and silk seller. Even better is the Artisan Sake Maker (☎ 604-685-7253; www.artisansakemaker.com; 1339 Railspur Alley; ⊗ 11:30am-6pm), who produces small batches of junmai sake right here (tastings are $2 each or $5 for three). You can sober up with a strong coffee at the Agro Café (p142), also a great spot for lunch.

EMILY CARR UNIVERSITY OF ART + DESIGN Map p89

www.ecuad.ca; 1399 Johnston St; admission free; ⊗ 10am-6pm; ⊟ 50

Named after BC's most famous historic painter (Emily Carr, 1871–1945), Vancouver's leading art school occupies a corrugated-metal factory complex near a cement plant. Nip into the Charles H Scott Gallery (☎ 604-844-3811; www.chscott.ecuad.ca; admission free; ⊗ noon-5pm Mon-Fri, 10am-5pm Sat & Sun) on your right for a glimpse of student and graduate work. There's also a portfolio show every May, where challenging photography, multimedia and the occasional oddball installation go on display. If you're an art lover, you'll also enjoy the school's excellent bookstore.

KIDS MARKET Map p89

www.kidsmarket.ca; 1496 Cartwright St; ⊗ 10am-6pm; ⊟ 50

A nightmare if you happen to stroll in by mistake, this two-story mini shopping mall for under-10s is bristling with kid-friendly stores, mostly of the toy variety. If your child's interests extend beyond Lego and Barbie, there are also retailers specializing in clothing, candy, magic tricks and arts and crafts. If it all gets a bit too much, you might try enticing your sprogs away from the shops to the huge Granville Island Water Park (admission free; ⊗ 10am-6pm mid-May–early Sep) just behind the market (or perhaps sneaking yourself to the nearby Granville Island Brewing for a swift libation).

GRANVILLE ISLAND ARTISAN TRAWL
Walking Tour

This stroll will take you around some of Vancouver's favorite artisan studios and arts and crafts galleries.

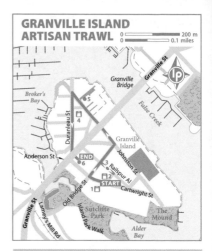

GRANVILLE ISLAND ARTISAN TRAWL

WALK FACTS

Start **Crafthouse**
End **Granville Island Brewing**
Distance **1km**
Time **1 hour**
Exertion **Easy**
Fuel stop **Granville Island Public Market**

1 Crafthouse

If you're entering the area from the main entrance on Anderson St, take the first right onto Cartwright St and dip into this shiny gallery (p123) of regional arts and crafts.

2 Gallery of BC Ceramics

Cross the street and check out this excellent showcase (p123) of locally produced artisan pottery. You'll find cool mugs and rustic teapots that will tempt your credit cards.

3 Railspur Alley

Duck along the little pathway beside the gallery and you'll hit this somewhat hidden back alley (p89). Peruse the excellent artisan stores here, including a sake maker.

4 Net Loft

Head to Old Bridge St at the end of Railspur Alley, then follow it to Johnston St. On your left is the Net Loft. It's lined with arts and crafts stores, including the recommended Edie Hats (p122) and Paper-Ya (p123).

5 Granville Island Public Market

Diagonally across the street from the Net Loft is the entrance to the public market (p88). It specializes in deli-style food stalls but always has additional artisan stands that are well worth a look. There's also a food court here if it's time for a snack.

6 Granville Island Brewing

To experience a different kind of artistry, end your visit with a guided tour of this famed local brewery (p88), where you'll be able to taste the creativity with a lip-smacking complement of beer samples.

Eating p142; Shopping p124; Sleeping p201

While clamorous Broadway is lined with shops and restaurants, it's never been the kind of alluring destination street its name implies. That's probably because this West Side strip is too long to have a single identity: the vastly different neighborhoods of Kitsilano and SoMa each claim sections as their own, while it also intersects with artsy South Granville and the old Fairview neighborhood.

Predominantly residential, Fairview rises from the south side of False Creek and was originally surveyed by the CPR's Lauchlan Hamilton in the 1880s. When he climbed the forested incline and looked back over the mountain-framed vista, he coined the name 'Fairview.' Now studded with clapboard houses that date from only a few years after Lauchlan's visit, the area is also home to Vancouver's City Hall, the region's second-best art deco tower after downtown's Marine Building (p57). It's also easier than ever to reach this part of town, since the new Canada Line runs right through the Cambie St heart of it.

If you have a sedentary approach to nature, pull up a bench among the trees and flowers of Queen Elizabeth Park or dip into VanDusen Botanical Garden, a Vancouver favorite. Alternatively, you can spend a sunny afternoon at a baseball game at Nat Bailey Stadium (p191).

South Granville (the strip of Granville St running south of the Granville Bridge as far as W 16th Ave) has been a popular shopping and dining district for years. Recently it's also become a destination for gallery hoppers – particularly on the uphill area before Broadway known as 'South Granville Rise,' which houses some of the city's best contemporary art galleries. They mainly feature leading local artists: it's a good place to drop a few thousand dollars on an up-and-coming painter.

The entire South Granville area is a manageable afternoon excursion from the downtown core, and is especially good if you like shopping but hate malls: the retailing thoroughfare here is reminiscent of a bustling high street in a mid-sized European town and is home to some of the city's best boutique, food and gift shops. You'll find fashion stores, interiors outlets and the kind of tempting knickknack joints where you can easily drop $50 without even thinking about it. Save some money for dinner, though: some of Vancouver's best restaurants, including Vij's (p143) and West (p142), line the street (or nestle just off the main drag) here.

For more information on South Granville, visit www.southgranville.org. Transit access to Fairview is via buses 9 and 15, and the Canada Line SkyTrain stations Broadway-City Hall and King Edward. Bus 10 runs along Granville St.

VANDUSEN BOTANICAL GARDEN
Map opposite

www.vandusengarden.org; 5251 Oak St; adult/child/senior & youth $9.75/5.25/7.25, reduced off-season; ⊗ 10am-4pm Nov-Feb, 10am-5pm Mar & Oct, 10am-6pm Apr, 10am-8pm May, 10am-9pm Jun-Aug, 10am-7pm Sep; ☒ 17

Vancouver's favorite ornamental green space, this 22-hectare idyll is a web of paths weaving through dozens of small, specialized gardens: the Rhododendron Walk blazes with color in spring, while the Korean Pavilion is a focal point for a fascinating Asian plant collection. There's also a fun Elizabethan maze and an intriguing menagerie of marble sculptures. Free tours are offered daily at 2pm. VanDusen is also one of Vancouver's top Christmastime destinations, complete with thousands of twinkling fairy lights illuminating the dormant plant life. Check the website to see what's in bloom seasonally.

top picks
LATE-OPENING ATTRACTIONS

- Vancouver Art Gallery (p56) – until 9pm Tuesday
- Vancouver Lookout (p57) – until 10.30pm mid-May to mid-September
- Museum of Anthropology (p101) – until 9pm Tuesday mid-January to mid-October
- Museum of Vancouver (p98) – until 8pm Thursday
- Bloedel Floral Conservatory (p94) – until 9pm Saturday and Sunday, May to August

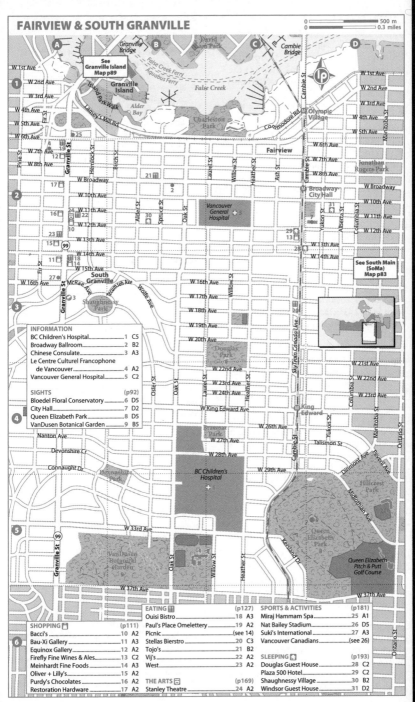

FAIRVIEW & SOUTH GRANVILLE

INFORMATION
BC Children's Hospital	1 C5
Broadway Ballroom	2 B2
Chinese Consulate	3 A3
Le Centre Culturel Francophone	
de Vancouver	4 A2
Vancouver General Hospital	5 C2

SIGHTS (p92)
Bloedel Floral Conservatory	6 D5
City Hall	7 D2
Queen Elizabeth Park	8 D5
VanDusen Botanical Garden	9 B5

SHOPPING (p111)
Bacci's	10 A2
Bau-Xi Gallery	11 A3
Equinox Gallery	12 A2
Firefly Fine Wines & Ales	13 C2
Meinhardt Fine Foods	14 A3
Oliver + Lilly's	15 A2
Purdy's Chocolates	16 A2
Restoration Hardware	17 A2

EATING (p127)
Ouisi Bistro	18 A3
Paul's Place Omelettery	19 A2
Picnic	(see 14)
Stellas Bierstro	20 C3
Tojo's	21 B2
Vij's	22 A2
West	23 A2

THE ARTS (p169)
Stanley Theatre	24 A2

SPORTS & ACTIVITIES (p181)
Miraj Hammam Spa	25 A1
Nat Bailey Stadium	26 D5
Suki's International	27 A3
Vancouver Canadians	(see 26)

SLEEPING (p193)
Douglas Guest House	28 C2
Plaza 500 Hotel	29 C2
Shaughnessy Village	30 B2
Windsor Guest House	31 D2

QUEEN ELIZABETH PARK Map p93

www.vancouverparks.ca; W 33rd Ave & Cambie St; admission free; ⏰ 24hr; 🚌 15

The city's highest point – it's 167m above sea level and has panoramic views of the mountain-framed downtown skyscrapers – this 52-hectare park claims to house specimens of every tree native to Canada. Sports fields, manicured lawns and two formal gardens keep the locals happy, and you'll likely also see wide-eyed couples posing for their wedding photos. Check out the synchronized fountains at the park's summit, where you'll also find a hulking Henry Moore bronze called *Knife Edge – Two Piece*. If you want to be taken out to the ball game, the recently restored Nat Bailey Stadium (p191) is a popular summer-afternoon haven for baseball fans.

BLOEDEL FLORAL CONSERVATORY
Map p93

☎ 604-257-8584; www.vancouverparks.ca; Queen Elizabeth Park; adult/child/senior & youth $4.76/2.43/3.33; ⏰ 9am-8pm Mon-Fri, 10am-9pm Sat & Sun May-Aug, 10am-5pm Sep-Apr; 🚌 15

Cresting the hill in Queen Elizabeth Park, this triodetic domed conservatory – an ideal indoor warm-up spot on a rainy day – is the area's green-fingered centerpiece. It has three climate-controlled zones with 400 plant species, dozens of koi carp and many free-flying tropical birds, including parrots and macaws: ask for a free brochure to help you identify the exotic flora and fauna. At the time of writing, the conservatory was under threat of closure due to funding issues so call first before you head over.

CITY HALL Map p93

www.vancouver.ca; 453 W 12th Ave; admission free; ⏰ 8:30am-5pm Mon-Fri; Ⓜ Broadway-City Hall

Art deco fans should save time for a stroll through the marble-lined lobby of one of Vancouver's best architectural gems. Completed in 1936, its highlights include a mirrored ceiling, streamlined signs, cylindrical lanterns and embossed elevator doors. Duck inside one of the elevators to peruse their intricate inlaid wood design, then check out the handsome heritage homes on surrounding Yukon St and W 12th Ave. If you're on a deco roll, also hit downtown's lovely Marine Building (see p57).

SOUTH GRANVILLE STROLL
Walking Tour

Artsy types can scratch their gallery itch along Granville St – most galleries occupy the compact uphill stretch known as South Granville Rise – while mall-avoiding shopping fans will enjoy perusing the many stores and boutiques here.

1 South Granville Rise

Start your stroll at the intersection of Granville St and W 6th Ave (bus 10 from downtown stops right here) and walk uphill past the many contemporary galleries lining the street, including Equinox Gallery (p124).

2 Granville St & Broadway

Continue up Granville St until you reach the intersection with Broadway. This is the neighborhood's bustling heart and you can head in any direction to explore the shops and restaurants that abound here.

3 Restoration Hardware

If you've decided to continue along Granville, cross over W Broadway and you'll soon hit this popular interior and housewares store (p125), where you can pick up some design tips for your apartment.

4 Purdy's Chocolates

Continue walking a couple more blocks until you reach the intersection with W 11th Ave. On the corner you'll find the city's favorite home-grown chocolate purveyor (p125). Consider stopping for a choc-covered ice-cream bar.

WALK FACTS

Start South Granville Rise
End Stanley Theatre
Distance 700m
Time 45 minutes
Exertion Easy
Fuel stop Coffee shops dot the intersection between Broadway and Granville St

5 Vij's

Cross over and head down W 11th Ave for half a block. On your right, you'll see Vij's (p143), the city's favorite Indian restaurant. If you don't have time for dinner, it has a great café next door.

6 Stanley Theatre

Amble back to Granville. Turn left and you'll soon be standing outside the Stanley (p178). Consider catching a show or keep strolling south along Granville to peruse the heritage mansions of Shaughnessy Heights (opposite).

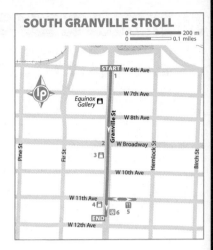

SOUTH GRANVILLE STROLL

KITSILANO

Drinking p159; Eating p143; Shopping p125; Sleeping p202

One of Vancouver's most attractive and established neighborhoods, Kitsilano – or 'Kits' as every local calls it – is a former hippie enclave where the counterculture flower children grew up to reap large mortgages and professional jobs. They still practice yoga and advocate organics, of course, but they're more than willing to pay top dollar for the privilege. The hybrid SUV was invented for the kind of people who now live here.

The area was named after Chief Khatsahalono, leader of the First Nations village of Sun'ahk, which occupied the seafront stretch now designated as Vanier Park. In 1901 the local government displaced the entire community, sending some families to the Capilano Indian Reserve on the North Shore and others to Squamish. The colonials replaced them with a vengeance.

The first Kits streetcar service in 1905 triggered an explosion of housing construction, from the 'Vancouver Box' (two-story wood-framed homes) to low-rise apartment buildings and expansive, fully fledged estates. During the 1950s and '60s many of these airy heritage mansions were converted into rooming houses popular with university students, sparking the 'beatnik ghetto' feel that transformed the district. Fueled by pungent BC bud, counterculture political movements and edgy newspapers mushroomed here, a drive that created the *Georgia Straight,*

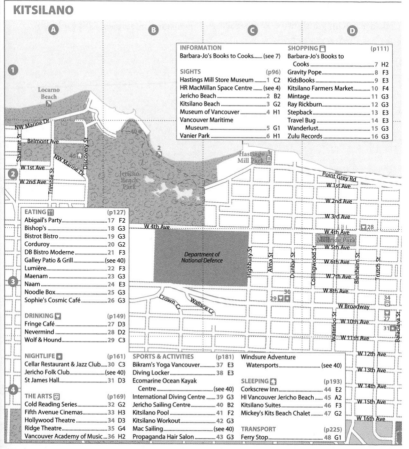

KITSILANO

INFORMATION
Barbara-Jo's Books to Cooks....... (see 7)

SIGHTS (p96)
Hastings Mill Store Museum 1 C2
HR MacMillan Space Centre ...... (see 4)
Jericho Beach 2 B2
Kitsilano Beach 3 G2
Museum of Vancouver 4 H1
Vancouver Maritime
   Museum 5 G1
Vanier Park 6 H1

SHOPPING (p111)
Barbara-Jo's Books to
   Cooks 7 H2
Gravity Pope 8 F3
KidsBooks 9 E3
Kitsilano Farmers Market............. 10 F4
Mintage 11 G3
Ray Rickburn 12 G3
Stepback 13 E3
Travel Bug 14 E3
Wanderlust 15 G3
Zulu Records 16 G3

EATING (p127)
Abigail's Party............................... 17 F2
Bishop's 18 G3
Bistrot Bistro 19 G3
Corduroy 20 G2
DB Bistro Moderne 21 F3
Galley Patio & Grill ....(see 40)
Lumière 22 F3
Maenam 23 G3
Naam 24 E3
Noodle Box................................... 25 G3
Sophie's Cosmic Café 26 G3

DRINKING (p149)
Fringe Café 27 D3
Nevermind 28 D2
Wolf & Hound 29 C3

NIGHTLIFE (p161)
Cellar Restaurant & Jazz Club.... 30 C3
Jericho Folk Club.......................(see 40)
St James Hall 31 D3

THE ARTS (p169)
Cold Reading Series....................... 32 G2
Fifth Avenue Cinemas.................... 33 H3
Hollywood Theatre 34 D3
Ridge Theatre 35 G4
Vancouver Academy of Music.... 36 H2

SPORTS & ACTIVITIES (p181)
Bikram's Yoga Vancouver.............. 37 E3
Diving Locker 38 E3
Ecomarine Ocean Kayak
   Centre ....(see 40)
International Diving Centre 39 G3
Jericho Sailing Centre.................... 40 B2
Kitsilano Pool 41 F2
Kitsilano Workout......................... 42 G3
Mac Sailing ....(see 40)
Propaganda Hair Salon 43 G3

Windsure Adventure
   Watersports ....(see 40)

SLEEPING (p193)
Corkscrew Inn............................... 44 E2
HI Vancouver Jericho Beach 45 A2
Kitsilano Suites............................. 46 F3
Mickey's Kits Beach Chalet 47 G2

TRANSPORT (p225)
Ferry Stop.................................... 48 G1

Vancouver's leading latter-day listings newspaper, and a little group of antinuclear protesters that a few years later became Greenpeace.

Kits today is a fun fusion of groovy patchouli and slick retail therapy, particularly along W 4th Ave and Broadway. These two primary commercial strips are lined with distinctive, sometimes quirky shops and a full menu of excellent restaurants. Also, the neighborhood's beaches and museums rank among the best in the city. You can buy a combined Explore Pass (adult/child $30/24)

top picks

BEACHES

- Third Beach (p64)
- Kitsilano Beach (p98)
- English Bay Beach (p66)
- Jericho Beach (p98)
- Wreck Beach (p103)

for all three museums at any of the three attractions. The area's top annual event is the ever-popular Bard on the Beach Shakespeare festival (p178), where the North Shore mountains form a backdrop to a tented stage.

For more information on the area, visit www.kitsilano4thavenue.com. Transit access to Kits is via buses 2, 4, 9 and 22.

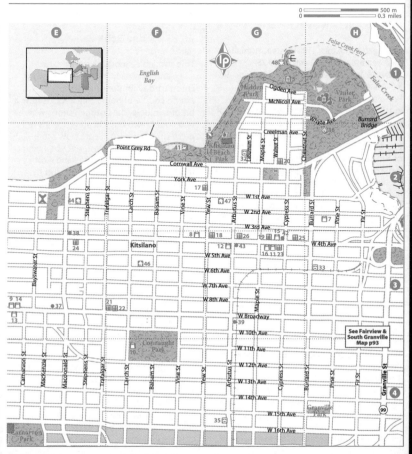

MUSEUM OF VANCOUVER Map pp96-7

www.museumofvancouver.ca; 1100 Chestnut St; adult/child/student & senior $12/8/10; ⊙ **10am-5pm Tue-Wed & Fri-Sun, to 8pm Thu;** 🚌 **22**

One of the three well-established educational attractions clustered together in Vanier Park, the recently rebranded MOV has upped its game with cool new temporary exhibitions and regular late-opening parties aimed at an adult crowd. It hasn't changed everything, though. There are still colorful displays on local 1950s pop culture and 1960s hippie counterculture – a reminder that Kits was once the grass-smoking center of Vancouver's flower-power movement – plus plenty of hands-on stuff for the kids, including weekend scavenger hunts and fun workshops.

HR MACMILLAN SPACE CENTRE
Map pp96-7

www.spacecentre.com; 1100 Chestnut St; adult/child, youth, student & senior $15/10.75; ⊙ **10am-5pm Jul & Aug, 10am-3pm Mon-Fri, 10am-5pm Sat & Sun Sep-Jun;** 🚌 **22**

Popular with packs of marauding school kids – expect to have to elbow them out of the way to push the flashing buttons – this high-tech science center illuminates the eye-opening world of space. There's plenty of fun to be had battling aliens, designing a spacecraft or strapping yourself in for a simulator ride to Mars, and there are also movie presentations on all manner of spacey themes. There's a stand-alone observatory (open weekends, weather permitting, entry by donation) across from the main entrance, and a popular planetarium running weekend laser shows (tickets $10.75) with music by the likes of Led Zeppelin and Pink Floyd.

VANCOUVER MARITIME MUSEUM
Map pp96-7

www.vancouvermaritimemuseum.com; 1905 Ogden Ave; adult/child & senior $11/8.50; ⊙ **10am-5pm May-early Sep, 10am-5pm Tue-Sat, noon-5pm Sun mid-Sep–Apr;** 🚌 **22**

The final member of the triumvirate – it's a five-minute walk west from the Museum of Vancouver – this library-quiet attraction combines dozens of intricate model ships with some detailed re-created boat sections and a few historic vessels. The main draw is

the *St Roch,* a 1928 Royal Canadian Mounted Police Arctic patrol sailing ship that was the first vessel to navigate the legendary Northwest Passage in both directions. The A-frame museum building was actually built around this ship and evocative free tours of the vessel are offered.

KITSILANO BEACH Map pp96-7

cnr Cornwall Ave & Arbutus St; 🚌 **22**

Mega-popular Kits Beach faces English Bay and has a strong claim to being the city's favorite summertime hangout. The wide, sandy expanse flanking the water here attracts buff Frisbee tossers and giggling volleyball players, as well as those who just like to preen while they're catching the rays. The beach is fine for a dip, though serious swimmers should dive into the heated 137m Kitsilano Pool (p189), one of the world's largest outdoor saltwater pools.

WEST 4TH AVENUE Map pp96-7
🚌 **4**

This strollable smorgasbord of stores (p125) and restaurants (p143) may have your credit card whimpering for mercy after a couple of hours. Since Kits is now a bit of a middle-class utopia, shops where you could once buy cheap groceries or grow-op paraphernalia are now more likely to be hawking designer yoga gear, hundred-dollar hiking socks and exotic (and unfamiliar) fruits from around the world. It's nice to look – although your resolve may buckle at some of the excellent themed bookshops and clothing stores. It's also a great place for a coffee stop and you're never far from the beach if you want to tote a picnic instead.

JERICHO BEACH Map pp96-7
north foot of Alma St; 🚌 **4**

An activity-lover's idyll – see p186 for ideas – Jericho is also great if you just want to putter along the beach, clamber over driftwood logs and catch stunning panoramic vistas of downtown Vancouver sandwiched between the water and the looming North Shore mountains. It's also popular with sunset fans. Check out the nearby Hastings Mill Store Museum (☎ 604-734-1212; 1575 Alma St; admission by donation; ⊙ 11am-4pm Tue-Sun mid-Jun–mid-Sep, 1-4pm Sat & Sun mid-Sep–mid-Jun). Built in Gastown in 1865, this ancient structure is Vancouver's oldest surviving building. It was floated over here in the 1930s and is now home to pioneer-era and First Nations exhibits.

VANIER PARK Map pp96–7
west of Burrard Bridge; ☼ 24hr; ☐ 22
Winding around Kitsilano Point and eventually connecting with Kits Beach, waterfront Vanier Park is more a host site than a destination. Home to three museums, it's also the evocative venue for the tents of the annual Vancouver International Children's Festival (p13) and the Bard on the Beach (p178) Shake-speare extravaganza. If you want to avoid the sweaty crush in English Bay during the Celebration of Light (p15) fireworks, bring your blanket and spread out here; you'll have great views of the aerial shenanigans among a convivial and family-friendly crowd. The park is also a good picnic spot – bring some takeout from Granville Island (a 15-minute stroll away via the seawall) and watch the kite flyers strut their stuff.

KITSILANO FOOD-FOR-THOUGHT HOP
Walking Tour
This walk will introduce you to the Kitsilano neighborhood and two of its main obsessions: culture and dining.

1 Barbara-Jo's Books to Cooks
Kick things off on W 2nd Ave (near the intersection with Burrard St) at this great cook-themed bookshop (p125). You can pick up a tome or two from famed local chefs (see the boxed text, p135).

2 Wanderlust
Stroll west to Burrard St, turn left and walk two blocks south until you reach W 4th Ave. Cross over and head up W 4th until you come to the city's biggest travel book store (p125). Duck inside for some LP books and mosquito repellant.

3 Zulu Records
Cross over and you'll be in front of one of Vancouver's favorite indie record shops (see the boxed text, p120). It's well worth a few minutes to browse the vinyl among the local musos here.

4 Sophie's Cosmic Café
You're in the heart of the Kits shopping district here, so spend some time checking out what's on offer. Once you've had your fill, drop by Sophie's (p145), a retro diner with a great line in heaping brunches and hearty comfort-food lunches.

WALK FACTS

Start Barbara-Jo's Books to Cooks
End Gravity Pope
Distance 1km
Time 1.5 hours
Exertion Easy
Fuel stop Sophie's Cosmic Café

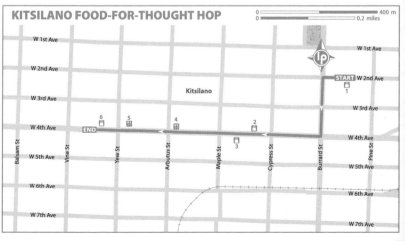

KITSILANO FOOD-FOR-THOUGHT HOP

5 Bishop's

On the next block, you'll spot the unassuming entrance to one of Vancouver's best restaurants (p144). Although you're probably not hungry yet, consider coming back later for an amazing showcase of perfect West Coast seasonal cuisine served in elegant surroundings – if you asked anyone at Barbara-Jo's for dining tips, they would likely have recommended this place.

6 Gravity Pope

Instead, pack your appetite away for the moment and drop into one of the area's favorite trendy clothing stores (p126). Women and men are treated as clothes-loving equals here.

Sleeping p202

The giant University of British Columbia (UBC; ☎ 604-822-2211; www.ubc.ca) is more than just your average college campus. Its 402-hectare grounds are part of an area called the University Endowment Lands and are set amid rugged forest. Three of the city's most treasured and wild beaches – Locarno, Spanish Banks and Wreck – are located around this area. The tranquil Nitobe Memorial Garden and sweeping UBC Botanical Garden flourish nearby. And one of the world's foremost First Nations museums nestles along the clifftop: the Museum of Anthropology, with its amazing indigenous artifacts and wealth of totem poles. There's also a modern art gallery and a brand new natural history museum. As if that wasn't enough to keep the 45,000 students from ever doing any work, the campus is studded with intriguing public artworks and is home to the Chan Centre (see the boxed text, p171), one of the city's best concert halls.

Although UBC is often referred to locally as being in Point Grey, technically it's not part of the City of Vancouver. The provincial government's ministry of municipal affairs administers the area, which harks back to the 1908 University Loan Act, when the government set up the site for the province's first university.

Even though the area was heavily logged from 1861 to 1891, it wasn't clear-cut, mainly because many of the trees were too difficult to reach. This allowed the remaining trees to generate substantial regrowth, hence the remarkable forests standing here today. With the creation of the Pacific Spirit Regional Park in 1988 (administered by MetroVancouver), an area almost twice the size of Stanley Park has been preserved for future generations.

For visitors, the campus is a tranquility break from the busy downtown core, and even if you're not studying here there's more than enough to keep you occupied for a half-day or so. There's also an array of accommodation. And if you feel like running free with nature, consider dropping your pants and joining the crowd at Wreck Beach, Vancouver's popular naturist hangout.

Consider a free campus walking tour (☎ 604-822-8687; www.ceremonies.ubc.ca/tours; departs north end of Student Union bldg; ✆ 10am & 1pm Mon-Fri mid-May–mid-Aug) to get your bearings. Transit access to UBC is via the 99B-Line express bus or regular buses 4, 9, 17 and 41.

SAVE YOUR DOSH

As well as the combined entry deal available for the Botanical Garden and the Nitobe Memorial Garden (see below), you can also save a few bucks with the new UBC Attractions Passport (adult/child/family $24/20.50/60). Covering entry to both gardens plus the popular Museum of Anthropology, it includes additional discounts for the Greenheart Canopy Walkway, as well as giving you deals on parking, dining and shopping on campus. The passport is on sale at all the attractions it covers.

MUSEUM OF ANTHROPOLOGY
Map p102

www.moa.ubc.ca; 6393 NW Marine Dr; adult/child & senior $14/12, $7 after 5pm Tue; ✆ 10am-5pm Wed-Mon, 10am-9pm Tue mid-Jan–mid-Oct, closed Mon mid-Oct–mid-Jan; 🚍 99B-Line
Recently reopened after an extensive $55 million renovation that doubled its size, Vancouver's best museum houses Canada's most important northwest coast aboriginal artifact collection, including full-size Haida houses and a spectacular array of totem poles set against a dramatic cliffside window. The expansion enables many non–First Nations exhibits to finally see the light of day, including jaw-dropping European ceramics and Cantonese opera costumes (no, you can't try them on).

There's such depth here that taking one of the free guided tours – there are three per day – is highly recommended. Also check out the gift shop and its lovely First Nations arts and crafts.

BOTANICAL GARDEN Map p102

www.ubcbotanicalgarden.org; 6804 SW Marine Dr; adult/child/youth $8/4/6, combined with Nitobe Memorial Garden $12/6/10; ✆ 9am-4:30pm Mon-Fri, 9:30am-4:30pm Sat & Sun, reduced off-season; 🚍 99B-Line, then C20
You'll find a giant collection of rhododendrons, a fascinating apothecary plot and a winter green space of off-season bloomers in this 28-hectare complex of themed gardens. The attraction's new

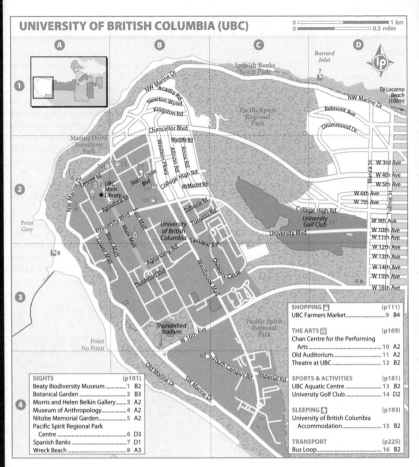

UNIVERSITY OF BRITISH COLUMBIA (UBC)

0 ————————— 1 km
0 ————————— 0.5 miles

Burrard Inlet

To Locarno Beach (100m)

Spanish Banks Beach Park

NW Marine Dr

Acadia Rd

Newton Wynd

Kingston Rd

Chancellor Blvd

Pacific Spirit Regional Park

Belmont Ave

Drummond Dr

Marine Drive Foreshore Park

Wycliffe Rd

Knox Rd

Allison Rd

Western Pkwy

College High Rd

Student Union Blvd

McMaster Rd

UBC Main Library

Agricultural Rd

University Blvd

Crescent Rd

NW Marine Dr

East Mall

Dalhousie Rd

Toronto Rd

University of British Columbia

Fairview Ave

West Mall

Main Mall

Lower Mall

Agronomy Rd

Thunderbird Blvd

Westbrook Mall

Osoyoos Circle

Point Grey

W 3rd Ave
W 4th Ave
W 5th Ave
W 6th Ave
W 7th Ave
W 9th Ave
W 10th Ave
W 11th Ave
W 12th Ave
W 13th Ave
W 14th Ave
W 15th Ave
W 16th Ave

Blanca St

Tolmie St

College High Rd

University Golf Club

University Blvd

Thunderbird Stadium

W 16th Ave

Pacific Spirit Regional Park

Point No Point

Old Marine Dr

Youth Campus Rd

Imperial Rd

SW Marine Dr

Greenheart Canopy Walkway (www.greenheartcanopy walkway.com; adult/child/youth/senior $20/6/14/16; 9am-5pm) lifts visitors 17m above the forest floor on a 308m guided eco tour. Walkway tickets include garden entry.

NITOBE MEMORIAL GARDEN Map above

www.nitobe.org; 1895 Lower Mall; adult/child/ youth $8/4/6, combined with Botanical Garden $12/6/10; 10am-4pm, reduced off-season; 99B-Line, then C20

Exemplifying Japanese horticultural philosophies, this verdant tranquility oasis includes a Tea Garden – complete with ceremonial teahouse – and a Stroll Garden that reflects a symbolic journey through life, with its little waterfalls and languid koi carp. Named after Dr Inazo Nitobe, a scholar whose mug appears on Japan's

¥5000 bill, consider a springtime visit for the florid cherry blossom displays.

MORRIS AND HELEN BELKIN GALLERY Map above

www.belkin.ubc.ca; 1825 Main Mall; admission free; 10am-5pm Tue-Fri, noon-5pm Sat & Sun; 99B-Line

This excellent little gallery specializes in contemporary and often quite challenging pieces – which explains the billboard-style depiction of an Iraqi city outside, complete with the caption 'Because there was and there wasn't a city of Baghdad.' Inside, you can expect a revolving roster of traveling shows plus chin-stroking exhibits from a permanent collection of Canadian avant-garde works.

top picks

GARDENS

- Dr Sun Yat-Sen Classical Chinese Garden (p78)
- VanDusen Botanical Garden (p92)
- Bloedel Floral Conservatory (p94)
- UBC Botanical Garden (p101)
- Nitobe Memorial Garden (opposite)

BEATY BIODIVERSITY MUSEUM
Map opposite

www.beatymuseum.ubc.ca; 2212 Main Mall; 🚍 99B-Line

Only open for public preview visits during research for this book, UBC's newest attraction showcases the university's wealth of natural history exhibits, including two million specimens that have never before been available for public viewing. Fossil, fish and herbarium galleries are included but the museum's main draw is the 25m blue whale skeleton, artfully displayed in a two-story glass gallery. The whale washed ashore on Canada's eastern coastline and was trucked across the country – to much media curiosity – in 2009.

PACIFIC SPIRIT REGIONAL PARK
Map opposite

cnr Blanca St & W 16th Ave; admission free; ☼ dawn-dusk; 🚍 99B-Line

This stunning 763-hectare park – the city's largest – cuts a wide swathe across the peninsula. Stretching from Burrard Inlet on one side to the North Arm of the Fraser River on the other, it's a green buffer zone between the campus and the city. A smashing spot to hug some trees and explore (there are 54km of walking, jogging and cycling trails), you'll also find Camosun Bog wetland (Map pp54-5; accessed by a boardwalk at 19th Ave and Camosun St), a haven for native bird and plant species. Visit the Park Centre (W 16th Ave; ☼ 10am-5pm Mon-Sat) for maps and info on the park's many features.

WRECK BEACH Map opposite

www.wreckbeach.org; 🚍 99B-Line, then C20

Follow Trail 6 into the woods then head down the steep steps to the water and you'll find Vancouver's only official naturist beach, complete with a motley crew of counterculture locals, independent vendors

and sunburned regulars. The pants-free bunch are in a continuing battle with the university over the building of residential towers that threaten their privacy, so be sure to offer your support as you peel off. Time your visit well and you can take part in the annual Bare Buns Fun Run (p15). And if you fancy connecting with other local naturists during your stay, check in with the Van Tan Nudist Club (☎ 604-980-2400; www.vantan.ca) for events, including regular swimming meets at local pools.

SPANISH BANKS Map opposite

cnr NW Marine Dr & Blanca St; 🚍 44, then C19

This tree-backed public beach (make sure you keep your clothes on at this one) is a popular locals' hangout – they're the ones jogging past in Lululemon outfits – as well as being a good spot to unpack a picnic and perch on a log to enjoy some sigh-triggering waterfront vistas. The sandy stretch was named after English Bay's 1792 meeting between British mariner Captain George Vancouver and his Spanish counterpart Dionisio Galiano.

UBC CAMPUS & GARDENS WALK
Walking Tour

This walk will introduce you to the UBC campus, combining its leading cultural attractions with its celebrated gardens.

1 Museum of Anthropology

Start your visit at Vancouver's best museum (p101), where you'll gain a deep appreciation for the culture and artistry of the region's original First Nations residents.

2 Morris and Helen Belkin Gallery

Cross NW Marine Dr and head down West Mall, turning left on Crescent Rd then right onto Main Mall. On your left is this free-entry gallery (opposite), which houses an impressive modern art collection.

3 UBC Asian Centre

Continue southwards along Main Mall, then turn right onto Memorial Rd. Continue on the downhill incline of Memorial until, on your right, you come to the rock garden of the UBC Asian Centre. The boulders here are inscribed with Confucian philosophies.

UBC CAMPUS & GARDENS WALK

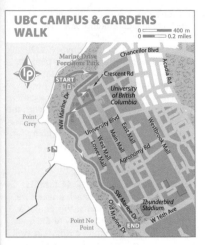

0 ⎯⎯⎯ 400 m
0 ⎯⎯⎯ 0.2 miles

4 Nitobe Memorial Garden

Continue along Memorial and ahead you will see the entrance of this formal Japanese garden (p102). Spend some time here immersing yourself in the site's subtle yet deeply meaningful design.

WALK FACTS

Start Museum of Anthropology
End Botanical Garden
Distance 3km
Time 1.5 hours
Exertion Moderate
Fuel stop Bring a snack

5 Wreck Beach

Return to NW Marine Dr and continue south-eastwards for about 1km. If you're feeling adventurous, look for the signs through the forest that indicate Trail 6. Follow the trail until you reach the waterfront, where you can disrobe – you're on Vancouver's official naturist beach (p103).

6 Botanical Garden

Continue your walk (don't forget to put your clothes back on first) along NW Marine Dr until it becomes SW Marine Dr. Near the intersection with W 16th Ave, you'll find the lovely botanical garden (p101), complete with its nature-hugging canopy walkway.

METRO VANCOUVER

Eating p146; Sleeping p203

Metro Vancouver – sometimes referred to as Greater Vancouver or the Lower Mainland – is chock full of looming mountains, crenulated coastal parks, wildlife sanctuaries, historic attractions and characterful communities, mostly within a 45-minute drive of downtown Vancouver. North Vancouver and West Vancouver together make up the North Shore, located across Burrard Inlet from Vancouver proper. For more information on the North Shore, visit www.vancouversnorthshore.com. In contrast, Richmond (and its charming Steveston enclave) lies directly south of Vancouver via Hwy 99. It's now easily accessible from the city via the Canada Line SkyTrain line.

NORTH VANCOUVER

Nestled between Indian Arm and West Vancouver, 'North Van' is centered on the clutch of tower blocks you can see shimmering across the Burrard Inlet from downtown. While its glory days as a trading port and shipbuilding center are long gone, it's an intriguing and SeaBus-accessible spot to spend the afternoon: this is the home of several of the region's top outdoor attractions but it also has its own wanderable town center. If you're looking for a walking route, head north up Lonsdale Ave from the quay (it's very steep but it's lined with pit stop coffee shops), turn west through Victoria Park and then amble back downhill to the waterfront along Chesterfield Ave.

For additional information on what to do here, peruse the visitor section of the municipal website (www.cnv.org). Transit access to the community is via the handy SeaBus (p230) service from Vancouver's Waterfront Station – a short trip that's worth making just for the views alone.

CAPILANO SUSPENSION BRIDGE
Map pp54-5

www.capbridge.com; 3735 Capilano Rd; adult/child/youth/senior $29.95/10/18.95/27.95, reduced off-season; ☉ 9am-5pm Jan–mid-Mar & Nov, 9am-6pm mid-Mar–Apr & Oct, 9am-7pm May & Sep, 8:30am-8pm Jun-Aug, 10am-9pm Dec; 🚌 236 from Lonsdale Quay

As you walk gingerly out onto one of the world's longest (140m) and highest (70m) suspension bridges, swaying gently over the roiling waters of tree-lined Capilano Canyon, remember that the thick steel cables you are gripping are safely embedded in huge concrete blocks on either side. That should steady your feet – unless there are teenagers stamping across to scare the oldsters. It's the region's most popular attraction – hence the summertime crowds and relentless tour buses. The grounds here include rainforest walks, totem poles and a network of smaller bridges strung between the trees, called Treetops Adventure. Drop by the souvenir shop, one of BC's biggest, for First Nations artworks and 'moose dropping' choccies.

GROUSE MOUNTAIN Map pp54-5

www.grousemountain.com; 6400 Nancy Greene Way; Skyride adult/child/youth/senior $39.95/13.95/23.95/35.95; ☉ 9am-10pm; 🚌 236 from Lonsdale Quay

Calling itself the 'Peak of Vancouver,' this mountaintop perch offers smashing views of the downtown towers, shimmering in the water below you. In summer, Skyride gondola tickets to the top include access to lumberjack shows, alpine hiking trails and a grizzly-bear refuge. Pay extra for the zipline course ($105) or new Eye of the Wind tour ($25), which takes you to the top of a 20-story wind turbine tower for spectacular views of the region. You can also reduce the gondola fee by hiking the ultra-steep Grouse Grind (see the boxed text, p184) up the side of the mountain – you have to pay $10 to get back down on the Skyride, though. In winter, Grouse also becomes the locals' favorite snowy playground (p187).

MT SEYMOUR PROVINCIAL PARK
Map pp54-5

www.bcparks.ca; 1700 Mt Seymour Rd; admission free; ☉ dawn-dusk

A popular, rustic retreat from the downtown clamor, this giant, tree-lined park is suffused with more than a dozen summertime hiking trails that suit walkers of most abilities (the easiest path is the 2km Goldie Lake Trail). Many trails wind past lakes and centuries-old Douglas firs

WORTH THE TRIP: BURNABY

Immediately east of Vancouver via Hastings St, Burnaby – the birthplace of Michael J Fox – is a no-frills residential suburb with an elongated strip-mall feel. Luckily, there are a handful of attractions to keep you away from the shops. Check in with Tourism Burnaby (☎ 604-419-0377; www.tourismburnaby.com) for tips on what to do here.

Nestled among Burnaby's labyrinth of residential side streets, tranquil Deer Lake Park (Map pp54-5; admission free; 🕑 dawn-dusk) is crisscrossed with verdant meadow and waterfront walks, and also offers boat rentals. Nearby, the popular Burnaby Village Museum (Map pp54-5; www.burnabyvillagemuseum.ca; 6501 Deer Lake Ave; adult/child/youth $12/6/9; 🕑 11am-4:30pm May-Aug) re-creates the atmosphere of a BC pioneer town with replica homes and businesses of the time and a wonderfully restored 1912 carousel. Entry to the museum is half-price on Tuesdays and it's also open off-season for special Christmas and Halloween displays.

Topping Burnaby Mountain, Simon Fraser University (Map pp54-5; www.sfu.com; 8888 University Dr) is the Lower Mainland's second main campus community. Visitor attractions here include the Museum of Archaeology & Ethnology (Map pp54-5; admission free; 🕑 10am-4pm Mon-Fri) and the SFU Gallery (Map pp54-5; admission free; 🕑 10am-4pm Tue-Fri, noon-5pm Sat).

---

and offer a true break from the city. This is also one of the city's three main winter playgrounds (p187). Drivers can take Hwy 1 to the Mt Seymour Pkwy (near the Second Narrows Bridge) and follow it east to Mt Seymour Rd.

LYNN CANYON PARK Map pp54-5
www.lynncanyon.ca; Park Rd; admission free; 🕑 7am-9pm May-Aug, 7am-7pm Sep-Apr; 🚌 229 from Lonsdale Quay
Set amid a dense bristling of ancient trees, the main feature of this provincial park is its swinging suspension bridge, a free alternative to Capilano. Not quite as long or high as its tourist-magnet rival, it provokes the same jelly-legged reaction as you sway over the river 50m below – and it's also far less crowded and commercialized. There are hiking trails, swimming areas and picnic spots around the park to keep you busy once you've done the bridge. The Ecology Centre (www.dnv.org/ecology; 3663 Park Rd; admission by donation; 🕑 10am-5pm Jun-Sep, noon-4pm Mon-Fri, 10am-5pm Sat & Sun Oct-May) houses interesting displays on the area's rich biodiversity, including dioramas and video presentations.

LONSDALE QUAY Map pp54-5
www.lonsdalequay.com; 123 Carrie Cates Ct; 🕑 9am-7pm; SeaBus from Waterfront Station
As well as being a transportation hub – this is where the SeaBus from downtown docks and you pick up transit buses to Capilano, Grouse and beyond – this waterfront facility built for Expo '86 houses a colorful indoor market. The region's second-best market (after Granville Island), this one is a popular spot for fresh fruit and glassy-eyed

top picks

FOR CHILDREN

- Capilano Suspension Bridge (p105)
- Vancouver Aquarium (p62)
- Miniature Railway & Children's Farmyard (p62)
- Second Beach Pool (p189)
- Science World (p78)
- HR MacMillan Space Centre (p98)
- Vancouver International Children's Festival (p13)
- Port Authority Interpretation Centre (p57)
- BC Sports Hall of Fame & Museum (p71)
- SeaBus (p230)
- Kidsbooks (p125)
- Maplewood Farm (below)
- Knight Camp (p232)
- Kitsilano Beach (p98)
- Gulf of Georgia Cannery (p109)
- Granville Island Water Park (p90)

whole fish on the main floor and trinkets and clothing on the 2nd floor. There's also a lively food court and a couple of sit-down restaurants. It's a nice afternoon jaunt from the city, with many visitors scooping up an ice cream and lingering over the boardwalk vistas of downtown.

MAPLEWOOD FARM Map pp54-5
www.maplewoodfarm.bc.ca; 405 Seymour River Place; adult/child & senior $6/3.50; 🕑 10am-4pm Apr-Oct, closed Mon Nov-Mar; 🚌 239 from Lonsdale Quay, then C15
One of the region's most popular family-friendly sites, this farmyard attraction

includes plenty of hands-on displays plus a collection of over 200 domestic animals. Your wide-eyed kids will have the chance to pet a few critters, watch the daily milking demonstration and feed some squawking, ever-hungry ducks and chickens. The highlight is the daily (around 3:30pm) 'running of the goats,' when the starving hairballs streak from the paddock to their barn for dinner.

CAPILANO SALMON HATCHERY
Map pp54-5
4500 Capilano Park Rd; admission free;
☼ 8am-4pm Nov-Mar, 9am-4.45pm Apr & Oct, 8am-7pm May & Sep, 8am-8pm Jun-Aug
Located in Capilano River Regional Park, about 2km north of the Capilano Suspension Bridge, this fish farm is run by the Federal Department of Fisheries and Oceans to protect valuable Coho, Chinook and Steelhead salmon stocks. Visit from July to November – October, when the Chinooks return, is the optimum month – and you'll catch adult salmon swimming through fish ladders past the rapids in an heroic effort to reach their spawning grounds upstream, after which they promptly die in a scripted lifecycle that must have been written by Samuel Beckett. Eye-level tanks display the creatures and enlightening exhibits help explain the entire mysterious process. Drivers head north along Capilano Rd, then turn left onto Capilano Park Rd and continue for 1km.

WEST VANCOUVER

Often referred to as the region's richest neighborhood, there's much more to 'West Van' than the mega homes perched imperiously on the cliffs overlooking the water. Take a 250 bus from downtown Vancouver and within 15 minutes you'll be trundling along Marine Dr among the village-sized enclaves of Ambleside and Dundarave. Alight anywhere along the route, wander around the stores and cafés and jump back on the bus whenever you're ready to return to town: it's an easy and surprisingly accessible half-day out.

While the area's attractions aren't the biggest must-sees around – unless you count Park Royal, Canada's first shopping mall – the neighborhood's truly inviting green spaces include Lighthouse Park and Whytecliff Park. It's also home to Cypress Provincial Park, arguably Metro Vancouver's best skiing mountain (see p187).

For information on West Vancouver, visit www.westvancouver.ca. Transit access to West Vancouver from downtown is via bus 240, 250, 251, 252 or 257.

CYPRESS PROVINCIAL PARK
Map pp54-5
www.bcparks.ca; Cypress Bowl Rd; admission free;
☼ dawn-dusk
Around 8km north of West Van via Hwy 99, Cypress offers some great summertime hikes, including the Baden-Powell, Yew Lake and Howe Sound Crest trails, which

WORTH THE TRIP: DEEP COVE

Take the Dollarton Hwy exit off Hwy 1 and go east – right if you just crossed Second Narrows Bridge, left if you're driving toward it. Stop in Cates Park to enjoy the views of Belcarra Regional Park across the waters of Burrard Inlet, or follow the road as it turns left and becomes Deep Cove Rd.

The road will pass close to some ultrarich homes before making a right turn, leading you down through the quaint hamlet of Deep Cove (Map pp54-5). A strip of galleries, gift shops, and pizza and gelato cafés leads down to the rocky beach, which is one of the most deeply relaxing parts of the Lower Mainland. Fuel up with a scrummy yeast-free donut at Honey's (4373 Gallant Ave; mains $4-8), then take part in the region's leading activity and the main reason many keep coming back here.

An ideal spot for kayak virgins, the waters of Deep Cove are glassy calm and the setting, around North America's southernmost fjord, couldn't be more tranquil. Deep Cove Canoe & Kayak Centre (p185) will show you how to paddle and take you around the lovely Indian Arm area on a guided tour.

Nearby Cates Park provides another vantage point from which to see Indian Arm. It's best known as the place where novelist Malcolm Lowry, author of *Under the Volcano*, lived with his wife from 1940 to 1954: a walk dedicated to him meanders past the spot where his squatter's shack once stood. The park also shelters the remains of the Dollar Lumber Mill (in operation from 1916 to 1942), a 15m First Nations war canoe, forest walks and a sandy beach.

Deep Cove can be accessed via buses 211 and 212.

plunge through forests of cedar, yellow cypress and Douglas fir and wind past little lakes and alpine meadows. In winter, the park's Cypress Mountain (p187) resort area – site of the snowboard and freestyle skiing events at the 2010 Olympic and Paralympic Winter Games – makes this one of the city's favorite snowbound playgrounds. From downtown Vancouver, drivers should cross the Lions Gate Bridge to the Upper Levels Hwy via Taylor Way in West Vancouver. Follow the signs to the park entrance.

LIGHTHOUSE PARK Map pp54-5
cnr Beacon Lane & Marine Dr; admission free;
🕐 **dawn-dusk;** 🚌 **250**
Some of the region's oldest and most spectacular trees live within this accessible 75-hectare park, including a rare stand of original coastal forest and plenty of those gnarly, copper-trunked arbutus trees. It's ideal for a romantic picnic, and you'll find plenty of doe-eyed couples hogging the grass here. About 13km of hiking trails crisscross the area, including a recommended trek that leads to the rocky perch of the Point Atkinson Lighthouse, where you'll come across some shimmering, camera-worthy views over Burrard Inlet and the nearby tree-covered islands. If you're driving from downtown, turn left on Marine Dr after crossing the Lions Gate Bridge to reach the park.

WEST VANCOUVER SEAWALL Map pp54-5
🚌 **250**
Take bus 250 from downtown Vancouver and hop off on Marine Dr at the intersection with 24th St. Peruse the charming clutch of stores and coffee shops in Dundarave Village here, then stroll downhill to the waterfront. Drink in the panoramic coastline views from Dundarave Pier, then weave eastwards along the shore-hugging Centennial Seawalk route. West Van's favorite promenade, you'll pass joggers, blue herons and public artworks before the 2km paved walkway comes to a stop. From here, head back up to the Marine Dr shops or weave over to Ambleside Park where you'll find a dramatic First Nations welcome figure facing the water.

HORSESHOE BAY Map pp54-5
🚌 **257**
The small coastal community of Horseshoe Bay marks the end of West Vancouver and

top picks
VANCOUVER STROLLS

- Coal Harbour Seawall (p66)
- Stanley Park Seawall (p62)
- South False Creek Seawall (p82)
- West Vancouver Seawall (left)
- Steveston waterfront (opposite)

the start of trips to Whistler, via the Sea-to-Sky Hwy (Hwy 99), or Vancouver Island, Bowen Island and the Sunshine Coast via the BC Ferries (p227) network. It's a pretty village with great views across the bay and up Howe Sound to distant glacial peaks. Cutesy places to eat and shop line the waterfront on Bay St, near the marina, where you can also take a whale-watching boat trek with Sewell's Sea Safari (p237).

WHYTECLIFF PARK Map pp54-5
7100 block, Marine Dr; admission free;
🕐 **dawn-dusk;** 🚌 **250**
Just west of Horseshoe Bay, this is an exceptional little park right on the water. Trails lead to vistas and a gazebo, from where you can watch the boat traffic in Burrard Inlet. The rocky beach is a great place to play, go for a swim or scamper over the large rocks protruding from the beach. The park is also popular with scuba fans (p186) and is regarded as one of the best dive spots in the Lower Mainland.

RICHMOND & STEVESTON
Many Vancouverites say they don't like driving to Richmond – the flat, landmark-free vistas and unfamiliar street names apparently make it confusing – but with the arrival of the new Canada Line SkyTrain link, the region's modern-day Chinatown is suddenly far more accessible from downtown. Hop onboard and head down the line for a half-day of Asian shopping malls – centered on the Golden Village area – followed by a taste-trip through some of the best contemporary Chinese, Japanese and Vietnamese restaurants in North America. If you only have time to come here once, don't miss the Summer Night Market (see the boxed text on p118).

Alternatively, head to Richmond's southwest corner and you'll find waterfront

Steveston village, a popular destination for sunset-viewing locals. It's also a hot spot for great fish-and-chips. Drive here from Vancouver via Hwy 99 (take the Steveston Hwy exit) for an early evening stroll along the boardwalk. For information on Richmond and Steveston, check www.tourismrichmond.com.

GULF OF GEORGIA CANNERY
Map pp54-5

www.gulfofgeorgiacannery.com; 12138 4th Ave, Steveston; adult/child/senior $7.80/3.90/6.55; 10am-5pm Feb-Oct; M Richmond-Brighouse, then bus 410

Once you've perused the boats hawking the day's fresh catch, check out Steveston's excellent cannery museum, illuminating the sights and sounds (and smells) of the region's bygone era of labor-intensive fish processing. Most of the machinery remains – polished and cleaned of its permanent film of blood and fish oil – and there's an evocative focus on the people who used to work before the plant closed in 1979. You'll hear recorded testimonies from old workers percolating through the air like ghosts and see large black-and-white blow-ups of some of the staff who spent their days immersed in entrails in order to roll thousands of cans down the production line. Take one of the free hourly tours, often run by former cannery workers.

BRITANNIA SHIPYARD Map pp54-5

www.britannia-hss.ca; 5180 Westwater Dr, Steveston; admission free; 10am-6pm Tue-Sun May-Sep, 10am-4pm Sat, noon-4pm Sun Oct-Apr; M Richmond-Brighouse, then bus 410

After you've done the cannery, hit Steveston's lovely waterfront boardwalk – complete with art installations evoking the area's bustling fishing sector – and within 15 minutes you'll stroll into the area's other national historic site. Not as slick as the cannery, it's nevertheless a fascinating complex of creaky old sheds housing dusty tools, boats and reminders of the region's maritime past. Check out the preserved Murakami House, where a large Japanese family lived before being unceremoniously interned during the war. Make sure you ask the volunteers plenty of questions: they have some great stories to tell.

KUAN YIN TEMPLE Map pp54-5

www.buddhisttemple.ca; 9160 Steveston Hwy, Steveston; admission free; 9:30am-5:30pm; M Richmond-Brighouse, then bus 403

Called simply the 'Buddhist Temple' by most, this attractive classical Chinese complex is an intriguing stop. The highlight is the sumptuous Gracious Hall, complete with deep-red exterior walls and a gently flaring orange porcelain roof. Check out the colorful 100m Buddha mural and the

WORTH THE TRIP: FORT LANGLEY NATIONAL HISTORIC SITE

Little Fort Langley's tree-lined streets and 19th-century storefronts make it one of the Lower Mainland's most picturesque historic villages, ideal for an afternoon away from Vancouver. Its main historic highlight is the colorful Fort Langley National Historic Site (☎ 604-513-4777; www.pc.gc.ca/fortlangley; 23433 Mavis Ave; adult/child/senior $7.80/3.90/6.55; 9am-8pm Jul & Aug, 10am-5pm Sep-Jun), perhaps the region's most important old-school landmark.

A fortified trading post since 1827, this is where James Douglas announced the creation of BC in 1858, giving the site a legitimate claim to being the province's birthplace. With costumed re-enacters, re-created artisan workshops and a gold-panning area that's very popular with kids – they also enjoy charging around the wooden battlements – this is an ideal place for families who want to add a little education to their trips.

If you need an introduction before you start wading into the buildings here, there's a surprisingly entertaining time travel–themed movie presentation on offer. And make sure you check the website before you arrive: there's a wide array of events that bring the past evocatively back to life, including a summertime evening campfire program that will take you right back to the pioneer days of the 1800s.

If you're driving from Vancouver, take Hwy 1 east for 40km, then take the 232nd St exit north. Follow the signs along 232nd St until you reach the stop sign at Glover Rd. Turn right here, and continue into the village. Turn right again on Mavis Ave, just before the railway tracks. The fort's parking lot is at the end of the street.

If traveling by transit, take the SkyTrain to Surrey Central Station, then transfer to bus 501, 502 or 320 to Langley. Transfer in Langley to the C62 and alight at the intersection of 96 Ave and Glover Rd. The fort is a signposted 400m walk from here.

golden, multi-armed Bodhisattva figure here. The surrounding landscaped garden with its sculptures and bonsai trees is another highlight, but allow yourself time to enjoy a lip-smacking veggie lunch in the ground-floor cafeteria. You don't have to be a Buddhist to visit and the monks are highly welcoming if you just want to have a look around.

top picks

- **Regional Assembly of Text** (p119)
- **Mountain Equipment Co-op** (p120)
- **Dutch Girl Chocolates** (p122)
- **Edie Hats** (p122)
- **Erin Templeton** (p118)
- **Granville Island Public Market** (p123)
- **Richmond's Summer Night Market** (p118)
- **Smoking Lily** (p119)
- **Gravity Pope** (p126)
- **Red Cat Records** (p120)

SHOPPING

The joys of shopping in Vancouver used to be limited to selecting a thick winter coat (if you lived here) or picking up some maple-sugar cookies (if you were visiting). But the city's retail therapy opportunities have developed dramatically in recent years – and we're not just talking about more chain stores. Once you've visited Vancouver's main attractions and checked out the dining scene, it's well worth buying an extra suitcase and hitting the stores – just be sure not to limit yourself to the malls and explore a little off the beaten path in shopping hot spots like Gastown, South Main (SoMa) and Kitsilano.

You'll find cool independent fashion designers who can transform you into a pale and interesting muse; record stores where you can delve into the undiscovered pantheon of great local music; galleries where you can splash some cash on First Nations artists; and specialist bookshops that cater to every interest, selling everything from gay-lit to travel guides and kids' books. In fact, there's really no excuse for buying boring souvenirs at all.

Keep in mind that the strong Canadian dollar means Vancouver is not the bargain-hunter's paradise it has been in the past, especially when you factor in the taxes (see below) that will be mercilessly added at the checkout.

OPENING HOURS

Typical retail shopping hours are 10am to 6pm Monday to Saturday, and noon to 5pm Sunday – some shops close on Sundays, though. The indie shops of SoMa and Gastown often open later – around 11am on weekdays – while downtown shops and malls sometimes close later, especially during the peak summer and Christmas seasons. In the reviews in this chapter, only shop opening hours that deviate dramatically from these standard times are noted.

CONSUMER TAXES

The prices on most goods in shops do not include tax, which is added when you take the item to the cash register to pay. The old GST and PST taxes were replaced by the HST (Harmonized Sales Tax) in 2010; the current rate is 12% for the vast majority of items. See p238 for more information on this tax.

DOWNTOWN

Centered on lively Robson St – Vancouver's leading mainstream shopping promenade and the home of most major chains – the city's downtown core is a strollable outdoor mall of grazing shoppers moving between their favorite stores with an ever-growing clutch of bags. High fashion, shoes and jewelry are the mainstays here, and there are also plenty of coffee shops if you need to stop and count your money. Head south along Granville St from the intersection with Robson St and you'll find an emerging enclave of fashionable urban streetwear shops: this is where you can pick up those limited-edition Puma runners you've always wanted. For luxe labels such as Tiffany, Burberry and Louis Vuitton, head to the area around the Burrard and Alberni Sts intersection.

BIRKS Map pp58-9   Accessories
www.birks.com; 698 W Hastings St; Ⓜ Waterfront
A Vancouver institution since 1879 – hence the landmark freestanding clock outside – Birks crafts exquisite heirloom jewelry and its signature line of timepieces. It's an upscale place, similar to Tiffany & Co in the USA, and ideal for picking up that special something in a classy, blue embossed box for a deserving someone back home.

top picks

SHOPPING STRIPS

- Main Street (p119)
- Water Street (p116)
- W 4th Avenue (p125)
- Robson Street (left)
- Commercial Drive (p121)

GOLDEN AGE COLLECTABLES

Map pp58-9   Bookstore

www.gacvan.com; 852 Granville St; 🚍 10

If you're missing your regular dose of
Emily the Strange or you just want to blow
your vacation budget on a highly detailed
life-size model of Ultra Man, head straight
to this Aladdin's cave of the comic-book
world. While the clientele is unsurprisingly
dominated by males of a certain age, the
staff are friendly and welcoming –
especially to wide-eyed kids buying their
first *Archie*.

MACLEOD'S BOOKS

Map pp58-9   Bookstore

455 W Pender St; Ⓜ Granville

From its creaky floorboards to those skuzzy
carpets and ever-teetering piles of books,
this legendary locals' fave is the best place
in town to peruse a cornucopia of used
tomes. From dance to occult – plus a travel
section that included a vintage past edition
of this book on our visit – it's the ideal spot
for a rainy-day browse. Check the windows
for posters of local readings and artsy
happenings.

CHERRY BOMB   Map pp58-9   Clothing

841 Granville St; 🚍 10

Printing ironic, often retro designs onto
American Apparel T-shirts is the main
activity at this hipster hangout. If you're not
cool enough for a Mr T or old-school AC/DC
graphic, head to the back of the store and
check out the museum-like array of vintage
clothing and accessories. Where else are

you going to find that replica Evel Knievel
jumpsuit you've always wanted?

HOLT RENFREW   Map pp58-9   Clothing

**www.holtrenfrew.com; 737 Dunsmuir St;
Ⓜ Granville**

Vancouver's swankiest clothing and
accessories department store; high-end
label lovers flock here to peruse the
artfully presented D&G, Armani and Issey
Miyake togs and accoutrements arrayed
over several floors. Service is personal and
particular from staffers often better dressed
than their customers. The awesome
end-of-season sales are recommended.

PACIFIC CENTRE

Map pp58-9   Clothing, Accessories

**www.pacificcentre.ca; cnr Howe & W Georgia Sts;
🕒 10am-7pm Mon, Tue & Sat, 10am-9pm Wed-Fri,
11am-6pm Sun; Ⓜ Granville**

If rain curtails your street shopping
activities, duck inside this handily located
central mall. You'll find all the usual chain
and department store suspects, plus
highlights like H&M, Purdy's Chocolates
and Harry Rosen. You can also check your
email for free at the Apple Store. There's a
large food court if you need a pit stop from
all that retail therapy.

ROOTS   Map pp58-9   Clothing

www.canada.roots.com; 1001 Robson St; 🚍 5

Basically a maple leaf–emblazoned
version of the Gap, Roots designs athletic
streetwear that's unmistakably Canadian;
its retro-styled jogging pants, hoodies and

SHOP THE MUSEUM

As if all the regular stores in Vancouver weren't enough to keep your shopping reflexes twitching nervously, the city's
museums and galleries also offer some unexpected buying opportunities. You don't have to visit the attraction to visit
its shop, and keep in mind that you're helping to fund the institutions you're buying from. Perhaps the best of all the
city's museum stores, the Museum of Anthropology (p101) has a fantastic array of First Nations and international
indigenous artworks, ranging from elegant silver jewelry to fascinating masks. Back downtown, the Vancouver Art
Gallery (p56) gift shop is like a lifestyle store for artsy types, with clever contemporary coasters, vases and knickknacks
to adorn your home, as well as large art books to leave on your coffee table and impress guests. There are also some
good educational toys here.

Toys are similarly a large part of the selection at the Vancouver Aquarium (p62), where your sprog will instantly fall
in love with the vast shoal of cuddly sharks, otters and starfish. If you have a tricky young teen to buy for back home,
pick up a Shark Pool Predator – an inflatable pool toy that doubles as a squirt gun. Even better: you can adopt an animal
for them – although they won't get to look after it at home. Kids are also well served at Science World (p78), where
there are lots of pocketmoney-priced items, including the entertainingly revolting freeze-dried ice cream for astronauts.
Finally, if you make it to the Vancouver Police Museum (p74), you can buy crime scene bandages, knuckle-duster coffee
mugs and blood-splattered evidence knives – try explaining that to customs when you arrive back home.

toques (if you don't know what that is, this is the place to find out) are ever-popular. If you can't find this store, there are additional outlets – usually in malls – throughout the city.

TRUE VALUE VINTAGE CLOTHING

Map pp58-9   Clothing

710 Robson St; 🚃 5

'Value' is a bit of a misnomer since the used duds at this subterranean cave of cool-clothing kitsch are sometimes fairly pricey. But if you really need that 1950s bowling shirt or Jimi Hendrix tour hat, you'll pay anything, right? Bargains are to be had on the musty-smelling sale racks.

MINK CHOCOLATES

Map pp58-9   Food & Drink

**www.minkchocolates.com; 863 W Hastings St;
Ⓜ Waterfront**

If chocolate is the main food group in your book, follow your candy-primed nose to this designer choccy shop in the downtown core. Select a handful of souvenir bon-bons – little edible artworks embossed with prints of trees and coffee cups – then hit the drinks bar for the best velvety hot choc you've ever tasted.

SIKORA'S CLASSICAL RECORDS

Map pp58-9   Music Store

**www.sikorasclassical.com; 432 W Hastings St;
Ⓜ Granville**

Sikora's blows away the classical inventory of mainstream music stores with its giant list of CD/DVD titles, plus hundreds of LPs for all those traditionalists out there. Opera, organ, choral, chamber and early music are represented, and there's a section devoted to Canadian musicians. The staff are highly knowledgeable and can point you to a hot Mahler or Rachmaninov recording at the drop of a hat.

WEST END

An eclectic and vibrant district of restaurants and coffee shops, the West End also has more than a few stores that are worth nosing around if you have a spare afternoon. The majority of the most distinctive businesses here are located on Davie St and are tailored toward the area's large gay community, but you can also expect bookstores, bakeries, wine shops and just about everything else to be offered

along the way. The western end of Robson St delivers some interesting Asian stores; this is the place to pick up oddball Japanese candies and cans of Pocari Sweat.

TEN THOUSAND VILLAGES

Map pp68-9   Arts & Crafts

www.tenthousandvillages.ca; 929 Denman St; 🚃 5

A fair-trade boutique where purchases support the work of artisans in low-income countries around the world, you'll find stationery from Bangladesh, baskets from Vietnam and a plethora of hammocks, drums, clothing and unusual handicrafts. Pick up a far more worthwhile Vancouver souvenir than those maple-syrup cookies and confuse everyone back home.

BOOK WAREHOUSE

Map pp68-9   Bookstore

**www.bookwarehouse.ca; 1051 Davie St;
🕙 10am-10pm; 🚃 6**

This busy outlet of Vancouver's favorite independent bookstore chain is one of several branches around the city. Prices are discounted on most titles and there's a good travel section and big stocks of new releases, contemporary faves and perennial classics. Look out for regular sales and pre-announced shipments of 'hurt books' – new tomes with minor dings and major discounts.

LITTLE SISTER'S BOOK & ART EMPORIUM

Map pp68-9   Bookstore

**www.littlesisters.ca; 1238 Davie St;
🕙 10am-11pm; 🚃 6**

One of the only gay bookshops in western Canada, Little Sister's is a large bazaar of queer-positive tomes, plus magazines, DVDs and gifts. Proceeds of designated books support the store's long-running legal battle against Canada Customs for its seizures of imported items. A good place to network with the local 'gayborhood.'

LULULEMON ATHLETICA

Map pp68-9   Clothing

www.lululemon.com; 3118 Robson St; 🕙 10am-9pm Mon-Sat, 11am-8pm Sun; 🚃 5

The flagship downtown store of the Vancouver-based chain that made ass-hugging yoga wear a mainstream fashion, this is the shop for that archetypal West Coast look.

BOOZE STORES

If you're planning a party in your hotel room, you might need a little alcoholic sustenance to keep things moving along swimmingly. Luckily, Vancouver has plenty of government-run liquor stores – see www.bcliquorstores.com for locations – as well as a large round of private cold beer and wine shops to slake your thirst. Like pubs, not all booze stores are created equal; the following are among the city's best:

Brewery Creek (Map p83; www.brewerycreekliquorstore.com; 3045 Main St, SoMa; 3) This Main St favorite is especially revered for its excellent array of bottled beer, covering choice tipples from BC and beyond. You'll find plenty of intriguing brews, from Flying Dog Pale Ale to Saskatoon's Black Cat Lager.

Firefly Fine Wines & Ales (Map p93; www.fireflyfinewinesandales.com; 2857 Cambie St, Fairview & South Granville; Broadway-City Hall) While there's a great choice of interesting beers here, this popular spot is a magnet for wine buffs. They come for the sterling selection of international treats, superb service from highly knowledgeable staff and, of course, the regular tastings.

Marquis Wine Cellars (Map pp68-9; www.marquis-wines.com; 1034 Davie St, West End; 6) Small and friendly, this boutique wine shop has a real snob-free approach to its products, which makes it a great place to hit if you can't tell the difference between a pinot noir and a pinot grigio. Expert staff and regular tastings are part of the mix – also check its website for wine education events.

Signature BC Liquor Store (Map pp68-9; www.bcliquorstores.com; 768 Bute St, West End; 5) The 'Signature' in the name means this well-located shop – just off Robson St at Bute – is one of the larger-format BC government liquor stores. You'll find a big selection of pretty much anything you might want to imbibe, including a back wall of regional and international beers and a large array of wines from around the world.

Sporty tops and pants for ladies are the collection's backbone, but menswear is also part of the mix – at least that can be your excuse as you head in here to meet attractive local women.

KONBINIYA JAPAN CENTRE
Map pp68-9   Food & Drink
www.konbiniya.com; 1238 Robson St; 11am-1am Sun-Thu, 11am-2am Fri & Sat; 5
At a point on Robson St where the generic chain stores dry up and the Asian businesses begin, this is the kind of colorful, chaotic, even tacky store frequently seen in Tokyo's clamorous suburbs. It's the best place in town for Pocky chocolate sticks, wasabi-flavored Kit Kats and Melty Kiss candies, hence the homesick language students shuffling around the aisles. If your accommodation is self-catering, this is a good place to pick up cheap noodles and curry mixes.

YALETOWN

Colonizing the area's evocative old brick warehouses, this chichi district is lined with high-end designer boutiques – it's worth a window-shopping stroll even if your budget isn't up to buying much. It's no surprise that there's a Mini Cooper showroom here – the

car is a popular fashion accessory in this part of town – but Yaletown isn't just about designer gear for beautifully airbrushed people: there's an art gallery and bookstore here, too.

COASTAL PEOPLES FINE ARTS
GALLERY Map p72   Arts & Crafts
www.coastalpeoples.com; 1024 Mainland St; Yaletown-Roundhouse
This museum-like store showcases an excellent array of Inuit and Northwest Coast aboriginal jewelry, carvings and prints. Focusing on the high-art side of aboriginal crafts, the exquisite items here are ideal if you're looking for a very special souvenir for someone back home – they can ship the totem poles if you can't fit them in your suitcase.

BASQUIAT Map p72   Clothing
www.basquiat.ca; 1189 Hamilton St; Yaletown-Roundhouse
A minimalist but pricey unisex clothing joint where you'll need all your credit cards to buy an outfit. Despite the price tags, the service is excellent and the carefully chosen selection of international labels is top-notch: look out for Ian, Dondop, Montesano and beyond. Since fashion is followed closely here, the end-of-season sales are truly excellent.

BROOKLYN CLOTHING Map p72 · Clothing
www.brooklynclothing.com; 418 Davie St;
Ⓜ Yaletown-Roundhouse
Proving that Yaletown men are just as aesthetically focused as women, this hipster menswear boutique is the perfect spot to upgrade your style from that New Romantic look you've been sporting since 1983. Local designers are well represented – check out the achingly cool T-shirts – and there are dozens of jeans styles so you can finally nail that perfect fit.

LOLA HOME & APPAREL
Map p72 · Clothing, Housewares
www.lolahomeandapparel.com; 1076 Hamilton St;
Ⓜ Yaletown-Roundhouse
A browser's delight, this visually appealing 'lifestyle boutique' is a firm Yaletown favorite, especially among the ladies. Resembling a pastel-painted French shop from the Victorian era, it showcases modern-day designers who have incorporated antique and vintage aesthetics into their contemporary clothing lines: think Victorian soap leaves jostling for space with contemporary silk dresses.

GASTOWN

While the main Water St thoroughfare is ideal for executing all your souvenir shopping obligations – especially if you're looking for maple-leaf-themed T-shirts and chocolate 'moose dropping' candies – the side streets and alternative walkways of Gastown are increasingly lined with hip designer stores, making this area a downtown rival to SoMa in the indie shopping stakes. Save time to wander off the beaten path and you'll be surprised at how many times your credit cards start twitching.

CANNABIS CULTURE
HEADQUARTERS Map p76 · Accessories
www.cannabisculture.com; 307 W Hastings St;
🚌 10
For arguments in support of legalization and the campaign to release cannabis advocate Marc Emery from prison for distributing marijuana, duck into the friendly shop and offices of the BC Marijuana Party, in an area of town still known as 'Vansterdam.' With books, hemp clothing and associated paraphernalia, the

top picks

INDIE DESIGNER WEAR

- Erin Templeton (p118)
- Lynn Steven Boutique (opposite)
- Smoking Lily (p119)
- Twigg & Hottie (p120)
- John Fluevog Shoes (opposite)

store also houses a back room where (for $5) you can use the vaporizers to chill out with like-minded buddies.

HILL'S NATIVE ART Map p76 · Arts & Crafts
www.hills.ca; 165 Water St; 🕚 9am-9pm;
Ⓜ Waterfront
Launched in 1946 as a small trading post on Vancouver Island, Hill's flagship store has many First Nations carvings, prints, ceremonial masks and cozy Cowichan sweaters, and traditional music and books of historical interest. Artists are often found at work in the 3rd-floor gallery. There are many souvenir stores on Water St, but this is the one if you want to find something special and artistic.

BLOCK Map p76 · Clothing
www.theblock.ca; 350 W Cordova St; 🚌 8
Colonizing this Gastown strip long before it was fashionable, this browse-worthy men's and women's boutique still has plenty of reasons for a visit. Check out the ever-changing array of clothes and shoes by designers like Nudie and Bloch London, and save time to peruse the ultra-cool jewelry, much of it crafted by local artisans.

DELUXE JUNK Map p76 · Clothing
www.deluxejunk.com; 310 W Cordova St; 🚌 8
A treasure trove of antique glories, from flapper dresses to sparkly evening shoes and even the occasional old-school wedding outfit, this is one of the city's best vintage clothing stores. Mostly serving discerning females, there are also essential outfits for passing blokes, including cummerbunds and Hawaiian shirts (not usually worn together). Check out the vintage cigarette holders – perfect for that 1940s dinner party you're time traveling back to.

CLOTHING SIZES

Women's clothing

Aus/UK	8	10	12	14	16	18
Europe	36	38	40	42	44	46
Japan	5	7	9	11	13	15
USA	6	8	10	12	14	16

Women's shoes

Aus/USA	5	6	7	8	9	10
Europe	35	36	37	38	39	40
France only	35	36	38	39	40	42
Japan	22	23	24	25	26	27
UK	3½	4½	5½	6½	7½	8½

Men's clothing

Aus	92	96	100	104	108	112
Europe	46	48	50	52	54	56
Japan	S		M	M		L
UK/USA	35	36	37	38	39	40

Men's shirts (collar sizes)

Aus/Japan	38	39	40	41	42	43
Europe	38	39	40	41	42	43
UK/USA	15	15½	16	16½	17	17½

Men's shoes

Aus/UK	7	8	9	10	11	12
Europe	41	42	43	44½	46	47
Japan	26	27	27½	28	29	30
USA	7½	8½	9½	10½	11½	12½

Measurements approximate only; try before you buy

LYNN STEVEN BOUTIQUE

Map p76 — Clothing

www.lynnsteven.com; 225 Carrall St; 🚌 8
An austere-looking white interior enlivened by a tower of paperbacks fashioned into a changing room, this excellent women's boutique is popular with under-30s coolsters looking for classic casual togs that will stand the test of time. Tops and jeans from designers in Toronto, New York and LA (including McGinn) dominate, but expect to also be tempted by the vegan bags from Montréal. Friendly service.

OBAKKI Map p76 — Clothing

www.obakki.com; 44 Water St; 🚌 8
Making excellent use of its brick-lined heritage space location, this handsome unisex clothing boutique looks more like an art gallery inside with its polished concrete floors and spruce wood-block tables. It pitches itself as elegant yet casual.

SHOE FRENZY

If you're a woman in Vancouver, you'll start to get itchy feet sometime in early April every year. But rather than a sudden desire to hit the road and start traveling, your tingling toes are telling you that the city's biggest sartorial event for feet is about to take place. When the Army & Navy (Map p76; www.armyandnavy.ca; 36 W Cordova St, Gastown; 🚌 8) department store's annual 12-day shoe sale kicks-off, there's always a long, excited queue of hundreds of local ladies ready to get in. Those who've waited in line for hours have the chance to hit — usually at maximum velocity — the shiny pyramids of deeply discounted designer footwear from the likes of Guess, Christian Dior and Jimmy Choo. As screams of delight emanate from those staggering around with armfuls of must-have shoes, a handful of sheepish husbands and boyfriends hang around in corners wondering how they can escape.

Unleash your credit cards for a full menu of highly contemporary made-in-North-America designs with a hint of mod-Asian influence.

JOHN FLUEVOG SHOES Map p76 — Footwear

www.fluevog.com; 65 Water St; Ⓜ Waterfront
Real Vancouverites own at least one pair of shoes from this local footwear legend, now firmly established in this cavernous flagship store (there's an older but smaller shop at 837 Granville St, downtown). Pick up that pair of thigh-hugging dominatrix boots you've always wanted or settle on some designer-twisted brogues that look exactly like chunky Dr Martens on acid.

CANADIAN MAPLE DELIGHTS

Map p76 — Souvenirs

www.mapledelights.com; 385 Water St; Ⓜ Waterfront
It might seem like a chore but if you have to pick up souvenirs for all those greedy friends back home, this is an ideal one-stop-shop. Specializing in all manner of maple syrup–flavored goodies (think maple sugar, maple tea, maple leaf–shaped candy, maple tree–growing kits etc), it also stocks vacuum-packed salmon for those who don't have a sweet tooth. There are several additional large souvenir stores on this street.

CHINATOWN

While this multisensory, ever-colorful area used to be more for looking than actually buying – how many live frogs, bags of dried fish or lizards splayed on sticks do you usually buy? – it's become part of East Vancouver's gentrification drive in recent years. Alongside the traditional apothecaries and grocery stores, you'll now find a smattering of Gastown-style indie stores catering to the area's newer influx of artsy hipsters. It's not all changing, though: the Chinatown Night Market (p79) is still one of the neighborhood's best retail attractions.

ERIN TEMPLETON Map p79   Accessories
www.erintempleton.com; 511 Carrall St;
Ⓜ Stadium-Chinatown
There's a funky array of vintage and consignment clothing and jewelry here, but the stars of the show are the leather bags, belts, hats and purses made on-site by Erin herself from new and recycled materials (she trained in shoemaking at a London college). They're the kind of must-have items that are hard to resist, no matter how many you already have back home.

BLIM Map p79   Arts & Crafts
www.blim.ca; 115 E Pender St; 🚍 19
This popular arts and crafts resource center is well worth a look if you need to scratch

your creative urge while you're here. You'll find supplies and space to make your own thing – from buttons to knitted scarves – or you can just peruse the gallery and shopping spaces to pick up something someone else has already labored over (you can always tell people back home you made it yourself). There's a lively list of workshops, events and film nights here, too.

PEKING LOUNGE Map p79   Arts & Crafts
www.pekinglounge.com; 83 E Pender St; 🚍 19
If you're a visiting antiques fan with an interest in old-school Chinese pieces, this is the place for you. Presented like artworks in a lounge-cool contemporary boutique setting, you'll enjoy perusing the price tags on intricately-carved dark wood chairs and armoires. Check out the lovely silk and linen cushions (new, rather than antique) and consider buying an extra suitcase so you can take some home.

TEN LEE HONG ENTERPRISES
Map p79   Food & Drink
500 Main St; 🚍 3
This authentic Chinese tea and herb shop is a great place to buy supplies of good green, red, white and black teas. The friendly staff – women in cool pink pantsuits – are used to dealing with curious Westerners: they'll instruct you in

RICHMOND'S SUMMER NIGHT MARKET

Much bigger than Vancouver's Chinatown version (p79), Richmond's Summer Night Market (Map pp54-5; www.summernightmarket.com; 12631 Vulcan Way, Richmond; ⏰ 7pm-1am Fri & Sat, 7pm-midnight Sun mid-May–mid-Oct) has around 300 vendors and offers a multisensory glimpse of what Hong Kong–style bazaars are all about. Don't eat anything before arriving and you can taste-trip among the 60 or so steamy food stalls. The highlight of an evening out here, they offer savory treats such as fish balls, shrimp dumplings, duck wraps, twirled potatoes, vegetarian gyoza (fried Japanese dumplings) and grilled squid. Most dishes cost from $3 to $6. Highlight vendors are the comparatively gourmet Roaming Dragon (go for its Korean short-rib tacos) and Sumo Bites (the sukiyaki beef rice burgers are recommended).

For dessert, drop by one of the Korean stands and watch the staff make Dragon's Beard Candy, then take some with you as you amble around the remainder of the market – rows of neon-lit stalls hawking everything from $15 Asian DVD blockbusters, to a myriad of colored iPhone covers to the occasional Samurai sword. On top of all the frenzied bartering, Canto pop percolates the air from the surrounding speakers.

If you've had your fill of kitsch shopping, there's also a live stage where dog shows, fish-ball eating contests and yoga demonstrations will keep you entertained (or not). Even if you don't buy anything, the market is a colorful, sense-pricking place to browse for an hour or two and will likely be an unforgettable highlight of your trip.

If you're coming by bus from downtown Vancouver, take the Canada Line SkyTrain to Richmond-Brighouse Station. From there, transfer to the 430 Metrotown bus. If you're driving, head south from Vancouver on Knight St, take the Knight St Bridge and turn right onto Bridgeport Rd once you hit Richmond. Head toward the giant IKEA store and you'll start to see the crowds.

the art of how to brew and will also serve you samples so you can find your favorite tipple.

SOUTH MAIN (SOMA)

Studding the stretch along Main St past 20th Ave, SoMa's shopping appeal lies in its unique clothing and accessories boutiques: this is Vancouver's must-see area for locally owned independent stores. Many showcase the exciting creative skills of hot regional designers, fuelling the renaissance of an area once known for its grungy, down-at-heel appearance. This is also a great place to hang out if you want to meet the city's coolsters and pick up on their fashion sense. You'll find many of the same crowd at the monthly Portobello West market (p82). Finally, west of Main St along Broadway, you'll find 'fleece central,' a couple of blocks of outdoor gear stores clustered around the Mountain Equipment Co-op behemoth.

LAZY SUSAN'S Map p83   Accessories
www.lazysusansonline.com; 3647 Main St; 🚌 3
An eclectic Aladdin's cave lined with tempting trinkets like Scrabble-tile earrings, reproduction old-school greeting cards and obsolete ties transformed into coin purses, it's hard to walk away from here without buying that kitsch-perfect gift for someone back home – possibly a cactus-shaped teapot or a broach resembling a palm tree.

RUBBER RAINBOW CONDOM COMPANY Map p83   Accessories
3851 Main St; 🚌 3
Formerly in the West End, this fun, funky condom and lube store serves all manner of experiment-inviting accessories, including studded, vibrating and 'full-fitting strawberry flavored' varieties. Ask for a

top picks

VINTAGE CLOTHING

- Deluxe Junk (p116)
- Mintage (p126)
- Front & Company (right)
- True Value Vintage Clothing (p114)
- Cherry Bomb (p113)

selection pack if you're going to be in town for a while – you never know how lucky you might get.

REGIONAL ASSEMBLY OF TEXT
Map p83   Arts & Crafts
www.assemblyoftext.com; 3934 Main St; 🚌 3
The epitome of South Main eccentricity, this ironic antidote to the digital age was founded by pen-and-paper-loving art school grads. Ink-stained fans flock here to stock up on Little Otsu journals, handmade pencil boxes and American Apparel T-shirts printed with typewriter motifs. Check out the tiny under-the-stairs reading room showcasing cool underground art, and don't miss the monthly letter-writing club (7pm, first Thursday of every month), where you can sip tea, scoff cookies and hammer away on those vintage typewriters.

EUGENE CHOO Map p83   Clothing
www.eugenechoo.com; 3683 Main St; 🚌 3
Behind the double-fronted, blue-painted exterior of this local favorite beats the heart of a store that pioneered the emergence of Main St as Vancouver's hip clothing capital. Once a grungy vintage-clothing shop, it's now a hotbed of local designer duds for the city's slim-fit set. Handmade shoes and tailored suits are recommended here, and this is one of the only stores in town that has stocked Freitag messenger bags.

FRONT & COMPANY
Map p83   Clothing, Housewares
www.frontandcompany.ca; 3772 Main St; 🚌 3
A triple-fronted store covering all the bases, the largest section here contains trendy consignment clothing (where else can you find that vintage velvet smoking jacket?). Next door houses new, knowingly cool housewares, while the third area includes must-have gifts and accessories such as manga figures, peace-sign ice trays and nihilist chewing gum (flavorless, of course).

SMOKING LILY Map p83   Clothing
www.smokinglily.com; 3634 Main St; 🚌 3
Quirky art-school cool rules here, with skirts, belts and halter-tops whimsically accented with prints of ants, skulls or the periodic table. Men's clothing is slowly creeping into the mix, with fish, skull and tractor T-shirts and ties. It's hard to imagine a better souvenir than the silk tea cozy

printed with a Pierre Trudeau likeness. It's a fun spot to browse and staff are friendly.

TWIGG & HOTTIE Map p83   Clothing
www.twiggandhottie.com; 3671 Main St; 🚌 3
Just across from Smoking Lily and named after owners Glencora Twigg and Christine Hotton, this wood-floored nook showcases distinctive garments (plus idiosyncratic jewelry) for women from Canadian designers: it's *the* place to find something that nobody else is wearing back home. If you're in a budgeting mood, peruse the Steals and Deals rack at the back.

VANCOUVER SPECIAL Map p83 Housewares
www.vanspecial.com; 3612 Main St; 🚌 3
An irresistible, white-walled interiors store that appeals to design-minded individuals with its carefully chosen array of Pantone mugs, molded plastic side tables and glossy architecture books. It's the kind of place you can easily spend an hour just browsing: the problem is you'll almost certainly find something – an Alessi bottle opener perhaps? – that you just can't live without.

EUROPE BOUND TRAVEL OUTFITTERS Map p83   Outdoor Gear
www.europebound.com; 195 W Broadway; 🚌 9
Among the plethora of outdoor stores clustering for economic warmth around the

nearby MEC campfire, Europe Bound offers a more branded approach to its selection, including reliable labels such as Columbia, North Face and Canada Goose. Whether you're looking for winter jackets, hydration daypacks, cycling accessories, maps or travel guidebooks, you'll find most of it on the racks here.

MOUNTAIN EQUIPMENT CO-OP
Map p83   Outdoor Gear
www.mec.ca; 130 W Broadway; 🚌 9
Cavernous granddaddy of Vancouver outdoor stores, grown hikers have been known to weep here at the amazing selection of mostly own-brand clothing, kayaks, sleeping bags and clever camping gadgets: MEC has been turning campers into fully fledged outdoor enthusiasts for years. There's a good selection of regional and international maps and guidebooks, plus a climbing wall to test your new gear. You'll have to be a member to buy, but that's easy to arrange and only costs $5. Equipment – canoes, kayaks, camping gear etc – can also be rented here.

SPORTS JUNKIES Map p83   Outdoor Gear
www.sportsjunkies.com; 102 W Broadway; 🚌 9
If you're heading to this part of town to check out MEC (above), do what the locals do and drop in first to this nearby outdoor

---

VANCOUVER'S HIGH-FIDELITY HOT SPOTS

If you're one of those travelers who can't wait to hit the record stores when you visit a new town, you won't be disappointed with Vancouver. The city is crammed with vinyl-packing shops where you can rub shoulders with local musos and – maybe – find that rare Pathetic Flowers album that's been missing from your collection all these years. First place to check should be the dude selling stacks of used records leaned against the sidewalk in Robson Sq. If you don't have any luck with him, try these recommended faves:

Neptoon Records (Map p83; www.neptoon.com; 3561 Main St, SoMa; 🚌 3) Dedicated to new and used vinyl (and CDs), the city's oldest independent record store has still got it, which explains why bands frequently play freebie gigs here. Step through the teal green storefront and you'll find endless racks of browsable, well-priced treats, along with an ever-friendly owner who's happy to chat. There's also a fantastic selection of vintage band posters.

Red Cat Records (Map p83; www.redcat.ca; 4332 Main St, SoMa; 🚌 3) Owned and operated by a pair of Vancouver musicians, Red Cat is packed with rare and local CDs and vinyl, and the staff are happy to offer plenty of suggestions for how to tap into the local live scene.

Scratch Records (Map pp58-9; www.scratchrecords.com; 726 Richards St, Downtown; Ⓜ Vancouver City Centre) Initially a tiny specialist record store, Scratch has expanded over the past 20 years to become a record label, concert promoter and international distributor. But the store remains, its bins packed with 99% independent labels, obscure releases and vinyl that the staff know intimately.

Zulu Records (Map pp96-7; www.zulurecords.com; 1972 W 4th Ave, Kitsilano; 🚌 4) Routinely voted Vancouver's best indie music store, visiting musos can happily spend a rainy afternoon here sifting the racks of new and used vinyl and hard-to-find imports. Check out any of the 30,000 titles at the sweet listening booths with retro chairs.

gear and sports equipment consignment store. Along with the shelves of used boots and shoes near the door, you'll find racks of end-of-range new togs (this is the place for $5 Olympic Games T-shirts). Upstairs is a cornucopia of new and used equipment, from skis to snowshoes. If you know your prices, you can save a bundle here.

COMMERCIAL DRIVE

Like a counterculture department store stretched along both sides of one street, the Drive is Vancouver's 'anti Robson.' You'll find 17 blocks of eclectic, independent shopping here, ranging from ethical clothing stores to intelligent-minded bookshops. If the area sounds a little too earnest, keep in mind that Commercial also has plenty of frivolous shopping outlets where you can pick up handmade chocolates and pop-culture gifts for your friends back home. Coffee-shop central (see the boxed text on p158), the Drive is a great place to shop and sup on a sunny afternoon.

URBAN EMPIRE Map p86   Accessories
www.urbanempire.ca; 1108 Commercial Dr; 🚌 20
This wacky, all-out, kitsch trinket shop is just the kind of place you can pick up that Crazy Cat Lady action figure you've always wanted. Other must-haves include bacon-strip sticking plasters and dog-butt flavored chewing gum, which means you'll

have plenty of ideas for souvenirs for your friends back home.

WOMYNS' WARE Map p86   Accessories
www.womynsware.com; 896 Commercial Dr; 🚌 20
The welcoming staff at this low-key, ultra-friendly shop – which specializes in an eye-popping menu of women's sex toys – are happy to explain the workings of the 'family jewels' harness' or 'nun's habit flogger.' There's also a good array of books and some games to put the fun back into your sexual shenanigans. Fair-trade committed.

BIBLIOPHILE BOOKSHOP
Map p86   Bookstore
2010 Commercial Dr; 🚌 20
Serving the area's well-read bohemians, this great used-tome store is one of several bookish nooks along the Drive. Floor-to-ceiling stacks bulge with titles covering just about every subject, including a surprisingly good selection of Canadian fiction. The shop additionally sells a menagerie of folk art, which explains the random carved ornaments populating spots where books won't fit.

BAREFOOT CONTESSA Map p86   Clothing
www.thebarefootcontessa.com; 1928 Commercial Dr; 🚌 20
The newer satellite store of one of Main St's popular fashion mainstays, the Contessa is all about ladieswear for those who never

---

FARMERS MARKETS

A tasty cornucopia of BC farm produce hits the stalls around Vancouver from June to October. Seasonal highlights include crunchy apples, lush peaches and juicy blueberries, while home-baked cakes and treats are frequent accompaniments. Don't be surprised to see zesty local cheese and a few arts and crafts added to the mix. To check out what's on offer, visit www.eatlocal.org.

East Vancouver Farmers Market (Map pp54-5; north parking lot of Trout Lake Park, Commercial Dr; 🕙 9am-2pm Sat mid-May–mid-Oct; 🚌 20)

Kitsilano Farmers Market (Map pp96-7; Kitsilano Community Centre, 2690 Larch St, Kitsilano; 🕙 10am-2pm Sun mid-May–mid-Oct; 🚌 4)

Main Street Station Farmers Market (Map p79; Thornton Park, 1100 Station St, Chinatown; 🕙 3-7pm Wed early Jun-Sep; Ⓜ Main St-Science World)

UBC Farmers Market (Map p102; 6182 South Campus Rd, UBC; 🕙 9am-1pm Sat mid-Jun–Sep; 🚌 99B-Line)

West End Farmers Market (Map pp68-9; Nelson Park, btwn Bute & Thurlow Sts, West End; 🕙 9am-1pm Sat mid-Jun–mid-Oct; 🚌 5)

Winter Farmers Market (Map p86; Wise Hall, 1882 Adanac St, Commercial Dr; 🕙 10am-2pm 2nd & 4th Sat of month Nov-Apr; 🚌 20)

want to be a clone of a chain-store manne-quin. You'll find cute hats, frocks and tops from Canadian and international designers, plus a wall of sparkling baubles guaranteed to brighten up any rainy day.

DUTCH GIRL CHOCOLATES
Map p86   Food & Drink

1002 Commercial Dr; 🚌 20
This little creaky-floored shop is artfully draped with an Aladdin's cave of totally irresistible choc treats, many made in the kitchen you'll glimpse through the hatch out back. Pick up some milk, white or dark chocolate models of cars or tennis racquets, peruse the old-fashioned jars of liquorice sweeties or create a selection box of handmade truffles and bonbons from the cabinet by the counter. And if you're a visiting Netherlander pining for home, you can pick up all your fave branded Dutch confections right here.

LA GROTTA DEL FORMAGGIO
Map p86   Food & Drink

1791 Commercial Dr; 🚌 20
If you insist on eating something other than chocolate or ice cream, drop into this legendary deli, a holdover from the days when this was Vancouver's 'Little Italy.' Peruse the lip-smacking cheese selection then check out the wall of marzipan, olive oil and cream crackers. A good spot to gather some mighty fine picnic fixings, you can scoff the lot in nearby Grandview Park. Check out the ceiling: it's painted with clouds like the Sistine Chapel.

KALENA'S SHOES Map p86   Footwear
www.kalenashoes.com; 1526 Commercial Dr; 🚌 20
True to Commercial Dr's Italian heritage, Kalena's imports handsome top-quality leather shoes and boots from the old country. Well-crafted men's and women's styles can be had for reasonable prices and there's also a big area devoted to sale items. This is the kind of place where you'll pay $200 for a pair of brogues and they'll last you for a couple of decades.

DREAM DESIGNS Map p86   Housewares
www.dreamdesigns.ca; 956 Commercial Dr; 🚌 20
Visiting greenies will enjoy dipping into this mini eco department store that sells everything from yoga knickknacks to linen pajamas and hemp bed sheets. Check

out the local pottery selection and enjoy a calming chat with the staff about your favorite natural spa treatments.

WONDERBUCKS TRADING COMPANY
Map p86   Housewares

www.wonderbucks.com; 1803 Commercial Dr; 🚌 20
Dedicated to cut-price chic for homes that don't quite have million-dollar budgets, you can find everything here from bargain art prints to mod tablecloths. Always worth a peruse, especially if you have room in your luggage for that all-important floor-to-ceiling vase, it's a challenge to leave here without something in your bag (and we're not talking about shoplifting).

GRANVILLE ISLAND

Teeming with studios where artisans throw clay, blow glass and silversmith jewelry, Granville Island can easily keep you and your wallet occupied for a day. You'll find a surfeit of artisan studios and shopping nooks colonizing the old industrial buildings – head to the Net Loft, Railspur Alley or Granville Island Public Market if you're lacking direction. Make sure you explore as much as possible and duck down the back alleys to see artisans at work in their studios. Buskers also hang out here on summer afternoons, making this Vancouver's most convivial shopping area.

EDIE HATS Map p89   Accessories
www.ediehats.com; Net Loft, 1666 Johnston St; 🚌 50
A cozy and convivial mood-lit jungle of classic and contemporary headgear, squeeze in and try on a few panama hats and a couple of rainbow-colored toques (if you have to ask what a toque is, they'll know you're not Canadian). Staffers are ever-friendly and have an irregular habit of handing out choccies if they like the look of you.

UMBRELLA SHOP Map p89   Accessories
www.theumbrellashop.com; 1550 Anderson St; 🚌 50
Often the only outdoor gear you need in Vancouver is a good brolly to fend off the relentless rain. This family-run company started in 1935 and has just the thing, with hundreds of bright and breezy designs that should put a smile on the face of any torrentially drenched visitor. Duck inside,

choose a great umbrella then launch yourself back into the tempest.

CIRCLE CRAFT Map p89   Arts & Crafts
www.circlecraft.net; Net Loft, 1666 Johnston St; 🚌 50
This 35-plus-year-old cooperative hawks 100% BC arts and crafts, including sculptures from found objects, ceramics and sleek jewelry, with hand-sewn puppets and dolls thrown in (not literally) for good measure. Prices vary considerably but there's usually something here to suit most budgets.

CRAFTHOUSE Map p89   Arts & Crafts
www.cabc.net; 1386 Cartwright St; 🚌 50
At this bright and friendly nonprofit gallery run by the Craft Council of BC (CCBC), the shelves hold everything from glass goblets and woven scarves to hand-forged jewelry and lathe-turned wooden bowls – all produced by around 120 regional artisans. The gallery also keeps schedules of provincial craft shows.

GALLERY OF BC CERAMICS
Map p89   Arts & Crafts
www.bcpotters.com; 1359 Cartwright St; 🚌 50
The public face of the Potters Guild of BC exhibits and sells the striking works of its member artists, often at great prices. You can pick up one-of-a-kind ceramic tankards or swirly-painted French butter dishes – it also had some puffer fish–shaped teapots on our visit. The hot items are the cool ramen noodle cups, complete with holes for chopsticks.

MICHAEL DEAN JEWELLERY
Map p89   Arts & Crafts
www.michaeldeanjewellery.com; 1808 Boatlift Lane; 🚌 50
Pearls and Canadian diamonds feature prominently in the rings created by local artisan Michael Dean, who works on his shiny trinkets at this cozy little island studio. Partners in business and life, his wife Carole also creates her own jewelry and has a sparkling range of abstract designs on silver necklaces. If you're looking for an extra special pressie for someone back home, this is a good place to start.

PAPER-YA Map p89   Arts & Crafts
www.paper-ya.com; Net Loft, 1666 Johnston St; 🚌 50
A magnet for slavering stationery fetishists (you know who you are), this treasure trove of writing-related ephemera ranges from natty pens to quirky, hand-crafted greeting cards. In between, you'll find an intriguing undercurrent of kitsch-cool Japanese journals and reams of sumptuous washi paper. It's a store that makes you long for the return of traditional letter writing.

ORGANIX Map p89   Clothing
www.granvilleislandorganix.com; 1812 Boatlift Lane; 🚌 50
Showcasing hemp, bamboo fiber and organic cotton clothing for men, women and children, this popular spot lures green-hued locals and visitors. Expanding in the last couple of years, the store now has

INSIDER'S GUIDE TO THE GRANVILLE ISLAND PUBLIC MARKET

The shopping highlight of any trip to Granville Island is the covered public market (p88), a colorful cornucopia of more than 70 deli stands, produce stalls and ever-changing arts and crafts tables that's worth an afternoon of anyone's time. But rather than just wading in aimlessly – not that there's anything wrong with that – there are some highlights that should not be missed, particularly if you're looking for picnic fixings or searching for a souvenir of the region that isn't vacuum-packed salmon or maple-syrup cookies.

If you know your Darjeeling from your Hawaiian Rooibos (or you want to learn), head to the Granville Island Tea Company, where 150 varieties are steeped and brewed on site. You can pull up a stool here and sample with the locals and chatty servers. If you're collecting goodies for an alfresco lunch later in the day, drop by Oyama Sausage Company, complete with dozens of smoked sausages and cured meats (go for the duck leg confit). Nearby Dussa's Ham and Cheese stocks hundreds of curdy treats and some mouth-melting cold cuts – its Island Ham is recommended and it also has delicious pitted Nicoise olives, although you'll have to ask for them since they're not on display. The perfect place to buy a souvenir for a foodie back home, Edible BC stocks more than 800 finger-licking products from the Okanagan, Fraser Valley and Vancouver Island. Along with wine and fresh produce, you'll be tempted by Thomas Haas cookies, delicious lobster oil and mason jars filled with local preserves and wine-soaked cherries. It also runs lip-smacking market foodie tours that are highly recommended.

room for bedding and accessories (look out for cool wooden earrings from Billy Would Designs) as well as a range of excellent bamboo towels.

FAIRVIEW & SOUTH GRANVILLE

The main shopping action here is along South Granville. This includes the 'South Granville Rise' area of gallery shops between Granville Bridge and Broadway and the boutiques, specialist food stores and slick houseware emporiums (of the Pottery Barn and Williams-Sonoma variety) that dot both sides of the street past Broadway.

BAU-XI GALLERY Map p93   Arts & Crafts
www.bau-xi.com; 3045 Granville St; 🚊 10
One of the long-established galleries responsible for the city's artistic renaissance in recent years, Bau-xi – pronounced 'bo-she' – showcases the best in local artists and generally has prices to match its exalted position. The main gallery selection changes monthly and the focus is usually on original paintings, although prints, drawings and sculpture are also added to the mix on occasion.

EQUINOX GALLERY Map p93   Arts & Crafts
www.equinoxgallery.com; 2321 Granville St; 🚊 10
Another veteran of the South Granville scene, Equinox generally focuses on quality contemporary works from established Canadian and international artists. Some of the leading lights the gallery continues to showcase are Jack Shadbolt, Fred Herzog and Liz Magor, and, along with the canvasses, there's a commitment to sculpture and provocative installations.

top picks

CANDY

- Mink Chocolates (p114)
- Konbiniya Japan Centre (p115)
- Dutch Girl Chocolates (p122)
- Purdy's Chocolates (opposite)

HOT BLOG

Vancouver's burgeoning shopping arena sees regular openings of hot new designer stores, quirky homeware shops and artsy outlets where the latest trends are unfolding before your eyes. To get a heads-up on the latest developments in health, beauty and fashion before you hit the ground, visit Vitamin Daily (www.vitamindaily.com/vancouver), Vancouver's top shopping and lifestyle blog for women. Established by local fashion know-it-alls Sarah Bancroft and Tara Parker Tait, it's a continually updated fresh sheet – including a lively forum – where locals go to find out what's hot and what's not.

BACCI'S Map p93   Clothing, Housewares
www.baccis.ca; 2788 Granville St; 🚊 10
Combining designer women's clothing on one side and a room full of hard-to-resist trinkets piled high on antique wooden tables on the other, Bacci's is a dangerous place to browse. Before you know it, you'll have an arm full of chunky luxury soaps, embroidered cushions and picture-perfect coffee pots to fit in your suitcase.

OLIVER + LILLY'S Map p93   Clothing
www.oliverandlillys.com; 1520 W 13th Ave; 🚊 10
This small, white-walled women's clothing boutique just around the corner from the South Granville hubbub is an oasis of great designer duds. You'll find stylish but casual jeans and halter tops from the likes of Heidi Merrick, Ali Ro and Eze Sur Mer, as well as that must-have Madison Marcus Zeal dress that will knock 'em all out back home.

MEINHARDT FINE FOODS
Map p93   Food & Drink
www.meinhardt.com; 3002 Granville St; 🚊 10
The culinary equivalent of a sex shop for food fans, the narrow aisles at this swanky deli and grocery emporium are lined with international condiments, luxury canned goods and the kind of tempting treats that everyone should try at least once. Drop by for Christmas goodies or build your perfect picnic from the tempting bread, cheese and cold cuts selections. If you're salivating too much, check out Picnic (p143), Meinhardt's adjoining eatery for lunch.

PURDY'S CHOCOLATES

Map p93   Food & Drink

www.purdys.com; 2705 Granville St; 🚌 **10**

Like a beacon to the weary, this purple-painted chocolate purveyor stands at the corner of Granville and W 11th Ave calling your name. It's a homegrown BC business with outlets dotted like candy sprinkles across the city, and it's hard not to pick up a few treats for the road here. Among the favorites are the chocolate hedgehogs, peanut-butter daisies and sweet Georgia browns – roasted pecans wrapped in caramel and chocolate. Check out the sales racks after Christmas and Valentine's Day for dramatic bargains.

RESTORATION HARDWARE

Map p93   Housewares

www.restorationhardware.com; 2555 Granville St; 🚌 **10**

Filled with furnishings and interior flourishes that you wish you had in your house, this yuppie favorite also carries some kitsch-tastic reproduction toys and old-school gadgets, especially at Christmastime. Nothing is cheap here, except the bargain pile of dinged goods shamefully hidden near the washrooms at the back – check out the snobs looking down their noses at you as you dive in here head first.

KITSILANO

Lined with a happy surfeit of bookstores (none of them far from a coffee shop if you want to buy, sup and read at your leisure), Kits – especially along W 4th Ave west of Burrard St – is also home to some of the city's best boutique clothing and interior design stores. This is a highly pleasurable and ultra-relaxed neighborhood to browse among the independent retailers: there are plenty of foodie pit stops and the beach is a short downhill stroll away: perfect if you need to discuss your abundant purchases with some sympathetic driftwood.

BARBARA-JO'S BOOKS TO COOKS

Map pp96-7   Bookstore

www.bookstocooks.com; 1740 W 2nd Ave; 🚌 **4**

Traveling epicureans should salivate over to this bookstore, specializing in finger-licking food and wine tomes (see the boxed text on p135 for recommended titles by Vancouver chefs). There are also regular book-

top picks

BOOKSHOPS

- **KidsBooks** (below)
- **MacLeod's Books** (p113)
- **Wanderlust** (below)
- **Barbara-Jo's Books to Cooks** (left)
- **Book Warehouse** (p114)

reading events and cooking classes in the demonstration kitchen if you fancy rubbing shoulders with a culinary maestro or two – check its website for the schedule.

KIDSBOOKS Map pp96-7   Bookstore

www.kidsbooks.ca; 3083 W Broadway; 🚌 **9**

If you're wondering what your sprogs can read now that the *Harry Potter* series may be over, bring them here. Like a theme park for bookish kids, this fantastic child-friendly store – Canada's biggest kids' bookshop – has thousands of novels, picture books, history titles and anything else you can think of to keep them quiet. There are also regular readings by visiting authors and a selection of quality toys and games.

TRAVEL BUG Map pp96-7   Bookstore, Accessories

www.travelbugbooks.ca; 3065 W Broadway; 🚌 **9**

Lined with maps, guidebooks and travel literature (plus handy on-the-road accessories), this is the smaller of two excellent travel-related Kits bookstores. It's a browsable treat for those planning a trip or those who just like to imagine afar from a comfy armchair. Check the website for readings from sinewy travel writers just back from navigating the Amazon armed only with shoelaces and a toothpick.

WANDERLUST

Map pp96-7   Bookstore, Accessories

www.wanderlustore.com; 1929 W 4th Ave; 🚌 **4**

Neatly divided between guidebooks, maps and travel literature and a large array of travel accessories, this store has been inspiring itchy feet among the locals for years. While the travel book selection is deeper than any other in town, it's the gadgets that are most intriguing. Peruse the luggage, money belts and mosquito nets, then wonder how you ever got

WORTH THE TRIP: BC'S BIGGEST MALL

If the 'Wet Coast' downpours are making you stir crazy and the shops in the hotel lobby are just not cutting it, leave your umbrella behind and head to BC's largest shopping mall. An ever-expanding 470-store homage to materialism, the ginormous Metropolis at Metrotown (Map pp54-5; www .metropolisatmetrotown.com; ✆ 10am-9pm Mon-Fri, 9:30am-9pm Sat, 11am-6pm Sun; Ⓜ Metro-town) is the only shopping center you'll need to visit on this trip. Savvy shoppers arrive early in the morning to beat the crowds then rest their weary feet at the sprawling food court – Indian, Japanese and Chinese cuisines are recommended here. All the regular chain-store suspects are on site, as well as bookshops, cinemas, department stores and a large number of intriguing Chinese businesses clustered around the excellent Asian T&T supermarket. The mall is a 20-minute SkyTrain ride from downtown Vancouver – it's big enough to warrant its own station.

by without quick-drying underwear. The staff of seasoned travelers is super-knowledgeable if you just want to talk up your next big adventure.

MINTAGE Map pp96-7   Clothing
www.mintagevintage.com 1946 W 4th Ave; 🚍 4
Kitsilano's most popular vintage store has a great selection covering all the bases, including a good array of shoes, tops, jeans and that oh-so-perfect old-school summer dress. Prices can be a bit on the steep side for some items – worn T-shirts shouldn't be over $30, no matter which cool band they're proclaiming – but there are still some finds to be had and a couple of sale racks that are always worth perusing.

RAY RICKBURN Map pp96-7   Clothing
www.rayrickburn.com; 2100 W 4th Ave; 🚍 4
Proving that not all of Vancouver's independent clothing stores cater only to women, this excellent men's apparel shop is the ideal haunt for blokes who want to reinvent their look. Patronized by under-30s with an eye on style, you'll find sweaters, skinny jeans and rakishly appealing jackets from the likes of Ted Baker, Fred Perry and Paul Smith. That's right: it costs to look this good.

GRAVITY POPE Map pp96-7   Footwear
www.gravitypope.com; 2205 W 4th Ave; 🚍 4
This unisex temple of great footwear is a dangerous place to come if you have a shoe fetish – best not to bring more than one credit card. Quality and designer élan are the keys here and you can expect to slip into Vancouver's best selection of fashion-forward clogs, wedges, mules and classy runners. If you have any money left, head next door to Gravity Pope Tailored Goods, a boutique stuffed with stylish must-have men's and women's clothing.

STEPBACK Map pp96-7   Housewares
www.stepback.ca; 3026 W Broadway; 🚍 9
Always a pleasure to browse, this quirky store combines an inventory of trendy retro knickknacks – 1970s whiskey glasses, vintage suitcases, school exercise books etc – with reproduction items that look just as old. Among all the furniture, classic housewares and accessories, look out for the enamel kitchenware, leather journals and books of old-school classics (including some legendary children's titles that will take you right back to your kid-hood).

EATING

top picks

- Raincity Grill (p133)
- Judas Goat (p137)
- Chambar (p130)
- Bao Bei (p137)
- Habit Lounge (p139)
- Bishop's (p144)
- Vij's (p143)
- Deacon's Corner (p137)
- Guu with Garlic (p134)
- Maenam (p144)

What's your recommendation? www.lonelyplanet.com/vancouver

EATING

Dining out in Vancouver used to mean little more than a visit to national fast-food chain Tim Hortons for a chili bread bowl and a box of donut Timbits. Now arguably surpassing Montréal and Toronto for the title of best Canadian restaurant city, a seismic epicurean shift in recent years has delivered a rich and satisfying menu of options, with diversity and regional sourcing high on the list of ingredients.

Many of Vancouver's neighborhoods are heaped with a vast smorgasbord of authentic and highly welcoming ethnic cuisines, originally developed to sustain immigrants salivating for a taste of home. Locals now happily taste-trip through France, Mexico, Africa, India and Italy, surrender to Southeast Asia, gorge on Malaysian curries and Chinese dim sum, and frequent the best array of sushi and *izakaya* (Japanese pub) restaurants outside Japan.

Alongside this, the seasonal West Coast approach – also called Pacific Northwest cuisine – is enjoying a golden age. The tag was formerly just a fancy way of labeling a menu's salmon special, but the movement has been fueled by recent sustainability demands and increasing calls for locally sourced ingredients. Restaurants throughout the city are now foraging for suppliers who can bring them delectable taste-of-the-region flavors like Tofino swimming scallops, Fraser Valley duck and Salt Spring Island lamb – not to mention sweet heirloom tomatoes, juicy local blueberries and piquant regional cheeses.

Most exciting of all, these two dining movements have been rubbing fondly against each other in recent years. Vancouver has one of North America's best fusion dining scenes, meaning that top-notch eateries such as the East Indian Vij's (p143) stir contemporary West Coast flavors into their mix, while high-end West Coast favorites like Raincity Grill (p133) and West (p142) sprinkle their menus with knowing nods to the foodie approaches of other cultures.

For visitors, choosing where to park their taste buds can be bewildering – like stopping for lunch at a small cafe and being presented with a 50-page menu in small print – but the best way to approach what's on offer is to follow your nose around the neighborhoods. Top dining streets, where you can't throw a *kapamaki* (cucumber sushi roll) without hitting a good eatery, include downtown's Robson St, where the Stanley Park end is studded with North America's best Japanese *izakaya* scene; Yaletown's Hamilton and Mainland Sts, where swanky restaurants offer many romantic dining options; Gastown, where some of the city's most exciting resto-bars reside in heritage brick-built settings; Commercial Dr, where funky ethnic-flavored joints and great patios lure hungry locals and hipsters alike; and the West End's Denman and Davie Sts, where a huge and diverse array of well-priced midrange dining options await.

If the weather's fine, don't hesitate to eat alfresco. Vancouverites love to nosh outdoors amid their stunning environs, so patios and decks are widespread – some are heated and stay open throughout the year. Keep in mind that smoking isn't allowed in restaurants, even on patios. You can also pack your food for an impromptu picnic, with Stanley Park, Vanier Park and Kits Beach among the most popular spots – consider a sunset beach buffet and it will likely be one of your trip highlights.

You can easily pick up some takeout (or just keep your dining budget down) at some of Vancouver's best homegrown fast-food minichains. Check out the ubiquitous branches of Flying Wedge for heaping gourmet pizza slices; Steamrollers for ultra-bulging burritos; Vera's Burger Shack for great burgers; and Japadog, the city's beloved fusion tube steak stands. And keep your taste buds on high alert: at the time of writing, Vancouver was about to relax its stringent street food rules, allowing an array of additional vendors to tempt you (see the boxed text, p134).

Finally, it might be a good idea to do some homework before you hungrily hit the streets here. Tap into the latest restaurant openings and reviews in the *Georgia Straight* and *Westender* or pick up a free copy of either *Eat Magazine* or *City Food*. Alternatively, go online and salivate over some great local foodie blogs (see the boxed text, p140).

PRACTICALITIES
Opening Hours

Restaurants in Vancouver are usually open for lunch from 11:30am to 2:30pm, and most serve dinner daily from 5pm to 9pm or 10pm (often later on weekends). Many also serve weekend brunch, usually from 11am to 3pm. For those that serve breakfast, the time is around 7:30am to 10am. If restaurants take a day off – and not many do – it's usually Monday. Some restaurants may close early or on additional days in winter, and stay open later in summer if there's enough hungry traffic wandering the streets. Since there's a wide array of hours for eateries, the reviews in this chapter include full opening hours.

Booking Tables

As a general rule, the higher the prices on the menu, the more strongly reservations are advised. Without a reservation, try to show up for an early or late seating, say, before 5:30pm or just after 9pm. Downtown, Yaletown and Gastown are probably the most difficult neighborhoods to score an easy table at a higher-end joint. Whichever posh spot you end up in, you won't need to dress up, as even the smartest restaurants adopt a fairly casual dress code – this is the fleece capital of the world, after all. Phone numbers are included in reviews where booking ahead is recommended.

Taxes & Tipping

Taxes are the only unpleasant taste on the dining scene here. At the time of writing, the Harmonized Sales Tax (HST) was being introduced to British Columbia (BC), increasing the tax levy added to your bill from the old 5% GST to the new 12% HST rate. Unpopular with local restaurateurs and the subject of a province-wide petition against the new tax – which applies to almost all goods and services purchased here – there is a chance it may be repealed or reduced in the future. Also, you need to add a tip – 15% of the pre-tax bill is the standard. So, for example, if you order a burger ($7) and beer ($3), you'll end up paying a total of $12.70 ($1.20 HST plus $1.50 tip). At cafes where you order at the counter, a tip jar will often be displayed prominently: you can drop some change in here if you feel it's warranted.

Groceries

The indoor Granville Island Public Market (see the boxed text, p123) is as much a sightseeing experience as a destination for deli treats and picnic goodies (take a 10-minute seawall stroll west to Vanier Park to enjoy your grub alfresco). Now part of the giant Wholefoods empire, local chain Capers (Map pp68-9; ☎ 604-687-5288; 1675 Robson St; ⏱ 8am-10pm; ⏹ 5) is a popular pit stop for natural and organic groceries plus good takeout wraps and salads. Near the foot of the giant Shangri-La tower, Urban Fare (Map pp68-9; ☎ 604-648-2053; 1133 Alberni St; ⏱ 7am-10pm; ⏹ 5) is a yuppie supermarket that has a large takeout-food component.

If you're looking for a cheaper alternative, the city's thriftiest food store is the West End's No Frills (Map pp68-9; ☎ 604-682-4331; 1030 Denman St; ⏱ 9am-9pm ⏹ 5), piled high with no-name brands and cut-price fruit and veg. Small greengrocers and convenience stores also dot Commercial Dr, South Main and the West End. If your recipe calls for more obscure ingredients – say live frogs or a barbecued pig's head – make for Chinatown.

An excellent and ever-expanding menu of tasty farmers markets, showcasing crisp seasonal produce, can be found throughout the city in summer – see the boxed text on p121 for listings. And don't miss the Chinatown Night Market (p79) plus the much larger Richmond Summer Night Market (p118) with their lip-smacking hawker food.

DOWNTOWN

You can't throw a donut in the downtown core without hitting a restaurant. While there are plenty of midrange options and a smattering of celebrity-fave high-end joints radiating from Robson St, there are also some rewarding ethnic eateries and a few quirky backstreet joints hidden slightly off the beaten path. Try either end of Robson for Japanese and Korean diners or the Granville Strip for brunch-serving bars.

PRICE GUIDE

The following cost guide is used in this chapter's eating reviews:

$$$	over $25 per main dish
$$	$10 to $25 per main dish
$	under $10 per main dish

C RESTAURANT Map pp58-9   Seafood $$$

☎ 604-681-1164; www.crestaurant.com;
1600 Howe St; mains $28-40; ⊙ 11:30am-2:30pm
Mon-Fri, 5:30-11pm daily; 🚍 C21

This pioneering seafood restaurant
overlooking False Creek isn't cheap – drop
by for lunch if you want to budget a bit –
but its revelatory approach to regional
sustainable fish and shellfish makes it the
city's best seafood experience. You'll be
hard-pressed to find smoked salmon with
cucumber jelly served anywhere else,
but there's also a reverence for simple
preparation that reveals the delicate flavors
in dishes such as local side-stripe prawns
and Queen Charlotte scallops. Check ahead:
early evening three-course prix-fixe specials
are offered periodically.

LE CROCODILE Map pp58-9   French $$$

☎ 604-669-4298; www.lecrocodilerestaurant.com;
909 Burrard St, entrance on Smithe St; mains $22-
36; ⊙ 11:30am-2pm Mon-Fri, 5:30-10pm Mon-Sat;
🚍 22

Tucked along a side street in an
unassuming building that resembles a cast-
off from a shopping mall, this surprising
Parisian-style dining room is right up there
with the city's top-end best. Instead of
focusing on experimental shenanigans that
only please the chefs, it's perfected a menu
of classic French dishes, each prepared
with consummate cooking skill and served
by excellent wait staff. Try the braised
veal shank with wild mushrooms, washed
down with a smashing bottle from the
mother country.

CHAMBAR Map pp58-9   Belgian $$$

☎ 604-879-7119; www.chambar.com; 562 Beatty
St; mains $14-29; ⊙ 5:30pm-midnight;
Ⓜ Stadium-Chinatown

This romantic, brick-lined cave –
atmospherically lit by candles at night –
is a great place for a lively chat among
Vancouver's urban professionals. The
sophisticated Euro menu includes perfectly
prepared highlights like pan-seared
scallops and velvet-soft lamb shank, but
the delectable *moules et frites* (mussels and
fries) are the way to go. An impressive wine
and cocktail list (try a Blue Fig Martini) is
coupled with a great Belgian beer menu,
including its own Chambar Ale. For more
casual fare, check out Medina Café,
Chambar's daytime-only sister next door.

NU Map pp58-9   West Coast $$

☎ 604-646-4668; www.whatsnu.com; 1661
Granville St; mains $10-24; ⊙ 11am-1am Mon-Fri,
10:30am-1am Sat, 10:30am-midnight Sun; 🚍 C21

Tucked under Granville Bridge's north end,
this swish and knowing eatery looks like
a decadent 1970s hotel bar – the perfect
place to don your gold silk cravat. The
menu ranges from French-influenced
tasting plates to delectable West Coast
mains like Salt Spring mussels and grilled
bison. Don't forget a few cocktails,
preferably on the lovely wraparound
sunset-facing deck. And consider Sunday's
jazz brunch (from 10:30am, a popular
locals' favorite).

BIN 941 Map pp58-9   Fusion $$

www.bin941.com; 941 Davie St; dishes $9-15;
⊙ 5pm-2am Mon-Sat, 5pm-midnight Sun; 🚍 6

A hopping little spot that's packed almost
every night, cave-like Bin 941 kicked off
Vancouver's current small-plates fever. Not
resting on its laurels, it's still arguably the
best spot in town for late-night nibbles and
a few glasses of wine with friends – which
will quickly include the people squeezed
next to you at the adjoining small table.
Tuck into treats like sustainable tuna tartar
and beef tenderloin, but don't miss the
excellent crab cakes.

LA BODEGA Map pp58-9   Mediterranean $$

www.labodegavancouver.com; 1277 Howe St;
mains $8-12; ⊙ 4:30pm-midnight Mon-Fri,
5pm-midnight Sat, 5-11pm Sun; 🚍 10

It's all about the tasting plates at this
country-style tapas bar, one of the most
authentic Spanish restaurants in Vancouver.
Pull up a chair, order a jug of sangria and
decide on a few shareable treats from the
extensive menu – if you're feeling spicy,
the chorizo sausage hits the spot and the
Spanish meatballs are justifiably popular.
There's a great atmosphere here, so don't
be surprised if you find yourself staying for
more than a few hours.

TEMPLETON Map pp58-9   Burgers, Breakfast $$

http://thetempleton.blogspot.com; 1087 Granville
St; mains $8-12; ⊙ 9am-11pm Mon-Wed, 9am-
1am Thu-Sun; 🚍 10; ♿

A funky chrome-and-vinyl '50s diner with
a twist, Templeton chefs up plus-sized
organic burgers, addictive fries, vegetarian
quesadillas and perhaps the best hangover

cure in town – try the 'Big Ass Breakfast' and you won't need to eat for days. Sadly, the mini jukeboxes on the tables don't work, but you can console yourself with a waistline-busting chocolate ice-cream float. Beer here is of the local microbrew variety. Avoid weekend peak times or you'll be queuing for ages.

LA TAQUERIA Map pp58-9   Mexican $
www.lataqueria.ca; 322 W Hastings St; 4-taco combo $9.50; ⏰ 11am-8:30pm Mon-Wed, 11am-10pm Thu-Sat; 🚌 8

Arrive off-peak to avoid the crush at this delightful hole-in-the-wall and you'll be able to grab a perch at the turquoise-colored counter. Listening to the grassroots Mexican soundtrack and kitchen staff chatting in Spanish is the perfect accompaniment to a few superbly prepared soft tacos: go for the four-part combo and choose from fillings like grilled fish, pork cheeks and house-marinated beef, with top-notch, locally sourced ingredients. Vegetarians have some tasty choices (the veggie combo is cheaper than the meat combo) and great-value quesadillas are also available. Save room for a glass of cinnamony *horchata* (a milkshake-style traditional beverage).

GALLERY CAFÉ Map pp58-9   Cafe $
www.thegallerycafe.ca; 750 Hornby St; mains $5-10; ⏰ 9am-9pm Mon-Fri, 9:30am-6pm Sat & Sun; 🚌 5

The mezzanine level of the Vancouver Art Gallery (p56) is home to a chatty indoor dining area complemented by one of downtown's best and biggest outdoor patios. The food is generally of the salad and sandwiches variety, but it's well worth stopping in for a drink, especially if you take your coffee (or bottled beer) out to the parasol-forested outdoor area, where you can top up your tan and watch over the Robson St clamor.

JAPADOG Map pp58-9   Japanese, Fusion $
www.japadog.com; 530 Robson St; mains $5-8; ⏰ noon-7pm; 🚌 15

You'll have spotted the patient lunchtime line-ups at the three Japadog fusion hotdog stands around town (the one at the corner of Burrard and Pender Sts is usually the least crowded), but these celebrated, ever-*genki* Japanese expats also opened

top picks

CHEAP EATS

- Go Fish (p142)
- Japadog (left)
- La Taqueria (left)
- Hawkers Delight (p140)
- Theresa's (p141)

their own storefront here in 2010. The small menu is almost the same – think turkey smokies with miso-mayo sauce and bratwursts with onion, daikon and soy – but there's also a naughty choc-banana dessert dog. The tiny round tables are usually taken, but the take-out window does a roaring trade. Cash only.

GORILLA FOOD Map pp58-9   Vegetarian $
www.gorillafood.com; 436 Richards St; mains $4-7.50; ⏰ 11am-7pm Mon-Sat; 🚌 20

Like stepping into a shaded forest nook, this smashing little subterranean eatery is lined with woodsy flourishes and the kind of fresh-faced, healthy-living vegans who will make you want to adopt a new lifestyle. Organic raw food is the approach, which means treats such as seaweed wraps and pizza made from a dehydrated seed crust topped with tomato sauce, tenderized zucchini and mashed avocado. Make space for an icy almond shake dessert, and some carrot cake slathered with cashew cream.

FINCH'S Map pp58-9   Cafe $
www.finchteahouse.com; 353 W Pender St; mains $3-8; ⏰ 9-5pm Mon-Fri, 11am-4pm Sat; 🚌 4

If you want a seat at one of the dinged old dining tables, arrive off-peak at this ever-buzzing, often sunny corner cafe that has a 'granny-chic' look combining creaky wooden floors and junkshop bric-a-brac. You'll be joining in-the-know hipsters and creative-types who've been calling this their local for years. They come for the well-priced breakfasts (egg and soldiers is from $2.50) and a range of fresh-prepared baguette sandwiches and house-made soups. A quirky little hangout, this is a great spot for an afternoon cake and coffee, but be prepared to wait for a perch to call your own.

STANLEY PARK

If you haven't brought a picnic with you – the park has several welcoming beaches and some tree-fringed grassy expanses made for alfresco noshing – Vancouver's verdant green heart has four main dining options covering a range of budgets. Wherever you dine, try for a window seat so you can enjoy a side dish of dense forest canopy or panoramic sea-to-sky views.

FISH HOUSE IN STANLEY PARK

Map p63   Seafood $$$

☎ 604-681-7275, 877-681-7275; www
.fishhousestanleypark.com; 8901 Stanley Park Dr;
mains $20-33; ⏱ 11:30am-10pm Mon-Fri, 11am-
10pm Sat & Sun; 🚌 19
The park's fanciest dine-out, the double-patioed Fish House serves some of the city's best seafood. The menu changes based on seasonal availability but typical favorites include chili sablefish and cedar-planked char, while the fresh oyster bar is ever-popular with visiting shuckers. Weekend brunch is a highlight – salmon bagel Benedict is recommended – and if you haven't eaten enough already the desserts are also surprisingly creative: save room for chocolate lava cake, then run around the park four times to work it off.

TEAHOUSE Map p63   West Coast $$

☎ 604-669-3281, 800-280-9893; www
.vancouverdine.com; Stanley Park Dr, Ferguson
Point; mains $18-28; ⏱ 11:30am-10pm Mon-Sat,
10:30am-1pm Sun; 🚌 19
Returning to the name it started with in the 1930s, the former Sequoia Grill is a cheery spot to enjoy contemporary West Coast classics like pan-seared BC halibut and Fraser Valley duck, along with smashing sunset views over Burrard Inlet from its heated patio. A good place for weekend brunch – crab eggs Benedict is recommended – the park's Third Beach is a few steps away and is ideal for an evening saunter.

PROSPECT POINT CAFÉ

Map p63   Burgers, Fast Food $$

www.prospectpoint.ca; Stanley Park Dr; mains $9-
18; ⏱ takeout 9am-8pm, cafe 11am-8pm; 🚌 19
A typical family-style tourist eatery and takeout with an attractive forest-surrounded patio deck, this is the place

most Stanley Park visitors end up eating at – usually because their tour bus has dropped them outside to partake of the adjoining gift shop. The takeout includes all the usual menu suspects (think burgers, hot dogs and chicken strips), while the seated patio cafe adds slightly overpriced salmon, steak and fish-and-chips mains along with a full bar.

STANLEY'S PARK BAR & GRILL

Map p63   Burgers, Fast Food $$

www.stanleysbar.ca; 610 Pipeline Rd; mains $9-18;
⏱ 11am-8pm Jun-Sep; 🚌 19
Overlooking the gardens and the Malkin Bowl outdoor theater, this casual summer-only resto-bar in the Tudor-style pavilion building has the park's biggest outdoor patio, although the view is dense forest rather than rippling seafront. A comfort-food menu that mirrors the Prospect Point Café (they share the same owner) means everything from burgers to steaks as well as a good range of Whistler Brewing beers and cocktail slushies. This is a good spot for a relaxing drink at the end of your park visit.

WEST END

If you can walk along the West End's restaurant-packed streets without stopping to eat, you either have a newly installed stomach staple or the willpower of a particularly virtuous (and not very hungry) saint. But it's not just the sheer number of restaurants sardined along Robson, Denman and Davie Sts that is impressive; the vast variety and generally good value make this Vancouver's best midrange dining 'hood, where it's easy to be overwhelmed by the choices tempting your taste buds.

LE GAVROCHE Map pp68-9   French $$$

☎ 604-685-3924; www.legavroche.ca; 1616
Alberni St; mains $19-39; ⏱ 5:30-11pm; 🚌 5
Hidden along a residential side street, it's easy to overlook this lovely heritage-home restaurant that fuses West Coast ingredients with an array of classic and contemporary French approaches. Emphasizing *les fruits de mer* with practiced flair – check out the Alaska black cod with burnt orange and anise sauce – it's an excellent choice for a romantic dinner. Wine lovers should also rejoice: there's a fantastic selection here

that might just have you crying into your glass with gratitude.

COAST Map pp68–9   Seafood $$$

☎ 604-685-5010; www.coastrestaurant.ca; 1054 Alberni St; mains $17-30; ☽ 11:30am-1am Mon-Thu, 11:30am-2am Fri, 4:30pm-2am Sat, 4:30pm-1am Sun; 🚌 5

The move from its original Yaletown location has upped the size and coolness quotient of this buzzing seafood joint where Vancouver movers and shakers like to be seen scoffing a wide array of aquatic treats. Knowing reinventions of the classics include prawn or lobster flatbread pizzas, but it's the mighty seafood platter of local salmon, cod, scallops and tiger prawns that true fish nuts should indulge in. Fish-and-chips (try the red snapper variety) is $14 on Sundays and there's also an excellent raw bar with oysters a'plenty. After dinner, hit the adjacent O Lounge for a swanky cocktail.

RAINCITY GRILL Map pp68–9   West Coast $$$

☎ 604-685-7337; www.raincitygrill.com; 1193 Denman St; mains $17-30; ☽ 11:30am-2:30pm Mon-Fri, 10:30am-2pm Sat & Sun, 5-10pm daily; 🚌 5

This smashing English Bay restaurant was sourcing and serving unique BC ingredients long before the fashion for local Fanny Bay oysters took hold. It's a great showcase for fine West Coast cuisine; the weekend brunch here is a local legend, and the $30 three-course tasting menu served between 5pm and 6pm is a great fine-dining bargain. Make sure you also check out the wine list: it's one of the city's best. If you're on the move, drop by the take-out window (open 11:30am to 7pm) for $10 fish-and-chips, then hit nearby English Bay beach for a picnic.

LOLITA'S Map pp68–9   Mexican $$

www.lolitasrestaurant.com; 1326 Davie St; mains $18-25; ☽ 4:30pm-1am Mon-Fri, 11am-11pm Sat & Sun; 🚌 6

This lively cantina is ever-popular with in-the-know West End hipsters for good reason: a great place to find yourself late at night, its warm and mellow party vibe makes you feel like you're hanging out with friends in a bar at the beach. Turn your taste buds on with a few rounds of gold tequila or a fruity cocktail or three, but

top picks

SEAFOOD

- C Restaurant (p130)
- Coast (left)
- Go Fish (p142)
- Fish House in Stanley Park (opposite)
- Blue Water Café (p135)

make sure you take a booze respite with some spicy, fusionesque fare, including the wonderful halibut tacos. Return for a hangover-busting weekend tropical brunch.

IL NIDO Map pp68–9   Italian $$

www.cafeilnido.net; 780 Thurlow St; mains $17-25; ☽ 11:30am-2:30pm Mon-Fri, 5:30-10pm Mon-Sat; 🚌 5

Hidden in the courtyard of an old-school apartment building, this good-value Italian gem has a warm and casual ambience, a secret little patio and a menu of well-prepared Italian comfort foods. A great respite from the Robson St shops at lunchtime – check the daily pizza or pasta specials – it becomes a romantic, mood-lit nook at night, when the chatty patio is the place to be. Menu highlights include the house-made polpettine bison meatballs and the delectable lobster-stuffed ravioli.

SURA KOREAN CUISINE

Map pp68–9   Asian Fusion $$

1518 Robson St; mains $10-18; ☽ 11am-10:30pm Mon-Thu, 11am-2am Fri & Sat, 11am-12:30am Sun; 🚌 5

From the 1400-block of Robson St and around onto Denman and Davie Sts, you'll suddenly find yourself among a finger-licking smorgasbord of popular Korean and Japanese casual eateries. Originally catering to the homesick ESL students who still call the area home, Vancouverites have embraced this area as a great way to indulge in authentic Asian dining. A cut above its student-luring siblings, Sura offers awesome Korean comfort dishes in a white-walled, bistro-like setting. Try the spicy beef soup, kimchee pancakes and excellent *dolsot bibimbap* (beef, veggies and a still-cooking egg in a hot stone bowl).

GUU WITH GARLIC Map pp68-9 Japanese $$

www.guu-izakaya.com; 1689 Robson St; mains
$8-14; 🕒 5:30pm-midnight; 🚌 5
One of the many excellent Asian bistros,
sushi spots and noodle joints at Robson St's
West End tip, you'll be chilling with
the visiting ESL students at this highly
authentic and ever-welcoming *izakaya*.
Heaping hotpots and steaming noodle
bowls are on offer but it's best to
experiment with a few Japanese-bar tapas
plates, such as black cod with miso mayo,
deep-fried egg pumpkin balls or a finger-
lickin' basket of *tori-karaage* fried chicken
that will make you turn your back on KFC
forever. Garlic is liberally used in most
dishes, and it's best to arrive at the 5:30pm
opening time to be sure of a seat.

MOTOMACHI SHOKUDO
Map pp68-9 Japanese $$
740 Denman St; mains $8-14; 🕒 noon-11pm; 🚌 5
One of Vancouver's very best ramen
houses, this evocative but incredibly
tiny spot – there are fewer than 20 seats –
combines lightning fast service with perfect
comfort dishes. First-timers should try the
New Generation Miso Ramen, brimming
with bean sprouts, sweet corn, shredded
cabbage and barbecued pork. An added
plus is that most ingredients are organic.
If the line-up's long, try its older sister
noodlery a few doors south. Cash or debit
cards only.

MR PICKWICK'S Map pp68-9 Seafood $$
www.mrpickwicks.bc.ca; 1007 Denman St; mains
$8-13; 🕒 11:30am-11pm; 🚌 5; ♿
The city's best Brit-style fish-and-chippery
knows exactly how to make your favorite
comfort food – even the chips are chunkily
satisfying and you won't have to ask twice
for malt vinegar. As well as the classics,
batter-fried salmon and crunchy crab cakes
are excellent, while the house-made tartar
and lemon dill sauces are fresh and tangy.
Check the daily specials and try a draft Dead
Frog beer. The friendly service is outstanding
here and it's a great spot to bring your kids.

SUSHI MART Map pp68-9 Japanese $
www.sushimart.com; 1686 Robson St; mains $6-10;
🕒 11:30am-8pm Tue-Thu & Sun, 11:30am-9pm Fri
& Sat; 🚌 5
You'll be rubbing shoulders with chatty
young Asians at the large communal

STREET-FOOD RUMBLE

An obscure 1970s bylaw has, somewhat unbelievably,
restricted Vancouver's street-food offerings in recent
years to just two approaches: roasted chestnuts or hot
dogs. So while other cities – most notably Portland
in the US – have unfurled a full menu of fantastic
hawker stands to their hungry residents, Vancouverites have been restricted to nuts and tube steaks.
While the celebrated Japadog (p131) has taken
advantage of this by offering fusion, nori-covered
hotdogs to adoring queues of locals (kicking off a fad
for Mexican and Indian-fusion dogs in the process),
the city finally relented in mid-2010 by announcing a
year-long experiment to relax the ridiculous old rules
with 17 lip-smacking new vendors. While local taste
buds perked up in anticipation – anyone who's visited
Richmond's Summer Night Market (p118) knows just
how good the street-food scene here could be – it's
hoped that this is just the start of a golden age of
Vancouver street dining.

dining table here, one of the best spots in
town for a sushi feast in a casual setting.
Check the fresh-sheet blackboard showing
what's available and then tuck into expertly
prepared and well-priced shareable
platters of all your fave *nigiri*, *maki* and
sashimi treats. Wash it all down with a
large bottle of Sapporo or a hot sake
or two.

GRIND CAFE Map pp68-9 Cafe $
1500 W Georgia St; mains $5-8; 🕒 7am-4pm Mon-
Fri; 🚌 252
If all you really want is a fresh-prepared
sandwich, with a hearty bowl of soup or a
crispy green salad, this unpretentious
locals-secret is recommended. The service
here is excellent and the generously
filled sarnies – bulging wraps or thick-cut
doorstoppers – are great value: check the
blackboard when you walk in for the day's
combo special. A good spot for a cake and
coffee pit stop, also consider collecting a
bag lunch here for a picnic in Stanley Park
a few minutes walk away.

YALETOWN

A favorite hangout for Vancouver's rich and
beautiful people – if you really need to see a
lap dog carried in a designer handbag, this is
where it'll happen – Yaletown is a great area for
a splurge-worthy dinner. Stroll along Hamilton

and Mainland Sts and you and your gold credit card will be spoilt for choice. Luckily, style over substance is not the general rule here: even if you spend a little more than usual for your meal, it will be worth it.

CIOPPINO'S MEDITERRANEAN GRILL
Map p72   Italian $$$

☎ 604-688-7466; www.cioppinosyaletown.com; 1133 Hamilton St; mains $25-40; 🕑 5-10pm; Ⓜ Yaletown-Roundhouse

Not your standard Italian joint, this fine-dining Mediterranean eatery deploys the *cucina naturale* approach to cooking, which aims to reveal the delicate natural flavors of a range of regionally sourced ingredients. The warm wood and terra-cotta interior is the perfect setting in which to dip into West Coast dishes tweaked with Italian flourishes – try the lobster and crab cannelloni or spit-roasted duck breast – while the international wine list should keep you jolly all evening.

BLUE WATER CAFÉ Map p72   Seafood $$$

☎ 604-688-8078; www.bluewatercafe.net; 1095 Hamilton St; mains $22-44; 🕑 5pm-midnight; Ⓜ Yaletown-Roundhouse

Under the expert eye of chef Frank Pabst, this high-concept seafood restaurant has become Vancouver's best posh oyster bar and the pinnacle of Yaletown fine dining. House music gently percolates through the brick-lined, cobalt-blue interior, while seafood towers, arctic char and BC sablefish grace the tables inside and on the patio outside. If you feel like an adventure, head for the semicircular raw bar and watch the whirling blades prepare delectable sushi and sashimi, served with the restaurant's signature soya-seaweed dipping sauce.

GLOWBAL GRILL STEAK & SATAY
Map p72   Fusion $$$

☎ 604-602-0835; www.glowbalgrill.com; 1079 Mainland St; mains $17-40; 🕑 11:30am-1am Mon-Thu, 11:30am-2am Fri & Sat, 4pm-1am Sun; Ⓜ Yaletown-Roundhouse

Casting a wide net that catches the power-lunch, after-work and late-night fashionista crowds, this hip but unpretentious joint has a comfortable, lounge-like feel. Its menu of classy dishes fuses West Coast ingredients with Asian and Mediterranean flourishes – the prawn linguine is ace and

the finger-licking array of satay sticks is a recommended starter. Check the glass-walled meat cellar on the counter and choose your desired steak cut, and make sure you head to the back-room Afterglow bar (p153) for a nightcap.

top picks
VANCOUVER COOKBOOKS

The city's leading chefs and top restaurants have been sharing their tips and recipes with the locals in book form for years. Pick up one of these unique souvenirs of your visit at stores around town – for the tastiest selection, check out Barbara-Jo's Books to Cooks (p125).

- Ocean Wise Cookbook, Jane Mundy (2010) – created by the Vancouver Aquarium, Ocean Wise encourages restaurants and seafood purveyors across Canada to employ sustainable fishing practices. This book showcases great seafood recipes from chefs and eateries in Vancouver and beyond.
- Vancouver Cooks 2, Chefs' Table Society (2009) – seventy Vancouver-area chefs come together to offer more than 100 great recipes that give a true taste of the region and its cosmopolitan, sometimes eclectic dining approach. Look out for treats from Rob Feenie, Vikram Vij and Tojo Hidekazu, among others.
- Blue Water Café Seafood Cookbook, Frank Pabst (2009) – one of Vancouver's leading chefs, working the kitchen at one of its best restaurants (left), Pabst's book covers 80 aquatic recipes, from bigeye tuna tataki to periwinkles with stinging nettle puree. Impress your friends at your next dinner party.
- Vij's: Elegant and Inspired Indian Cuisine, Vikram Vij and Meeru Dhalwala (2006) – mirroring the authors' celebrated Indian restaurant (p143), the recipes here offer an exciting twist on the subcontinent's traditional meals, giving away the secrets to some of Vij's mouthwatering signature dishes.
- Fresh: Seasonal Recipes Made with Local Foods, John Bishop (2007) – a celebration of BC produce and its dedicated growers, this sumptuous 100-recipe book underlines Bishop's credentials as the city's leading sustainable restaurateur. Read it in his eponymous restaurant (p144) and he'll likely stroll over and sign it for you.

REGIONAL TASTING LOUNGE
Map p72   Fusion $$

☎ 604-689-8318; www.r.tl; 1130 Mainland St; mains $15-29; ⊙ 5-11pm Mon-Wed, 5pm-midnight Thu, 5pm-1am Fri & Sat; Ⓜ Yaletown-Roundhouse

An intimate, mood-lit dining room with an innovative menu approach: every three months it adds a new regional focus, which brings taste-bud-hugging treats from different parts of the world. Foodie focuses have included Italy, Spain, Greece and New Orleans, but there's always a selection of Pacific Northwest classics if you want to taste-trip BC, too. Small plates are popular here, so consider ordering to share. There's a three-course $29 tasting menu available daily plus a full bar: the cocktails here, including the lovely pistachio sour, are recommended.

EAT THAT BAR: GREAT DINE-OUT ALTERNATIVES

Due to Vancouver's murky and conflicting liquor laws, the labels 'bar' and 'restaurant' are often interchangeable here. But just because a bar has a large menu of greasy comfort food doesn't mean it's a great place to dine. Those watering holes where the eating is almost as good as the drinking are listed below, with cross-references to their reviews in the Drinking chapter.

Three Lions Café (p156)
Irish Heather (p156)
Cascade Room (p156)
Yaletown Brewing Company (p154)
Alibi Room (p155)
Black Frog (p155)
Steamworks Brewing Company (p155)
Whip (p157)

GASTOWN

Vancouver's oldest neighborhood is back on the menu for hungry travelers. After years of offering no more than seedy pub dives and a smattering of boring tourist-trap eateries, the heritage buildings are coming back to life with some of the city's most innovative gourmet hangouts and convivial comfort-food haunts. Make sure you also peruse the Gastown bar listings (see p154), since many of the area's bars are high on the must-eat-here list too. Things are changing rapidly down here, so keep your eyes peeled for regular new openings.

BONETA Map p76   Fusion $$$
☎ 604-684-1844; www.boneta.ca; 1 W Cordova St; mains $15-29; ⊙ 5:30pm-midnight; 🚌 4

Typifying Gastown's extensive transformation, this old bank building – one of the oldest in the city – now houses a bold-but-casual eatery where the chef's ever-fertile imagination is sparked by regional seasonal ingredients. Expect taste-tripping riffs like smoked bison carpaccio with sherry vinaigrette or grilled rack of lamb with curried cauliflower. There's a small but excellent wine selection but start with a cocktail or two: the bar is far from being an afterthought here and the mixologists are expert. Plans were afoot during research for this book for a possible move to a new location, so call ahead to check.

POURHOUSE Map p76   Fusion, West Coast $$
☎ 604-568-7022; www.pourhousevancouver.com; 162 Water St; mains $12-26; ⊙ 11am-1am Mon-Sat, 11am-midnight Sun; Ⓜ Waterfront

Like a cool reinvention of an old-school saloon (without the kitsch) this swank resto-bar has a solid spruce wood counter, century-old light fittings and a clever row of repurposed radiators dividing the drinking from the eating areas. If you're not just here for a tipple – reinvented classic cocktails like 'Gold Fashioned' are a specialty – aim for a table and tuck into gourmet comfort dishes like cassoulet-style pork and beans or local-beef sloppy joe.

NUBA Map p76   Middle Eastern $$
www.nuba.ca; 207 W Hastings St; mains $8-19; ⊙ 11:30am-11pm Mon-Wed, 11:30am-midnight Thu-Sat; 1-11pm Sun; 🚌 8

Tucked under the landmark Dominion Building, this hopping subterranean Lebanese restaurant attracts budget noshers and cool hipsters in equal measure. If you're not sure what to go for, have the good-value falafel plate ($9), heaped with hummus, tabboulleh, salad, pita and brown rice. It'll make you realize what wholesome, made-from-scratch food is supposed to taste like. More substantial fare – grilled lamb, Cornish hen etc – has been added to the menu since the eatery moved from its hole-in-the-wall site across the street, and there's also regular live music. Excellent service.

DEACON'S CORNER

Map p76   Burgers, Breakfast $

www.deaconscorner.ca; 101 Main St; mains $6-13;
🕑 7am-5pm Mon-Fri, 9am-5pm Sat & Sun; 🚌 8

The perfect Gastown combination of new
gentrification and old-school good value,
this lively neighborhood diner has been
luring Vancouverites to a grubby part of
town they've previously avoided. Locals
come for the large, hangover-busting
breakfasts (biscuits with sausage, gravy
and eggs is recommended if you want your
weekly calorific intake in a single meal),
while lunches include good-value grilled
sandwiches (go for the pulled pork) and
heaping fish-and-chips.

JUDAS GOAT Map p76   Fusion $

www.judasgoat.ca; 27 Blood Alley; plates $6-10;
🕑 5pm-midnight Mon-Sat; 🚌 4

This smashing 28-seat, mosaic-and-marble
nook became a local foodie favorite
soon after its 2010 opening. Named
after the goats used to lead sheep off
slaughterhouse trucks, it's nailed the art
of small, simply-prepared but invitingly
gourmet tapas treats like beef brisket
meatballs, lamb cheek wrapped in Savoy
cabbage and scallop tartare with pork
rinds. Like its Salt Tasting Room (p155) brother
next door, you'll also find a good (although
much shorter) wine and Spanish sherry
drinks list. Arrive off-peak to avoid line-ups:
there's a 90-minute time limit for diners.

CHINATOWN

Pender and Keefer Sts (between Columbia
St and Gore Ave) are your best bet for an
authentic Chinese meal, but there's more
than Asian dining to this rapidly evolv-
ing old neighborhood. Consider dropping
by for the weekend Summer Night Market
(p79), when steamy hawker stands will entice
your taste buds, and don't forget Richmond
(see p146), where there's a far larger array of
both traditional and new-wave Chinese
restaurants.

BAO BEI Map p79   Asian, Fusion $$

☎ 604-688-0876; www.bao-bei.ca; 163 Keefer St;
mains $10-18; 🕑 5:30pm-midnight Tue-Sat;
Ⓜ Stadium-Chinatown

This chic-but-welcoming Chinese brasserie
soon lured the hipsters when it opened in
2010. From its prawn and chive dumplings

top picks

ASIAN

- Maenam (p144)
- Bao Bei (left)
- Tojo's (p142)
- Guu with Garlic (p134)
- Phnom Penh (below)

to its addictive short-rib-filled buns, it's
brought a welcome contemporary flair
to eating out in the area, combined with
an innovative approach to dishes and
ingredients: top-of-the-range organic
meat and sustainable seafood are used
throughout. It's easy to find yourself
seduced by the relaxed, candlelit ambience,
especially if you hit the excellent cocktail
menu. Reservations not accepted so avoid
peak 7pm to 9pm dining times, if possible.

PHNOM PENH Map p79   Vietnamese $$

244 E Georgia St; mains $8-18; 🕑 10am-9pm Mon-
Thu, 10am-10pm Fri & Sat; 🚌 3

Arrive early or late to avoid the queues
at this locals' favorite eatery. The dishes
here are split between Cambodian and
Vietnamese soul-food classics, such as
crispy frogs legs, spicy garlic crab and
prawn and sprout filled pancakes. Don't
leave without sampling a steamed rice
cake, stuffed with pork, shrimp, coconut
and scallions, and washed down with an
ice-cold bottle of Tsingtao. This is the kind
of place that makes Vancouver Canada's
most authentic ethnic-food city.

ACME CAFE Map p79   Burgers, Breakfast $$

www.acmecafe.ca; 51 W Hastings St; mains $8-13;
🕑 8am-9pm Mon-Sat, 10am-9pm Sun; 🚌 8; ♿

The black-and-white, deco-style interior
here is enough to warm up anyone on a
rainy day – or maybe it's the comfy
booths and retro-cool U-shaped counter.
But it's not just about looks at this new
neighborhood fixture. The hipsters have
been flocking here since day one for good-
value hearty breakfasts and heaping
comfort-food lunches flavored with a
gourmet flourish: the meatloaf, chicken
club and shrimp guacamole sandwiches
are grand but why not drop by for an

afternoon coffee or Ovaltine plus a slab of house-baked fruit pie? Good kids menu.

HON'S WUN-TUN HOUSE

Map p79   Chinese $$
www.hons.ca; 268 E Keefer St; mains $6-18;
11am-11pm Sun-Thu, 11am-midnight Fri & Sat;
3

Part of the city's favorite Chinese-restaurant minichain, Hon's flagship Chinatown branch is suffused with inviting cooking smells and clamorously noisy diners. The giant, 300-plus menu ranges from satisfying dim sum brunches to steaming wonton soups, bobbing with juicy dumplings. For something different, try the congee rice porridge, a fancy-free soul-food dish that takes three hours to prepare and comes in seafood, chicken and beef varieties.

EVERYTHING CAFÉ Map p79   Cafe $

75 E Pender St; mains $5-9; 8am-6pm;
M Stadium-Chinatown;

Exemplifying Chinatown's rapid gentrification, this cool, recently opened pit stop would easily be at home on hipster-hugging South Main. Snag a perch at the window to watch the world go by, or sink into the studded leather bench running the length of one wall. A small but well-prepared array of coffees is available and there's an ever-growing menu of hunky sandwiches leaning heavily toward meat: the cold cuts are locally sourced. Cakes like the excellent chocolate banana bread pudding will lure your sweet tooth. Cooked lunches are available from 11am to 3pm and plans were afoot during research for this book to open in the evening.

NEW TOWN BAKERY & RESTAURANT

Map p79   Chinese $
158 E Pender St; dishes $5-9; 6:30am-8:30pm;
3

Arguably the area's best Chinese bakery, this lively, old-school diner specializes in steam buns, Chinese pastries and dim sum, served from giant steamers on the counter. The warm, moist barbecue pork buns are the bakery's signature snack and they make an ideal takeout – there's not much of an ambience here, so there's no real reason to stick around. The buns also come in several vegetarian varieties.

SOUTH MAIN (SOMA)

Renowned for alt-shopping options plus its independent bar and coffee-shop scene,

---

FESTIVAL TASTING MENU

Vancouver bulges like an overstuffed sushi roll with events for food and wine nuts. Time your trip right and you can add some enjoyable waist-expanding experiences to your visit.

If you're here in winter, make room for Dine Out Vancouver (p12), when the city's top restaurants offer two- or three-course tasting menus for $18, $28 or $38. There's a similar but more localized event in October called Taste of Yaletown, which promotes that area's excellent dining options.

Lovers of all things foodie should also drop by June's annual Eat Vancouver (www.eat-vancouver.com) festival. Western Canada's largest food and cooking event, the three-day extravaganza is dripping with culinary demonstrations, celebrity chef appearances and a tasting area where the city's leading restaurants ply their wares.

If you're more a fan of liquid lunches, stagger into town in March for the Vancouver Playhouse International Wine Festival (p13), where neophytes and tipple snobs can rub shoulders and pretend they're not getting drunk. Ale fans also have their own event with May's annual Vancouver Craft Beer Week (p13) staging sudsy tastings and food-pairings across the city.

If BC's cornucopia of regional produce intrigues, check into the annual, one-day Feast of Fields (www.feastoffields .com) events held in August and September at different locations across the region. With great local chefs serving fresh, finger-licking dishes at alfresco locations, the event highlights the importance of regional suppliers and sustainable farming. The $85 entry ticket – $15 for under-15s and free for kids under six – includes enough food, wine and beer samples to keep you full for days.

Also consider the University of British Columbia's weekend Apple Festival (www.ubcbotanicalgarden.org/events; adult/child under 12yr $3/free) in mid-October. It's a chance to sample as many seedy treats as you can cram in your mouth, ranging from regional favorites such as Spartan and Macintosh to unusual heritage strains including Ambrosia and Grimes Golden. And, of course, there's the longest peel contest, with prizes for whoever can peel the longest unbroken apple skin.

South Main is also an intriguing area for eclectic, one-of-a-kind dining experiences. Most radiate from the intersection with E Broadway, with additional pockets of tasty treats up to E 48th Ave, where the city's Little India area offers great value cheap-and-cheerful curry buffets. Make sure you also peruse the SoMa bar listings (see p156) since many of the area's drinkeries are also on the must-eat-here list.

top picks
VEGETARIAN

- Naam (p145)
- Gorilla Food (p131)
- Foundation (below)
- All India Sweets & Restaurant (p147)
- Theresa's (p141)

HABIT LOUNGE Map p83 — West Coast $$
www.habitlounge.ca; 2610 Main St; mains $10-18; 9am-midnight; 3

Since you're obviously craving a little 1970s retro, don your flares and hit the brown vinyl booths in this cool reproduction resto-bar – preferably with a view of the wall-mounted shagpile carpet. It's not all about looks, though: there's a menu of clever reinventions of old-school dishes – try the lamb meatloaf – and a funky little list of disassembled cocktails that come to your table in little 'bento boxes' of bottles: you follow the recipe card and shake them together. There's also an amazing array of 21 Canadian-made whiskies, and a very popular weekend brunch.

PUBLIC LOUNGE EATERY
Map p83 — West Coast $$
www.publiclounge.ca; 3289 Main St; mains $9-22; 4:30pm-midnight; 3

Oddly tucked between the Main St hubs of E Broadway and 20th Ave, this art-lined, candlelit little spot is worth the walk. Don't bother trying to find a space on the patio though – it's not only tiny but traffic-noisy. Instead, duck inside for a small wooden table facing the cheese and charcuterie board or perch at the L-shaped bar with a large bottle of Czechvar from the always-interesting booze list. Start with a plate of tasty tapas – along with the fresh board, the tenderloin steak bites are popular – then fill up on a delectable main of sesame-crusted tuna.

CRAVE Map p83 — West Coast $$
www.craveonmain.com; 3941 Main St; mains $9-18; 11am-10pm Tue-Fri, 9am-10pm Sat, 9am-9pm Sun; 3

One of Main St's best neighborhood haunts – especially on its hidden back patio – this often hopping resto-bar is an ideal end-of-day destination. The candlelit

tables and darkwood interior trigger a chilled out ambience (the friendly servers and good-value beer pitchers also help) and there's a menu of nicely tweaked comfort-food classics ranging from organic burgers to braised lamb shank with mashed potatoes. The velvet-soft chipotle-covered baby back ribs, however, is the menu winner.

CHUTNEY VILLA Map p83 — Indian $$
www.chutneyvilla.com; 147 E Broadway; mains $8-18; 11:30am-10pm Mon, Wed & Thu, 11:30am-11pm Fri & Sat; 9

Don't be surprised to get a hug from the owner when entering this warmly enveloping South Indian restaurant that lures savvy SoMa-ites with its lusciously spiced curries (the lamb poriyal is a favorite), best served with fluffy dosas to mop them up. There's an outstanding Sunday brunch combo of veggie curries and piping hot Indian coffee, plus a drinks list of bottled Indian beers, on-tap BC brews and fresh lime cordial. Come hungry, expect to share and stay long.

FOUNDATION Map p83 — Vegetarian $$
2301 Main St; mains $6-14; noon-1am; 3

This lively vegetarian (mostly vegan) noshery is where artsy students and chin-stroking young intellectuals like to hang. Despite the clientele, it's not at all pretentious (apart from the philosophical quotes adorning the walls) and its mismatched Formica tables are often topped with dishes like the giant, finger-licking Utopian Nachos, spicy black bean burgers or hearty house-made curries – called Revolutionary Rations on the menu. Vancouver's Storm Brewing beers are also served (go for the Scottish Cream Ale).

ARGO CAFE Map p83 Burgers, Breakfast $
1836 Ontario St; mains $6-10; ☻ **7am-4pm Mon-Fri;** ☒ **3**

Fronted by a jaunty painted exterior that suggests you're about to enter a youth club, the Argo is one of Vancouver's last genuine diner-style cafes. Vinyl booths, a warm welcome and heaping, home-cooked nosh (this is an especially good breakfast spot) are part of its charm and you'll be joined by an eclectic mix of manual workers and in-the-know office drones. Come back after the lunchtime rush for a slice of fruit pie and you'll have the place to yourself as the afternoon slides by.

HAWKERS DELIGHT Map p83 Asian $
4127 Main St; mains $4-8; ☻ **11am-9pm Mon-Sat;** ☒ **3**

This unassuming, no-frills hole-in-the-wall is easy to miss, but it's worth retracing your steps for a taste of highly authentic Malaysian and Singaporean soul food, all made from scratch at this family-run favorite. Peruse the photo-menu, with dishes such as aromatic coconut milk curry or yellow noodles with tofu and spicy sweet potato sauce, then head straight to the counter to order. The dishes are super-cheap, making this one of the city's best and most enduring cheap eats.

COMMERCIAL DRIVE

The center of East Vancouver's eclectic dining scene, the Drive – from the Commercial-Broadway SkyTrain Station to Venables St – is a strollable smorgasbord of adventurous dining. Combining ethnic soul-food joints, chatty streetside cafes and the kind of convivial pub-style hangouts that give the concept of 'neighborhood bar' a good name (see p157 for recommendations), this is the city's most sociable dine-out district. It's also Vancouver's patio capital, so if the weather's good, drop by for an alfresco meal.

REEF Map p86 Caribbean $$
www.thereefrestaurant.com; 1018 Commercial Dr; mains $11-17; ☻ **11am-11:30pm Mon-Wed, 11am-12:30am Thu & Fri, 10am-12:30am Sat, 10am-11:30pm Sun;** ☒ **20**

With its funkily bright interior, this is a perfect rainy-night haunt (which could be any time of the year in Vancouver). The Caribbean soul-food menu includes heap-

ing, stomach-lagging dishes like Bajan fried chicken and eye-poppingly spicy Jamaican curries, but don't ignore the cornmeal johnny cakes that usually arrive free at the table: you'll be planning your next visit as soon as you've finished them. Cocktails are a specialty (try the Dark & Stormy) and all are also available booze-free, which means you'll still be able to find your way home after you've eaten.

HAVANA Map p86 Latin $$
www.havanarestaurant.ca; 1212 Commercial Dr; mains $10-20; ☻ **11am-11pm Mon-Thu, 10am-midnight Fri, 9am-midnight Sat & Sun;** ☒ **20**

The granddaddy of dining on the Drive has still got it, hence its buzzing patio on most summer nights. It combines a rustic Latin American ambience – peruse the graffiti signatures scratched into the walls – with a roster of satisfying Afro-Cuban-southern soul-food dishes, with highlights ranging from yam fries to slow-roasted lamb curry and perfect platters of clams, mussels and oysters. Port, brandy and single malt color the drinks list but the mojito pitchers slide down very easily on those lazy, sunset-hugging evenings. Arrive early to beat the patio crowds.

WAAZUBEE CAFÉ Map p86 West Coast $$
www.waazubee.com; 1622 Commercial Dr; mains $8-20; ☻ **10:30am-1am Mon-Fri, 10am-1am Sat, 10am-midnight Sun;** ☒ **20**

This long, Bohemian bat cave is lined with huge painted murals, velvet curtains and recycled metal sculptures – check out that spoon chandelier. An equally eclectic menu (including plenty of vegetarian options) runs from sesame tuna sashimi to grilled

TOP BLOGS

Springing up like mushrooms after a downpour, hundreds of bloated bloggers have emerged in Vancouver in recent years to chart the city's ever-moving foodie waters. Check out Urban Diner (www.urbandiner.ca) for new openings and insider info; Cheap Appetite (www.cheapappetite.com) for recommendations on good-value eateries; and Vancouver Foodster (www.vancouverfoodster.com) for reviews and interviews. Also dedicate some quality cursor time to Scout Magazine (www.scoutmagazine.ca), a general interest local site with a strong emphasis on Vancouver's restaurant scene.

portobello mushroom burgers and maple chili-glazed wild salmon. There's also an impressive wine list and a good selection of BC beers, including Storm Scottish Ale, made just down the road.

TIMBRE Map p86 — Fusion $$

www.timbrerestaurant.com; 2068 Commercial Dr; mains $8-18; 🕒 4pm-midnight Mon-Fri, 11am-midnight Sat & Sun; Ⓜ Commercial-Broadway
A couple of blocks north of the SkyTrain station, this buzzy, wood-lined neighborhood resto-bar is a popular weekend brunch spot, when the hungover locals drop by to address their night-before excesses. The highlight of the main menu, though, is the Gut Strut Jambalaya, heaped with scallops, prawns and smoked chicken. The beer list might appeal if you're heading the hair-of-the-dog route – the bottled BC treats often include Phoenix Gold Lager and Phillips Blue Buck Ale – while Wednesday night is reserved for good-value beer and burger specials (usually around the $12 to $14 mark).

CLOVE Map p86 — Indian, Fusion $$

2054 Commercial Dr; tapas $4-14; 🕒 5-10pm Sun-Thu, 5-10:30pm Fri & Sat; 🚌 20
Not your traditional Indian eatery, expect wider Asian contemporary and fusion tapas influences here that will have you wondering exactly which ethnic food group you're dining from. Start with tender gyoza or some edamame wraps before moving on to the eye-rollingly good butter chicken (made with addictive candied almonds). Whatever you have, make sure you follow it with a delectable chai crème brûlée. The room is warm and intimate: hang at the long bar or canoodle at a tiny table.

THERESA'S Map p86 — Burgers, Breakfast $

www.theresaseatery.com; 1260 Commercial Dr; mains $4-8; 🕒 8am-2pm Mon-Wed, 8am-7pm Thu-Sun; 🚌 20
This homely, often-hopping cooperative-run joint (just the kind of commie spot you'd expect on the Drive) gives life a good name. Expect hearty, great-value organic breakfast dishes, each named after local streets – go for the 'Hastings' of eggs, bacon and lox and chase it with a house-made chai latte. Or drop by for lunch and tuck into an inventive house-made soup, rustic

top picks

ROMANTIC DINING

- Observatory (p146)
- Chambar (p130)
- Sandbar (below)
- Abigail's Party (p144)
- Le Gavroche (p132)

salad or the popular vegan burger – one of many vegetarian options on the menu.

LA CASA GELATO Map p86 — Fast Food $

www.lacasagelato.com; 1033 Venables St; single scoops $4.50; 🕒 11am-11pm; 🚌 20
If you've been skiing, cycling, kayaking or just on your feet all day exploring the neighborhoods, it may be time to cool down with an ice-cold treat. A visit to Vancouver's fave ice-cream joint should hit the spot, although you'll likely get brain-freeze trying to choose from the bewildering kaleidoscope of flavors – 508 at last count. All the usual suspects are available, but if you're feeling adventurous try the garlic or hot chili varieties.

GRANVILLE ISLAND

This waterfront ambler's idyll is sometimes overlooked as a dine-out destination. Between catching a show at a theater or grabbing a beer at one of the area's bars, you should plan for a convivial meal here, ideally with a sunset view of Burrard Bridge and the shimmering False Creek waterfront. If you just need a fuel-up, head to the public market (p88) with its smorgasbord of deli treats and its ever-popular food court.

SANDBAR Map p89 — Seafood $$$

☎ 604-669-9030; www.vancouverdine.com; 1535 Johnston St; mains $18-35; 🕒 11:30am-midnight Sun-Thu, 11:30am-1am Fri & Sat; 🚌 50
A vast array of West Coast seafood heads the menu at this long-established, high-ceilinged restaurant-with-a-view tucked under the iron arches of Granville Bridge. The fresh oysters are justifiably popular and they're best sampled on the fireplace-warmed rooftop deck – there's also a sushi bar if your raw mood continues. The giant

wine list is also something to write home about, but the urban professionals crowding the U-shaped bar on weekends seem more interested in quaffing cocktails. A good romantic dinner spot.

BRIDGES Map p89 West Coast $$
www.bridgesrestaurant.com; 1696 Duranleau St; mains $12-20; ⏰ 11am-10pm; 🚌 50
You'll easily spot this bright yellow bistro as you pass over the Granville Bridge on your way here. In summer it offers one of the best sunset patios in town from which to enjoy well-executed classics like seafood chowder, halibut and chips and thin-crust pizzas – the smoked-salmon variety is recommended. Also consider a pitcher of Granville Island Iced Tea (if you have enough friends to finish it). Diners can escape the patio clamor at the quieter, more upscale upstairs dining room (dinner only).

GO FISH Map p89 Seafood $
1505 W 1st Ave; mains $8-13; ⏰ 11:30am-6:30pm Wed-Fri, noon-6:30pm Sat & Sun; 🚌 50
A two-minute walk west along the seawall from the Granville Island entrance, this wildly popular seafood shack is one of the city's best fish-and-chip joints, offering a choice of halibut, salmon or cod encased in crispy golden batter. The smashing (and lighter) fish tacos are also highly recommended, while the ever-changing daily specials – brought in by the nearby fishing boats – often include praiseworthy scallop burgers or ahi tuna sandwiches. There's not much of a seating area, so pack your grub and continue along the seawall to Vanier Park for a picnic with the ever-watchful seagulls.

AGRO CAFÉ Map p89 Cafe $
www.agrocafe.org; 1363 Railspur Alley; mains $6-10; ⏰ 8am-7pm Mon-Fri, 9am-7pm Sat & Sun; 🚌 50; 📶
Seemingly known only to locals and Emily Carr Uni students, this slightly hidden cafe on Railspur Alley is a smashing coffee stop with a fair-trade commitment. But there's much more on offer here: tuck into a BC-brewed Back Hand of God Stout or a bulging ciabatta sandwich. And if you're hungry for a good start to the day, the heaping brekkies are a great fill-up (and a genuine good deal). In summer, sip your

Americano outside and watch the Granville Island world go by.

FAIRVIEW & SOUTH GRANVILLE

Bordered by SoMa to the east and Kitsilano to the west, the backbone of this area is Broadway, which is suffused with pockets of restaurants for much of its length. While many of these are of the cheap-and-cheerful neighborhood-eatery variety – you'll never have a problem finding budget noodleries and sushi joints here – there are some dining highlights that are worth getting off the bus for. Many of these cluster around the South Granville area that starts from the south side of Granville Bridge.

WEST Map p93 West Coast $$$
☎ 604-738-8938; www.westrestaurant.com; 2881 Granville St; mains $22-46; ⏰ 11:30am-2:30pm Mon-Sat, 5:30-11pm daily; 🚌 10
While this award-winning favorite lost its famous chef in 2008 (David Hawksworth's eponymous new downtown eatery was yet to launch at the time of writing), the sleek spot has retained its commitment to superb seasonal West Coast dining with ultra-attentive service and a great wine selection. Ideal for a romantic night out, menu highlights often include Queen Charlotte halibut and Pemberton Valley striploin, while the pastry chef delivers some of the best desserts in town. Before you leave, ask to try the sliding ladder attached to the wine shelves.

TOJO'S Map p93 Japanese $$$
☎ 604-872-8050; www.tojos.com; 1133 W Broadway; mains $19-26; ⏰ 5-11pm Mon-Sat; 🚌 9
Hidekazu Tojo's legendary skill with the sushi knife has created Vancouver's most revered Japanese restaurant, in a city that's probably the best in the world for this particular culinary art form outside Tokyo. Among his exquisite dishes are favorites such as lightly steamed monkfish, sautéed halibut cheeks and fried red tuna wrapped with seaweed and served with plum sauce. It's a sleek and sophisticated room and seats at both the sake bar and omakaze sushi bar can be hard to come by on weekend nights: book ahead by phone.

VIJ'S Map p93 Indian $$$

www.vijs.ca; 1480 W 11th Ave; mains $18-26;
🕐 5:30-10pm; 🚌 10

Just off S Granville St, ever-popular Vij's is
the high-water mark of contemporary East
Indian cuisine, fusing regional ingredients,
subtle global flourishes and classic ethnic
dishes to produce an array of innovative
flavors. The unique results range from
signature wine-marinated 'lamb popsicles'
to savor-worthy dishes like halibut, mussels
and crab in a tomato-ginger curry. The
adventurous should also try the *paranta*:
flat breads made with roasted ground
crickets. Reservations are not accepted:
avoid the queues by hitting Rangoli, the
adjoining take-out cafe. Plans were afoot
at the time of writing to move to a new
Cambie St location, so call ahead.

OUISI BISTRO Map p93 Fusion $$

www.ouisibistro.com; 3014 Granville St; mains
$10-22; 🕐 5pm-2am Mon-Fri, 11am-2am Sat &
Sun; 🚌 10

Vancouver's most authentic Creole and
Cajun menu in a casual, bar-style
setting, Ouisi (as in 'Louisiana') chefs up
adventurous dishes like habanero coconut
chicken, cornmeal-crusted trout and
vegetarian étouffée for those who like a
taste-tripping dinner – also consider one of
the New Orleanian sandwiches for a hearty
lunch. The large menu of accompanying
malts and bourbons plus regular live jazz
spices things up, while weekend brunch
offers hot fusion riffs on trad breakfast
dishes.

STELLA'S BIERSTRO Map p93 West Coast $$

www.stellasbeer.com; 3305 Cambie St; mains $8-
18; 🕐 11am-11:30pm Mon-Fri, 10am-11:30pm Sat
& Sun; 🚌 15

More of a sit-down restaurant than its
bar-esque older brother on Commercial Dr
(p157), this inviting bistro-style room
combines a wood-lined interior
(dominated by an imposing stag painting)
and two street-side patios. The more
extensive menu includes excellent maple
syrup–glazed pork loin chops, while
weekends draw locals looking for brunch
of the eggs Benedict and *huevos rancheros*
(ranch-style) variety. Befitting its Belgian-
beer background, there's also an
outstanding booze menu with continental
and Canadian treats a'plenty.

top picks

BREAKFAST

- Deacon's Corner (p137)
- Templeton (p130)
- Acme Cafe (p137)
- Paul's Place Omelettery (below)
- Sophie's Cosmic Café (p145)

PAUL'S PLACE OMELETTERY

Map p93 Breakfast $$

2211 Granville St; mains $8-12; 🕐 7am-3pm;
🚌 10; ♿

You'll be jostling for space with strollers
and chatty moms at this unassuming
breakfast joint near the south side of
Granville Bridge, but it's worth it: this cozy
place is far superior to most city bacon-
and-egg spots. The menu is short and
sweet, but it's grounded on 12 signature
omelets, including a chockablock
vegetarian option that will make carnivores
eye you jealously. It's a great place to
start the day before a wander down to
Granville Island, but there's also a lunch
menu of house-made burgers and
sandwiches.

PICNIC Map p93 Cafe $

3010 Granville St; mains $4-8; 🕐 8am-5pm Mon-
Sat, 10am-5pm Sun; 🚌 10

Adjacent to Meinhardt Fine Foods (p124),
this easy-to-miss little storefront opens into
a long and slender interior dominated by a
giant communal table. Pick up a breakfast
muffin and coffee at the front then join
the South Granvillites hunched over their
newspapers at the big table. The delectable
cake selection you noticed on your way in
will likely lure you back later in the day.
A good spot to fuel-up before a stroll
around the heritage mansions of nearby
Shaughnessy Heights.

KITSILANO

Kitsilano's two main arteries – W 4th Ave
and W Broadway – offer a healthy mix of
eateries: it's well worth the trek here to lounge
on a beach or stroll the shopping areas then
end your day with a rewarding meal. The
neighborhood's hippie past has left a legacy
of vegetarian-friendly restaurants, but Kits'

more recent wealth means that there are also some top-notch high-end eateries well worth a splurge.

LUMIÈRE Map pp96-7 — French $$$

☎ 604-739-8185; www.lumiere.ca; 2551 W Broadway; seasonal prix fixe from $65; ⏰ 5:30-10pm Sun-Wed, 5:30-11pm Thu-Sat; 🚍 9

With Iron Chef Rob Feenie's 2008 departure, few thought this multi-award-winning eatery would survive. But superstar New Yorker Daniel Boulud rolled in and reinvented the top-notch French and West Coast fusion eatery with dishes like Redbro chicken stuffed with truffles and the celebrated six-mushroom ravioli. The menu comprises multi-course tasting selections intended for savoring and the best way to go is the $65 three-course seasonal menu (you can add wine pairing for an extra $35). A sophisticated eatery, this is dining as an event.

BISHOP'S Map pp96-7 — West Coast $$$

☎ 604-738-2025; www.bishopsonline.com; 2183 W 4th Ave; mains $28-38; ⏰ 5:30-11pm; 🚍 4

A pioneer of superb West Coast cuisine long before the 'locavore' fashion took hold, modest but legendary chef-owner John Bishop – he'll almost certainly drop by your table to say hi – is still at the top of his game in this charming, art-lined little restaurant. Served in an elegant, white-tablecloth room, the weekly-changing menu can include stuffed rabbit loin, steamed smoked sablefish and the kind of crisp, seasonal veggies that taste like they've just been plucked from the ground. The service here is pitch-perfect, so stay a little longer and indulge in dessert: if you're lucky, it'll be sweet fried fig empanada with brown sugar ice-cream.

DB BISTRO MODERNE
Map pp96-7 — Burgers, West Coast $$

☎ 604-739-7115; www.dbbistro.ca; 2551 W Broadway; mains $17-27; ⏰ noon-2:30pm Tue-Fri; 11:30am-2:30pm Sat & Sun; 5:30-10pm Sun-Wed, 5:30-11pm Thu-Sat 🚍 9

Formerly Feenies, this transformed French-influenced contemporary bistro serves the city's best posh burger: a $28 bulging combination of sirloin patty and black truffles that couldn't be further from a Big Mac. The menu is brimming with additional comfort-food pleasures like coq au vin and

the excellent Berkshire pork tenderloin, while the weekend brunch highlight is a delicious lobster eggs Florentine that lures the esurient locals. Also look out here for regular good value prix-fixe deals.

MAENAM Map pp96-7 — Thai $$

☎ 604-730-5579; www.maenam.ca; 1938 W 4th Ave; mains $15-18; ⏰ noon-2:30pm Tue-Fri, 5-11pm Mon-Thu & Sun, 11am-1am Fri & Sat; 🚍 4

A swish, contemporary reinvention of the Thai-restaurant model, this is probably unlike any Thai eatery you've been to. Sophisticated, subtle and complex traditional and international influences flavor the menu in a room that has a laid-back modern lounge feel. Inviting exploration, you can start with the familiar (although even the pad Thai here is eye-poppingly different) but save plenty of room for something new: the *geng panaeng neua* beef curry is a sweet, salty and nutty treat suffused with aromatic basil. The mains are great value here, but why not share a few smaller plates (around the $8 to $10 range) instead?

ABIGAIL'S PARTY Map pp96-7 — Fusion $$

☎ 604-739-4677; www.abigailsparty.ca; 1685 Yew St; mains $14-24; ⏰ 9am-2:30pm Fri-Sun, 5:30pm-2am Mon-Sat; 🚍 22

A romantic little tapas and wine haunt that creates its own atmosphere depending on the crowd filling its handful of small, candlelit tables. The idea here is to sit back, order some tapas plates and explore the wine list at your leisure. The barbecue beef brisket and Moroccan chicken dishes are great if you're particularly hungry, but the lamb sausage corn dogs and duck confit sliders are ideal for sharing: although since you'll find three of each on the plates, a fight over the final one is highly likely. Make up with a bottle from the blackboard of ever-changing wine specials and an Abigail's Mohito or three.

BISTROT BISTRO Map pp96-7 — French $$

☎ 604-732-0004; www.bistrotbistro.com; 1961 W 4th Ave; mains $14-19; ⏰ 5-10pm Sun & Mon, 5-11pm Tue-Thu, 5pm-midnight Fri & Sat; 🚍 4

A charming, snob-free neighborhood bistro with a casual contemporary feel, the menu here combines traditional French recipes with seasonal local ingredients and simple, flavor-revealing preparations. Expect hearty nosh like apple-sweetened pork tenderloin still simmering in its skillet and the kind of robust boeuf bourguignon that makes lesser chefs weep. Great value, especially the Sunday to Thursday prix-fixe special.

CORDUROY Map pp96-7   West Coast $$
www.corduroyrestaurant.com; 1943 Cornwall Ave; mains $12-18; ⏰ 5:30pm-2am Mon-Sat; 🚌 22
It's easy to walk right past this tiny storefront but once you're inside you'll be pleased you discovered such a kitsch-cool spot. Slide onto a soft bench seat and peruse the oddball array of alleged artworks – junkshop pictures and carved masks – then order a house beer from the shingle-covered bar: if you're lucky, it'll be served in a boot-shaped glass. Interesting brews and tempting cocktails are offered, along with organic dinner treats like root-veggie fries and the excellent Better Than Your Mum's Meatloaf. There are often live music or open-mike nights during the week.

NOODLE BOX Map pp96-7   Asian Fusion $$
www.thenoodlebox.net; 1867 W 4th Ave; mains $9-14; ⏰ 11:30am-9pm Mon-Wed, 11:30am-10pm Thu-Sun; 🚌 4
Although Noodle Box hails from across the water in Victoria, its plans for world domination have taken hold in Vancouver, where its winning combination of freshly prepared, good-value Asian nosh has roused Kits locals from their high-end-dining ways. The company's kitsch-tastic take-out noodle boxes – almost a fashion accessory – helped spread the word, but diners keep coming back for Malaysian lamb curry, Thai chow mein and the ever-popular spicy Cambodian jungle curry.

GALLEY PATIO & GRILL
Map pp96-7   Burgers, Seafood $$
www.thegalley.ca; Jericho Sailing Centre, 1300 Discovery St; mains $8-16; ⏰ 9am-10pm Jun–early Sep, reduced hours off-season; 🚌 4
This is a terrific, unfussy perch at sunset, with its stunning views across the beach toward English Bay. Plop down in one of the plastic patio chairs (reservations are not accepted, so arrive early for the vista) then eyeball all the sailboats steering toward shore. The food is of the house-made comfort-food variety, with seafood dominating.

top picks

PATIOS

- Galley Patio & Grill (left)
- Havana (p140)
- Gallery Café (p131)
- Bridges (p142)
- Teahouse (p132)

It's a popular spot for fish-and-chips, but even better for halibut tacos and an ice-cream-cone chaser. There are usually a couple of BC wine offerings, along with some tasty local brews from R&B Brewing (the Sun God Wheat Ale is a recommended summer quaff).

NAAM Map pp96-7   Vegetarian $$
www.thenaam.com; 2724 W 4th Ave; dishes $8-14; ⏰ 24hr; 🚌 4
A rare and evocative relic of Kitsilano's hippie past, this vegetarian restaurant has the feel of a comfy, highly chatty farmhouse. It's not unusual to have to wait for a table here at peak times, but it's worth it for the hearty stir-fries, Mexican platters and sesame-fried potatoes with miso gravy. This is the kind of veggie spot where carnivores are also happy to dine. There's nightly live music, an array of great organic beers and a popular patio – it's covered, so you can cozy up here with a bowl of broth and still enjoy the rain.

SOPHIE'S COSMIC CAFÉ
Map pp96-7   Burgers, Breakfast $$
www.sophiescosmiccafe.com; 2095 West 4th Ave; mains $6-14; ⏰ 8am-9pm; 🚌 4; ♿
With its museum of garage-sale kitsch lining the walls, local legend Sophie's – the place with the giant chrome cutlery either side of the entrance – is a cheery diner with burgers, club sandwiches and big-ass milkshakes dominating the menu. There are also a few off-message gems such as BC oyster burgers. A highly popular breakfast and brunch spot – expect to queue on weekends – it's also worth dropping by mid-afternoon for some truck-stop coffee and a slice of pyramid-sized apple pie (you can jog up and down the hill to and from the beach to work it off).

METRO VANCOUVER

The North Shore has plenty of dining options if you've come over the Lions Gate Bridge for the day. Across the rest of the region, Richmond offers perhaps North America's most authentic traditional and contemporary Asian dining (plus some great fish-and-chips in Steveston), while Burnaby chefs up a fine-dining surprise or two. You won't go hungry, though: the Lower Mainland region is full of midrange and mom-and-pop eateries.

OBSERVATORY Map pp54-5 West Coast $$$
☎ 604-998-4403; www.grousemountain.com; Grouse Mountain, North Vancouver; mains $35-40; ⏱ 5-10pm; 🚌 236

Perched atop Grouse Mountain, the fine-dining Observatory serves up dishes of seared scallops and roasted beef tenderloin with some of the best views in BC – over the crenulated waterfront of Stanley Park and the twinkling glass towers of Vancouver far below. A perfect romantic dinner venue – you wouldn't be the first to propose here – there's also an excellent wine list if you suddenly need to console yourself. The atmosphere is more laid-back at the adjacent Altitudes Bistro (☎ 604-984-0661; mains $7-17; ⏱ 11:30am-10pm), which offers pub-style food in a casual ski-lodge setting.

FRAICHE Map pp54-5 West Coast $$$
☎ 604-925-7595; www.fraicherestaurant.ca; 2240 Chippendale Rd, West Vancouver; mains $28-40; ⏱ 11:30am-2:30pm & 5-10pm Mon-Fri, 10am-2:30pm & 5-10pm Sat & Sun; 🚌 256

You'll fall in love with the panoramic shoreline views over the city even before you start eating at this swanky locals' favorite. But it's worth removing your gaze from the mesmerizing vistas to focus on your plate. Perfect Pacific Northwest is the approach here, with typical highlights on the seasonal menu including roasted Steelhead or Qualicum Bay scallops served with lobster ravioli. If you fancy a taste of the high life without the price, drop in for lunch when many dishes are under $20, or try the weekend brunch (Dungeness crab cakes recommended).

PEAR TREE Map pp54-5 West Coast $$$
☎ 604-299-2772; www.peartreerestaurant.net; 4120 E Hastings St, Burnaby; mains $24-29; ⏱ 5-10pm Tue-Sat; 🚌 135

The surprisingly sleek contemporary interior here – belying its inauspicious location and discreet storefront – complements a menu of modernized, continental-influenced West Coast classics. Vancouverites are often shocked to find such a place in the 'burbs, but they quickly tell their friends about the amazing lobster cappuccinos and salmon with star anise butter sauce. Delectable desserts are also a feature here and the service is excellent.

HAKKASAN CONTEMPORARY CHINESE RESTAURANT
Map pp54-5 Chinese $$
www.hakkasan.ca; 2188 No 5 Rd, Richmond; mains $13-23; ⏱ 11:30am-2:30pm & 5:30-10pm Wed-Sun; 🚌 405

Like it says on the sign, this is a contemporary take on Chinese eateries, which means an upscale wine-bar-like interior that belies its location among a string of light industrial businesses. The menu combines traditional Hakka soul food and modern Cantonese dishes, with highlights including braised pork hock and scallops in a garlic-based sauce. The specialty, though, is the clay-pot-roasted salty chicken that arrives at your table wrapped in parchment paper.

POSH CHARCOAL COLLABORATION DINING Map pp54-5 Japanese $$
www.303-posh.com; 3779 Sexsmith Rd, Richmond; mains $11-16; ⏱ 11:30am-3pm & 5:30-11pm Mon-Thu, 11:30am-midnight Fri & Sat, 11:30am-11pm Sun; Ⓜ Aberdeen

This loungey little Japanese hot-pot spot in an unassuming strip-mall location is possibly the most fun you can have with a meal. Each table has a camping-style stove topped with a pan of soup broth: you order plates of delicate tofu, crisp veggies and thin-cut beef and cook it all yourself in the broth. The affordable all-you-can-eat sukiyaki approach invites experimentation, and you'll find yourself sampling lotus root and the oddly textured konjac tofu. Wash it all down with some smashing Pearl Sake and you'll soon be considering a job as a chef. Popular with younger Asian diners, you'll find lots of 20-somethings here on most nights.

AU PETIT CHAVIGNOL

Map pp54-5 Cafe $$

☎ 604-255-4218; www.aupetitchavignol.com; 843 E Hastings St; mains $8-16; ⏰ noon-11pm Mon-Fri, 11am-11pm Sat & Sun; 🚇 10

Oddly located on a humdrum strip of scruffy neighborhood shops, this exemplary cheese and wine restaurant is the best place in town to indulge your curd addiction. Twinned with the top-notch cheese shop next door, it's a loungey but unpretentious little room where the friendly staffers happily guide you through an eye-popping array of local and international cheese and charcuterie, available per-selection or in 'flights' of three or five. Expert wine accompaniments – Rieslings are favored – are also offered.

BURGOO BISTRO Map pp54-5 Fusion $$

www.burgoo.ca; 3 Lonsdale Ave, North Vancouver; mains $8-16; ⏰ 11am-11pm; 🚇 Lonsdale Quay

With the feel of a cozy, rustic cabin – complete with a large stone fireplace – Burgoo's menu of comfort foods with a twist aims to warm up those long North Van winter nights: the Guinness-infused Irish stew, spicy apricot lamb tagine or smile-triggering butter chicken with brown basmati rice would thaw a glacier from 50 paces. There's also a wide array of house-made soups and heaping salads. If all you fancy is a few beers, dip into the dark and hoppy Burgoo Brew or the rich and blackcurranty Middle Mountain Black Mead. There's also live jazz on Sunday nights to keep your toes tapping.

TOMAHAWK RESTAURANT

Map pp54-5 Burgers, Breakfast $$

www.tomahawkrestaurant.com; 1550 Philip Ave, North Vancouver; mains $8-16; ⏰ 8am-9pm Sun-Thu, 8am-10pm Fri & Sat; 🚇 240

A colorful blast from North Van's pioneering past, the family-run Tomahawk has been heaping its plates with comfort food since 1926. A bustling weekend brunch spot – if the massive Yukon bacon and eggs grease-fest or the frightening Skookum chief burger don't kill your hangover, nothing will – it's also great for lunch or dinner, when bulging burgers, chicken potpies and organic meatloaf hit the menu. As you waddle back out, peruse the surfeit of First Nations artifacts lining the walls.

SHANGHAI RIVER RESTAURANT

Map pp54-5 Chinese $$

7381 Westminster Hwy, Richmond; mains $6-18; ⏰ 11am-2:30pm, 5:30-11pm; Ⓜ Richmond-Brighouse

Grab a seat overlooking the kitchen window at this cavernous contemporary northern Chinese eatery and you'll be mesmerized by the intricate handiwork that goes into folding some of the best Vancouver-area dim-sum dumplings. Order plates to share here – one dish per person is the usual ratio – and be careful not to squirt everyone with the delicate but ultra-juicy pork or shrimp dumplings. The braised duck and ham soup is a great winter warmer, too. This place fills up at peak times, when it becomes animated with Chinese chatter. Note: the servers are often not fluent in English, so keep your orders simple.

ALL INDIA SWEETS & RESTAURANT

Map pp54-5 Indian $

www.allindiasweetsrestaurant.com; 6507 Main St; mains $6-13; ⏰ 11:30am-10pm; 🚇 3

One of a string of good-value Indian family diners lining Main St's Punjabi Market area, the All India wins with its impressive all-you-can-eat $10.95 vegetarian buffet, which includes lashings of naan bread and unlimited Indian sweets for dessert. The ambience – chipped 1980s tables and chairs – is nothing to write home about, but the welcome is warm and the food will fill you for a day. Meat dishes are also available from the menu – including goat *saag* (curry) and an excellent fish *masala* – but it's the buffet that lures most esurient noshers.

PAJO'S Map pp54-5 Seafood $

www.pajos.com; The Wharf, Steveston; mains $6-9; ⏰ 11am-dusk Feb-Nov; 🚇 402

It's hard to think of a better spot to enjoy fish-and-chips than the boat-bobbing wharf at Steveston. Luckily, this floating, family-run local legend fully delivers. After perusing the fresh catches on the backs of the nearby fishing boats, follow your nose and descend the ramp to Pajo's little ordering hatch. You'll be greeted by a friendly face and a menu more extensive than your average chippy. Go the traditional fresh-fried cod, salmon or halibut route (with secret-recipe tartar sauce) or mix things up with a yellowfin tuna burger and zucchini sticks.

DRINKING

top picks

- Alibi Room (p155)
- Railway Club (p151)
- Six Acres (p155)
- Cascade Room (p156)
- Three Lions Café (p156)
- Narrow Lounge (p156)
- Diamond (p154)
- Brickhouse (p156)
- St Augustine's (p157)
- Irish Heather (p156)

DRINKING

With swanky new lounges springing up across Vancouver like drunks at an open bar, and neighborhood pubs seemingly as popular as ever with those locals who like a quiet beery chat with friends at the end of the day, it's not hard to find a drink in this city. Visitors are welcome wherever the locals sup – just remember that it's table service at most places, rather than the Brit model of ordering at the bar.

Wherever you end up drinking, avoid the generic national brews by beery behemoths such as Molson and Labatt and head straight for the local selection. British Columbia (BC) is one of North America's frothiest microbrewing capitals and Vancouver serves up an impressive array of small producers well worth sampling (see the boxed text on p152). Ask your server for recommendations.

It's not all about beer, of course. Cocktail fans will find plenty of exotic tipples in bars and lounges here (see the boxed text, p154). And wine selections – check out offerings from Vancouver Island and the Okanagan – are spreading in depth and quality across the city like a spilled glass of pinot noir; see the boxed text opposite for top options.

If you've had a heavy night mixing it with the locals and your head feels like a melon on a toothpick, recover at one of the city's great coffeehouses. Although Vancouver was the home of the first Starbucks outside the US, there are plenty of quirky independent coffee stops here that could teach Starbucks' baristas a thing or two about great java.

Finally, if you need to pick up a bottle for an impromptu party in your hotel room, head to one of the many private or government-run liquor stores around the city. For a selection of the best, see p115.

PRACTICALITIES

Opening Hours

Pubs and bars that serve lunch usually open before midday, with swankier, lounge-style operations waiting it out until 5pm. Most drinkeries close sometime between midnight and 2am, although they are allowed to stay open until 3am and will do so if they're busy enough, particularly on weekends: if you're desperate for a late-night tipple, the Granville Strip is usually a safe bet. Coffeehouses typically open around 8am and often close before 9pm.

How Much?

Expect to pay $5 or $7 for a large glass of beer, but always ask if there are any daily specials. A glass of wine will set you back anything over $6, while cocktails often start at $6. Your bill will also include an added 12% Harmonized Sales Tax (HST), an extra that's enough to drive anyone to drink.

Tipping

Table servers expect around $1 per drink, 15% when you're buying a round. Even if you order and pick up your beverage at the bar, consider dropping your change in the prominently placed tip glass.

DOWNTOWN

The Granville Strip between Robson and Davie Sts is lined with popular bars where drinking to party is the main attraction. A short walk away, you'll find more discerning options in the West End (p152) and Yaletown (p153).

BACCHUS Map pp58-9 Bar

www.wedgewoodhotel.com; 845 Hornby St; 🚍 5

A roaring hearth on a chilly day is the main attraction at Bacchus, a decadent bar with a gentleman's club ambience on the lobby level of the Wedgewood Hotel & Spa (p195). Sink into a deep leather chair, adjust your monocle and listen to the piano player as you sip a signature Red Satin Slip martini of vodka, raspberry liqueur and cranberry juice. There's a good small-plate menu for the incurably esurient (go for the cheese).

UVA Map pp58-9 Bar

www.uvawinebar.ca; Moda Hotel, 900 Seymour St; 🚍 10

Possibly the city's best wine bar, this little nook combines a heritage mosaic floor and

150

top picks

WINE LISTS

- **UVA** (opposite)
- **Bacchus** (opposite)
- **O'Doul's** (p152)
- **Opus Bar** (p154)
- **1181** (p152)

swanky white vinyl chairs that add a dash of mod class. But despite the cool look, there's a welcome snob-free approach that will have you happily taste-tripping through a boutique drinks list carefully selected from Old and New World delights plus some exciting BC wines: go for the citrusy Joie Riesling. Combine your drinks with tasting plates from charcuterie to tangy cheese – make sure you have the sardine bruschetta.

CAFFÈ ARTIGIANO Map pp58-9   Cafe
www.caffeartigiano.com; 763 Hornby St; 5
An international award-winner for its barista skills and latte art, Artigiano has the locals frothing at the mouth with its satisfyingly rich java beverages. The drinks appear with leaf designs adorning their foam and there's a good side attraction of gourmet sandwiches and cakes. The small patio here is almost always packed – grab a table quickly if you see one – and the interior has a classy Tuscan look.

MARIO'S Map pp58-9   Cafe
595 Howe St; Ⓜ Burrard
A java-lover's favorite that only downtown office workers seem to know about, you'll wake up and smell the coffee long before you make it through the door here. The rich aromatic beverages served up by the man himself are the kind of ambrosia brews that should make Starbucks' drinkers weep – you might even forgive the incessant 1980s Italian pop music percolating through the shop as you sip on your perfect Americano.

DOOLINS Map pp58-9   Pub
www.doolins.ca; 654 Nelson St; 10
The best-looking Irish bar in Vancouver – take a quick tour of the cavernous wooden-beamed and stained-glass interior before

finding your perch and hitting the menu. Not surprisingly, Guinness tops the draft popularity stakes but you'll also find lesser-expected alternatives like Murphy's and Caffrey's. There's also an extensive pub grub menu (the pulled pork sandwich is good) plus live toe-tapping Celtic music most nights. Clamorous on weekends.

FOUNTAINHEAD PUB Map pp58-9   Pub
www.fountainheadpub.com; 1025 Davie St; 6
The area's loudest and proudest gay neighborhood pub, this friendly joint is all about the patio, which spills onto Davie St like an overturned wine glass. Expect to take part in the ongoing summer evening pastime of ogling the passing locals or retreat to a quieter spot inside for a few lagers (Red Truck Beer is recommended) or a naughty cocktail: anyone for a Sicilian Kiss or a Slippery Nipple?

LENNOX PUB Map pp58-9   Pub
800 Granville St; Ⓜ Vancouver City Centre
This narrow Granville St drinkery never seems to have enough tables to go around at the weekend, when the noise levels prevent all but the most rudimentary of conversations. It's a different story during the week, when calm is restored and you can savor a good roster of 15 drafts from Belgium and beyond – try the Leffe or Big Rock Grasshopper. The decor is reproduction old-school and the upstairs seating area is a popular couples' nook.

RAILWAY CLUB Map pp58-9   Pub
www.therailwayclub.com; 579 Dunsmuir St; Ⓜ Granville
A local-legend, pub-style music venue (p168), the upstairs 'Rail' is accessed via an unobtrusive wooden door next to a 7-Eleven. Don't be put off by the grungy-looking entrance: this is one of the city's friendliest bars and you'll fit right in as soon as you roll up to the bar – unusually for Vancouver, you have to order at the counter, since there's no table service. Expect regional microbrews from the likes of Tree Brewing and Central City (go for its ESB) and hit the hole-in-the-wall kitchen for late-night nosh, including burgers and quesadillas.

DRINKING DOWNTOWN

BC'S FROTHY MICROBREW RENAISSANCE

Finally starting to rival the massive Pacific Northwest craft brewing scene south of the border, British Columbia is in the midst of a golden age of regional beer-making. Luckily for Vancouver visitors, bars around the city are falling over themselves to showcase intriguing brews from around the province. Look out for taps from the following small BC beer producers:

Central City Brewing (www.centralcitybrewing.com)

Driftwood Brewing (www.driftwoodbeer.com)

Howe Sound Brewing (www.howesound.com)

Old Yale Brewing (www.oldyalebrewing.com)

Phillips Brewing (www.phillipsbeer.com)

R&B Brewing (www.r-and-b.com)

Red Truck Beer (www.redtruckbeer.com)

Russell Brewing (www.russellbeer.com)

Storm Brewing (www.stormbrewing.com)

Tree Brewing (www.treebeer.com)

Vancouver Island Brewery (www.vancouverislandbrewery.com)

Whistler Brewing (www.whistlerbeer.com)

If you're a real beer nut, check out the annual Vancouver Craft Beer Week (p13) and also connect with the local Campaign for Real Ale chapter (www.camravancouver.ca), which stages regular events throughout the year. Finally, weekly special kegs are tapped on Sunday at the Whip (p157), Monday at St Augustine's (p157) and Thursday at Yaletown Brewing Company (p154), while the Alibi Room (p155) is the best place in town to sample a wide array of tongue-tickling BC brews.

WEST END

This bustling neighborhood has plenty of pubs and bars, including several gay-friendly haunts along Davie St.

1181 Map pp68-9   Bar

www.tightlounge.com; 1181 Davie St; 🚍 6
The West End's coolest gay bar, this loungey spot combines a chatty, sofa-strewn front space with a cozy back area that feels a lot more intimate. Separating the two is a sidebar staffed by friendly servers ever-ready to offer you tips on the local scene: this is also where the singletons sit, so you can expect to be the subject of some flirty attention as soon as you arrive. There's a good wine list and plenty of tempting cocktails, including the signature 1181 Margarita, made with Cointreau and lime-infused tequila.

O'DOUL'S Map pp68-9   Bar

www.odoulsrestaurant.com; 1300 Robson St; 🚍 5
Live nightly jazz attracts savvy locals to the watering hole of the Listel Vancouver (p199)

hotel, where there's an impressive wine list of Old and New World classics and a surprisingly smashing BC beer selection from brewers like Crannog, Storm and Turning Point: go for the Hermann's Dark Lager. The shows are cover-free and you can also expect performers to drop by for some late-night jamming during the Jazz Festival (p14). Service is excellent here and there's also a good grease-free bar menu.

SYLVIA'S LOUNGE Map pp68-9   Bar

www.sylviahotel.com; 1154 Gilford St; 🚍 5
Attached to the permanently popular Sylvia Hotel (p200), this was Vancouver's first cocktail bar when it opened in the mid-1950s. Now a comfy, wood-lined neighborhood bar favored by in-the-know locals (they're the ones who are hogging the window seats as the sun sets over English Bay), it's a great spot for an end-of-day wind down. Go for a 1954 vodka and Chambord cocktail, along with a side-dish of seafood-stuffed mushrooms.

DELANY'S Map pp68-9 — Cafe
1105 Denman St; 🚌 5

A laid-back, wood-lined neighborhood coffee bar that's popular with the West End's gay community, Delany's is a good perch from which to catch the annual Pride Parade (p15), although you'll have to get here early if you want a front-row seat. The usual array of cookies and muffins will keep you fortified while you wait.

MELRICHE'S Map pp68-9 — Cafe
www.melriches.com; 1244 Davie St; 🚌 6; 🛜

With its mismatched wooden tables, hearty array of cakes and crowd of journal-writing locals hunkered in every corner, this is an ideal rainy-day nook. Warm your hands on a pail-sized hot chocolate and press your face to the condensation-soaked window to watch the Davie St locals bustling past. This is the kind of place where Morrissey would hang out on a wet Monday afternoon to check his emails.

CARDERO'S Map pp68-9 — Pub
www.vancouverdine.com; 1583 Coal Harbour Quay; 🚌 19

Between Coal Harbour's bobbing boats, Cardero's is a stellar waterfront pub with cozy leather sofas, a wood-burning fireplace and great marina-side views. The small bar has a good menu of comfort food (the oyster burger is excellent) and the booze selection showcases a dozen or so drafts, from Strongbow to local Red Truck Lager. There's live guitar music most weekday nights and a full seafood restaurant – with patio – parked alongside.

MILL MARINE Map pp68-9 — Pub
www.millbistro.ca; 1199 W Cordova St; Ⓜ Waterfront

The food here is nothing special, but the waterfront panoramic patio views of Coal Harbour and the North Shore mountains more than make up for it. There's a small but impressive beer selection – try the Whistler Brewing Pale Ale – as well as summer-friendly cocktail slushies, while the nosh is generally of the pizzas and pasta variety. If you're in this area on a sunny day, drop by: it's one of the best spots to catch a signature Vancouver vista – arrive before 5pm or you'll be wrestling the locals for a table.

top picks

PATIOS

- Mill Marine (left)
- Chill Winston (p154)
- Dockside Brewing Company (p158)
- Backstage Lounge (p158)
- Yaletown Brewing Company (p154)

PUMPJACK PUB Map pp68-9 — Pub
www.pumpjackpub.com; 1167 Davie St; 🚌 6

Glancing through the open window as you walk past here on a summer night tells you all you need to know about this popular gay pub: it's a great place to meet leather-clad, often hairy locals ever-ready to meet a new friend in town for a quick visit. Expect queues here on weekends as the local bears vie for a pick up or two.

YALETOWN

Where the city's rich and beautiful people come to sip martinis and exchange lap-dog stories, there's more to this brick-lined SoHo than swanky lounges.

AFTERGLOW Map p72 — Bar
www.glowbalgrill.com; 1082 Hamilton St; Ⓜ Yaletown-Roundhouse

Tucked at the back of Glowbal (p135), the city's tiniest lounge is an intimate, brick-lined room studded with low-slung couches and little white coffee tables: it feels like a den for fashionistas. Pull up a vinyl stool and you'll soon be experimenting with flirty cocktails or a selection from the restaurant's wine list. Take a break from all that quaffing with a handful of lip-smacking satay sticks or some black truffle popcorn.

GEORGE ULTRA LOUNGE Map p72 — Bar
www.georgelounge.com; 1137 Hamilton St; Ⓜ Yaletown-Roundhouse

One of hedonistic Yaletown's favorite haunts, George attracts the local glitterati with its perfectly executed high-concept cocktails – anyone for a Sazerac, featuring bourbon in an 'absinthe-washed glass'? Work your way down the menu as you hone your chat-up lines on the locals, or just sink into that lip-shaped sofa in the corner and try to figure out what the giant swirly glass thing above the bar is. Food-wise, it's all about tasty side-dishes (the pork buns are especially recommended), while the DJs hit the turntables on Wednesdays and Thursdays.

OPUS BAR Map p72   Bar
www.opusbar.ca; 350 Davie St; Ⓜ Yaletown-Roundhouse

Adjoining the lobby of the swanky Opus Hotel (p201), the bar here is divided between an area of loungey gold thrones and high bar stools alongside a classic Parisian-style wooden bar in the restaurant room. Both serve a roster of old-school and new-twist cocktails to immaculately coiffured women hoping to snag a passing movie star or wealthy stockbroker. Try the Opus 97 and consider a serving of pecorino fries.

YALETOWN BREWING COMPANY
Map p72   Brewery
www.drinkfreshbeer.com; 1111 Mainland St; Ⓜ Yaletown-Roundhouse

Entering from the street, there's a brick-lined brewpub on the left and a giant dining room on the right; both serve pints of on-site-made beer, but the restaurant adds a long menu of comfort foods. In summer the pub's tiny patio is a popular perch (the restaurant's is much larger), but in winter playing pool at the back of the barroom is recommended. Check to see if there's an unusual small-batch beer on offer, otherwise hit one of the mainstays: Brick & Beam IPA is recommended. Beer nuts should drop by at 4pm on Thursdays, when a special cask is tapped.

ATLANTIC TRAP & GILL Map p72   Pub
www.atlantictrapandgill.com; 118 Robson St; 🚌 15

Hanging on to the end of Robson St, this cheery East Coast tavern is a great spot to

top picks

COCKTAIL JOINTS

- Diamond (right)
- Cascade Room (p156)
- Keefer (opposite)
- George Ultra Lounge (p153)
- Opus Bar (above)

indulge in hearty seafood pub grub and a pitcher or three of Trap Lager, the house beer that's usually on special. The interior is comfy roadhouse but, in summer, make for the large patio and soak up some of the sunshine: you'll still be able to hear the Celtic-inspired bands that keep the party atmosphere going on Thursdays and Saturdays.

GASTOWN & CHINATOWN

Home to many of the best bars in the city, Gastown's atmospheric old brick buildings have been revitalized with some excellent and distinctive watering holes, making this an ideal spot for an easy pub crawl. And don't forget about Chinatown, which has a choice bar or two of its own.

CHILL WINSTON Map p76   Bar
www.chillwinston.ca; 3 Alexander St, Gastown; 🚌 4

Gastown's best patio is the highlight attraction of this large, brick-lined bar overlooking Maple Tree Sq. Snag a spot under a parasol on a sunny afternoon and you're unlikely to move much for the rest of the day. Drinks-wise, you'll find a wide array of tipples, from flirty cocktails to New World wines, as well as a good boutique selection of interesting beers from Quebec, Belgium, the UK and beyond. Refuel with some sharable tapas plates.

DIAMOND Map p76   Bar
www.di6mond.com; 6 Powell St, Gastown; 🚌 4

Look for the unassuming entrance and head upstairs and you'll suddenly find yourself in one of Vancouver's best and coziest cocktail bars. This high-ceilinged, renovated heritage room is studded with sash windows – try for a view seat – and while it's popular with local hipsters it's never pretentious. A list of perfectly nailed cocktails (try the warming Penicillin of blended scotch, peated scotch, ginger, lemon and honey) is welcoming, but you'll also find a roster of intriguing, Asian-focused tasting plates, such as pork gyoza and green-tea noodles.

KEEFER Map p79 Bar
www.thekeeferbar.com; 135 Keefer St, Chinatown;
Ⓜ Stadium-Chinatown

A dark, narrow and sophisticated new bar
that – along with nearby Bao Bei (p137) – is
changing the face of Chinatown from
old-school to mod-cool. Claimed by the
hipsters as soon as it opened in 2010,
you'll find an intriguing menu of extremely
well-crafted cocktails (they start north
of the $10 mark, so they should be) plus
Asian-fusion tapas. Try something new and
you're almost bound to be blown away (if
you need help, go for the Opium Sour or
Keefer Fizz).

SALT TASTING ROOM Map p76 Bar
☎ 604-633-1912; www.salttastingroom.com;
Blood Alley, Gastown; 🚊 4

Tucked along a cobbled back alley
reputedly named after the area's former
butcher trade, this chatty and atmospheric
little brick-lined wine bar offers around
100 interesting tipples, most of which are
unusually offered by the glass. Beer fans
will also find a small menu of treats,
including the excellent Anchor Liberty Ale.
From your communal table perch, you
should also peruse the giant blackboard of
house-cured meats and regional cheeses,
then go for a $15 tasting plate of three,
served with piquant condiments – go for
Brit-style piccalilli.

SIX ACRES Map p76 Bar
www.sixacres.ca; 203 Carrall St, Gastown; 🚊 4

Perfect for a shared plate of finger food, it's
just as easy to cover all the necessary food
groups with the extensive beer selection
here (at least that's what you should tell
yourself). There's a small, animated patio
out front but inside is great for hiding in a
chatty, candlelit corner and working your
way through an exotic array of bottled
brews, often including London Porter and
the rather marvelous Draft Dodger from
Phillips Brewing. Possibly the city's coziest
tavern-style bar, you can pull a board game
from the shelf for an extended stay.

STEAMWORKS BREWING COMPANY
Map p76 Brewery
www.steamworks.com; 375 Water St, Gastown;
Ⓜ Waterfront

The signature beer at this giant, edge-of-
Gastown microbrewery is Lions Gate Lager,
which is a good summer tipple, but the
Empress IPA is also worth a try. A favorite of
the after-work crowd, the pub downstairs
can get noisy, while upstairs is all about
serene views across to the North Shore. The
menu is packed with pub standards, but
the pizzas and fish-and-chips are standouts.
Drop by for the monthly Green Drinks social
(www.greendrinks.org/BC/Vancouver), where local
chatty enviro-types flirt with each other
over a few brews.

ALIBI ROOM Map p76 Pub
www.alibi.ca; 157 Alexander St, Gastown;
☽ closed Mon; 🚊 4

Vancouver's favorite craft brew bar, this
often-hopping brick-walled contemporary
tavern stocks an ever-changing roster
of around 25, mostly BC, beers from
celebrated breweries like Phillips,
Driftwood, Old Yale, Crannog, Central City
and beyond. Adventurous taste-trippers –
Main St hipsters and old-lag Camra drinkers
alike – enjoy the $9 'frat bat' of four
sample tipples: choose your own or ask to
be surprised. Food-wise, go for a side order
of skinny fries with chili garlic vinegar or
for something more filling try a bulging,
Pemberton-sourced burger.

BLACK FROG Map p76 Pub
www.blackfrog.ca; 108 Cambie St, Gastown;
Ⓜ Waterfront

A few steps from the Steam Clock but
occupying a side-street blind spot, this
smashing Edmontonian-run bar does
everything right, from its friendly staff to
its perfect pub-grub menu. In summer, aim
to bask on the wood-deck patio – covered
against the rain – and tuck into the full
array of Big Rock beers from across the
border in Alberta (Traditional Ale is the way
to go). Food-wise, favorites include hearty

top picks
HIDDEN GEMS

- Narrow Lounge (p156)
- Three Lions Café (p156)
- Brickhouse (p156)
- Black Frog (above)
- Sylvia's Lounge (p152)

burgers, sandwiches and baked Stilton, but consider the great two-person ploughman's lunch instead.

BRICKHOUSE Map p79 — Pub
730 Main St, Chinatown; 🚍 3
On a sketchy strip of Main St that most people avoid, you'd expect the Brickhouse to be just as skuzzy as the nasty-ass dive bars surrounding it. But stepping inside here is a revelation. In Vancouver's most eclectic bar, you'll find redbrick walls lined with Christmas lights and fish tanks. The room is studded with junk-shop coffee tables and sagging couches. Popular with artsy locals and in-the-know hipsters, it's like hanging out in someone's old-school den. Grab a Storm Scottish Ale at the bar, slide onto a perch and start chatting: you're bound to meet someone interesting.

CAMBIE Map p76 — Pub
300 Cambie St, Gastown; 🚍 4
While this increasingly gentrified area still has plenty of dodgy dive bars that are best avoided, the Cambie is a local legend that most Vancouverites love, even if they haven't been here for years. Summer nights on the raucous patio are grungy fun, but perching at a sticky bench table inside with the boozy-but-friendly regulars is a blast. You'll be treated to some of the cheapest suds – go for a Cambie Pale Ale – in town plus a $7.50 burger and beer deal that's seriously good value.

IRISH HEATHER Map p76 — Pub
www.irishheather.com; 210 Carrall St, Gastown; 🚍 4
After moving across the street from its original location, the Heather has become a slicker version of its former self. And while not all the old regulars are happy about the upgrade, it's still undeniably one of Vancouver's best gastropubs. Pull up a chair on the bar side – the floor is reclaimed Guinness barrels – and dip into a great list of Irish drafts and international bottled brews. Or head to the narrow room next door where the regular Long Table Series – beer and dinner for under $15 – has become a runaway success. A great spot for charcuterie plates or hearty, home-made fare like bangers and mash or steak and Guinness pie.

SOUTH MAIN (SOMA)
Combining convivial bars and cozy coffeehouse hangouts, cool South Main is the kind of area you can nurse a drink all afternoon while you type your latest epic poem on your Apple laptop.

CASCADE ROOM Map p83 — Bar
www.thecascade.ca; 2616 Main St; 🚍 3
A great way to fast-track your way in with the local hipsters, this is the perfect contemporary reinvention of the trad neighborhood bar. Choice bottled beers like Anchor Steam and Young's Double Chocolate Stout feature, but the excellent 50-strong cocktail list is recommended: try a Cascade Room Cocktail of bourbon, pressed apple, lime juice, vanilla bean, bitters and egg white. Food is of fine gastropub quality, with the wine-braised beef and bubble and squeak worthy of praise. Drop by on Mondays for quiz night.

NARROW LOUNGE Map p83 — Bar
www.narrowlounge.com; 1898 Main St; 🚍 3
Push through the door just around the corner on 3rd Ave – the red light above tells you if it's open or not – then descend into Vancouver's coolest small bar. Little bigger than a train carriage and lined with stuffed animal heads and junk-shop pictures, the hipster-luring Narrow is an atmospheric nook where the absence of windows means it always feels like midnight. Ask the friendly bar staff for recommendations (cocktails like the Bramble or beers including Blue Buck Ale are popular) and refuel with an 'unburger' – meatloaf on a baguette.

GENE CAFÉ Map p83 — Cafe
2404 Main St; 🚍 3; 🛜
Colonizing a slender, flatiron wedge of concrete floors and expansive windows, slide onto a chunky cedar bench here with your well-thumbed copy of *L'Etranger* and you might catch the eye of an available SoMa local. If not, console yourself with a perfectly made cappuccino and a chunky homebaked cookie (the fruit pies are recommended for additional consolation).

THREE LIONS CAFÉ Map p83 — Pub
www.threelionscafe.ca; 1 E Broadway; 🚍 9
Vying with the Irish Heather for the 'best Vancouver gastropub' title, this small,

Brit-owned bar has a dedicated local following. Pulling both Tetley and London Pride on tap – as well as a good array of bottled ciders – the service here is excellent and the food (including great pies, Indian-style curries and a truly smashing lamb burger) is made-to-order from locally sourced ingredients. Drop by for the excellent weekend breakfast or try the ever-popular quiz night held every second Tuesday. Good spot to watch soccer games on TV.

WHIP Map p83 · Pub
www.thewhiprestaurant.com; 209 E 6th Ave; 🚌 3
The wood-floored Whip fuses the best in pub and lounge approaches. There's a dare-inviting selection of seven martinis, each named after a deadly sin (lust is always recommended) and a good menu with tempting treats such as yam *frites* and pad Thai. But it's the beer that wins regulars, with choice drafts from R&B Brewing, Storm Brewing and Quebec's infamous Unibroue. Consider dropping by on a Sunday afternoon when it cracks open a guest keg.

COMMERCIAL DRIVE

If you like your drink served with a frothy head of lively bohemian locals, the Drive's funky neighborhood bars and expert independent coffeehouses are hard to beat. For more on the coffee culture here, see the boxed text, p158.

STELLA'S TAP & TAPAS BAR Map p86 · Bar
www.stellasbeer.com; 1191 Commercial Dr; 🚌 20
Leading the Drive's friendly neighborhood bars, Stella's is a pilgrimage spot for fans of great Belgian brews. Leffe and Stella Artois are on tap but it's the multipage bottled list that'll do you in. Try fruity Mort Subite Kriek, coppery Chimay Rouge, strong Golden Draak and dark X.O., a brooding, end-of-the-night beer made with cognac. And don't forget that other nutrient group: *moules et frites* (mussels and fries) is recommended, or a cone of addictive fries (served Euro-style with mayonnaise) is always a good idea. There's also a more food-forward Stella's on Cambie (see p143).

CAFÉ CALABRIA Map p86 · Cafe
www.cafecalabria.com; 1745 Commercial Dr; 🚌 20
When Vancouverites tell you that Commercial is the city's best coffee street,

this is one of the places they're thinking about. It tops a healthy handful of great cafes founded here by Italian immigrants, and these guys really know their java. Don't be put off by the chandeliers-and-statues decor (if Liberace had opened a coffee shop, this is what it would have looked like) – just order an espresso and biscotti and pull up a chair outside.

CAFE DEUX SOLEILS Map p86 · Cafe
www.cafedeuxsoleils.com; 2096 Commercial Dr; Ⓜ Commercial-Broadway
This rambling bohemian coffeehouse is a hip, healthy and child-friendly addition to the Drive. On sunny days, folks relax out-side with a beer, while acoustic musicians, performance poets and open-mike wan-nabes take the stage several nights a week (see p165). There are plenty of good-value vegetarian snacks and meals but this is a great spot if you just want to chill out and meet the counterculture locals.

PRADO CAFÉ Map p86 · Cafe
www.pradocafe.com; 1938 Commercial Dr; 🚌 20; 🛜
Eschewing the kitsch-heavy interiors of many Commercial Dr coffee shops, the comparatively austere Prado is the kind of place where minimalists sup in peace. But it's not just about aesthetics: the baristas here are serious about their fair-trade coffee, which – don't tell the Italians down the street – may be the best on the Drive. Consider a Nutella chocolate cookie for the road.

CHARLATAN Map p86 · Pub
www.thecharlatanrestaurant.com; 1447 Commercial Dr; 🚌 20
Reinventing the old Bukowski's bar, the charming Charlatan has quickly become a Drive favorite. In summer the windows are flung open and the tiny patio is crowded, while in winter it becomes a cozy joint to watch the game or just chat in a corner. The hearty food covers a wide array of comfort dishes, while the 20-strong draft beer selection runs the gamut from Strongbow to Sleemans. Food-wise, go with the pulled pork burger or brisket sandwich.

ST AUGUSTINE'S Map p86 · Pub
www.staugustinesvancouver.com; 2360 Commercial Dr; Ⓜ Commercial-Broadway

VANCOUVER'S CAFFEINE CAPITAL

Starbucks and Tim Hortons are as ubiquitous as rainy days in Vancouver but the 'Wet Coast' metropolis is also Canada's independent coffee-shop capital. And the best place to head for an eclectic java crawl on one of those dark, cloud-threatening afternoons is Commercial Dr. Colonized in the 1950s by Italian immigrants, the Drive was built on buzzing, family-run cafes. Now operated by later generations of their original owners, many still serve the kind of life-enhancing brews that put the chains to shame. But Vancouver's favorite coffee strip isn't just about the past: alongside the old-school java joints are latter-day indie haunts beloved of local hipsters.

First stop for coffee tourists should be the legendary Café Calabria (p157). Dotted with replica Roman statues under a ceiling painted like a Venetian mansion, it stays just the right side of kitsch – even when one of its owners suddenly bursts into song. And while a coffee at Calabria used to be a choice between strong or ultra-strong espresso, there's now a huge, expertly prepared menu for caffeine-loving sophisticates.

Soccer-lovers are also well served here. FIFA World Cup tournaments always turn the Drive into a flag-waving fiesta, with fans packing those coffee shops that screen live games. Join the good-natured partisans at Continental Coffee (Map p86; 1806 Commercial Dr) and you'll be swept up in the moment, especially when someone scores. It's not all about sports, though: Continental runs its own bean-roasting operation and percolates some of the city's very best java.

It's easy to spend a twitchy afternoon trawling the trad coffee bars here – Joe's Cafe (Map p86; 1150 Commercial Dr) and Abruzzo Cappuccino Bar (Map p86; 1321 Commercial Dr) are also popular – but the full Drive effect comes from mixing it up with the newer kids on the block.

Opened a few years back, JJ Bean (Map p86; 2206 Commercial Dr) is possibly the area's coziest hangout. Part of a small, Vancouver-only minichain, it has a woodsy, neighborhood-bar feel. Clamorous with convivial chat on most days, its high tables and bar stools will lure you in for a quick latte with friends…and you'll find yourself still there several hours later. Best to move to decaf, since a cappuccino overdose is not conducive to a regular heartbeat.

Slow your pulse at Prado Café (p157) a few blocks away. Illustrating just how vibrant the Drive's coffee culture is, this mod little joint has the kind of whitewashed walls and hardwood floors that look coldly austere from the outside. But push through the door and you'll find a highly welcoming spot behind the minimalist veneer.

Looking like a regular neighborhood sports bar from the outside, step inside St Aug's and you'll find the largest array of on-tap microbrews in the city. Most are from BC – look out for highlights from Salt Spring Brewing, Central City Brewing and Tin Whistle Brewing – but there's usually an intriguing selection or three from south of the border. Drop by for Monday evening's cask night and you'll find an extra special tipple on offer. The food is of the standard pub-grub variety and if you drink too much, the SkyTrain station is just a few steps away.

GRANVILLE ISLAND

After a day spent weaving around the public market and artisan stores, wind down at one of Granville Island's decidedly laid-back bars.

DOCKSIDE BREWING COMPANY
Map p89   Bar
www.docksidebrewing.com; Granville Island Hotel, 1253 Johnston St; 🚌 50
Dockside has been self-brewing treats such as Alder Bay Honey Lager and fruity,

hibiscus-toned Jamaican Lager for more than 30 years. Take your drinks outside to the recently upgraded patio for tranquil, awe-inspiring views of False Creek's boat traffic and the mountain-backed downtown skyline – this is what supping in Vancouver is all about. If it's raining, stay indoors by the fireplace and sink into a leather couch. If you're not sure which beer to have, try a six-sample tasting flight for $14.

BACKSTAGE LOUNGE   Map p89   Pub
www.backstagelounge.com; 1585 Johnston St; 🚌 50
This often-hopping Granville Island hangout serves up winning patio views and some cool local live bands (see p167). The bar is lined with more than 20 BC microbrew taps from the likes of Dead Frog, Lighthouse and Red Truck – Bowen Island Cream Ale is on special on Tuesdays for $3 – so you won't go thirsty as you taste-trip around the province. The tempting food menu includes a good tandoori-chicken pizza.

GRANVILLE ISLAND BREWING
TAPROOM Map p89   Pub

www.gib.ca; 1441 Cartwright St; ☻ **bar to 8pm;**
🚌 **50**

Canada's oldest microbrewery started here
in 1984, gradually expanding to become
a big player in city bars. Most of its beer is
now made off-site, but you can still take a
tour of the small brewery (p88) or just head
straight to its pub-style Taproom. Naturally,
you're duty bound to sample everything,
but the lightly-hopped Brockton IPA and
English Bay Pale Ale are popular, along
with two seasonal favorites: summertime's
Robson Street Hefeweizen and the vanilla-
tinged Lions Winter Ale.

KITSILANO

You can only hang out at the beach and
wander among the shops in Kits for so long.
After a while, the bars will start to call your
name. Don't be afraid to listen.

FRINGE CAFÉ Map pp96-7   Pub
www.fringecafe.ca; 3124 W Broadway; 🚌 **9**

An ever-friendly locals' hangout, the
tiny Fringe is a reminder of Kitsilano's
counterculture heritage, from its funky,
memorabilia-lined walls to its chatty, bar-
propping regulars. Russell Brewing beers –
here called Ugly Boy Lager and Dirty Girl
Pale Ale – are usually on special, but
there's also a surprisingly large array of
international bottled brews that usually
includes everything from Tyskie to Tuborg.

If you're hungry, head for the Sherpa's Pie,
the best of several hearty house-cooked
entrées on the one-page menu.

NEVERMIND Map pp96-7   Pub
3293 W 4th Ave; 🚌 **4**

Casual-but-cavernous, this dark,
subterranean bar is popular with University
of British Columbia (UBC) students. They
come for the cozy log-lined back room –
there's also a large patio outside for
summer quaffing – and a large drinks list
that covers all the bases. Sleeman and
Okanagan Springs beers are available but
there's also a large and well-priced
cocktail selection – some are available by
the pitcher for group imbibing. The food
menu is equally intriguing, having
standard burgers and pizzas alongside
lesser-expected recommendations like
mahi mahi tacos.

WOLF & HOUND Map pp96-7   Pub
www.wolfandhound.ca; 3617 W Broadway; 🚌 **4**

One of the city's best Irish bars, this
perfectly comfy pub is also popular with
assignment-avoiding UBC students. It's not
surprising they can't tear themselves away:
there's a den-like back room to watch
sports, cover-free Celtic music on Friday
and Saturday and a menu of comfort-food
classics: go for the lamb stew or steak
and Guinness pie. Harp, Kilkenny and
Smithwick's Red Ale join Ireland's fave
stout on the beer list: you can try all four in
a sampler that's the same price as a pint.

NIGHTLIFE

top picks

With a reputation for spending their leisure time sipping chamomile macchiatos, indulging in an extra session of yoga or gorging on naughty rice cakes, you'd be forgiven for thinking that healthy-living Vancouverites don't really know how to kick it. In fact, hedonism is never far from the minds of most locals, which might explain the sweet-smelling substances wafting toward you on even the most respectable-looking streets.

But if you've come to the city in search of a rocking good night out, you'll need to dig a little. Although the Granville St entertainment strip between Robson and Davie Sts is Vancouver's traditional night-out area – and it's great if you like big clubs, big noise and big crowds – there are plenty of additional pockets of fun for fans of comedy, clubbing and great live music.

To find out what's on and where, pick up a free copy of the weekly *Georgia Straight*, the city's best listings newspaper. The *Westender* and the West Coast Life section of the *Vancouver Sun* also tap into local happenings. All three hit the streets on Thursdays.

PRACTICALITIES
Opening Hours
Nightclubs usually open their doors at 9pm (although they don't really get going until 11pm) and most stay open until 3am or 4am. Few clubs are open every day (many close Monday to Wednesday) and most are liveliest on Friday and Saturday. Acts at live-music venues typically hit the stage after 9pm.

How Much?
Expect to pay $5 to $20 for entry to many clubs, with weekends being top-price time. The cover charge at live-music venues can range from nothing at all to $35+, although there are many where $10 is the norm.

COMEDY
Vancouverites apparently have a sense of humor, but the city's live comedy scene is not very large. Along with a couple of dedicated clubs, some regular stand-up and improv nights are staged at venues across the city where you can laugh at some hilarious hockey and beaver in-jokes – check the *Georgia Straight* to see what's coming up. If you really need a good guffaw, drop by the annual Vancouver Comedy Fest (p16) or chuckle yourself silly at the International Fringe Festival (p16), where comic plays and stand-up shows hit Granville Island. Big-name acts – from Eddie Izzard to Jerry Seinfeld – often visit the city and, like touring bands, they take the stage at major venues such as the Orpheum Theatre, Queen Elizabeth Theatre and Richmond's River Rock Show Theatre.

COMEDY MIX Map pp58-9
www.thecomedymix.com; Century Plaza Hotel, 1015 Burrard St, downtown; 🕐 8:30pm Tue-Thu, 8:30pm & 10:30pm Fri & Sat; 🚍 2
The former Yuk-Yuk's venue in the basement of the Century Plaza Hotel mixes Tuesday's pro-am night with Wednesday's local talent showcase before the visiting headliners take the small stage for the rest of the week. If you're happy for food to erupt from your sniggering mouth at any moment, tapas-style nosh is also available from the bar.

COMEDY MONDAYS Map pp68-9
www.jlounge.ca; 1216 Bute St, West End; 🕐 8pm & 10pm Mon; 🚍 6
The kicking upstairs J Lounge in the West End stages regular events throughout the week for its predominantly gay (and gay-friendly) clientele, but Monday is comedy night. Cackle like a queen at 8pm's Tops & Bottoms, when 'Canada's only queer improv troupe' hits the little stage. Then stick around until 9pm or 10pm for the week's stand-up headliners, usually drawn from the local talent pool.

KITTY NIGHTS Map p83
www.kittynights.com; Biltmore Cabaret, 2755 Prince Edward St, SoMa; 🕐 9pm Sun; 🚍 9
Taking over the hipster-fave Biltmore on Sunday evenings, this ever-popular big night out – hosted by The Purrrfessor and Burgundy Brixx – is like an old-school variety show…with a rather saucy spin. The acts include a full roster of New York–style burlesque dancers and you can expect

some teasing audience participation from your wise-cracking hosts. Arrive early: those geeky males working in IT who haven't seen a girl all week tend to hog the best seats.

VANCOUVER THEATRESPORTS LEAGUE Map p89

☎ 604-738-7013; www.vtsl.com; The Improv Centre, 1500 Duranleau St, Granville Island; ⏱ 7:30pm & 9pm Wed, 7:30pm & 9:15pm Thu, 8pm, 10pm & 11:45pm Fri & Sat; 🚌 50
The city's most popular improv group stages its energetic romps – sometimes connected to themes such as Shakespeare or *Star Trek* – at a swanky new venue a couple of blocks from its old site. The format remains the same, though: if you're sitting near the front, expect to be picked on, unless you're naked – they tend to leave you alone if you're naked. The recommended 11:45pm Friday and Saturday shows are commendably ribald.

CLUBBING

While downtown's Granville Strip draws the barely clad booties of most mainstream clubbers, there are other, less limelight-hogging areas that cater to just about every musical peccadillo. Cover charges usually run from $5 to $20 ('the ladies' are often free before 11pm) and dress codes are frequently smart-casual – ripped jeans and sportswear will not endear you to the bouncers looking for people to send home. Bring ID to get in: most clubs accept over-19s but some want you to be over 25. You can put yourself on the VIP list (no waiting, no cover) at the websites of individual clubs or via www.clubvibes.com and www.clubzone.com. Doors generally open around 9pm or 10pm and most close at around 3am or 4am.

top picks

GAY JOINTS

AUBAR Map pp58-9

www.aubarnightclub.com; 674 Seymour St, downtown; ⏱ Wed-Sat; Ⓜ Granville
Top 40, hip-hop and house blast from the speakers at this popular, mainstream near-Gastown haunt, complete with three bars and a smallish dance floor. Drop in on Friday for Sensual, a mash-up of R&B and old-school pop, or save yourself for Rockstar Saturday, when the locals writhe around each other with abandon.

BAR NONE Map p72

www.dhmbars.ca; 1222 Hamilton St, Yaletown; Ⓜ Yaletown-Roundhouse
Yaletown's favorite haunt for young professionals has a scrubbed beatnik appearance, but within its exposed-brick-and-beam shell the main topic of conversation is perfect cocktails and real estate prices. The great and good come to sip and sway at Thursday's Straight Goods night (rap, hip-hop and $4 highballs) followed by Metro Fridays ('80s, '90s and contemporary mixes).

CAPRICE Map pp58-9

www.capricenightclub.com; 967 Granville St, downtown; ⏱ Wed-Sat; 🚌 10
Originally a movie theater – hence the giant screen evoking its Tinseltown past – upscale Caprice is one of the best mainstream haunts on the Granville Strip. The cavernous two-level venue is a thumping magnet for all the local preppies and their miniskirted girlfriends, while the adjoining resto-lounge is great if you need to rest your eardrums and grab a restorative cocktail and bite to eat. Expect to line up here on weekends, when the under-25s visiting from the suburbs dominate.

CELEBRITIES Map pp58-9

www.celebritiesnightclub.com; 1022 Davie St, downtown; ⏱ Tue-Sat; 🚌 6
The city's other main gay club (also see Odyssey, p164), Celebrities hosts a series of sparkling, sometimes sequined event nights throughout the week, including a raucous Red Hot Wednesday drag night and Saturday's Release, a massive dance party, when go-go dancers, live singers and occasional circus performers strut for your viewing pleasure. If you're on a budget, Tuesday is $3 highball night.

FORTUNE SOUND CLUB Map p79

www.fortunesoundclub.com; 147 E Pender St, Chinatown; ☾ Wed-Sat; 🚌 10

The city's best club has transformed a grungy old Eastside location – formerly the legendary Ming's Chinese Restaurant – into a slick space with the kind of genuine staff and younger, hipster-cool crowd rarely seen in Vancouver nightspots. Slide inside and you'll find a giant dance floor bristling with party-loving locals just out to have a good time. Expect a long wait to get in on weekends: it's worth it, though, for Happy Ending Fridays when you'll possibly dance your ass off.

ODYSSEY Map pp58-9

www.theodysseynightclub.com; 1251 Howe St, downtown; 🚌 6

This ever-popular gay club, combining regular drag nights on Wednesday and Sunday with a host of ever-changing special events throughout the week, is a thumpingly fun night out. Of course, you don't have to be gay to dance here, but it certainly helps if you're planning to meet someone (which almost everyone here is). The vibe is entertainingly risqué – hence Thursday night's Shower Power, when local beefcakes lather up in front of the slavering crowds.

POST MODERN Map p76

www.donnellynightclubs.ca; 7 Alexander St, Gastown; ☾ Thu-Mon; Ⓜ Waterfront

Despite the name, you're more likely to be discussing Yaletown condo prices than Foucault at this sleek and comparatively pricey lounge-club. Attracting an over-25s

crowd with money to burn on decadent cocktails, it's a good pit stop between the cool bars of Gastown: this is a very popular night-out neighborhood so weekend queues can be overly long. The main light-panel dance floor is quite small, and it's especially crowded for Friday's rap, indie dance and classic remix night.

REPUBLIC Map pp58-9

www.donnellynightclubs.ca; 958 Granville St, downtown; 🚌 10

If you make it this far up Granville, you're in for a loungey change of pace from the noisy clubs at the Robson St end; Republic attracts those sophisticated over-25s who have strayed all the way from Yaletown. Start your visit with a cocktail on the 2nd-floor patio while you look over the human wreckage of staggering late-night drunks. Then hit the dance floor, open nightly. Sunday is reggae and ska classics, while Saturday offers pulsing dance shenanigans.

ROXY Map pp58-9

www.roxyvan.com; 932 Granville St, downtown; ☾ nightly; 🚌 10

A raucous old-school nightclub that still has plenty of fans – including lots of partying youngsters who seem to be discovering it for the first time – this brazen old hussy is downtown's least pretentious dance space. Expect to be shaking your booty next to near-teenage funsters, kid-escaping soccer moms and UBC students looking for a bit of rough. On Sunday, don your buttless chaps and drop by for a wild western night out.

ALTERNATIVE NIGHTS OUT

Tired of the usual bar and club scene? Try these quirky substitutes:

Pub quiz at Cascade Room (p156) or Three Lions Café (p156)

Green Drinks at Steamworks Brewing Company (p155)

FUSE at Vancouver Art Gallery (p56)

Friday night at Hastings Racecourse (see the boxed text, p191)

Letter-writing social club at Regional Assembly of Text (p119)

Smoking with the hookah crowd at the Persian Tea House (Map pp58-9; www.persianteahouse.ca; 668 Davie St, downtown; 🚌 10)

SoMa's Royal Canadian Legion (Map p83; 2655 Main St, SoMa; 🚌 3), where the seniors and local coolsters share the dinged tables, shuffleboard and cheap beers. Don't miss Wednesday's karaoke night.

SHINE Map p76
www.shinenightclub.com; 364 Water St, Gastown; Ⓥ Wed-Sat; Ⓜ Waterfront

With music from electro to funky house and hip-hop, Gastown's sexy subterranean Shine attracts a younger crowd and is divided into a noisy main blue room and an intimate cozy cave red room with a 40ft chill-out sofa. The club's Bonafide Saturday indie disco and electro rave night is justifiably popular, while Wednesday's reggae, glitch and dubstep is slightly more chill.

VENUE Map pp58-9
www.venuelive.ca; 881 Granville St, downtown; Ⓥ Thu-Sat; 🚌 8

Redesigned from its previous incarnation as the Plaza Club, the removal of the obtrusive central bar has opened up a much larger dance floor here. The music is of the mainstream variety – Saturday's pop, rock and bass night is best – and the crowd includes plenty of nonlocals in from Surrey and New Westminster for their weekly big night out. This is also a live-music venue on some evenings – check the website to see what's coming up.

LIVE MUSIC

Vancouver's ever-eclectic live-music scene includes blues, jazz, folk and a double A-side of local and visiting indie acts. Superstar performers typically hit the stages at sports stadiums and downtown theaters – with inflated ticket prices to match – while smaller bands crowd the broom-closet dressing rooms at a rag-tag of little venues and bars around town, some of which are known only to the locals. If you want to plug into the city's grassroots sounds, check out the muso blogs and list of hot Vancouver acts in the Background chapter (see p28).

Hot venues here include the Commodore, Biltmore Cabaret, the Rickshaw Theatre and the Railway Club: to find out what they're scheduling while you're in town, pick up a copy of the *Georgia Straight* (or go to www.straight.com) or visit www.livevan.com. Alternatively, check in with the record stores listed on p120 – Zulu Records and Red Cat Records are your best bet, since they're experts on the local scene and they sell tickets to shows around the city. For the usual lofty fees, Ticketmaster (www.ticketmaster.ca)

NOT QUITE HOLLYWOOD...
If you're staggering along the Granville Strip after one too many tipples, take a breather by laying on the sidewalk. Cover yourself by telling your friends that you're closely perusing the brass discs embedded there – they might even believe you. The BC Hall of Fame's Starwalk emulates the slightly better known Hollywood version by celebrating famous names from the region's performing back catalogue. Look out for Diana Krall, Randy Bachman, Dal Richards and Red Robinson – if you don't recognize them, nip into the nearby Orpheum Theatre, which has a wall of photos depicting the near-300 inductees.

also hawks tickets and has a handy website calendar of what's coming up.

Of course, Vancouver isn't just about rock and roll. While this chapter also covers folk, jazz and blues, you'll find a full exploration of the classical side of things in the Arts chapter (see p170).

FOLK & WORLD

Touch base with the Rogue Folk Club (www.roguefolk.com), which presents dozens of annual shows and networking events for local and visiting folksters. Most of its shows are staged at Kitsilano's St James Hall (Map pp96-7; 3214 W 10th Ave). If you're here in July, indulge in the weekend-long Vancouver Folk Music Festival (p15) at Jericho Beach.

CAFÉ DEUX SOLEILS Map p86
www.cafedeuxsoleils.com; 2096 Commercial Dr; Ⓥ 9pm; Ⓜ Commercial-Broadway

A neighborhood hangout for the Drive's artsy bohemian bunch, this gallery-like coffeehouse and vegetarian eatery hosts poetry slams, open-mike and improv comedy nights as well as live music almost every evening – check the website to see what's on. The eclectic menu of tunesmiths can include anything from singer-songwriters to folk doyens and world-music performers.

JERICHO FOLK CLUB Map pp96-7
www.discoverysailing.org/folksong.html; Jericho Sailing Centre, 1300 Discovery St, Kitsilano; Ⓥ 7:30pm Tue; 🚌 4

Hosted by the Jericho Folk Club in this convivial beachfront sailing center, local folkies start their regular Tuesday-night event at 7:30pm with a fun drop-in jam session. The evening then progresses to an open-mike hour – make sure you bring your tambourine – and concludes with a headline act that's guaranteed to have your toes tapping and your beard growing.

PACIFIC BLUEGRASS JAM NIGHT
Map p83

www.pacificbluegrass.bc.ca; ANZA Club, 3 W 8th Ave, SoMa; ⏲ 7:30pm Mon; 🚍 9

The weekly public jam session for local bluegrass nuts, everyone is welcome to watch or join in with their instruments – all skill levels are fully welcome by this ever-friendly bunch. A great way to meet Vancouver fiddle-huggers, this foot-stomping night out upstairs at the ANZA Club takes place throughout the year, with a summer break to rest those weary plucking fingers.

JAZZ & BLUES

Hep cats should touch base with the Coastal Jazz & Blues Society (www.coastaljazz.ca), which orchestrates shows around the city throughout the year. It also runs the hugely successful Vancouver International Jazz Festival (p14), with its Canadian and international megastar shows plus free outdoor concerts. It also helped establish the smaller but highly successful Burnaby Blues & Roots Festival (www.burnabybluesfestival.com) in Deer Lake Park, which takes place every August. For something a little different, drop by St Andrew's Wesley United Church (Map pp58-9; www.standrewswesleychurch.bc.ca; 1012 Nelson St, downtown; 🚍 2) at 4pm on Sundays for a free Jazz Vespers performance.

CAPONES RESTAURANT & LIVE JAZZ CLUB Map p72

☎ 604-684-7900; www.caponesrestaurant.net; 1141 Hamilton St, Yaletown; no cover; Ⓜ Yaletown-Roundhouse

A convivial restaurant venue – think quality pastas and excellent thin-crust pizzas – with a strong roster of regular mainstream jazz and blues, this popular Yaletown haunt is an ideal spot if you're hungry for dinner and a show. House pianists and trios are the mainstay performers but funky blues dogs regularly hit the eardrums of chatty diners, most often on Sundays.

CELLAR RESTAURANT & JAZZ CLUB
Map pp96-7

☎ 604-738-1959; www.cellarjazz.com; 3611 W Broadway, Kitsilano; 🚍 9

A serious muso venue where you're required to keep the noise down and respect the performers on the tiny corner stage, this subterranean 70-seat resto-club is as close as you'll get in Vancouver to a classic jazz venue. Known for showcasing hot local performers, as well as some great touring acts, the atmospheric spot lures aficionados from across the region with its mix of mainstream and edgier fare. On Tuesdays, entry is free and there are good beer specials.

LIBRA ROOM Map p86

www.libraroom.com; 1608 Commercial Dr; 🚍 20

This glowing, brick-and-art-lined long room is a great spot for a relaxing, chatty dinner over a martini or three. Even better is the roster of nightly music, when two hopping jazz bands hit the stage (not at the same time, luckily) to deliver a mellow, toe-tapping sidedish to keep you in the mood. The kind of place you'd happily stay into the wee hours – they'll probably kick you out around 1am – it's one of Commercial Dr's best music venues.

O'DOUL'S Map pp68-9

www.odoulsrestaurant.com; 1300 Robson St, West End; 🚍 5

Free nightly jazz attracts locals and visitors to the Listel Vancouver hotel's laid-back resto-bar (see p152), a romantic, ambient-lit venue showcasing hot soloists, trios and quartets from the city and beyond. The focus is mainstream, but there's always a great buzz here during the Jazz Festival, when performers drop by to jam into the wee hours. Excellent wine menu plus some great BC beers.

YALE Map pp58-9

www.theyale.ca; 1300 Granville St, downtown; 🚍 10

A sassy unpretentious old gal with a large stage, a devoted clientele and a beer-sticky dance floor, the grunge-tastic Yale is possibly western Canada's best blues venue. Photos of past performers Koko Taylor, Junior Wells and even John Lee Hooker adorn the grubby brick walls, while latter-day regulars on the big stage include local fave Jim Byrnes, who holds court here like a king. Many shows are free here – check the website calendar for details.

ROCK & ALTERNATIVE

Local indie musicians seem to permanently bemoan the loss of favored Vancouver live venues over the years – goodbye forever Marine Club and Richards on Richards – but the city still has plenty of spots to catch a show and new ones crop up on a fairly regular basis. Support old lags like the Railway Club and Media Club, but save time to dip into exciting newer venues like the Biltmore Cabaret and the Rickshaw Theatre.

To see what's on during your stay, check the *Georgia Straight* or the online rosters of promoters Live Nation (www.livenation.com) and Sealed With a Kiss (www.sealedwithakisspresents.com). Along with the following venues, they stage visiting acts at the cavernous Rogers Arena (GM Place; p57) and the classical Orpheum Theatre (see the boxed text, p171) among others. For a good listing of local shows, dip into www.livevan.com.

ANZA CLUB Map p83
www.anzaclub.org; 3 W 8th Ave, SoMa; 🚍 9
This wood-built community hall – which has the ambience of a worker's club without the edge – is popular with East Vancouver hipsters and old-school hippies who have been coming here for years. Along with its eclectic roster of quiz and darts nights in the Tiki Lounge, there's a popular filmmaking club in the main hall (see the boxed text, p175) plus regular DJ and live-music events – check the website for calendar details.

BACKSTAGE LOUNGE Map p89
www.thebackstagelounge.com; 1585 Johnston St, Granville Island; 🚍 50
This lively, dark-interiored Granville Island haunt has been a mainstay of the local night-out scene for years, with its daily booze specials, DJ-led dance nights and a great chill-out patio. The live music – Monday's open mike, Wednesday's singer-songwriters, and local bands the rest of the week – keeps things hopping. Check the huge array of BC microbrew drafts lining the bar if the open-mike night drives you to drink.

top picks

LIVE-MUSIC VENUES

- Biltmore Cabaret (below)
- Commodore (below)
- Railway Club (p168)
- Rickshaw Theatre (p168)
- Media Club (p168)

BILTMORE CABARET Map p83
www.biltmorecabaret.com; 2755 Prince Edward St, SoMa; 🚍 9
One of Vancouver's best alt venues has only been open in its present incarnation for a few years but it's already a firm favorite. The SoMa crowd comes for its nightly-changing smorgasbord of Vancouver and visiting indie bands that can range from the Wintermitts to Tribal Soiree and Attack in Black (what do you mean you've never heard of them?). When there are no bands, DJ, poetry and film nights keep things lively, as well as Sunday's highly popular Kitty Nights burlesque show (p162).

COBALT Map p79
www.thecobalt.ca; 917 Main St, Chinatown; 🚍 3
Vancouver's punk, hardcore and metal fans almost swallowed their tongue studs in anger when the owners of this insalubrious Eastside hotel kicked out the legendary Wendy Thirteen, promoter of the city's alternative music scene, who had been scheduling acts here to great, spit-lobbing acclaim for years. The 'new' venue has yet to take off with the old crowd but it still schedules live acts – not all of them hard-core – almost every night.

COMMODORE Map pp58–9
www.livenation.com; 868 Granville St, downtown; 🚍 10
Up-and-coming local bands know they've finally made it when they play the city's best mid-sized music venue, a lovingly restored art deco ballroom that still has the bounciest dance floor in town – courtesy of stacks of tires placed under its floorboards. If you need a break from your moshing shenanigans, collapse at one of the tables lining the perimeter, catch your breath with a bottled Stella from the back bar then plunge back in.

MALKIN BOWL Map p63

www.malkinbowl.com; Stanley Park; 🚌 19

Formerly used only as the summertime venue for Theatre Under the Stars musicals (p180), this smashing Stanley Park stage has become an increasingly popular spot for alfresco live music. Elvis Costello, Franz Ferdinand and the Flaming Lips have had audiences (and those skulking around the fences outside) jumping up from the grass to punch the air…or partake of the aroma of naughty BC cigarettes wafting through the crowd. Check the website for this year's Concerts in the Park menu and book ahead.

MEDIA CLUB Map pp58-9

www.themediaclub.ca; 695 Cambie St, downtown; Ⓜ Stadium-Chinatown

This intimate, low-ceilinged indie space tucked underneath the back of the Queen Elizabeth Theatre books inventive local acts that mix and match the genres, so you may have the chance to see electro-symphonic or acoustic metal groups alongside power pop, hip-hop and country bands – although probably not on the same night. A great place for a loud night out (earplugs not supplied), this rivals the Railway Club and the Rickshaw for catching up-and-coming Vancouver acts.

PAT'S PUB Map p79

www.patspub.ca; 403 E Hastings St, Chinatown; 🚌 10

Saved from gentrification annihilation by its grungy location, the recently revived Pat's Pub was once a hopping jazz club. Now focusing mostly on thrasher, rockabilly and ska bands (do the names Raygun Cowboys and Napalm Willy ring any bells?), there's also a surprisingly good bar and beer menu (the own-made Pat's Classic Lager is always cheap). Music is mostly on Fridays and Saturdays.

RAILWAY CLUB Map pp58-9

www.therailwayclub.com; 579 Dunsmuir St, downtown; Ⓜ Granville

The old-school Rail is perfect for grabbing a beer in a traditional Brit-pub setting (see p151), but what really makes it special is its enduring commitment to the indie music scene. Its little stage has seen dozens of rising stars launch their careers and it's still the best place in town to catch passionate, consistently high-quality acts, ranging from folk to metal to bluegrass to polka. If you don't like what's on, just slink to the back bar. Arrive before 7pm and there's no cover charge, but since this goes to the bands, you might like to pay it anyway.

RICKSHAW THEATRE Map p79

www.rickshawtheatre.com; 254 E Hastings St, Chinatown; 🚌 10

This recently renovated old venue has been completely revamped from its grungy old self (it used to be called the Shaw), showing that Eastside gentrification can be positive. In fact, the Rickshaw has quickly become the stage of choice for local and visiting punk and metal bands – acts like Propagandhi and Dillinger Escape Plan, plus BC lads 3 Inches of Blood – that are more used to playing in dive-bar hellholes when they hit town. Expect a mega moshpit experience with plenty of action.

RIVER ROCK SHOW THEATRE Map pp54-5

☎ 604-247-8562; www.riverrock.com; 8811 River Rd, Richmond; Ⓜ Bridgeport

Handily located on the new Canada Line, the River Rock Casino's swanky on-site theater specializes in nostalgic music acts from the easy listening and older rock periods of music history. If you're wondering where Nazareth, Chicago or Robert Cray play when they hit town, this is it. The menu here sometimes includes a few surprises, like Blondie, just to show that you're turning into your parents. Visiting comedians including Jay Leno and Tim Allen have also appeared here.

WISE CLUB Map p86

www.wisehall.ca; 1882 Adanac St, Commercial Dr; 🚌 20

This comfortably grungy former church hall is a friendly neighborhood gem that's close to the heart of in-the-know locals, who flock here to catch live ska, salsa, improv shows and the occasional hip-hop DJ night – check the eclectic schedule for events or just hang out in the lounge (ask the bartender to sign you in as a guest). It's a great place to mix with cool East Vancouverites; the bouncy floor here brings out the moshpit desires in the most reluctant of dancers.

THE ARTS

top picks

THE ARTS

It's easy to think that Vancouver's Lycra-clad locals are a bunch of philistines when it comes to culture – how can opera and ballet fans also enjoy off-road mountain biking? – but in reality the city is a major regional center for artsy pursuits. On the highbrow side, there's an enormous array of classical music (below) on stage here, while dance (p172) is one of the city's Canada-leading specialties. There are also dozens of theater troupes (p178) across Vancouver, covering Shakespeare to challenging contemporary works and everything in between. And even though the Lower Mainland region is a popular location for Hollywood movie shoots, there's also a relatively healthy domestic movie scene (p173) and a great love among the locals for art-house productions. Finally, if you're in the mood for something a little more eclectic, the city is home to some regular spoken-word events (p177), including poetry and story slams.

To tap into the local scene, grab a copy of the *Georgia Straight,* and also check the *Westender* and the West Coast Life section of the *Vancouver Sun.* All three appear on Thursday every week. Make sure you also check the city's festival calendar (p12) before you arrive: Vancouver is home to some excellent annual arts events that can satisfy the most hungry of traveling culture vultures.

CLASSICAL MUSIC

Vancouver has a rich and resonant classical music scene, with particular strengths in baroque and chamber music. Along with recitals at downtown churches, the spectacular Orpheum Theatre and the swanky, state-of-the-art Chan Centre at the University of British Columbia (UBC), the city hosts festivals for fans of many genres. These include the frequently fascinating New Music Festival (p16) and the giant Music-Fest Vancouver (p15). The following societies and orchestras stage shows across the city.

EARLY MUSIC VANCOUVER
www.earlymusic.bc.ca; times & locations vary
Devoted to the performance and study of baroque music from the Middle Ages to the late Romantic era – often played on instruments authentic to the period – this lively recital society stages a popular summer festival (p15) as well as a rolling roster of concerts throughout the year, usually from September to May. Talks, workshops and events are also offered, so bring your lute in case there's a jam night.

FRIENDS OF CHAMBER MUSIC
www.friendsofchambermusic.ca; Vancouver Playhouse, downtown; Oct-Apr; M Stadium-Chinatown
Taking over downtown's Vancouver Playhouse (see the boxed text opposite) for intermittent Tuesday evening (plus some Sunday afternoon) performances, the Friends stages a tasty menu of shows from international visiting musicians. It's the kind of roster where you'll see chamber musicians from the Lincoln Center one week and the Berlin Philharmonic wind quintet the next.

NATIONAL BROADCAST ORCHESTRA
www.nbo.ca; Chan Centre for the Performing Arts, UBC; times vary; 99B-Line
Formed from the disbanded CBC Radio Orchestra – killed by funding cuts at the national broadcaster in 2008 – the new NBO tours the country but calls the Chan Centre for the Performing Arts (see the boxed text opposite) its home. Expect a full slate of intriguing shows, including plenty that champion Canadian composers.

PACIFIC BAROQUE ORCHESTRA
www.pacificbaroque.com; times & locations vary
Dedicated to baroque music from the 17th and 18th centuries, this thrilling Vancouver orchestra is highly regarded across North America. Its mandate is to perform the music the way it was originally written, which means using antique or authentic replica instruments and researching the prevalent techniques and styles of the period. Expect to hear plenty of violins and violas, accompanied by visiting harps and harpsichords, as you listen to fresh versions of works by composers such as Bach, Handel and Mozart.

PERFORMING ARTS VENUES

Few of the city's performance groups – from orchestras to dance troupes to theater companies – have their own venue, with most booking space and sharing from the same array of stages across the city. The following venues are the most likely spots for your cultural big night out.

- Centennial Theatre (Map pp54-5; ☎ 604-984-4484; www.centennialtheatre.com; 2300 Lonsdale Ave, North Vancouver; 🚍 230)
- Centre in Vancouver for Performing Arts (Map pp58-9; ☎ 604-602-0616; www.centreinvancouver.com; 777 Homer St, downtown; Ⓜ Stadium-Chinatown)
- Chan Centre for the Performing Arts (Map p102; ☎ 604-822-9197; www.chancentre.com; 6265 Crescent Rd, UBC; 🚍 99B-Line)
- Cultch (Vancouver East Cultural Centre; Map p86; ☎ 604-251-1363; www.thecultch.com; 1895 Venables St, Commercial Dr; 🚍 20)
- Fei & Milton Wong Experimental Theatre (Map p76; ☎ 778-782-9149; http://sfuwoodwards.ca; 149 W Hastings St, Gastown; 🚍 7)
- Firehall Arts Centre (Map p76; ☎ 604-689-0926; www.firehallartscentre.ca; 280 E Cordova St, Gastown; 🚍 7)
- Kay Meek Centre (Map pp54-5; ☎ 604-913-3634; www.kaymeekcentre.com; 1700 Mathers Ave, West Vancouver; 🚍 251)
- Old Auditorium (Map p102; ☎ 604-822-0182; www.music.ubc.ca; 6344 Memorial Rd, UBC; 🚍 99B-Line)
- Orpheum Theatre (Map pp58-9; ☎ 604-665-3050; www.vancouver.ca/theatres; 884 Granville St, downtown; 🚍 4)
- Performance Works (Map p89; ☎ 604-687-3020; www.gicculturalsociety.org; 1218 Cartwright St, Granville Island; 🚍 50)
- Queen Elizabeth Theatre (Map pp58-9; ☎ 604-665-3050; www.vancouver.ca/theatres; 609 Cambie St, downtown; Ⓜ Stadium-Chinatown)
- Roundhouse Community Arts & Recreation Centre (Map p72; ☎ 604-713-1800; www.roundhouse.ca; 181 Roundhouse Mews, cnr Davie St & Pacific Blvd, Yaletown; Ⓜ Yaletown-Roundhouse)
- Vancouver Playhouse (Map pp58-9; ☎ 604-873-3311; www.vancouverplayhouse.com; cnr Hamilton & Dunsmuir Sts, downtown; Ⓜ Stadium-Chinatown)
- Vogue Theatre (Map pp58-9; ☎ 604-569-1144; www.voguetheatre.com; 918 Granville St, downtown; 🚍 10)
- Waterfront Theatre (Map p89; ☎ 604-685-3005; www.gicculturalsociety.org; 1412 Cartwright St, Granville Island; 🚍 50)

VANCOUVER CHOPIN SOCIETY

www.chopinsociety.org; locations vary; ☯ Oct-May
One of the city's smaller musical societies, this dedicated group is a must for fans of the French-born Polish piano composer. It usually stages five or six signature piano recitals from famed national and international soloists (they often add the works of other composers to their performances). Lectures are sometimes also offered to satisfy the hunger of slavering Chopin musos (you know who you are).

VANCOUVER NEW MUSIC SOCIETY

www.newmusic.org; times & locations vary
Excitingly innovative and focusing on all manner of contemporary and new composing – from opera to electronica to mixed media – the society's performances are often an adventure in unfamiliar soundscapes. Coordinating a program of regional and visiting acts, its short annual festival (p16) takes place in October. Book ahead for a Soundwalk – a free listening tour uncovering the city's complex everyday musical soundscape.

VANCOUVER RECITAL SOCIETY

www.vanrecital.com; locations vary; ☯ Oct-Apr
This group brings in some big international names – think Yo-Yo Ma, Lang-Lang or Daniel Hope (although not usually on the same bill) – for performances across the city, but it also nurtures up-and-coming hot musicians destined to be the next big classical thing. Straddling opera and orchestral works, you can expect to see great vocal soloists and celebrated ensembles wowing the locals.

VANCOUVER SYMPHONY ORCHESTRA

☎ 604-876-3434; www.vancouversymphony.ca; times & locations vary

Led by popular maestro Bramwell Tovey, the city's stirring symphony orchestra serves up accessible classics and 'pops.' Shows to look out for include Symphony Sundays and film nights (when live scores are performed to classic movies), plus visits from revered soloists. There's also a series of themed light matinees and Kids' Koncerts to entice children from their Justin Bieber–loving ways. Concerts often take place at the Orpheum Theatre (see the boxed text, p171), but the orchestra frequently unpacks its kettledrums at auditoriums across the Lower Mainland.

DANCE

Vancouver is a major center for Canadian dance, offering an esoteric array of classical ballet and edgy contemporary fare. The city is home to more than 30 professional companies as well as many internationally recognized choreographers. To touch base with the region's hotfoot crowd, pirouette over to the Dance Centre. If you time your Vancouver visit well, you can also hit one of the region's key dance festivals: March's Vancouver International Dance Festival (p13) and July's Dancing on the Edge (p14).

BALLET BC

☎ 604-732-5003; www.balletbc.com; Queen Elizabeth Theatre, downtown; ⏰ times vary; Ⓜ Stadium-Chinatown

Despite almost folding due to financial problems in 2009, the region's premier dance troupe has resurrected itself with renewed determination. Under artistic director Emily Molner, the 15-dancer group continues to reinvent classic money-spinners like *Giselle* and *Swan Lake* while thrusting ahead with challenging new contemporary works. Ballet BC mainly performs at the Queen Elizabeth Theatre (see the boxed text, p171) from September to April.

DANCE CENTRE Map pp58-9

www.thedancecentre.ca; 677 Davie St, downtown; ⏰ times vary; 🚌 4

Vancouver's dance headquarters, this cleverly reinvented old bank building offers a kaleidoscopic array of activities that arguably makes it Canada's foremost dance center. Home to resident companies – Ballet BC is based here – it also houses classes, workshops, performances and events throughout the year. For visiting dance nuts, there's almost always something on worth seeing (check the website). If you're really lucky the biennial Dance in Vancouver showcase of British Columbia's best contemporary offerings will be on during your visit.

HOLY BODY TATTOO

www.holybodytattoo.org; times & locations vary

Formed by dancers Noam Gagnon and Dana Gingras, the internationally acclaimed Holy Body Tattoo has been performing riveting, edge-of-your-seat pieces to contemporary-dance fans around the world for two decades. Most of their self-choreographed works still start out in Vancouver. They can sometimes be found at the Cultch (see the boxed text, p171), if they're not gallivanting around the globe.

IN-THE-KNOW MUSIC SHOWS

If you've enjoyed the tranquility of a visit to the lovely Dr Sun Yat-Sen Classical Chinese Garden (p78), consider dropping by on a balmy summer night for its Enchanted Evenings Concert Series. Staged alfresco from July to early September (usually on Fridays), the international performers range from jazz to world music to gospel. Shows are very popular so book ahead, unless you're one of the turtles in the large pond – they usually get free entry.

Also consider Music in the Morning (www.musicinthemorning.org; Vancouver Academy of Music, 1270 Chestnut St, Kitsilano) where artists – from solo pianists to classical guitarists to visiting string quartets – give short introductory talks over coffee at 10am followed by the kind of stirring, life-enhancing performances that really set you up for the day.

The success of that series led organizers to add two additional events for music lovers. The same venue is used for Composers & Coffee, where musicians and experts discuss a composer and explore his or her work via performance. In addition, a series of bite-sized, one-hour, early-evening concerts – under the Rush Hour banner – has also been launched, with performers hitting the stage at CBC Radio's Studio One (Map pp58-9, 700 Hamilton St, downtown).

Expect a host of multimedia fireworks to accompany the show.

KAREN JAMIESON DANCE
www.kjdance.ca; times & locations vary
Striking contemporary choreography and cross-cultural First Nations themes are just two of the hallmarks of this innovative troupe, founded in 1983. The group's work has taken on a more mystical quality in recent years, reinterpreting its older canon and mixing it with some moving new works. Performing at various locations around the city, the troupe often hits the stage at festivals, including Dancing on the Edge and the Vancouver International Dance Festival.

FILM
Vancouver is a shimmering silver screen of independent, second-run and art-house movie theaters. You'll have no trouble catching the latest mindless blockbuster at a multiplex in the afternoon, followed by a depressing, subtitled dirge about French taxi drivers in the evening. Cheer yourself up the next day with an Omnimax movie that will have you soaring over the Grand Canyon or ducking and diving through the Great Barrier Reef. For cinema listings and special-event schedules, check the weekly *Georgia Straight* or daily *Vancouver Sun*, or visit www.cinemaclock.com to see what's on at all area theaters.

Try not to miss the Vancouver International Film Festival (p16) in late September, where you can rub shoulders with local moviemakers and catch some of the world's most exciting art-house pictures. If it's not on while you're here, drop by the Vancity Theatre (p175), where flicks, lectures and movie events are staged throughout the year.

If you're inspired to direct your own searing indictment of whatever takes your fancy, you might want to look into enrolling at the Vancouver Film School (Map pp58-9; www.vfs.com; 198 W Hastings St, downtown), which has programs in animation, game design and visual effects.

TICKETS
First-run movie tickets cost up to $12.50 for adults, less for students and seniors, with matinees (shows before 6pm) often a couple of dollars cheaper. Tuesday is discount day at many cinemas, which means it's often the

top picks
ARTS FESTIVALS
- Vancouver International Film Festival (p16)
- Vancouver International Fringe Festival (p16)
- Vancouver International Writers and Readers Festival (p16)
- MusicFest Vancouver (p15)
- PuSh International Performing Arts Festival (p12)

busiest night of the week. Admission to second-run theaters, repertory cinemas and art-house joints typically costs from $6 to $12.

CINEMARK TINSELTOWN Map p79
www.cinemark.com; 88 W Pender St, Chinatown;
Ⓜ Stadium-Chinatown
A Vancouver favorite, Tinseltown – incongruously located on the 3rd floor of a usually empty Chinatown shopping mall – combines blockbuster and art-house offerings, screened in a convivial but high-tech multiplex setting. Comfy, stadium seating is the norm here and it's the ideal place to shelter on a rainy Vancouver day, especially with its bottomless-coffee-cup policy. Drop by for the first showing of each movie on any day when all tickets are $8, or hit the crowded all-day-Tuesday discount day ($8.75).

FIFTH AVENUE CINEMAS Map pp96-7
www.festivalcinemas.ca; 2110 Burrard St, Kitsilano;
🚌 44
The popular Fifth Avenue screens indie, foreign flicks and blockbuster Hollywood schlock (those Kitsilano locals might look like intellectuals but they enjoy *Iron Man* as much as anyone else). Moviegoers can belly up to the lobby cappuccino bar for above-par baked goods before the show. A non-mandatory $12.50 annual membership provides about 15% savings on tickets throughout the year, while on Tuesday seats are $8 for everyone. Also check out the loveseats, where you can lift the padded divider and snuggle up with your movie buddy.

GRANVILLE 7 Map pp58-9
www.empiretheatres.com; 855 Granville St,
downtown; 🚌 10

ALFRESCO FILM NIGHTS

While drive-in movie theaters in Canada are about as common these days as Canuck Oscar winners, Vancouverites have fully embraced a burgeoning new summertime trend for catching a film or two outside. Grab your friends, a blanket and some picnic snacks and arrive early for a good spot at the grassy, free-entry screenings organized by FreshAirCinema (www.freshaircinema.ca). Venues often include Yaletown's David Lam Park and Coal Harbour's Harbour Green Park and the big-screen action usually covers fave flicks like *ET, Hairspray* or *Ghostbusters*. Click through to the Facebook page via its website for listings of upcoming shows.

Alternatively, it's hard to beat Stanley Park for a movie backdrop. Which is just as well, since Monsters in the Meadow (Map p63; www.vancouverparks.ca; ☽9pm) screens scary B-movie classics in its Creperly Meadow area near Second Beach every August. The free-entry movies often include the scream-triggering likes of *Godzilla, King Kong* or *Creature from the Black Lagoon*. It'll be chilly once the sun goes down (although you may be trembling in fright), so bring a sweater. Flashlights are also recommended so you can find your way back out of the park after the show.

And for those who can't get enough of Andrew McCarthy and Molly Ringwald, Hastings Racecourse (see the boxed text on p191) stages Flashback to the '80s, free outdoor screenings of evergreen nostalgic flicks like *Teen Wolf, Top Gun* and *Breakfast Club* after the last horse race on Fridays in June and July.

The remaining vestige of a once-thriving cluster of cinemas lining both sides of downtown's old entertainment strip, the Granville 7 might not be around much longer – which probably explains why the escalators are hardly ever switched on – but it still screens a good selection of mainstream and second-run flicks. Empire Theatres, its new owners, have recently reduced the ticket price to an enticing $7.99 for all shows ($5.99 on Tuesdays).

HOLLYWOOD THEATRE Map pp96-7
www.hollywoodtheatre.ca; 3123 W Broadway, Kitsilano; ▣9

Two-thirds blockbuster and one-third art house make up the roster here, showing exactly where the funding for this popular local theater comes from. Tickets are a great deal, especially since they include two shows – double bills are every evening and on weekend afternoons. Bucking the trend, Monday night is cheap night here, when you can catch two movies for just $6.

OMNIMAX THEATRE Map p79
www.scienceworld.ca; 1455 Quebec St, Chinatown; Ⓜ Main St-Science World

Now the only mammoth-format screen in town, following the demise of the CN Imax at Canada Place, this Science World cinema will have you swaying in your seat with its roster of neck-cracking, if rather worthy, documentaries – the ones that always fly the camera over a soaring clifftop vantage point to keep you awake.

Occasionally, reformatted Hollywood movies of the *Spiderman* or *Harry Potter* ilk are added to the mix.

PACIFIC CINÉMATHÈQUE Map pp58-9
www.cinematheque.bc.ca; 1131 Howe St, downtown; ▣4

This beloved nonprofit repertory cinema operates like an eclectic ongoing film festival with a daily-changing program of movies. A $3 annual membership is required – pick it up at the door – before you can skulk in the dark with the chin-stroking movie buffs, who would name their children after Fellini and Bergman if they ever averted their gaze from the screen long enough to have relationships. Although it's $9.50 to catch a flick here, you can watch two movies a night for just $11.50. The high point of the year is August's annual classic film noir season.

RIDGE THEATRE Map pp96-7
www.festivalcinemas.ca; 3131 Arbutus St, Kitsilano; ▣16

A local community fave, mixing foreign films and Hollywood fare, this is a lively and convivial cinema in which to hang out with the locals. Check out the retro building's glass-enclosed 'crying room,' where parents can take wee noisemakers and still watch the movie without disturbing other patrons. Unlike most cinemas, where the food typically has the nutritional value of a hockey puck, the concession here serves organic fruit.

RIO THEATRE Map p86
www.riotheatre.ca; 1660 E Broadway, Commercial Dr; Ⓜ Commercial-Broadway
A recently restored 1980s movie house with very comfy seats, the one-screen Rio shows one Hollywood blockbuster every night. Even better are its extras: there's a baby-friendly screening for parents and their mewling progeny every other Wednesday, while Friday night brings a midnight double bill of classics like *A Clockwork Orange, Back to the Future* and, of course, the *Rocky Horror Picture Show* – there's a $2 discount if you arrive in costume. Check the website for additional special events. All matinees are $7, as are all Tuesday shows.

SCOTIABANK THEATRE Map pp58-9
www.cineplex.com; 900 Burrard St, downtown; 🚌 2
Downtown's shiny nine-screener was big enough to attract its own corporate sponsor when it opened in 2005, but it's actually the city's Cineplex chain flagship. It's the most likely theater to be screening the latest must-see *Harry Potter* sequel or in-your-face comic-strip action flick. In contrast, it also shows occasional live broadcast performances from major cultural institutions like London's National Theatre and New York's Metropolitan Opera. For 3-D movies, add an extra $3 to your ticket price. There are no matinee or Tuesday discounts here.

VAN EAST CINEMA Map p86
2290 Commercial Dr; Ⓜ Commercial-Broadway
This balconied old-school cinema shows an eclectic schedule of critically acclaimed

THE NEXT EISENSTEIN
Visiting movie nuts with a penchant for making their own flicks – or just chewing the fat with those who do – should unspool their film over at one of Vancouver's coolest underground hangouts. Held every month at the community hall ANZA Club (p167), the Celluloid Social Club (www.celluloidsocialclub .com; 🕑 7:30pm Wed, mid-month) is a drop-in for local filmmakers and video artists who want to show their shorts to anyone who happens to turn up. The results – seven mini-epics are shown over the course of a couple of hours – are always interesting, and the screenings are followed by a few beers and a chance to rub shoulders and chat with the local auteurs.

new and classic movies (plus second-run blockbusters to keep the money rolling in), with occasional late-night screenings and special events such as moviemaker lectures. It's a handy five-minute stroll north of the Commercial-Broadway SkyTrain station; continue on up the road after the show and discuss the flick at one of Commercial's chatty bars (see p157).

VANCITY THEATRE Map pp58-9
www.viff.org; 1181 Seymour St, downtown; 🚌 4
The state-of-the-art headquarters of the Vancouver International Film Festival screens a wide array of movies throughout the year in the kind of auditorium that cinephiles dream of: think generous legroom, wide arm rests and great sight lines from each of its 175 seats. It's a place where you can watch a four-hour subtitled epic about a dripping tap and still feel

FILM FESTIVALS
While the leading lady of the city's film-festival scene is the giant Vancouver International Film Festival (p16), several supporting players hit city screens throughout the year. Butter up your popcorn at one or two of these:

DOXA Documentary Film Festival (www.doxafestival.ca) May's nine-day celebration of the very best in documentary filmmaking from around the world.

Vancouver Asian Film Festival (www.vaff.org) Emerging and established North American–Asian filmmakers screen works over four days in November.

Vancouver International Mountain Film Festival (www.vimff.org) A week of movies in February about mountain culture and sports.

Vancouver Latin American Film Festival (www.vlaff.org) Held in September, it's a week of movies illuminating the region's rich culture and social issues.

Vancouver Queer Film Festival (www.queerfilmfestival.ca) Western Canada's largest film event by and for gays and lesbians; held in August around the same time as Pride Week (p15).

comfortable. Check the ever-changing schedule for shows and special events, and remember that a $2 annual membership is mandatory. Double bills are available most nights (adult/student $13/11).

OPERA & CHORAL

Twinned with its classical repertoire (p170) and staged at similar venues around the city, Vancouver has quite a soaring array of options for those who enjoy operatic or choral performances. Check the websites of the following groups and societies to see what's on the menu during your visit.

VANCOUVER BACH CHOIR

www.vancouverbachchoir.com; Orpheum Theatre, downtown; ⏲ times vary; 🚌 4
The city's largest nonprofessional choir, this 150-strong, all-ages group can lift the spirits on the soggiest of Vancouver days. Performing five concerts annually at the gorgeous Orpheum Theatre (see the boxed text, p171), its Christmastime 'Sing Along Messiah' is guaranteed to raise the hairs on the back of your neck as you join in to try and raise the roof on the auditorium.

VANCOUVER CANTATA SINGERS

www.vancouvercantatasingers.com; times & locations vary
Renowned as the city's leading semi-professional exponent of baroque choral pieces – receiving critical acclaim from across the country – the Vancouver Cantata crew also keeps things current by commissioning and performing works by new composers. Clearing its collective throat at churches and auditoria across the city, its concert series usually runs late October to early May.

VANCOUVER CHAMBER CHOIR

www.vancouverchamberchoir.com; locations vary; ⏲ late Sep–May
Vancouver's top professional choir is an award-winning ensemble of 20 singers recognized around the world for its diverse repertoire, interpretive skills and performing excellence. In addition to busy touring and recording commitments, the choir performs a hotly anticipated season at venues around the city. The concerts are rarely less than outstanding, the styles range from chant to folk song, traditional to avant-garde, a cappella to orchestra or jazz trio.

VANCOUVER MEN'S CHORUS

www.vancouvermenschorus.ca; times & locations vary
Canada's first gay chorus when it was set up 25 years ago, this highly regarded and ever-entertaining troupe has since gained national and international recognition as well as massive popularity around the city. Expect a full menu of spirit-raising concerts at venues throughout the Lower Mainland, with light classics, tear-jerking ballads and Broadway showstoppers often part of the mix.

VANCOUVER OPERA

www.vancouveropera.ca; locations vary; ⏲ Oct–May
The city's well-regarded opera company stages four annual productions at the Queen Elizabeth Theatre (see the boxed text, p171) during its season. While the shows are typically traditional productions of well-known favorites such as *Pagliacci* and *La Bohème* – complete with lavish sets and costumes – there are usually some less mainstream or even edgy offerings to keep things interesting.

VANCOUVER'S THEATRICAL GRAND DAME

If you're lucky enough to catch a show at the Orpheum Theatre (Map pp58–9; ☎ 604-665-3050; www.vancouver.ca/theatres; 884 Granville St, downtown; 🚌 4), be prepared to gasp when you enter the auditorium. Built in 1927 and now designated a national heritage site, the sumptuous Spanish baroque interior of multiple arches topped by an ornate painted dome harkens back to a time when theaters offered a fantasy escape from reality. But the beautiful old gal isn't just a well-preserved relic. In fact, she's steeped in theatrical history. Originally part of a Chicago-headquartered chain of vaudeville houses, stars who have hit the boards before the near-3,000 seats here have included Bob Hope, Shirley MacLaine and Harry Belafonte – check out the commemorative wall plaques around the stage door out back and you'll find an A-Z of names from entertainment history.

SPOKEN WORD

Vancouver's under-the-radar spoken-word events can run from free readings at local libraries to poetry slams at cool cafes and lectures at theaters and halls around the city. If you're a visiting bookworm, check into the readings and discussions staged during October's annual Vancouver International Writers and Readers Festival (p16), or time your visit for the one-day, late-September Word on the Street (www.thewordonthestreet.ca), when authors, poets and publishers cluster around the Vancouver Public Library (p60), offering readings, recitals and plenty of lovely books to buy.

COLD READING SERIES Map pp96-7

www.evolvingartscollective.com; Billy Bishop Legion, 1407 Laburnum St, Kitsilano; ⏰ 7:15pm Thu mid-Jun–early Sep; 🚌 16

Visiting actors are cast on the spot – they'll audition you on the night if you feel the urge – to read through an always-changing selection of new plays, movie scripts and TV pilots submitted by nervous local writers. It's like a workshop with an audience and it can be a recipe for a fun night out if you're a creative type who likes to watch.

JOY KOGAWA HOUSE Map pp54-5

www.kogawahouse.com; 1450 W 64th Ave, Marpole; ⏰ times vary; 🚌 10

Saved from demolition in 2006 by a hardy band of literary volunteers and the deep pockets of the Land Conservancy Trust (funds are still required to renovate the property), the modest bungalow where celebrated Japanese Canadian poet and novelist Kogawa grew up now has a writer-in-residence program and a drive to become a pilgrimage spot for local and visiting bookworms. There's a calendar of varied readings, workshops and events on its website.

PANDORA'S COLLECTIVE

www.pandorascollective.com; times & locations vary

Promoting self-expression through literature, this busy group stages events throughout Vancouver, including open-mike readings, poetry nights and 'word whips,' where you're given 15 minutes to write some engaging prose on a given cue.

Locations are usually coffeehouses around the city. Check the collective's website for upcoming events and consider its annual Summer Dream Literary Arts Festival, a day of readings and bookish shenanigans in Stanley Park.

PHILOSOPHERS' CAFÉ

www.sfu.ca/philosopherscafe; times & locations vary

This is a popular series of engaging philosophical discussions staged at restaurants, cafes and galleries in Vancouver and across the Lower Mainland. You can listen to the theories being espoused or wade in with your own crackpot ideas. Each night has a different theme, which might include 'freedom and jazz' or 'painting is dead,' for example. The moderated discussions are often brain-fizzingly lively – consider dressing up as Marx and sitting at the back chuckling to yourself. Check website for dates, themes and locations.

ROBSON READING SERIES Map pp58-9

www.robsonreadingseries.ubc.ca; UBC Library/Bookstore, Plaza Level, 800 Robson St, downtown; ⏰ times vary; 🚌 5

This ongoing encyclopedia of readings and literary events – free-entry, with refreshments provided – is mostly held in the subterranean UBC bookstore underneath downtown's Robson Sq (it's near the Vancouver Art Gallery, if you need a landmark). Canadian novelists, poets and creative non-fiction writers dominate and there's a strong emphasis on Q&A and sociable chitchat: now's your chance to thrust that 1800-page *Lord of the Rings* sequel into someone's hands.

VANCOUVER POETRY SLAM Map p86

www.vancouverpoetryhouse.com; Cafe Deux Soleils, 2096 Commercial Dr; ⏰ Mon night; Ⓜ Commercial-Broadway

If you thought poetry was a tweedy, soporific experience, drop by one of the events organized by the Vancouver Poetry House at Cafe Deux Soleils (p157) for a taste of high-speed, high-stakes slamming. The expert performers will blow your socks off with their verbal dexterity, which often bears more than a passing resemblance to rap. Every fourth Monday is Youth Slam, for the 13 to 22 age group.

OLYMPIC GREASEPAINT

While many Vancouverites were lost to the gold medal hockey pursuit at the city's 2010 Olympic and Paralympic Winter Games, it was another event that made some locals even more excited. The giant Cultural Olympiad that ran alongside the Games was a 600-show smorgasbord of artsy shenanigans that had many tearing their hair out as they tried to catch as much of it as possible. From a laser light spectacular over English Bay to a Montréal electro-funk rave and a performance from world-leading flamenco dancer María Pagés, there was so much to see that some didn't catch any of the sports at all. And while there were dozens of nightly free music shows – with the likes of K'naan, Feist and Bryan Adams among many others – arguably the best show of all was a two-night rock concert featuring Elvis Costello and Lou Reed interpreting the songs of Neil Young. They were backed by a giant band of Canadian musicians including Ron Sexsmith and members of Metric and Broken Social Scene, who all grinned like happy kids when Reed strutted his stuff in front of them.

THEATER

From mainstream to fringe, theater thrives in Vancouver: luvvies can catch an important new work from a Canadian playwright one night and follow it up the next evening with a quirky off-the-wall production in an intimate studio space. While the season generally runs from October to May, there are a couple of choice theatrical events that ensure the greasepaint is a year-round smell here.

These include summertime's Bard on the Beach (right), where locals pack the tents of Vanier Park for atmospheric retellings of *Hamlet, King Lear* et al, January's PuSh International Performing Arts Festival (p12) and September's Vancouver International Fringe Festival (p16).

If challenging is your theatrical bag and you're in town for a while, consider a See Seven (www.seeseven.bc.ca) pass, which gives you entry to seven out of 11 shows from some of the city's leading independent theater companies for just $97.

TICKETS

Ticketmaster (☎ 604-280-4444; www.ticketmaster.ca) is not surprisingly the standard agent for many theatrical productions here, although some theaters prefer to bypass it. For advance regular-price tickets and same-day half-price tickets, try the homegrown Tickets Tonight (☎ 604-684-2787; www.ticketstonight.ca). In addition, discounts are normally available for students, seniors and children – ask theater box offices for details.

ARTS CLUB THEATRE COMPANY
www.artsclub.com; times & locations vary
Musicals, international classics and works by contemporary Canadian playwrights

are part of the mix at this leading theater company. If you're curious about West Coast theatrics, look out for plays by Morris Panych, BC's favorite playwright son. The company's three performance spaces are the Granville Island Stage (Map p89; 1585 Johnston St, Granville Island; 🚌 50), the nearby and more intimate Revue Stage (Map p89; 1601 Johnston St, Granville Island; 🚌 50) and the refurbished 1930s Stanley Theatre (Map p93; 2750 Granville St, South Granville; 🚌 10).

BARD ON THE BEACH
☎ 604-739-0559, 877-739-0559; www .bardonthebeach.org; Vanier Park, Kitsilano; 🕓 Jun-Sep; 🚌 22
Watching Shakespeare performed while the sun sets against the mountains looming through the open back of a tented stage is a singular Vancouver highlight. An enduring favorite summer pastime for city culture hounds, there are usually three Bard plays, plus one Bard-related work (*Rosencrantz and Guildenstern are Dead,* for example), on offer. Free pre-show talks are staged before Tuesday-night performances, along with special opera, fireworks and wine night packages throughout the run. For more, see the boxed text opposite.

BOCA DEL LUPO
www.bocadellupo.com; times & locations vary
Dedicated to the creation of new works of physical theater using collaborative processes and interactions between the performers and audience, this cutting-edge experimental troupe fuses international approaches with its team of local actors. New theater is the name of the game here, and the company often brings in collaborators from across the country (or the world) to keep things fresh.

CAROUSEL THEATRE Map p89
www.carouseltheatre.ca; Waterfront Theatre, Granville Island; ⏰ times vary; 🚌 50

Performing at Granville Island's Waterfront Theatre (see the boxed text, p171), this smashing child-focused theater company stages some great, wide-eyed fantasy productions that adults often enjoy just as much as their kids. Adaptations of children's classics such as *The Wind in the Willows* have featured in the past, with clever versions of Shakespeare works added to the mix for older children. There's also an excellent kids theater school in summer if you're traveling with a young thesp.

CULTCH (VANCOUVER EAST CULTURAL CENTRE) Map p86
www.thecultch.com; 1895 Venables St, Commercial Dr; ⏰ times vary; 🚌 20

This once-abandoned 1909 church near Commercial Dr has been a gathering place for performers and audiences since being officially designated as a cultural space in 1973. But following a comprehensive $14 million renovation that was completed in 2009, the Cultch (as everyone calls it) has become one of the city's best performance spaces and the performance jewel of the Eastside. Appearing on the charming Historic Theatre main stage is an ever-eclectic roster of local and visiting drama plus music and dance troupes. After the show, hang around in the lobby wine bar to mull over the show and chat with the locals.

FIREHALL ARTS CENTRE Map p76
www.firehallartscentre.ca; 280 E Cordova St, Gastown; ⏰ times vary; 🚌 7

One of the leading players in Vancouver's independent theater scene, this intimate, studio-sized venue is located inside a historic fire station. It presents culturally diverse contemporary drama and dance, with an emphasis on showcasing emerging talent. An important venue during the annual Dancing on the Edge festival (p14), there's also a convivial licensed lounge onsite where visiting drama fans discuss the scene over a few beers.

GATEWAY THEATRE Map pp54-5
www.gatewaytheatre.com; 6500 Gilbert Rd, Richmond; ⏰ Oct-Apr; 🚌 407

The Lower Mainland's third-largest theater company (and Richmond's only professional live theater), the state-of-the-art Gateway has two stages and runs a full roster of shows during its season. Slick productions of contemporary favorites and older classics – there's usually at least one musical here per season – occupy the main stage, while intriguing and more challenging work fills the studio space, including some premieres of bold new plays.

PLAYHOUSE THEATRE COMPANY
☎ 604-873-3311; www.vancouverplayhouse.com; Vancouver Playhouse, downtown; ⏰ Oct-May; Ⓜ Stadium-Chinatown

Mainstream and generally 'safer' in its selection than the city's edgier companies,

---

ALL THE WORLD'S A (TENTED) STAGE

There's no doubt that if Shakespeare was alive today, he'd definitely be a West Coast surfer dude, spending most of his time bumming around local beaches. Well maybe not, but Vancouver's annual Bard on the Beach festival (opposite) catches a little of that spirit with a summer-long theatrical run that's arguably the city's most successful and enduring arts event.

Under the creative guidance of twinkle-eyed actor-manager Christopher Gaze – a local luvvie legend; see p33 for an interview – the 20-year-old festival (known simply as 'Bard' among the locals) has grown faster than the pile-up of dead bodies accumulating at the end of *Hamlet*. Attendance has increased from just 6000 visitors in 1990 – when there was one play and 35 performances – to well over 90,000 in 2009, when fours plays and more than 200 shows were performed.

The not-for-profit company now employs 30 professional actors every season, plus expert directors, technicians and designers. There's also a dedicated team of 200 volunteers to keep order on show nights. Alongside its 520-seat Mainstage tent (quaintly, patrons still have to mark their unnumbered seats with Post-it notes provided at the door), the smaller Douglas Campbell Studio Stage was added to the temporary village in 1999. Before catching a show, the audience spends its time here sipping wine from the bar tent or poking around the Bard-related gift shop – the perfect place to pick up that *Macbeth* manga comic or quill-wielding Shakespeare action figure.

THEATRICALS YOUNG & OLD

Several of Vancouver's colleges and universities incorporate lively drama departments, offering some excellent productions at great prices. If you're a visiting theater buff on a budget, smell the greasepaint at one of these recommended student playhouses.

Exit 22 (Map pp54-5; www.capilanou.ca/theatre; Capilano University, 2055 Purcell Way, North Vancouver; 251) North Van's Cap Uni is home to this well-established theater company, affiliated with its drama department, which performs at a smashing 372-seat performance space. Its season – often featuring comedies, classics and contemporary works – runs from October to March, with the theater used by touring musicians the rest of the time.

Studio 58 (Map pp54-5; www.langara.bc.ca/studio58; Langara College, 100 W 49th Ave, SoMa; M Langara-49th Ave) Named after the room number of the theater space at Langara College campus, which is a two-block walk from the Canada Line SkyTrain station, Studio 58 has grown to become one of western Canada's most respected theater companies, hiring professional directors to work on each of its four annual productions. You might catch musicals, Shakespeare or Canadian premieres here.

Theatre at UBC (Map p102; www.theatre.ubc.ca; Frederic Wood Theatre, 6354 Crescent Rd, UBC; 99B-Line) UBC's drama students, grads and faculty stage their biggest shows here, but they also have two studio theaters where they try out more challenging fare. The season usually runs September to March, with each production lasting around a week. Expect a roster of classics and contemporary plays.

And if you want to hang out at the other end of the age range, check out the Performing Arts Lodge Theatre (Map pp68-9; www.palvancouver.org; 581 Cardero St, West End; 19), located in a swanky new Coal Harbour condominium block reserved for retired performance artists. While the building's smashing upper-floor studio space hosts an eclectic array of visiting, sometimes-challenging shows throughout the year, the audience is often full of old luvvies who look like they might have a few good stories to tell about the profession during the interval.

Vancouver's pre-eminent city-run theater troupe performs in the purpose-built Vancouver Playhouse (see the boxed text, p171). Its six-play season includes original Canadian and international works featuring top-tier regional actors and directors. There's often a crowd-pleasing classic musical thrown into the mix as well. Productions here are slick and impressive.

THEATRE UNDER THE STARS Map p63

☎ 604-734-1917; www.tuts.ca; Malkin Bowl, Stanley Park; ☉ mid-Jul–mid-Aug; 19 Stanley Park's old-school Malkin Bowl is an atmospheric open-air venue in which to catch a summertime show. The season never gets too serious, usually featuring two enthusiastically performed Broadway musicals, but it's hard to beat the location, especially as the sun fades over the trees peeking from behind the stage. Increasingly, the venue is being used for music – see p168 for details.

TOUCHSTONE THEATRE COMPANY

www.touchstonetheatre.com; locations vary; ☉ Nov-Apr One of Vancouver's most vital and refreshing theater companies, Touchstone has been treading the local boards for more than 30 years. It's never lost touch with its commitment to nurture and stage contemporary Canadian theater and it often premieres new work by local writers or stages the first regional productions of important national works. The company performs around the city – check the website to see what it's up to during your visit.

SPORTS & ACTIVITIES

top picks

SPORTS & ACTIVITIES

Vancouverites have a passion for the outdoors – it's hard not to when the outdoors is staring you in the face everywhere you look. But the variety of easily accessible activities here is what really impresses: this truly is a city where you can ski in the morning and hit the beach in the afternoon, although it would make for quite a tiring day out. In between, you could hike through a rainforest, swim in a giant saltwater pool, windsurf along the coastline or kayak to your heart's content – and it really will be content with a sunset backdrop of mirrored skyscrapers and the tree-lined wilderness of the looming mountains.

If that all sounds a little *too* active, sports fans of the armchair variety will likely enjoy the city's spectator options – from hockey to horse racing to roller derbies – while those who just like to be pampered have plenty of opportunities to hit a day spa or two and build a deep and meaningful relationship with a massage table. If you indulge a little too much at the city's bars and restaurants, don't forget there are lots of gyms to lick you back into shape.

ACTIVITIES

It's hard *not* to be active in Vancouver, with its plethora of outdoorsy resources as well as its full menu of indoor facilities for those rainy days when you still want to raise your heart rate. Pick up an activity guide by the Vancouver Board of Parks & Recreation (www.vancouverparks.ca) from the Tourism Vancouver Visitor Centre (p239) or head to the board's website for comprehensive listings covering facilities and courses.

Canada's favorite outdoor-activities megamart, Mountain Equipment Co-op (p120) rents all sorts of gear and has weekend specials where you collect the goods at 3pm Thursday, bring them back by 1pm Monday and only pay for Saturday and Sunday rental. Visit its website (www.mec.ca) for a calendar of local events and activities, ranging from group hikes to guided kayak paddles.

CYCLING & MOUNTAIN BIKING

Vancouver is a cycle-friendly city with a good network of designated bike routes. See p226 for info and resources on biking in the city. You can also touch base on local bike issues via Momentum (www.momentumplanet.com) magazine, available free online.

The city's favorite (ie most crowded) cycling route is the one-way 8.8km Stanley Park seawall, where cyclists (plus joggers, walkers and bladers) have to keep their eyes on the road rather than stare open-mouthed at the sea-to-sky vistas. After circling the park to English Bay, you can pedal on along the north side of

False Creek toward Science World, where the route turns up the south side of False Creek to Granville Island, Kitsilano Beach and, finally, the University of British Columbia (UBC). This extended route is around 25km.

If you're more of a mountain biker and you can't wait to hit some mud-splattering trails, the North Shore is striped with fantastic options. Mt Seymour (www.bcparks.ca) offers excellent forested runs, including Salvation, Pangor and Bridal Path, each with boulders, logs and bridges to keep you challenged. First-timers should consider the 10km Seymour Valley Trailway, which has only a few uphills and offers great views of Mt Seymour as well as the occasional deer. And if you fancy tackling one of the region's all-time fave courses, consider Pipeline trail on Mt Fromme. Its 2km course is packed with beams, rocks, ladders and boardwalks and it links to the popular 48km Baden Powell Trail, which stretches scenically across the region.

For more information on local mountain-biking experiences, check in with the North Shore Mountain Biking Association (www.nsmba.ca). And for an introduction to biking in the area, consider a guided tour with Endless Biking (www.endlessbiking.com; tours from $115).

The following businesses rent or service bikes.

BAYSHORE RENTALS Map pp68-9
www.bayshorebikerentals.ca; 745 Denman St, West End; per hr/8hr $6/22.80; ☀ 9am-9pm May-Aug, 9am-dusk Sep-Apr; ☐ 19
One of several rival businesses taking advantage of their Stanley Park

proximity, the folks here will rent you just about anything to get you rolling around the seawall. The 21-speed mountain bikes are its bread and butter, but it also hires in-line skates, tandems (you know you want one) and rugged baby strollers for parents who like to jog with their sprogs.

COVE BIKE SHOP Map pp54-5
www.covebike.com; 1389 Main St, North Vancouver; ⏰ 9:30am-5pm; 🚌 250
The North Shore's favorite store for hardcore mountain bikers, the Cove doesn't rent bikes but it sells and services for the area's serious bike dudes. An excellent spot to rub shoulders with the region's biking fraternity, it's worth dropping in for a chat and some expert tips on area trails.

DENMAN BIKE SHOP Map pp68-9
www.denmanbikeshop.com; 710 Denman St, West End; ⏰ 10am-5pm Sun & Tue, 10am-6pm Fri & Sat, 9am-6pm Mon, 9am-7pm Wed & Thu; 🚌 19
If you've brought your own wheels with you and need a tune-up or repair, this is perhaps the best spot in the city to get some help. The owners are real bike aficionados – hence the tempting array of '50s-style cruisers for sale – and they can tell you all you need to know about tapping into the local bike scene.

RECKLESS BIKE STORES Map p89
www.reckless.ca; 1810 Fir St, Granville Island; per hr/5hr $8.25/29.50; ⏰ 9:30am-7pm Mon-Fri, 9:30am-6pm Sat, 10am-6pm Sun; 🚌 50
The friendly folk at Reckless have been big players in the city's bike community for years, sponsoring events and supporting initiatives across the region. There's a good selection of rental cruisers and mountain bikes and staff can provide maps of regional road routes. Located in a no-man's-land of mismatched businesses near the entrance to Granville Island, there's also a Yaletown location (Map p72; 110 Davie St; ⏰ 9:30am-7pm Mon-Sat, 10am-6pm Sun).

SPOKES BICYCLE RENTALS Map pp68-9
www.vancouverbikerental.com; 1798 W Georgia St, West End; adult per hr/6hr from $7.15/21.43; ⏰ 8am-9pm Jul & Aug, reduced off-season; 🚌 19
On the corner of W Georgia and Denman Sts, the recently expanded Spokes is the biggest of the bike shops crowding this stretch – these are the guys mostly

top picks

SPORTY SHENANIGANS

- Ski or snowboard at Cypress, Grouse or Seymour mountains (p187)
- Cycle the mountain-bike trails of the North Shore (opposite)
- Kayaking at Deep Cove (p185)
- Hike the sweat-triggering Grouse Grind (p184)
- Take a saltwater swim at Kitsilano Pool (p189)

responsible for all those tourists wobbling across the nearby road as if they've never ridden a bike in their lives. It can kit you and your family out with all manner of bikes, including cruisers, tandems and kiddie one-speeds. Also rents in-line skates.

GOLF

Vancouverites love to swing their sticks, and the city's mild climate allows for year-round putting. Green fees for 18-hole courses average $40 to $60 (early-bird specials are often available) and many courses have highly convivial clubhouses where you can hang with the locals and their dimpled balls. For information on the regional scene, check in with Golf British Columbia (www.golfbritishcolumbia.ca).

FRASERVIEW GOLF COURSE
Map pp54-5
☎ 604-257-6921; www.vancouverparksgolf.ca; 7800 Vivian Dr, South Vancouver; green fees adult/youth/senior $57/28.50/40, weekends extra; ⏰ dawn-dusk; par 72, 6700yd; Ⓜ 29th Ave Station, then bus 29
Surrounded by mature trees, this city-run facility near E 54th St overlooks the Fraser River and consistently wins awards for being one of Canada's best public courses. Its clubhouse serves a full menu and you can also grab a consolatory beer if you've been hacking unsuccessfully all day.

GLENEAGLES GOLF COURSE
Map pp54-5
☎ 604-921-7353; www.westvancouver.ca/golf; 6190 Marine Dr, West Vancouver; green fees adult/youth/senior $22/16/18; ⏰ dawn-dusk; par 35, 2800yd; 🚌 250
This picturesque but challenging nine-hole public course has a long history and must

have been named by a fan of the Great Game. Nestled between the mountains and sea near Horseshoe Bay, its lovely views entice many to keep coming back. Beware of the third hole, known as Cardiac Hill. A new clubhouse was recently added.

LANGARA GOLF COURSE Map pp54-5

☎ 604-257-8357; www.vancouverparksgolf.ca; 6706 Alberta St, South Cambie; green fees adult/ youth/senior $52/27/37, weekends extra; ☼ dawn-dusk; par 71, 6260yd; Ⓜ Langara-49th Ave
Another city-owned facility (near W 49th St), with large rolling greens and narrow fairways, Langara is regarded as a challenging course. You can practice a few strokes on the putting green before you hit the main attraction.

UNIVERSITY GOLF CLUB Map p102

☎ 604-224-1818; www.universitygolf.com; 5185 University Blvd, UBC; green fees adult & youth/ senior $59/48; ☼ dawn-dusk; par 72, 6157yd; 🚍 99B-Line
Tucked inside UBC's giant Pacific Spirit Regional Park, this popular and attractive course has been luring locals of all skill levels to knock off early from work for 80 years. The tree-lined 13th hole will have you reaching for your camera, and there's a driving range and an excellent clubhouse restaurant – as well as the cool BC Golf Museum behind the 17th tee.

HIKING

Hiking opportunities abound in the regional and provincial parks here. A rite of passage for many, the Grouse Grind (see the boxed text, right) is the most infamous. Lighthouse Park (p108) and Whytecliff Park (p108) are scenic gems with gentle trails to tramp around. Many locals agree that Mt Seymour Provincial Park (p105) has the area's best hiking, though the Cypress Provincial Park (p107) and Pacific Spirit Regional Park (p103) certainly rank up there, as well.

If you're heading to any of the North Shore parks, be prepared for continually changing mountain conditions – the weather can alter suddenly here and a warm sunny day in the city might not mean it's going to be the same, or stay the same, in the mountains. Take along a warm waterproof jacket, wear sturdy shoes and a hat, and carry a water bottle.

MOTHER NATURE'S STAIRMASTER

If you're finding your vacation a little too relaxing, head over to North Vancouver and join the sweaty throng snaking – almost vertically – up the Grouse Grind trail. The entrance is near the parking lot, across the street from where slightly more sane visitors to Grouse Mountain (p105) pick up the Skyride gondola to the summit. Around 3km, the steep, rock-studded forest trek will likely have your joints screaming for mercy within 15 minutes as you focus on the feet of the person in front of you. Most people take around an hour to reach the top, where they collapse like gasping fish on the rocks. If you're feeling energetic, you might want to try and beat the record of Vancouverite Sebastian Albrecht who nailed the trail 14 times in one day in 2010. Things to keep in mind if you're planning to join the 110,000 who hike the Grind every year: take a bottle of water, dress in thin layers so you can strip down, and bring $10 with you: the trail is one way, so when you reach the summit you have to pay a special rate to take the Skyride back down – your consolation is that you get to enjoy the summit's many attractions for free in exchange for your exploding calves.

ICE SKATING

If you were inspired by the 2010 Winter Olympics and want to practice your sequined ice-dance routines, Vancouver has several facilities where no one would mind at all. If you're up at Grouse Mountain (p105) in winter, there's a small outdoor rink where you'll be fighting the five-year-olds for ice time. The city also has several good-value indoor public rinks. Hillcrest Park's Vancouver Olympic Centre, which housed curling events during the Games, was being re-created as a legacy project during research for this book. When it reopens in 2011, its facilities will include a swanky new public ice rink – check progress on the project via www.vancouverparks.ca.

BRITANNIA COMMUNITY CENTRE
Map p86

www.britanniacentre.org; 1661 Napier St, Commercial Dr; adult/child/senior $5.10/2.52/3.57, skate rental $2.57; ☼ 8am-9pm Mon-Thu, 8:30am-7pm Fri, 9am-5pm Sat, 10am-4pm Sun; 🚍 20
Handily open for skaters all year round, this popular community-center rink offers skate lessons and a weekly roster of regulars, including Monday's women-only drop-in

hockey, Thursday's late-night co-ed drop-in hockey and Wednesday evening's adults-only skate (the perfect place to meet your new ice-dance partner).

WEST END COMMUNITY CENTRE
Map pp68-9

www.westendcc.ca; 870 Denman St, West End; adult/child/senior $5.10/2.52/3.57, skate rental $2.57; ⏰ 9am-10pm Mon-Thu, 9am-9pm Fri, 9am-5pm Sat, 10am-5pm Sun winter-early Spring; 🚌 5
This busy and bustling community center, with a full range of events, activities and classes to keep the locals on their toes, has its main hall transformed into an ice rink for the winter and early spring. You don't have to pack your skates because rentals are available. Like all the city-owned rinks, public skating times vary, so call ahead for the latest schedule.

KAYAKING
It's hard to beat the joy engendered by a sunset paddle around the coastline here, with the sun sliding languidly down the mirrored glass towers that forest the skyline. With its calm waters, Vancouver is a popular spot for both veteran and novice kayakers. For an alternative, try a tranquil, sigh-inducing summer excursion around the glassy waters of Deep Cove.

DEEP COVE CANOE & KAYAK CENTRE
Map pp54-5

☎ 604-929-2268; www.deepcovekayak.com; 2156 Banbury Rd, North Vancouver; 2hr/5hr rental $30/63; ⏰ 9am-6pm; 🚌 212
Enjoying Deep Cove's sheltered waters, this is an ideal – and idyllic – spot for first-timers to try their hand at paddling. The staff here will gently show you all you need to know on a three-hour introductory course ($80), where you'll learn that getting in and out of the boat are the hardest parts. For those with a little more experience, the center also offers rentals and some smashing guided tours (the full-moon tour is recommended). Check the website for regular events, including Tuesday's popular race nights.

ECOMARINE OCEAN KAYAK CENTRE
Map p89

☎ 604-689-7575, 888-425-2925; www.ecomarine.com; 1668 Duranleau St, Granville Island; 2hr/24hr

$36/69; ⏰ 9am-6pm Jun-early Sep, 10am-6pm mid-Sep–May; 🚌 50
Headquartered on Granville Island, the friendly folk at Ecomarine offer guided tours (from $59) and equipment rentals. At the center's Jericho Beach branch (Map pp96-7; ☎ 604-222-3565; Jericho Sailing Centre, 1300 Discovery St; ⏰ 9:30am-dusk late Apr-early Sep; 🚌 4), they also organize events and seminars where you can rub shoulders with local paddle nuts. From June to September, you'll find them renting additional kayaks from the old bath house building on English Bay Beach.

ROCK CLIMBING
There's rock climbing close to Vancouver at places such as Juniper Point in West Vancouver's Lighthouse Park (p108) and the bluffs overlooking Indian Arm in Deep Cove (p107). Serious climbers, however, head up Hwy 99 to Squamish (p219) to scale the mighty Stawamus Chief. The BC Mountaineering Club (www.bcmc.ca) offers programs and courses and is a good way to network with the local upwardly mobile community.

In the city, Vancouverites are restricted to indoor climbing centers, which generally charge around $15 to $20 for entry; courses are extra. Recommended centers – both with additional kid-friendly programs – include the following:

CLIFFHANGER VANCOUVER Map p83
www.cliffhangervancouver.com; 670 Industrial Ave, SoMa; ⏰ 10am-10:30pm Mon, noon-10:30pm Tue-Thu, noon-10pm Fri, 10am-9:30pm Sat & Sun, reduced off-season; Ⓜ Main St-Science World
The city's newest indoor-climbing center has a chatty, welcoming vibe and offers tons of courses for beginners and more advanced climbers alike. The popular two-hour intro course ($69) is ideal if you're a climbing virgin. The facility has 15,000 sq ft of terrain and 53 top ropes.

EDGE CLIMBING CENTRE Map pp54-5
www.edgeclimbing.com; Suite 2, 1485 Welch St, North Vancouver; ⏰ 1-11pm Mon-Fri, noon-9pm Sat & Sun; 🚌 240
This high-tech North Van facility has a large climbing gym with more than 15,000 sq ft of climbing surfaces for those who like hanging around for fun. There are plenty of courses, from introductory level

to advanced classes where you can learn all about diagonalling and heel-and-toe hooking. If you enjoy this, you can drive straight from here to the Stawamus Chief in Squamish.

RUNNING

For heart-pounding runs (or even just an arm-swinging speed walk), the 8.8km Stanley Park seawall remains the city's number-one circuit. It's mostly flat, apart from a couple of uphill sections where you might want to hang onto a passing bike. Among the park's less-crowded interior trails, the 2km trek around Lost Lagoon is among the best. If you still have plenty of energy when you reach the end, carry on running along the seawall into the West End: you'll soon hit the False Creek route that will take you all the way around the water to Granville Island and beyond. UBC is another popular running destination, with tree-lined trails marked through Pacific Spirit Regional Park.

Tap into the city's Lycra-clad jogging fraternity by dropping into the Running Room (Map pp68-9; www.runningroom.com; 679 Denman St, West End; 🕑 9:30am-9pm Mon-Fri, 9:30am-6pm Sat, 8:30am-5pm Sun; 🚊 19), a store where steely-calved perambulators and those hitting the streets for the first time come to hang out. As you swap training regimes and choose your next pair of well-supported athletic shoes, ask about the regular clinics and group runs it

---

RUNNING THE CITY

Elite runners, regular joggers and the kind of people who would normally rather have a beer than pull on jogging shoes join together once a year for Vancouver's 10km Sun Run (www.sunrun.com). North America's second-biggest street race – numbers creep up every year and currently hover around 55,000 – the April event is like a gargantuan rolling street parade, complete with laughing locals, bands that buoy your spirits along the route and a party-like group hug that awaits the triumphant at the end, when everyone tucks into bagels and yogurt while rubbing their aching muscles. It's a great way to see the city, too – you'll wind into Stanley Park, over the Burrard Bridge and through residential streets where the cheering locals will be out in force. And the satisfaction as you limp toward the finish line – usually with some stirring music to trigger a final sprint – will live with you long after you return home.

---

organizes. You can also find out about races in the region.

SAILING & WINDSURFING

English Bay gets some good winds whipping through, attracting summertime sailors and windsurfers to duke it out over the water. For lessons and equipment rentals, Jericho Sailing Centre (Map pp96-7; 1300 Discovery St, Kitsilano; 🚊 4) is the best place in town. Several companies are based here, along with the Galley Patio & Grill (p145), where the patio sunset views are among the best in the city. Hardcore windsurfers and kiteboarders also head to Squamish Spit (p219), where the winds are fiercer.

The following companies occupy the Jericho Sailing Centre:

MAC SAILING Map pp96-7

☎ 604-224-7245; www.macsailing.com; rental per hr $35-50; 🕑 9am-7pm Mon-Fri, noon-6pm Sat & Sun, reduced off-season; 🚊 4
This excellent operation, catering to sailing veterans and newbies who want to learn the ropes, has six boats available for rent – the super-fast and easy-to-sail Hobie Getaway is recommended. Lessons – which usually run for four days – are also offered and some are tailored specifically for kids.

WINDSURE ADVENTURE WATERSPORTS Map pp96-7

☎ 604-224-0615; www.windsure.com; board/skim-board rental per hr $18.58/4.64; 🕑 9am-8pm Apr-Sep; 🚊 4
For those who want to be at one with the sea breeze, Windsure specializes in kiteboarding, windsurfing and skimboarding and offers lessons and equipment rentals. Novices are more than welcome here: the two-hour windsurfing introductory group lesson ($52) is recommended.

SCUBA DIVING

Despite extremely cold temperatures, the North Shore waters have a lot to offer divers, although the general consensus is that you can find more comfortable diving elsewhere in the province. Among the most popular dive areas near the city is Whytecliff Park (p108), which contains an underwater reserve that's best explored between October and April. Divers in this area will need a 6mm neoprene wetsuit as temperatures below the thermocline stay at about 10°C (50°F). If you're a real dive nut, consider hitting Nanaimo, on the east coast of Vancouver Island, where you'll encounter wolf eels, Pacific octopus and two sunk-to-order navy vessels – see www.divenanaimo .travel for further information.

Back in Vancouver, outfitters including the following offer equipment, training and trips:

DIVING LOCKER Map pp96-7

☎ 604-636-2681; www.divinglocker.ca; 2745 W 4th Ave, Kitsilano; rentals from $60, courses from $75; 🕑 10am-6pm Mon-Fri, 10am-5:30pm Sat, 10am-4pm Sun; 🚌 4

A long-established favorite with local snorkelers and scuba divers, the Diving Locker is not just for experienced practitioners. Along with its regular series of PADI training courses, there's a great introductory course ($75, including equipment) for first-timers. There are also specialist kids courses for aquatically inclined youngsters.

INTERNATIONAL DIVING CENTRE Map pp96-7

☎ 604-736-2541; www.diveidc.com; 2572 Arbutus St, Kitsilano; rentals from $55, courses from $79; 🕑 10am-7pm Mon-Fri, 10am-6pm Sat & Sun; 🚌 16

Equipment rentals and courses are part of the mix here, but the center also organizes regular trips around the region that can take you to revered dive sites on the Sunshine Coast and off Vancouver Island – treks to the sunken HMCS *Cape Breton* near Nanaimo are especially recommended.

SKIING & SNOWBOARDING

While Whistler (p214) is the regional king of the snowy hill, there are excellent alpine skiing and snowboarding areas as well as cross-country skiing trails on the edge of the city, less than 30 minutes from downtown. The season typically runs from late November to early April. Following are the three main powder kegs.

CYPRESS MOUNTAIN Map pp54-5

www.cypressmountain.com; West Vancouver; adult/child/youth $44.76/21.90/36.19; 🕑 9am-4pm Dec, 9am-10pm Jan-Mar

Around 8km north of West Van via Hwy 99, Cypress Provincial Park (p107) transforms into Cypress Mountain ski resort in winter, attracting well-insulated sporty types with its 53 runs, popular snowshoe trails and a snowtubing course. Handsomely upgraded as the venue for the 2010 Winter Olympics snowboarding and freestyle skiing events, new facilities include a fancy lodge and huge improvements to popular runs like Hutch, Windjammer and Lower Panorama (where Canada won its first Olympic gold on home soil). If you don't want to drive here, consider taking the seasonal Cypress Mountain Shuttle Bus (www.cypresscoachlines.com).

GROUSE MOUNTAIN Map pp54-5

www.grousemountain.com; 6400 Nancy Greene Way, North Vancouver; Skyride adult/child/youth/senior $39.95/13.95/23.95/35.95; 🕑 9am-10pm mid-Nov–mid-Apr; 🚌 236 from Lonsdale Quay

Vancouver's favorite wintertime hangout (see p105 for summertime info), family-friendly Grouse offers 26 ski and snowboard runs, an outdoor ice-skating rink and a large helping of Christmastime shenanigans – if you're looking for Santa in Vancouver, this is where you'll find him. Night skiing is popular here, there are plenty of lessons available for beginners and the forested snowshoe trails are magical. There are some good dining options if you just want to relax, and there's a wolf habitat area if you'd like to get close to wildlife without having it eat you.

MT SEYMOUR Map pp54-5

www.mountseymour.com; 1700 Mt Seymour Rd, North Vancouver; adult/child/youth $42/21/35; 🕑 9:30am-10pm Mon-Fri, 8:30am-10pm Sat & Sun Dec-Apr

A year-round outdoorsy hangout for Vancouverites (see p105), the third branch of the region's winter playground network has a 23-run ski and snowboarding area, plus an eight-run toboggan spot and four-lane tubing course. The snowshoe trails and tours are also popular – check out the nighttime snowshoeing and fondue tour ($55). Seymour is usually far less crowded than Grouse and you're much more likely to meet the locals. There's no transit service to the park, so if you don't want to drive, hop on the seasonal shuttle from Lonsdale Quay ($6 each way).

SNOWSHOE SHENANIGANS

If you lack the pose-worthy skills for the ski and snowboard slopes around Vancouver but you'd still like to gambol through the powder, snowshoeing is an ideal alternative – especially since the only requirement is the ability to walk. If you can manage that, head to Grouse Mountain (p187; there are also trails at the other two resort mountains), where you can rent shoes and hit the 10km of winding trails in Munday Alpine Snowshoe Park.

Within minutes, you'll feel like you're the only person on the mountain, as the fading voices are replaced by the crunch-crunch of ice-caked snow, along with the ever-present cawing of scavenging ravens – you might also glimpse an eagle or two. Passing through the forest of mountain hemlocks and Pacific silver fir trees – many with straggles of moss hanging from them like Marxian beards – you'll sometimes break into open ground where you'll catch some stunning panoramic views. Burnaby Mountain, topped by Simon Fraser University, is usually visible, while the ghostly face of Mt Baker can often be glimpsed shimmering 130km away.

Continuing upward, you'll eventually hit the park's broad Evian Express Trail. The route overlooks the silver surface of Capilano Reservoir far below and the distant crags of Vancouver Island on the watery horizon. Once you've had enough, head downhill (at a rate of knots) to the lodge for a well-deserved Granville Island brew or two.

HEALTH & FITNESS

You might think Vancouver is the perfect place to mumble the 'I can't go for a run today because it's raining' excuse. Wrong. The city hosts a sweaty kit bag full of gyms, yoga and Pilates studios, and offers other indoor ways to stay fit. You'll also find recommendations for spas and beauty salons in this section.

GYMS

Private gyms charge up to $30 per day: ask about weekly or monthly membership if you're sticking around. Vancouver's community centers charge around $5 to use their workout rooms, and the same for aerobics or other fitness classes. The West End Community Centre (p185) is a convenient option, with both a fitness facility and classes. Contact the Vancouver Board of Parks and Recreation (www.vancouverparks.ca) for details of other community centers offering fitness programs.

FITNESS WORLD Map pp68-9

www.fitnessworld.ca; 1185 W Georgia St, West End; ⊙ 24hr Mon-Fri, 8am-7pm Sat, 8am-9pm Sun; Ⓜ Burrard
Known as 'Fatness World' by locals, this West End 2nd-floor gym – you'll see the bedraggled staggering back to their apartments after overdoing it – has long opening hours, so you can usually find some quiet time. Hop on a running machine by the window and work out while you look down over the unfit masses below. The company has several other city branches.

KITSILANO WORKOUT Map pp96-7

www.kitsilanoworkout.com; 1923 W 4th Ave, Kitsilano; ⊙ 24hr Sun-Fri, 7am-10pm Sat; 🚌 4
You can exercise among the stringy fitness nuts and 'yummy mummies' of Kitsilano at this highly popular gym. If you want to mix up your routine, regular classes include step, yoga, Pilates and belly dancing – dance aerobics is a specialty here. After you've reached your sweat quotient, you can nip along the street to Sophie's Cosmic Café (p145) and blow all your hard work.

YWCA HEALTH & WELLNESS CENTRE Map pp58-9

www.ywcahealthandfitness.com; 535 Hornby St, downtown; ⊙ 6am-10pm Mon-Fri, 8am-5:30pm Sat & Sun; Ⓜ Burrard
Despite its name, this excellent downtown gym is open to men and women. It has three studios with wood-sprung floors, and combined and women-only weight rooms, a cardio room, steam room, meditation room and a 25m pool. There are also kickboxing, cycling, Pilates and other classes. A day membership ($18) gets you access to all.

SWIMMING

Ten beaches around the city are fine for swimming and have lifeguards on duty from May to early September (11:30am to 8:45pm). Among the best are Second Beach (p64), Third Beach (p64), English Bay Beach (p66) and Kitsilano Beach (p98).

Kits is usually the busiest of the lot – as many as 10,000 people may hit the sand here on a hot summer day. It gets less crowded the further you move toward UBC. Vancouver's waters are never exactly warm; they reach a high in summer of around 21°C (70°F).

If you prefer to swim in fish-free waters, Vancouver's best public pools include the following:

KITSILANO POOL Map pp96-7
www.vancouverparks.ca; 2305 Cornwall Ave, Kitsilano; adult/child/youth $5.10/2.52/3.57; ⏰ 7am-8:30pm Mon-Fri, 10am-8:45pm Sat & Sun Jun-Aug, reduced off-season; 🚌 22
This giant, heated 137m saltwater outdoor pool provides the best dip in town. It has a designated kids' area, where young families often teach their kids to swim, and some lanes so you can practice your laps.

SECOND BEACH POOL Map p63
www.vancouverparks.ca; cnr N Lagoon Dr & Stanley Park Dr, Stanley Park; adult/child/youth $5.10/2.52/3.57; ⏰ 10am-8:45pm mid-Jun–Aug, reduced off-season; 🚌 19
This outdoor pool shimmers like an aquamarine right beside the beach. It has lanes for laps but you'll be weaving past kids on most summer days; the kids take over here during school vacations, making it very hard to get anywhere near the waterslide.

UBC AQUATIC CENTRE Map p102
www.aquatics.ubc.ca; 6121 University Blvd, UBC; adult/child $4.95/4.75; ⏰ 7:30am-10pm Mon-Fri, 10am-9pm Sat, 10:30am-9pm Sun, reduced off-season; 🚌 99B-Line
The city's best indoor pool is on the UBC campus, so it's a bit of a hike from downtown. Also, the students take precedence in the water so you'll have to plan your visit around them – check the website for the latest schedules. If you negotiate those obstacles, you'll find a 50m pool, saunas and exercise areas for public use.

VANCOUVER AQUATIC CENTRE
Map pp68-9
www.vancouverparks.ca; 1050 Beach Ave, West End; adult/child/youth $5.10/2.52/3.57; ⏰ 6:30am-8pm Mon, Wed & Fri, 6:30am-9:30pm Tue & Thu, 8am-9:30pm Sat, 10am-4:45pm Sun; 🚌 6
At Sunset Beach beside the Burrard Bridge (the concrete monstrosity that looks like a

nuclear bunker), this busy aquatic center has a 50m pool, whirlpool, diving tank and sauna. There's also a gym if you want to continue your exercise purge.

YOGA
Yoga is hugely popular in Vancouver, as you'd expect in the city that birthed Lululemon Athletica (p114) and made yoga wear into a fashion statement. Most of the city's community centers (see p232), including those in the West End, Coal Harbour and Yaletown, offer drop-in classes.

BIKRAM'S YOGA VANCOUVER
Map pp68-9
☎ 604-662-7722; www.bikramyogavancouver .com; Suite 101, 1650 Alberni St, West End; drop-in session $20; ⏰ 7am-8pm Mon, Wed & Fri, 10am-8pm Tue & Thu, 8am-6pm Sat & Sun; 🚌 5
Dynamic yoga performed in a heated room, Bikram is a 26-asana series designed to warm and stretch muscles, ligaments and tendons. It is reputedly good at providing relief for arthritis, back problems and other chronic conditions. Also has a Kitsilano branch (Map pp96-7; 2861 W Broadway; ⏰ 6am-9:30pm Mon-Fri, 7:30am-7:45pm Sat & Sun).

FLOW WELLNESS Map pp58-9
☎ 604-682-3569; www.yyoga.ca; 888 Burrard St, downtown; drop-in session $15; M Burrard
This large and popular studio offers around 150 classes per week covering all manner of approaches. Spend some time figuring out which one would be best for you from a menu including Yoga Mechanics, ESL Yoga (for visiting students) and Yoga for Stiff Guys (don't ask). Alongside the stretching classes, there's a roster of additional wellness treats, from Thai massage to Shiatsu therapy.

BEAUTY SALONS
Expect to pay at least $50 for a haircut and style (plus a tip of 15% to 20%). Try to make appointments at least a day in advance.

AXIS Map pp68-9
☎ 604-685-0200; www.axishairsalons.com; 1111 W Georgia St, West End; ⏰ 10am-6pm Mon-Fri; M Burrard
A local favorite, this slick Vancouver minichain has both veteran stylists and

newbie creatives who can be a little more daring. If you want to save money, go for a trainee and you'll get up to half off the top price (although hopefully not half off your locks). If they can't fit you in here, there are other locations at 757 W Hastings St and 1386 W Pender St.

PROPAGANDA HAIR SALON
Map pp96-7

☎ 604-732-7756; www.propagandasalon.com; 2090 W 4th Ave, Kitsilano; ☺ 10am-6pm Mon-Wed & Sat, 10am-8pm Thu & Fri, 10am-5pm Sun; ☐ 4
Propaganda features excellent hair washing complete with relaxing scalp massages. The staff is a mix of trendy and cool but stylistically sensible hair professionals, and hey, dogs are welcome inside to help their owners make those all-important new-look decisions.

SUKI'S INTERNATIONAL Map p93

☎ 604-738-7713; www.sukis.com; 3157 S Granville St, South Granville; ☺ 9am-6pm Sat-Wed, 9am-9pm Thu & Fri; ☐ 10
If you're jealous of all those stunningly coiffed people you keep seeing in the clubs here, don't get mad, get even. They generally get their 'dos and colors at Suki's, the city's fave salon minichain. There are three other Suki's around the region.

SPAS

Given Vancouver's healthy lifestyle, it's no wonder that spas flourish here. Expect to pay upwards of $85 for an hour-long massage and at least $30 for a 'quickie' facial. It is usual to add a tip in the 15% to 20% range.

ABSOLUTE SPA AT THE CENTURY
Map pp58-9

☎ 604-648-2772; www.absolutespa.com; Century Plaza Hotel, 1015 Burrard St, downtown; ☺ 8:30am-9pm; ☐ 2
This popular, hotel-based day spa has a calming earth-toned interior and offers a full menu of treats from facials to hydrotherapy to make-up sessions in its nine treatment rooms. If you need a boost after your long-haul flight, try the grapefruit jet lag recovery body wrap (from $95). Men-only treatments also available. There are four other Absolutes dotted around the region.

MIRAJ HAMMAM SPA Map p93

☎ 604-733-5151; www.mirajhammam.com; 1495 W 6th Ave, South Granville; ☺ 11am-7pm Tue & Wed, noon-8pm Thu & Fri, 10am-6pm Sat, 2-6pm Sun; ☐ 10
Canada's only hammam is based on the real Middle Eastern deal. Step into the arched and tiled interior for a steam followed by *gommage* (a full-body scrub with authentic black Moroccan soap, starting at $99). Men are only admitted from 4pm to 8pm Thursday and 2pm to 6pm Sunday; it's women only the rest of the time.

SKOAH Map p72

☎ 604-642-0200; www.skoah.com; 1011 Hamilton St, Yaletown; ☺ 10:30am-7:30pm Mon-Fri, 10am-7pm Sat & Sun; Ⓜ Yaletown-Roundhouse
'No whale music and no bubbling cherubs,' as they say at this tongue-in-cheek, trying-hard-not-to-be-pretentious spa. There are deep-cleansing masks, facial massages, scalp massages, foot 'facials' and muscle stimulation treatments, all done by your 'personal skin care trainer.' Skoah also sells its own line of all-natural products. There's a second location in Burnaby's Metrotown mall.

SPA UTOPIA Map pp58-9

☎ 604-641-1351; www.spautopia.ca; Pan Pacific Vancouver, 999 Canada Place, downtown; ☺ 9am-9pm Tue-Fri, 9am-5pm Sat-Mon; Ⓜ Waterfront
Welcome to the height of luxury. Spa Utopia is just that: a perfect world of relaxation and pampering specializing in 'spa suites,' where you hold court in a private, hotel-style room while various treatments and their practitioners come your way. There is a massive range of

GO-GO GIRLS

Taking off faster than a freewheeling skate from the top of Lonsdale Ave, Vancouver's hottest new alternative sports league is the Terminal City Rollergirls (www .terminalcityrollergirls.com). Join the hipster fans cheering the all-female amateur flat-track roller derby teams as they whistle around at breakneck speeds. Most bouts – between teams with names like Riot Girls and Bad Reputations – take place at Richmond's Minoru Arena. Tickets are $10 in advance or $15 on the door.

treatments; the ultra-relaxing Earth Mud Bath ($127) is recommended.

SPECTATOR SPORTS

Vancouver's sports scene is tightly entwined with the city's culture, and if residents aren't engaging in some sort of sporting activity themselves, they're likely to be watching one. Hockey generates the most madness. Despite the fact the Vancouver Canucks have yet to win a Stanley Cup, hope springs eternal. And just remember: those pesky Toronto Maple Leafs haven't won a Cup since 1967, so Vancouver fans needn't feel too bad.

Canadian football is also popular; to the uninitiated, it looks like American football, but with key differences best summed up as 'longer, wider and faster.' The BC Lions is the local team, and it's done a pretty good job in recent years. Vancouver does have a baseball team, the minor-league Vancouver Canadians, which serves as the training ground for Major League Baseball's (MLB) Oakland As. However, games are more about the nostalgic summertime ambience than serious sports watching. On the rise is the city's Vancouver Whitecaps soccer team, joining Major League Soccer (MLS) in 2011.

TICKETS & RESERVATIONS

Ticketmaster (www.ticketmaster.ca) sells advance tickets, but be aware of the extra fees. You can also pick up tickets at Tickets Tonight (www.ticketstonight.ca) or the box offices of the venues listed here. Scalpers congregate on the corner of W Georgia and Beatty Sts for Rogers Arena events and at the Expo Blvd entrances for BC Place events.

BASEBALL

VANCOUVER CANADIANS Map p93
www.canadiansbaseball.com; Nat Bailey Stadium, 4601 Ontario St, Fairview; tickets $10-22; ☉ Jun-Sep; Ⓜ King Edward, then bus 33
The minor-league farm team to the MLB's Oakland As, the Canadians play at the recently refurbished but still charmingly old-school Nat Bailey Stadium, by Queen Elizabeth Park. It's known as 'the prettiest ballpark in the world' thanks to its mountain backdrop. Afternoon games – called 'nooners' – are perfect for a nostalgic bask in the sun. Hotdogs and beer rule the

menu, but there's also sushi and fruit – this is Vancouver, after all.

FOOTBALL

BC LIONS Map p72
www.bclions.com; Empire Field & BC Place Stadium, 777 Pacific Blvd, Yaletown; tickets $35-85; ☉ Jun-Nov; Ⓜ Stadium-Chinatown
The Lions is Vancouver's team in the Canadian Football League (CFL), arguably a more exciting game than its US counterpart. The Lions team has had some decent showings in the last few years, winning the Grey Cup championship most recently in 2006. The team relies on its jump-out-of-your-seat offense. Tickets are easy to come by – unless the boys are laying into their Calgary rivals.

HOCKEY

VANCOUVER CANUCKS Map pp58-9
www.canucks.com; Rogers Arena (GM Place), 800 Griffiths Way, downtown; tickets $55-131.50; ☉ Oct-Apr; Ⓜ Stadium-Chinatown
The city's beloved National Hockey League (NHL) team toyed with fans in 1994's thrilling Stanley Cup finals before losing Game 7 to the New York Rangers, triggering local riots. But love runs deep and 'go Canucks go!' is still boomed out from packed-to-capacity Rogers Arena at every game. Book

STADIUM SWITCH-EROO

The venue for the 2010 Winter Olympics opening and closing ceremonies, BC Place Stadium (p71) is Vancouver's main sports arena. While a new $500 million retractable roof was being fitted during the research for this book, its resident sports team – the BC Lions – was forced to play its games at a new outdoor 27,500-seat temporary venue in East Vancouver called Empire Field (Map pp54-5). If the refurbished BC Place doesn't quite meet its expected reopening schedule (fingers are crossed for late 2011) by the time you visit, you might be checking out this alternative venue. Luckily, it's an easy 15-minute number-10 bus ride east of downtown. Despite being a new-build, the temporary stadium has a lot of history to live up to: it's situated on the site of the old Empire Stadium, where Roger Banister and John Landy both broke the four-minute mile at the 1954 Empire Games. The former stadium was demolished in the early 1990s, but it was the old home of both the BC Lions and the Vancouver Whitecaps soccer team – which is just as well, since the Whitecaps will also be playing here until taking up residency in the newly-lidded BC Place once it's finished.

your seat way before you arrive in town or just head to a local bar for some game-night atmosphere.

VANCOUVER GIANTS Map pp54-5

www.vancouvergiants.com; Pacific Coliseum, 100 N Renfrew St, East Vancouver; tickets $19.50-21.50; ⊙ Sep-Apr; 🚌 16

If you can't score Canucks tickets, the Western Hockey League's (WHL) Vancouver Giants is a good-value alternative. Games are held at the Pacific Coliseum and often have a buzzy locals feel with lots of families and die-hard fans, all united in awaiting the next big punch-up on the ice. Tickets cost a lot less than Canucks ones, unless you factor in the beer you'll be sipping throughout the game.

SOCCER

VANCOUVER WHITECAPS Map p72

www.whitecapsfc.com; Empire Field & BC Place Stadium, 777 Pacific Blvd, Yaletown; tickets from $21.50; ⊙ Apr-Oct; Ⓜ Stadium-Chinatown

Rejected in its attempts to build a new waterfront stadium, the Whitecaps team will be moving from its old Burnaby home to downtown's BC Place once it's been refurbished. Until then, the team that's been promoted to the MLS from the 2011 season plays at the temporary Empire Field venue.

lonely planet Hotels & Hostels

Want more sleeping recommendations than we could ever pack into this little ol' book? Craving more detail – including extended reviews and photographs? Want to read reviews by other travellers and be able to post your own? Just make your way over to **lonelyplanet.com/hotels** and check out our thorough list of independent reviews, then reserve your room simply and securely.

SLEEPING

top picks

SLEEPING

Although there are 25,000 hotel, B&B and hostel rooms in Metro Vancouver, the city is colonized by tourists in summer months, so booking ahead is a smart move – unless you want to be sleeping with your head on a damp log in Stanley Park. With rates at their highest in July and August, there are some genuinely good deals in spring and fall, when you can avoid the school-holiday crush and join the locals in enjoying a day or two of wild 'Wet Coast' rainfall.

While the 2010 Winter Olympics triggered a rash of slick new hotel developments – including the Shangri-La and the Fairmont Pacific Rim – not all the newbies managed to open in time for the gold rush. The revamped Hotel Georgia, a few steps from the venerable Hotel Vancouver, was still under wraps during research for this book but it promises to be one of the city's swankiest new sleepovers.

Vancouver is not just about high-end hotels, of course. There are many good midrange options, especially in the downtown core, as well as pockets of homely heritage B&Bs in the West End and Kitsilano. If you want to be closer to the forests and mountains yet not too far from downtown, the North Shore is also a good alternative. And for those on a limited budget, there are hostels scattered across the city, as well as some good student-style digs out at the University of British Columbia (UBC).

From high end to budget, lodgings are increasingly adding free wireless internet access to their offerings, while spas, pools, air-conditioning and laundry facilities are more sporadically applied: see the symbols in each listing to see what's available and call ahead to find out what's new. Also note that some reviews include family-friendly (👶) and pet-friendly (🐾) symbols.

Accommodation reviews here are arranged by neighborhood and then by budget – most expensive first. Quoted prices are for the height of the summer season, but rates can drop by as much as 50% in the off-season and many hotels also offer good-value packages that might include restaurant deals, spa treatments or entry to local attractions – check hotel websites to see what's on offer.

Alternatively, save time by checking online or calling for the many deals, packages and accommodation services offered via Tourism Vancouver (☎ 604-966-3260, 877-826-1717; www.tourismvancouver .com) and Hello BC (☎ 800-435-5622; www.hellobc.com).

Be aware that there are some significant additions to most quoted room rates. You'll have to pay 12% HST (Harmonized Sales Tax), plus an additional hotel room tax of 2%. In addition, many hotels charge a destination marking fee of around 1.5%. In total, these extras can amount to as much as 16.5%. Many hotels, particularly in the downtown core, also charge parking fees that are often between $10 and $20 per night. You can avoid this by staying at B&Bs, which generally don't charge for parking.

BOOKING B&BS

B&Bs across the city run from homely rooms in residential neighborhoods that start at under $100 per night to sumptuous, antique-lined heritage mansions at prices over $200, where every pampering treat is offered. The average is around $150 and you can expect a warm welcome and plenty of friendly personal attention. It's not all smiles, though: some B&Bs require a two-night minimum stay – especially on summer weekends – and cancellation policies can cost you an arm and a leg if you decide not to turn up.

There are several handy regional agencies that allow you to search and book Vancouver-area properties online. These generally show photos and available amenities at local properties and can save you a lot of time when you're on the road. You can do your pre-trip homework via the recommended agencies BBCanada (www.bbcanada.com) or BC Bed & Breakfast Innkeepers Guild (www.bcsbestbnbs.com).

TIPPING

Bellhops typically get $2 to $5 for hailing you a cab at the front of the hotel and up to $5 for carrying your bags to your room. Housekeepers can be tipped $2 to $5 per night of your stay, although this is entirely optional.

DOWNTOWN

With few B&B options – head to the West End if you want an antique-lined, home-style sleepover – the downtown area is bristling with swanky hotel towers, and also has a handful of refurbished heritage properties and a couple of party-central hostels. You'll be within staggering distance of many of the city's best nightlife options and have a smorgasbord of good restaurants. Be aware that some front-facing rooms can be noisy; request a quieter back room if you're a light sleeper.

FAIRMONT PACIFIC RIM
Map pp58-9   Hotel $$$

☎ 604-695-5300, 888-264-6877; www.fairmont.com/pacificrim; 1038 Canada Place; r from $350; Ⓜ Waterfront; ✖ 🛜 🖳

Handily located across from the convention center expansion, this chic 400-room property opened just in time for the Olympics. Check out the wrap-around text art installation on the exterior glass, then nip inside to the elegant white lobby. While many rooms have city views, the ones with waterfront vistas will blow you away, especially as you sit in your jetted tub or cube-shaped Japanese bath with a decadent glass of bubbly. High-tech flourishes include iPod docks and Nespresso machines, but the rooftop swimming pool should take up most of your time.

PAN PACIFIC VANCOUVER
Map pp58-9   Hotel $$$

☎ 604-662-8111, 800-663-1515; www.vancouver.panpacific.com; 999 Canada Place; r from $329; Ⓜ Waterfront; ✖ 🖳 🖳

This deluxe convention hotel inside Canada Place starts with a cavernous lobby, complete with its own clutch of totem

top picks

HOTEL SPAS

- Shangri-La Hotel (p198)
- Century Plaza Hotel & Spa (p196)
- Pan Pacific Vancouver (above)
- Wedgewood Hotel & Spa (p195)
- Fairmont Hotel Vancouver (p195)

poles. The large rooms, many with panoramic views across Burrard Inlet, are no less impressive and come with rich maple-wood furnishings and the kind of beds where the linen thread-count is off the scale. The three on-site restaurants include the recommended Five Sails. And if you need any more pampering, the on-site Spa Utopia (p190) is one of the city's best.

FAIRMONT HOTEL VANCOUVER
Map pp58-9   Hotel $$$

☎ 604-684-3131, 866-540-4452; www.fairmont.com/hotelvancouver; 900 W Georgia St; r from $300; Ⓜ Burrard; ✖ 🖳

Built in the 1930s by the Canadian Pacific Railway company, this sparkling grand dame is a Vancouver landmark. Despite the snooty provenance, the hotel carefully balances comfort with elegance: the lobby is decked with crystal chandeliers but the rooms have an understated business hotel feel. If you have the budget, check in to the Gold Floor for a raft of pampering services. And if you'd rather not pay for internet access, join the President's Club loyalty program for free and it won't cost you a penny.

WEDGEWOOD HOTEL & SPA
Map pp58-9   Boutique Hotel $$$

☎ 604-689-7777, 800-663-0666; www.wedgewoodhotel.com; 845 Hornby St; r from $275; 🖳 5; ✖ 🖳

The last word in personalized boutique luxury, the elegant Wedgewood is dripping with top-hatted charm. The friendly staff is second to none, the rooms are stuffed with reproduction antiques and the balconies enable you to smirk at the grubby plebs shuffling past below. Steam up your monocle with a trip to the spa – where a shiatsu massage should work off those sore shopping muscles – then hang out around the fireplace in the lobby bar with a signature cocktail or three.

ST REGIS HOTEL

Map pp58-9   Boutique Hotel $$$

☎ 604-681-1135, 800-770-7929;
www.stregishotel.com; 602 Dunsmuir St; r from
$219; Ⓜ Granville; ⊠ ▢ ⊚

Unrecognizable from its former incarnation,
the completely transformed St Regis has
become an art-lined boutique sleepover in
a 1913 heritage shell. The rooms
(befitting its age, almost all seem to be
a different size) exhibit a loungey élan,
complete with leather-look wallpaper,
earth-tone bedspreads, flatscreen TVs and
multimedia hubs. Check out the furniture,
too: it's mostly reclaimed and refinished
from the old Hotel Georgia. Rates include
breakfast and access to the nearby gym.
Rentable iPads are also available ($25 per
day).

METROPOLITAN HOTEL

Map pp58-9   Boutique Hotel $$$

☎ 604-687-1122, 800-667-2300;
www.metropolitan.com/vanc; 645 Howe St; r from
$205; Ⓜ Burrard; ⊠ ⊚ ⊠ ✿

This swish boutique property has a cool
contemporary take on style that will
appeal to urban sophisticates. It's also right
in the heart of downtown for those who
like to be close to all the action. Bold
modern artworks add a splash of color to
the atmospheric, subtly decorated rooms,
and there's a good on-site restaurant, an
indoor pool and a squash court to keep
you busy. Excellent service.

L'HERMITAGE HOTEL

Map pp58-9   Boutique Hotel $$$

☎ 778-327-4100, 888-855-1050; www
.lhermitagevancouver.com; 788 Richards St; r from
$190; Ⓜ Vancouver City Centre; ⊠ ▢ ⊠

Another new boutique sleepover, this
well-located property is divided between
longer-stay suites that attract visiting movie
industry–types and regular guests just
dropping in for the night. Whichever you
are, you'll find a contemporary designer
feel combined with artsy flourishes in the
rooms – some of which offer full kitchens –
along with a library-style common lounge
with its own secret garden terrace and
adjoining lap pool.

CENTURY PLAZA HOTEL & SPA

Map pp58-9   Hotel $$

☎ 604-687-0575, 800-663-1818; www.century
-plaza.com; 1015 Burrard St; r/ste from $169/229;
⊟ 2; ⊠ ✿

Renovated in recent years, this centrally
located tower sleepover combines standard
business hotel–style rooms (many with
handy kitchenettes) plus a raft of on-site

VANCOUVER'S HISTORIC SLEEPOVERS

While shiny new towers are *de rigueur* for Vancouver hotels these days, the city has a heritage of older sleepover spots
with bags of character and plenty of stories to tell (if they could talk, that is).

Leading the pack is the lovely, ivy-shrouded Sylvia Hotel (p200), which celebrates its centenary in 2012. Originally
designed as an apartment building and named after the first owner's daughter, this West End landmark was converted
into an apartment hotel during the 1930s when the city was in the grip of the Great Depression. By the late 1940s, it
had transformed into a regular hotel and in 1954 its lobby became the home of Vancouver's first cocktail bar — you
can visit the bar (p152) today, although it's moved on from its cocktail-exclusive heyday. Local rumor has it that Errol
Flynn propped up the bar here once or twice during a prolonged bender just before dying of a heart attack in the city
in October 1959.

While the Sylvia was designated as a local heritage building in 1975, it's not the only historic hotel in town. The
Canadian Pacific Railway company built a string of castle-like sleepovers across Canada around the turn of the 19th
century. The idea was to encourage rich travelers to vacation on the fledgling cross-country rail system, stopping off at
sumptuous sleepovers along the way. Several of these grand hotels still exist – Victoria's Empress Hotel (p214) and
Quebec's Chateau Frontenac are the most famous examples – and you'd be forgiven for thinking that the equally glam
Hotel Vancouver (now called the Fairmont Hotel Vancouver; p195) is another. In fact, the city's grand dame sleepover
was the third building to have that name. The first was a large, wood-framed structure at Granville and W Georgia Sts
that opened in 1888. It was superseded, on the same spot, by the second in 1916. This was a much more elaborate
structure, deploying an Italianate style that included turrets and a grand arched entrance. However, it wasn't to last.
During the Great Depression, a third Hotel Vancouver was built – the current one at W Georgia and Burrard Sts – as a
make-work project for unemployed locals. It opened in 1937. After serving as a barracks during WW2, the second and
arguably more attractive hotel was torn down in 1949.

amenities: there can't be many North American hotels that have both their own spa and comedy club, Comedy Mix (p162). There's also an indoor pool and steam room, and you're just a couple of downhill blocks from the Robson St shops.

MODA HOTEL Map pp58-9   Hotel $$
☎ 604-683-4251, 877-683-5522; www.modahotel .com; 900 Seymour St; d from $159; 🚇 10; 🛜
A white-fronted, boutique-ish property one block from the Granville St party area – that means you should request a back room if you want to sleep. The refurbished, mostly small rooms have loungey flourishes without quite being designer cool: think cheap mod furnishings and bold paintwork. The bathrooms have also been given a swanky makeover, while the flatscreen TVs are handy if you can't handle another night on the town. Alternatively, pad down to the excellent on-site wine bar UVA (p150) for a nightcap.

VICTORIAN HOTEL Map pp58-9   Hotel $$
☎ 604-681-6369, 877-681-6369; www.victorianhotel.ca; 514 Homer St; r with private bathroom from $149, with shared bathroom from $129; Ⓜ Granville; 🛜
Housed in a pair of renovated older properties, the high-ceilinged rooms at this lovely, Euro-style pension combine glossy hardwood floors, a sprinkling of antiques, an occasional bay window and plenty of heritage charm. Bathrobes and summer fans are common but the best rooms are in the newly renovated extension, where raindrop showers, marble bathroom floors and flatscreen TVs add a luxe dimension. Go for room 203: a spacious corner room with views and a cool mod chair. Rates include continental breakfast.

KINGSTON HOTEL Map pp58-9   Hotel $$
☎ 604-684-9024, 888-713-3304; www.kingstonhotelvancouver.com; 757 Richards St; s/d/tw $115/145/160; Ⓜ Granville; 🖳
While some recent revamping has taken place, most of the 52 rooms at this 1910-built Euro-style pension are still conventionally basic, except for the recommended rooms with bathrooms, which have new furniture, flatscreen TVs and fresh floral bedspreads. Everything is clean and well-maintained, though, and rates include continental breakfast. There's also a large

and popular adjoining bar with an excellent patio plus a handy coin laundry service if it's time to wash your crinkly undies.

URBAN HIDEAWAY GUESTHOUSE
Map pp58-9   Guesthouse $$
☎ 604-694-0600; www.urban-hideaway.com; 581 Richards St; d/tw/ste $109/129/149; Ⓜ Granville; 🖳
This supremely cozy (but fiendishly well-hidden) home-away-from-home is a good value word-of-mouth favorite. Tuck yourself into one of the seven comfy rooms (the loft is recommended) or spend your time in the lounge areas downstairs. There's a free-use computer, a library of 500 DVDs for the big-screen TV and a plant-lined patio with a barbecue. Laundry is free, as are the loaner bikes, or you can just hang out with house cats Pippin and Nemo. Breakfast fixings (eggs, bacon etc) are provided: you cook it yourself in the well-equipped kitchen. Bathrooms are mostly shared, although the loft's is private.

ST CLAIR HOTEL Map pp58-9   Hostel $
☎ 604-684-3713, 800-982-0220; www.stclairvancouver.com; 577 Richards St; r from $44; Ⓜ Granville; 🖳 🛜
This well-located combination hostel and budget hotel is a real find, so don't be put off by the grubby-looking staircase that leads up to it. You'll discover a surprisingly large, nautical-themed interior that feels like being below deck in a long, narrow ship. Each of the three floors has an array of slightly-dinged but clean private rooms, all with sinks, and ranging from doubles to quads (some with bunks). There are books, shower facilities and a computer ($1 per 30 minutes) on each level, plus small kitchens with microwaves and fridges. And if you're wondering about the maritime theme: the

top picks
CHEAP SLEEPS

- St Clair Hotel (above)
- YWCA Hotel (p201)
- Samesun Backpackers Lodge (p198)
- HI Vancouver Central (p198)
- Buchan Hotel (p200)

property was built in 1911 for travelers taking ships to and from Asia.

HI VANCOUVER CENTRAL

Map pp58-9 Hostel $

☎ 604-685-5335, 877-203-4461; www.hihostels.ca/vancouver; 1025 Granville St; dm/r from $33.50/83; 🚌 10;

Across from the Samesun (they both have the same Granville St noise issues, so snag a back room), this warren-like sleepover is calmer than its party-loving rival. Enjoying some of the benefits of its past incarnation as a hotel – air-conditioning, small dorms with sinks and natty yellow decor – there are dozens of individual rooms for privacy fans (some with bathrooms). Continental breakfast is included – kitchen facilities are limited to microwaves here – and there's a brimming roster of social activities.

SAMESUN BACKPACKERS LODGE

Map pp58-9 Hostel $

☎ 604-682-8226, 877-972-6378; www.samesun.com; 1018 Granville St; dm/r $29.50/71; 🚌 10;

Expect a party atmosphere at this lively 200-bed hostel in the heart of the Granville St nightclub area – ask for a back room to avoid the raucous weekend street life or just head down to the on-site bar (naughtily called the Beaver) to join the beery throng. The dorms are comfortably small and there's a large kitchen for your mystery meat pasta dishes – free continental breakfast or a $2 cooked breakfast is also available. There's a strong line-up of social events, from poker nights to free walking tours, so check the roster daily.

WEST END

Vancouver's B&B central, the West End is dripping with clapboard heritage houses that tend toward the high-end range of comfortable. The main draw is that you're within walking distance of the downtown bustle without the attendant noise; the West End is crisscrossed with quiet residential streets but is also ringed with shops and restaurants. And Stanley Park is on your doorstep, enticing you for a sunset seawall stroll.

SHANGRI-LA HOTEL

Map pp68-9 Hotel $$$

☎ 604-689-1120; www.shangri-la.com; 1128 W Georgia St; r from $345; Ⓜ Burrard;

Occupying the lower 15 floors of Vancouver's tallest building, the first North American property of this ultra-luxe Asian hotel chain offers chic, mood-lit rooms (some surprisingly compact and others palatially large) lined with artwork and dark-wood paneling. Pampering extras include L'Occitane products, TVs embedded in bathroom mirrors and automatic blinds so you can shower behind the floor-to-ceiling windows without being seen from outside. Service is second-to-none throughout and Market, the on-site restaurant, is a winner even among those not staying here.

LODEN VANCOUVER

Map pp68-9 Boutique hotel $$$

☎ 604-669-5060, 877-225-6336; www.theloden.com; 1177 Melville St; r from $249; Ⓜ Burrard;

The definition of class, the stylish Loden is the real designer deal – and one of the first new boutique properties in years to give Yaletown's Opus a run for its money. The 70 rooms combine a knowing contemporary élan with luxe accoutrements like marble-lined bathrooms and those oh-so-civilized heated floors. The attentive service is top notch, while the glam Voya is one of the city's

VANCOUVER'S TALLEST HOTEL TOWER

Standing at the corner of Thurlow and W Georgia Sts and craning your neck skywards to the building dominating the intersection is a somewhat futile gesture. However hard you try, you won't see much of the rooftop garden sitting up top: the city's loftiest manmade green space, it resides at the apex of what became Vancouver's tallest building when it opened its doors in 2009.

Housing an ultra-luxury hotel (see left) on its first 15 floors, the Shangri-La is a sheer 201m glass box that beats the city's previous record-holder – the dark-glassed One Wall Centre at 1088 Burrard St – by more than 50 meters. Slick condominiums occupy the rest of the building above the hotel, including one 'penthouse estate' that reputedly sold for $15 million. Check out the raised box blip that sticks out a little from the rest of the building's mirror-like fascia: its location marks the previous height limit for buildings in the city.

around town in style in the hotel's
complimentary London taxicab.

ENGLISH BAY INN Map pp68-9 B&B $$$

☎ 604-683-8002, 866-683-8002; www
.englishbayinn.com; 1968 Comox St; r from $199;
🚌 5; 🛜

Each of the six, antique-lined rooms in this
Tudoresque B&B near Stanley Park has a
private bathroom and two have sumptuous
four-poster beds: you'll think you've arrived
in Victoria, BC's determinedly Olde English
capital, by mistake. There's complimentary
port in the parlor, a secluded garden for
hanging out with your copy of the London
Times, and a three-course breakfast –
arrive early to snag the alcove in the
upstairs dining room.

BARCLAY HOUSE B&B

Map pp68-9 B&B $$$

☎ 604-605-1351, 800-971-1351; www
.barclayhouse.com; 1351 Barclay St; d from $195;
🚌 5; 🛜

This magnificent bright-yellow Victorian
heritage property (built in 1904) has a
sophisticated boutique twist on the usual
B&B approach. Rather than a mothballed
museum look – think delicate and overly
chintzy antiques – the five rooms have a
loungey, designer feel and are lined with
local modern artworks. Home comforts
haven't been lost to aesthetics, though,
and four of the five rooms have deep
soaker tubs.

LISTEL VANCOUVER

Map pp68-9 Boutique Hotel $$

☎ 604-684-8461, 800-663-5491;
www.thelistelhotel.com; 1300 Robson St;
d from $169; 🚌 5; 🛜

A sophisticated, self-described 'art hotel,'
the Listel attracts grown-ups with its on-
site installations and package deals with
local art galleries. There's original artwork,
including some First Nations creations, in
the rooms, which all have a relaxing,
mood-lit West Coast ambience. Artsy
types should also check out the small
lobby-accessed gallery. The hotel's
bar, O'Doul's (p152), hosts nightly free
jazz shows.

BLUE HORIZON HOTEL

Map pp68-9 Hotel $$

☎ 604-688-1411, 800-663-1333;
www.bluehorizonhotel.com; 1225 Robson St;
r from $159; 🚌 5; 🛜

Despite being a 1960s tower, the
exceptionally well-maintained Blue
Horizon still feels modern. Rooms have
the kind of quality, business-hotel
furnishings common in pricier joints and
all are corner suites – each has a balcony,
with the top floors looking across to
English Bay or the North Shore. The on-site
restaurant has a summertime patio – look
for the blueberry pancakes at breakfast –
while you couldn't be better located:
the hotel is right on the city's main
shopping strip.

ARTSY HOTELS

While visiting art-lovers might find it difficult to roll out a sleeping bag and kip among the exhibits at the Vancouver
Art Gallery, there are some places in town that positively encourage it (*sans* sleeping bag). The city's artsiest sleepover,
the Listel Vancouver (p199) has a curatorial arrangement with local galleries and museums that means its corridors
are lined with display cases of local art – First Nations carvings or contemporary abstract works – while many of its
rooms eschew generic landscapes in favor of limited-edition prints. Even better is its hidden gallery. Opposite the front
desk, head up the steps and you'll find – between the lobby and the bar – a small exhibition room. The micro-gallery
displays a revolving array of works (giant photos from Africa were recent highlights) and there's always something worth
a look. Adding to its creative credentials, the hotel even produced its own anthology of short stories with contributions
from Douglas Coupland and William Gibson, among others.

Guests who stay at the Shangri-La Hotel (opposite) should also be bookish, since on their pillow they'll find a copy
of the 1930s novel *Lost Horizons,* which details the discovery of a hidden utopia in the Himalayas. Alongside its own
impressive wall-mounted art collection, the best artsy contribution the Shangri-La made to the city was creating the
Vancouver Art Gallery Offsite just outside the hotel's entrance. This new free-access public art area includes a couple
of eye-catching alfresco art shows every year. These have so far included a series of giant photos of Chinese children and
a clutch of highly detailed scale models of cannery sheds that recall the area's fishing industry past.

SLEEPING WEST END

EMPIRE LANDMARK HOTEL
Map pp68-9   Hotel $$
☎ 604-687-0511, 800-830-6144;
www.empirelandmarkhotel.com; 1400 Robson St;
r from $135; 🚌 5; 🛜

Housed in a generic tower block, the
Landmark has rooms with a slightly dated
business-hotel look, despite being recently
renovated. All rooms have balconies –
ask for one with a view of English Bay or
Stanley Park – and there's a raft of
amenities, including a gym and business
center. Save time for a cocktail (meals are
better value elsewhere) at the lofty
revolving restaurant on the 42nd floor,
which has some of the city's best
panoramic views.

RIVIERA HOTEL Map pp68-9   Hotel $$
☎ 604-685-1301, 888-699-5222;
www.rivieraonrobson.com; 1431 Robson St;
r from $119; 🚌 5; 🛜

One of several slightly dinged but well-
located apartment-style hotels crowding
the Robson St and Broughton St
intersection, the best deals at this mid-sized
concrete tower are the spacious one-
bedroom suites. Complete with full
kitchens (there are plenty of eateries
nearby if you don't want to cook), they
easily fit small families. The slightly
scuffed 1980s furnishings are nothing
to write home about but some of the
higher back rooms have good views.
Parking is free and there are on-site laundry
facilities.

SYLVIA HOTEL
Map pp68-9   Hotel $$
☎ 604-681-9321; www.sylviahotel.com;
1154 Gilford St; s/d/ste from $110/165/195;
🚌 5

Built in 1912 and named after the original
owner's daughter, the ivy-covered Sylvia
enjoys a prime location overlooking English
Bay. Generations of guests keep coming
back – many request the same room every
year – for a dollop of Old World charm plus
a side order of first-name service. There's
a wide array of comfortable room
configurations to suit every need here: the
best are the 12 apartment suites, each with
full kitchens and waterfront panoramas.
If you don't have a room with a view,
decamp to the lounge (p152) to nurse a beer
and watch the sunset.

top picks

HOTEL BARS

- Loden Vancouver (p198)
- Opus Hotel (p201)
- Sylvia Hotel (below)
- Listel Vancouver (p199)
- Shangri-La Hotel (p198)

BUCHAN HOTEL Map pp68-9   Hotel $
☎ 604-685-5354, 800-668-6654; www
.buchanhotel.com; 1906 Haro St; r from $86; 🚌 5

The cheap and cheerful, 1926-built Buchan
has bags of charm and is steps from
Stanley Park. Along corridors lined with old
prints of yesteryear Vancouver, its budget
rooms – most with shared bathrooms – are
clean and cozy, although some furnishings
have seen better days. The pricier rooms are
correspondingly prettier, while the east-side
rooms are brighter. There's a comfy guest
lounge and the extras here include storage
facilities for bikes and skis as well as laundry
machines. Friendly front desk.

HI VANCOUVER DOWNTOWN
Map pp68-9   Hostel $
☎ 604-684-4565, 888-203-4302;
www.hihostels.ca/vancouver; 1114 Burnaby St;
dm/r from $33.50/83.25; 🚌 6; 🖥 🛜

It says 'downtown' in the name but this
purpose-built hostel is in the West End, a
short walk from the center of all the action.
Much quieter than the HI Central (families
are welcome here), the dorms are all small
and rates include continental breakfast.
There's bike storage, a full kitchen and free
movies in the TV room, plus free regional
tours with Erik, a near-legendary HI
volunteer who's been introducing visitors
to Vancouver for years. You can take his
tours from any of the three local HIs. The
front deskers are ultra-friendly here.

YALETOWN

Lined with fancy bars and restaurants,
Yaletown claims to be Vancouver's 'little
SoHo'. That may be a bit of a stretch – it's
not really cutting edge or bohemian enough to
be quite so cool – but this is still an excellent
location for a sleepover. You'll be just a couple
of blocks from the Granville St entertainment

area and you'll also find plenty of great places to eat, drink and shop just steps from your hotel bed.

OPUS HOTEL Map p72 — Boutique Hotel $$$

☎ 604-642-6787, 866-642-6787; www.opushotel .com; 322 Davie St; r from $249; Ⓜ Yaletown-Roundhouse; ✖ ☐ 🛜 ♿
International celebs looking for a place to be seen should look no further. The city's original designer boutique sleepover has been welcoming the likes of Justin Timberlake and that bald bloke from REM for years: slip on your sunglasses and hop in the hotel's complimentary BMW courtesy car and you'll fit right in. The paparazzi dodgers come for the chic suites – think mod furnishings and feng-shui bed placements – and the luxe bathrooms with clear windows overlooking the streets (visiting exhibitionists take note). A model of excellent service, there's a stylish on-site bar (p154) and restaurant as well as a small gym.

GEORGIAN COURT HOTEL

Map p72 — Hotel $$
☎ 604-682-5555, 800-663-1155; www .georgiancourt.com; 773 Beatty St; r from $169; Ⓜ Stadium-Chinatown; ✖ 🛜 ♿
A recent makeover for this discreet, European-style property hasn't changed its classic, old-school approach to high service levels and solid, dependable amenities. The spruced-up standard rooms have new carpets and curtains but the spacious, apartment-style corner suites, with their quiet recessed bedrooms, are recommended. There's a small on-site fitness room, while the top-quality William Tell restaurant draws plenty of local diners. A popular sleepover for visiting bands, keep your eyes peeled for celebs in the lobby.

YWCA HOTEL Map p72 — Hostel $

☎ 604-895-5830, 800-663-1424; www.ywcahotel .com; 733 Beatty St; s/d/tr $69/86/111; Ⓜ Stadium-Chinatown; ✖ ☐ 🛜 ♿
This popular tower block is one of Canada's best Ys. Accommodating budget-hugging men and women, it's a bustling place with a communal kitchen on every other floor, some shared bathrooms and rooms ranging from compact singles (they feel like college study rooms) to group-friendly larger quarters. All units feel a little institutionalized, but each has a handy sink

top picks
CELEB-SPOTTING SLEEPOVERS

- Opus Hotel (left)
- Pan Pacific Vancouver (p195)
- Georgian Court Hotel (left)
- Loden Vancouver (p198)
- Wedgewood Hotel & Spa (p195)

and refrigerator. Rates include day passes to the YWCA Health & Wellness Centre (p188), a 10-minute walk away. This is a good option for families – kids get a toy when they check in.

GRANVILLE ISLAND, FAIRVIEW & SOUTH GRANVILLE

While shopping-friendly Granville Island has just one lodging option (it's ideal if you want to enjoy a retreat-like location with water-front views that's also close to the city action), Fairview has some good B&Bs and a couple of recommended hotels. Transit from these areas to the downtown core is generally good.

PLAZA 500 HOTEL Map p93 — Hotel $$

☎ 604-873-1811, 800-473-1811; www .plaza500.com; 500 W 12th Ave, Fairview; r from $160; Ⓜ Broadway-City Hall; ✖ 🛜
With some sterling views overlooking the downtown towers framed by the region's looming mountains, rooms at the tower-block Plaza 500 have received a makeover in recent years, delivering a more modern aesthetic – think lounge-contemporary business hotel. It's a look that's taken to the max in FigMint, the property's Euro-chic on-site resto-bar. Rates include passes to a nearby gym and there's a new Canada Line SkyTrain station a couple of blocks away that can whisk you to Yaletown and downtown in a few minutes.

GRANVILLE ISLAND HOTEL

Map p89 — Boutique Hotel $$
☎ 604-683-7373, 800-663-1840; www .granvilleislandhotel.com; 1253 Johnston St, Granville Island; r from $159; 🚐 50; ✖ ☐ ♿

This gracious boutique property hugs the quiet eastern tip of Granville Island and enjoys great views of False Creek and the mirrored Yaletown towers. You'll be a five-minute walk from the island's public market, with plenty of additional dining, shopping and theater options right on your doorstep. Characterized by contemporary West Coast decor, the rooms feature exposed wood and soothing earth tones. There's also a cool rooftop Jacuzzi, while the on-site brewpub makes its own distinctive beer (the Jamaican Lager is recommended).

WINDSOR GUEST HOUSE Map p93 B&B $$
☎ 604-872-3060, 888-872-3060; www.dougwin .com; 325 W 11th Ave, Fairview; r from $105, with shared bathroom from $95; Ⓜ Broadway-City Hall; 🛜

This handsome 1895 wood-built mansion has a lived-in, homey feel, complete with a charming veranda and stained-glass windows. The rooms vary greatly in size and some have shared bathrooms. The recommended top floor 'Charles Room' is quaint and quiet with a patio – shared with the next room – overlooking downtown. A filling cooked breakfast is included, along with free off-road parking. The owners have an additional B&B called Douglas Guest House (456 West 13th Ave) nearby.

SHAUGHNESSY VILLAGE Map p93 Hotel $
☎ 604-736-5511; www.shaughnessyvillage.com; 1125 W 12th Ave, Fairview; s/d $79/101; 🚌 9; 🅿

This immaculate, entertainingly kitsch sleepover – think pink carpets, flowery sofas and maritime memorabilia – describes itself as a tower block 'B&B resort.' Despite the old-school approach,

top picks
UNEXPECTED HOTEL PERKS

- On-site comedy club – Century Plaza Hotel & Spa (p196)
- London taxicab courtesy car – Loden Vancouver (p198)
- Landscaped garden with crazy golf – Shaughnessy Village (above)
- Dog available for walking – Fairmont Hotel Vancouver (p195)

the hotel is perfectly shipshape, right down to its clean, well-maintained rooms, which, like boat cabins, are lined with wooden cupboards and include microwaves, refrigerators and tiny private bathrooms. Extras include cooked breakfasts, an outdoor pool, a large laundry and, of course, a large display of petrified wood.

KITSILANO & UNIVERSITY OF BRITISH COLUMBIA (UBC)

Vancouver's original hippie haven has moved on since the flower children used to hang out here smoking naughty cigarettes. The counterculture rebels who stayed behind now own some of the city's most expensive heritage properties. Some of these have become popular B&Bs that are walking distance to the beaches and close to browseable shops and good restaurants. Head further west for some great budget options at UBC.

CORKSCREW INN Map pp96-7 B&B $$
☎ 604-733-7276, 877-737-7276; www .corkscrewinn.com; 2735 W 2nd Ave, Kitsilano; d from $180; 🚌 2; 🛜

Rising above the city's array of polished, creaky-floored heritage B&Bs, this immaculate, antique-lined property looks like it has a drinking problem: it houses hundreds of corkscrews, some of them centuries old (look out for the one with the skull-shaped handle). Aside from the boozy paraphernalia, this 1912 Craftsman property has five lovely art-themed rooms (we like the art deco room) and is an ideal sleepover for traveling wine nuts (guests receive a souvenir corkscrew). Three-night minimum stay in summer.

KITSILANO SUITES
Map pp96-7 Self-catering Suites $$
☎ 778-833-0334; www.kitsilanosuites.com; 2465 W 6th Ave, Kitsilano; ste $149-229; 🚌 9; 🛜

If you want to pretend you're a well-to-do Kits local, stay at this shingle-sided arts and crafts house divided into three smashing self-catering, home-from-home suites. Although a century old, each has been immaculately renovated and is lined with modern appliances without spoiling their heritage feel: think hardwood floors, claw-foot bathtubs and stained-glass windows. Each has a full kitchen (a handy welcome pack is included so you can chef up your first breakfast) and there are shops and restaurants a short walk away on W 4th Ave. A three-night minimum rule often applies and weekly rates are available.

MICKEY'S KITS BEACH CHALET
Map pp96-7   B&B $$

☎ 604-739-3342, 888-739-3342; www
.mickeysbandb.com; 2142 W 1st Ave, Kitsilano;
r $135-175; 🚍 2; 🛜 ♿

Eschewing the heritage-home approach of most B&Bs in Kitsilano, this modern, Whistler-style chalet has three rooms and a tranquil, hedged-in garden terrace. Behind its slender, chimney-dominated exterior, its accommodations – including the gabled, top-floor York Room – are decorated in a comfortable contemporary style, but only the York Room has a private bathroom. It's a family-friendly place: the hosts can supply toys, cribs and even help arrange babysitters. Rates include continental breakfast.

UNIVERSITY OF BRITISH COLUMBIA ACCOMMODATION
Map p102   Hostel, Hotel $, $$

☎ 604-822-1000, 888-822-1030; www
.ubcconferences.com; 5961 Student Union Blvd,
UBC; hostel r from $35, apt r from $49, ste from
$179; 🚍 99B-Line; 🛜

You can pretend you're still a student by staying on campus at UBC. The wide variety of room types includes good-value one or two-bedded rooms at the Pacific Spirit Hostel; private rooms in shared four- to six-bed apartments at Gage Towers (most with great views); and the impressive, hotel-style West Coast Suites with flatscreen TVs and slick wood and stone interiors. Most rooms are available May to August only but the West Coast Suites are offered year-round and have kitchenettes, twin beds and wi-fi.

HI VANCOUVER JERICHO BEACH
Map pp96-7   Hostel $

☎ 604-224-3208, 888-203-4303; www.hihostels
.ca/vancouver; 1515 Discovery St, Kitsilano; dm/r
from $30/76.25; 🕑 May-early Oct; 🚍 4; 🖥 🛜

One of Canada's largest hostels looks like a Victorian hospital from the outside and it's in a great location – especially if you're here for the sun-kissed Kitsilano vibe and

the surfing and kayaking at nearby Jericho Beach (downtown is a 20-minute bus ride away). The basic rooms make this the least palatial Vancouver HI, but handy extras include a large kitchen, licensed Jerry's Cove Café and bike rentals (there are lots of trails nearby). If you're not a fan of snorers, plan ahead and book one of the nine sought-after private rooms.

METRO VANCOUVER

Across the Burrard Inlet, North Vancouver and West Vancouver (particularly the former) have a smattering of lodging options for those who like to be closer to the mountains and yet only a short hop from downtown. You're also in a good spot if you plan to explore further afield to Whistler. South of the city, Richmond is close to the airport so you can roll from bed and make that early-morning flight without even waking up.

PINNACLE HOTEL AT THE PIER
Map pp54-5   Hotel $$

☎ 604-986-7437; www.pinnaclehotelatthepier
.com; 138 Victory Ship Way, North Vancouver;
r from $169; SeaBus to Lonsdale Quay; 🔀 🛜 🖥

Just to prove that not all Olympics-inspired hotel openings were in downtown Vancouver, North Van's swanky new Pinnacle is an excellent new option if you want to stay on this side of the water and hop over to the city center on the SeaBus, just a few minutes walk away. Rooms are furnished with understated elegance – the hotel balances itself nicely between business and leisure travelers – with calming pastel hues favored over bold colors. Fitness buffs will enjoy the property's large gym and pool. Harbor-view rooms are recommended but they cost a little extra.

THISTLEDOWN HOUSE B&B
Map pp54-5   B&B $$

☎ 604-986-7173, 888-633-7173; www.thistle
-down.com; 3910 Capilano Rd, North Vancouver;
r $165-295; 🕑 Feb-Nov; 🚍 236

Located on the road to Grouse Mountain, this romantic, adult-oriented 1920s Craftsman-style house is a notch above standard B&Bs: just check its gourmet breakfast menu. Among its elegantly decorated rooms, the most palatial suite – called Under the Apple Tree – is surprisingly secluded and includes a

AIRPORT ALTERNATIVES

Staying near the airport in Richmond is not required since downtown Vancouver is only a 25-minute Canada Line SkyTrain ride away. But if you're a dogged plane spotter or have an early-morning flight to catch (or a late-night one to recover from), you might want to consider these two recommended options:

Delta Vancouver Airport (Map pp54-5; ☎ 604-278-1241, 888-890-2322; www.deltavancouverairport.ca; 3500 Cessna Dr, Richmond; r from $169; 🛜 🖵 🐾) Situated on 9 acres fronting the Fraser River and a five-minute drive from the airport, the Delta has standard, comfortable, business-class rooms. It provides a 24-hour airport shuttle (or free taxi during the wee hours), a 24-hour health club and an outdoor pool. Check online for price-lowering package deals.

Fairmont Vancouver Airport (Map pp54-5; ☎ 604-207-5200, 866-540-4441; www.fairmont.com/vancouverairport; Vancouver International Airport, Richmond; r from $199; 🖵 🖵) You can wave from the overhead walkway to the harried economy-class plebs below as you stroll toward the lobby of this luxe airport hotel in the US departure hall. This is a great option for boarding long-haul flights in a Zen-like state of calm – if you've booked an economy-class seat yourself, you're in for a rude awakening after staying here. The rooms are elegantly furnished with high-end flourishes including remote-controlled curtains and marble-lined bathrooms.

beautiful fireplace, sunken sitting room, Jacuzzi and large windows opening onto a private patio. The owners are friendly and helpful and intent on making your stay in the region as comfortable as possible – join them for afternoon tea and a chat during your stay.

LONSDALE QUAY HOTEL
Map pp54-5   Boutique Hotel $$
☎ 604-986-6111; www.lonsdalequayhotel.com; 123 Carrie Cates Ct, North Vancouver; d/ste $149/189; SeaBus to Lonsdale Quay; 🖵
Recently renovated, this well-located sleepover – it's right by the market near the SeaBus terminal – has upgraded its rooms with granite bathroom counters and (in the higher-end executive rooms and suites) flatscreen TVs, new artworks and dark-wood furnishings. You can also work

off your vacation excesses in the gym. Free wired high-speed internet access.

GROUSE INN Map pp54-5   Motel $$
☎ 604-988-1701, 800-779-7888; www.grouseinn.com; 1633 Capilano Rd, North Vancouver; s/d/ste from $79/99/129; 🖵 236; 🖵 🐾 🐾
Resembling a stuccoed shopping mall from the outside, this family-friendly motel is a favorite among winter skiers and summer hikers and is suffused with amenities, including a restaurant, outdoor pool and free continental breakfast. Rooms (some with kitchens) have bright and breezy interiors – especially if you like busy, 1980s-style bedspreads – and they come in a wide array of configurations, including Jacuzzi suites and larger rooms for groups. A good spot for kids, it has a playground and can also arrange local babysitters.

DAY TRIPS & EXCURSIONS

DAY TRIPS & EXCURSIONS

Wherever you wander in Vancouver, the rest of the province seems to be calling you from almost every corner. It could be the snow-capped crags peeking at you between the glass towers of downtown; the region's dense and ancient forests waving at you from the other side of an inlet; or the nearby islands whispering your name as you stroll along the waterfront. Your best response to all these enticements is to go with the flow. Vancouver may be an enjoyable place to visit but it's the surrounding treasures that truly make it a great vacation destination – if you don't get away to one or two of these while you're here, you haven't really seen British Columbia (BC).

Victoria, the provincial capital, and Whistler, BC's favorite outdoor playground, are the region's big-ticket locales and both are possible day trips if you're on a tight timeline, although an overnight trip is preferable, if you can manage it.

The former has a reputation as a tweed-curtained 1950s evocation of old-empire England, but this image has slowly receded in recent years. The city's iconic landmark buildings are still there, but the tourist-trap olde-world restaurants and Tudor-framed shops have been reinvigorated with a new generation of funky eateries and businesses, without abandoning the charming aesthetic that draws two million visitors yearly.

Whistler is North America's top ski resort and is fast becoming a year-round destination with its menu of summertime adrenaline-rush activities. Despite getting all gussied up as the 'host mountain' for the recent Olympic and Paralympic Winter Games, the town retains a bit of a nonconformist image and draws people from all walks of life. You can see baggy-pants-wearing snowboarders, muddied-up mountain bikers and women in business suits all downing coffee within a few meters of each other.

En route to Whistler along winding Hwy 99, Squamish is the place to go for rock climbing and eagle spotting. The colorful Southern Gulf Islands lure art fans and retreat seekers with their bewitching bluffs, bays and teensy, often quirky communities. And for those who think they have no time for excursions when visiting the region, consider Bowen Island, little more than a stone's throw from West Vancouver, or Buntzen Lake, just an hour from the city and a breathtaking natural spot that's far from the madding tourist crowds.

The accommodation prices listed in this chapter are for peak season, which runs from late May to early September. Whistler is the exception, when December to February is the prime time, with prices to match.

OUTDOOR ACTIVITIES

Tottering around Vancouver's Stanley Park seawall on a rented bike does not count: you really have to dive head first (not always literally) into the activity side of BC's outdoor wonderland if you want some stories to tell when you get back home. Highlights include scuba diving or kayaking (try a sunset kayak tour) in Victoria (p208), where you should also hop on a bike: the city constantly brags about having more cycling routes than any other in Canada.

For breadth of activities, you can't beat Whistler (p214) – especially if your idea of thrills includes screaming like a banshee or wetting yourself (or both). In summer, the popular alpine resort attracts zipliners, hikers, rock climbers and white-water rafters, while winter delivers action from skiing to snowboard-ing to nighttime snowshoeing. If you prefer rock climbing in the morning and a choice of kiteboarding or mountain biking in the afternoon, Squamish (p219) is ideal. Alternatively, if you're just craving a quick nature break from the city, Buntzen Lake (p220) is a breathtaking tree-hugger's fave.

PLANES, TRAINS & BOATS

While getting around is usually the least exciting part of any vacation, in BC the reverse is true. The region is blessed with some great transportation options that also turn out to be among the best ways to encounter the forests, islands and coastlines for which the province is justly famous. You'll understand exactly what we mean if you take a 35-minute floatplane trip (p209) between Vancouver and Victoria:

you'll be glued to the window watching the forested islands and expansive ocean slide past below. You'll likely fall in love with Mother Nature again if you make the return trip via BC Ferries (opposite), where you can stand on deck and sigh as deeply as you want. The operator also runs services between the Southern Gulf Islands (p223), which tend to be even more peaceful and laid-back. Slow-travel fans will also enjoy the scenic Rocky Mountaineer Whistler Sea to Sky Climb (p215) service that winds between the resort and North Vancouver. (If you're a true train nut, drop by the giant West Coast Railway Heritage Park – see p219 – home to BC's favorite steam engine and a rolling cavalcade of historic locomotives.)

ISLAND HOPPING

You won't go wrong visiting any of the region's main islands, so let time be the deciding factor. If you only have half a day, sample the 'Happy Isle,' Bowen (p220), a 20-minute ferry ride from West Vancouver and a fine place for a quick hike or nautical-style pint. Vancouver Island's Victoria (right) can be visited in a day, but it'll be a long-ass one, so consider spending at least a night. You can also use Victoria as a base for traveling further afield: Vancouver Island is ripe for exploring and is relatively drivable, or you can take the train as far as Courtenay, stopping at the colorful communities en route.

The Southern Gulf Islands (p221) recharge the soul with their aquamarine skies seemingly close enough to touch. The islands aren't that far away, but the infrequent ferries mean you should give yourself plenty of time to get around – it's never too late to adopt the slower-paced island approach to life. The BC Ferries (p223) network services all of these places, and the ride itself – as the boat slithers through a labyrinth of lighthouse-punctuated islands – can be just as rewarding as the destination. The operator sells a special SailPass aimed at island-hoppers: check its website for the latest prices and information.

WILDLIFE WATCHING

The most popular BC excursion for those who want to commune with nature is a whale-watching trip (p212) from Victoria, usually a three-hour boat tour where mostly orcas are viewed. But keeping your eyes peeled wherever you are in BC can also reveal a few wildlife surprises: BC Ferries' services often slip past seals and the occasional whale pod (the captain will announce anything worth getting your camera out for); Victoria's Beacon Hill Park (opposite) is home to a few bold raccoons; and it's not too difficult to spot a marmot or two diving between the rocks around Whistler (p214). In the wilderness, of course, anything goes: near Tofino, the Pacific Rim National Park (p213) has rainforests of huge cedar and fir trees and is home to a teeming mass of critters large and small. Take a guided wildlife trek here and you'll find out all about them.

VICTORIA

BC's ivy-covered, picture-postcard capital was long touted as North America's most English city. This was a surprise to anyone who actually came from Britain, since Victoria promulgated a dreamy version of England that never really was: every garden (complete with the occasional palm tree) was manicured; every flagpole flew the Union Jack; and every afternoon was spent sipping imported Marks & Spencer tea from bone-china cups.

Thankfully this sleepy theme-park version of Ye Olde England has gradually faded in recent years. Fuelled by an increasingly younger demographic, a quiet revolution has seen lame tourist pubs, eateries and stores transformed into the kind of brightly painted bohemian shops, wood-floored coffee bars and surprisingly innovative restaurants that would make any city proud. It's worth seeking out these enclaves on foot, but activity fans should also hop on their bikes: Victoria has more cycle routes than any other Canadian city.

Centered on the twin Inner Harbour landmarks of the Parliament Buildings and the Fairmont Empress Hotel, downtown Victoria is compact and strollable. Stretching north from here, Government St is the main shopping promenade (especially for souvenirs) and it leads to Bastion Square, lined with historic buildings now colonized by cafes and restaurants. At the northern edge of downtown, Victoria's small Chinatown is the oldest in Canada. Just south is Market Square, adjoined by the funky LoJo shopping area. Once you've got your bearings, you're ready to go.

The excellent Royal BC Museum (www.royalbcmuseum.bc.ca; 675 Belleville St; adult/child $14.29/9.06; 10am-5pm) is the best in the province and should be a highlight of any visit here. It's an evocative introduction to the prehistoric and human history of the region – the old woolly mammoth diorama still packs a punch. Don't miss the museum's stirring First Nations gallery and pioneer town re-creation.

Across the street, the handsome, multiturreted Parliament Buildings (www.leg.bc.ca; 501 Belleville St; admission free; 8:30am-5pm May-Sep, 8:30am-5pm Mon-Fri Oct-Apr) offers more history and an entertaining 30-minute tour (free; 9am-5pm Mon-Thu, 9am-6pm Fri-Sun May-Sep, 9am–5pm Mon-Fri only Oct-Apr), where costumed Victorians will regale you with plenty of quirky stories about the old dame. Consider coming back in the evening, when the building's handsome exterior is lit up like a Christmas tree.

Even if you're not staying there, it's well worth strolling through the nearby Fairmont Empress Hotel (p214) as if you own the place. You can stop for afternoon tea ($44 to $55 per person), a pricey but popular experience that attracts many tourists, or just walk haughtily through and continue your stroll up Government St.

The buskers here will keep you entertained as you duck into Rogers' Chocolates (www.rogerschocolates .com; 913 Government St) for some dessert-sized Victoria Creams, or indulge in a different kind of sustenance at the revered Munro's Books (www .munrobooks.com; 1108 Government St). If it's a Sunday in summer, the Government St Market (www.pin.ca /market; 1600-block Government St; 11am-5pm Sun May-Sep) will be open, offering an eclectic mix of street performers and craft stalls.

This end of the city (Fisgard St) is the doorstep of Chinatown, complete with chatty grocery-store and trinket-shop owners, as well as Fan Tan Alley – a narrow passageway between Fisgard St and Pandora Ave that's a mini-warren of traditional and trendy stores hawking cheap-and-cheerful trinkets, cool used records and funky artworks. Consider signing up with Hidden Dragon Tours (250-216-1370; www.oldchinatown.com; 541 Fisgard St; adult/child $29/14.50) for a three-hour evening lantern tour of the area, where you'll learn all about opium dens and the hardships of 19th-century immigration.

Close by, the brightly painted former colonial buildings on Lower Johnson St have been repainted and occupied by Victoria's best independent shops; this area is now called LoJo and is worth an hour or so of anyone's time. You'll find hemp clothing stores, one-off design boutiques and a couple of good coffee shops. Among the best stores here is Smoking Lily (www.smokinglily.com; 569a Johnson St), an ultra-tiny micro storefront specializing in locally designed clothing for the pale and interesting set.

If you're still hungry for activities (and you haven't run out of time), Beacon Hill Park is the city's best outdoorsy hangout – enter on Douglas St and check out the windswept trees along the dramatic cliff top. You'll find a marker for Mile 0 of the Trans-Canada Hwy here, alongside a statue of Terry Fox, the heroic, one-legged runner whose attempted cross-Canada trek gripped the nation in 1981. It's not far to the Emily Carr House (www.emilycarr.com; 207 Government St; admission by donation; 11am-4pm

TRANSPORTATION: VICTORIA

Direction 100km southwest

Travel time Three to 3½ hours (including ferry) by vehicle; 35 minutes by floatplane or helicopter; 25 to 35 minutes by plane

Air Services by Air Canada (www.aircanada.ca) arrive from Vancouver International Airport (from $73, 25 minutes, up to 21 daily) at Victoria International Airport (www.victoriaairport.com), 26km north of the city. Much more convenient, Harbour Air Seaplanes (www.harbour-air.com) services arrive in the Inner Harbour from downtown Vancouver ($145, 35 minutes) throughout the day. Similar routes are serviced via helicopter by Helijet (www.helijet .com).

Bus From Vancouver, Pacific Coach Lines (www.pacificcoach.com) services arrive, via ferry, several times daily. The Victoria Regional Transit (www.busonline.ca) bus 70 runs from Swartz Bay ferry terminal to downtown (adult/child $2.50/1.65).

Car Drive from downtown Vancouver to the BC Ferries Tsawwassen terminal – via S Oak St, Hwy 99 and Hwy 17 – then board the Victoria ferry. From Swartz Bay on Vancouver Island, take Hwy 17 into Victoria (32km).

Ferry Services from BC Ferries' (www.bcferries.com) Tsawwassen terminal on the mainland (adult/child/vehicle $14/7/46.75, 90 minutes) arrive at Swartz Bay every hour between 10am and 7pm in summer (reduced hours in winter).

VICTORIA

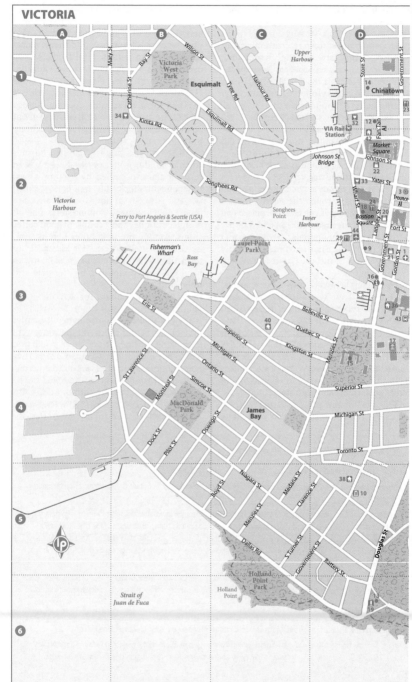

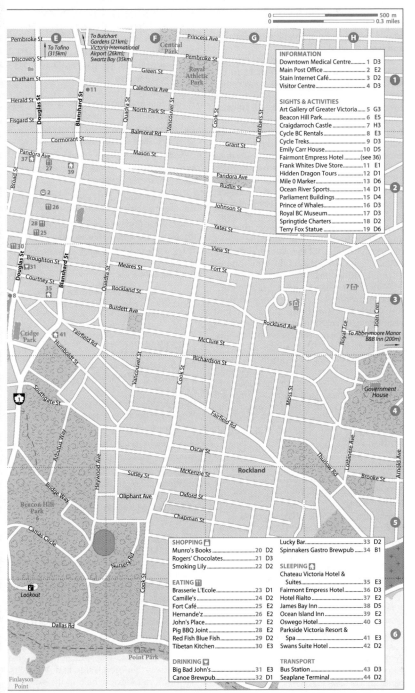

INFORMATION

Downtown Medical Centre	1	D3
Main Post Office	2	E2
Stain Internet Café	3	D2
Visitor Centre	4	D3

SIGHTS & ACTIVITIES

Art Gallery of Greater Victoria	5	G3
Beacon Hill Park	6	E5
Craigdarroch Castle	7	H3
Cycle BC Rentals	8	E3
Cycle Treks	9	D3
Emily Carr House	10	D5
Fairmont Empress Hotel	(see 36)	
Frank Whites Dive Store	11	E1
Hidden Dragon Tours	12	D1
Mile 0 Marker	13	D6
Ocean River Sports	14	D1
Parliament Buildings	15	D4
Prince of Whales	16	E3
Royal BC Museum	17	D3
Springtide Charters	18	D2
Terry Fox Statue	19	D6

SHOPPING 🛍

Munro's Books	20	D2
Rogers' Chocolates	21	D3
Smoking Lily	22	D2

EATING 🍴

Brasserie L'Ecole	23	D1
Camille's	24	D2
Fort Café	25	E2
Hernande'z	26	E2
John's Place	27	E2
Pig BBQ Joint	28	E2
Red Fish Blue Fish	29	D2
Tibetan Kitchen	30	E3

DRINKING 🍷

Big Bad John's	31	E3
Canoe Brewpub	32	D1

Lucky Bar	33	D2
Spinnakers Gastro Brewpub	34	B1

SLEEPING 🛏

Chateau Victoria Hotel & Suites	35	E3
Fairmont Empress Hotel	36	D3
Hotel Rialto	37	E2
James Bay Inn	38	D5
Ocean Island Inn	39	E2
Oswego Hotel	40	C3
Parkside Victoria Resort & Spa	41	E3
Swans Suite Hotel	42	D2

TRANSPORT

Bus Station	43	D3
Seaplane Terminal	44	D2

Tue-Sat May-Sep), the birthplace of BC's best-known painter, complete with re-created period rooms and displays on the artist's life and work.

If her swirling nature-dominated canvases appeal, drive or take transit bus 11 to the **Art Gallery of Greater Victoria** (www.aggv.bc.ca; 1040 Moss St; adult/child $13/2.50, by donation 1st Tue of every month; ☉ 10am-5pm Mon-Wed, Fri & Sat, 10am-9pm Thu, noon-5pm Sun, reduced off-season), where you'll find many Carr paintings on display, along with a revolving roster of additional shows. The nearby **Craigdarroch Castle** (www.thecastle.ca; 1050 Joan Cres; adult/child $13.75/5; ☉ 9am-7pm mid-Jun–Aug, 10am-4:30pm Sep–mid-Jun) is also worth a stop. A handsome, 39-room landmark built by a 19th-century coal baron, this multiturreted stone mansion is dripping with period architecture and antique-packed rooms. Climb the tower's 87 steps (checking out the stained-glass windows en route) for views of the snow-capped Olympic Mountains.

With all the rugged natural beauty in BC, it's a bit ironic that one of the province's top tourism draws is the 20 hectares of elaborate manicured foliage at **Butchart Gardens** (www.butchartgardens.com; 800 Benvenuto Ave; adult/child/youth $28.10/2.86/14.05; ☉ 9am-10pm mid-Jun–Aug, earlier closing at other times), 21km north of Victoria in Brentwood Bay. With its year-round kaleidoscope of colors, the grounds are divided into separate garden areas – the tranquil **Japanese Garden** is a favorite. Summer can be crowded but the Saturday-night fireworks display (July and August) makes it all worthwhile.

Victoria is a whale-watching center and is also home to kayaking and diving operators and has plenty of bike routes, so if you're looking for a bit more action from your visit, check out the following:

Cycle BC Rentals (☎ 250-380-2453; www.cyclebc.ca; 685 Humboldt St; rental per hr/day $7/24; ☉ 9am-6pm) Bike rentals.

Cycle Treks (☎ 250-386-2277; www.cycletreks.com; 1000 Wharf St; tours from $99; ☉ 9:30am-6pm Mon-Sat) Leads six-hour seafront-themed cycling tours.

Frank Whites Dive Store (☎ 250-385-4713; www.frankwhites.com; 1620 Blanshard St; ☉ 9am-5:30pm) Scuba equipment rentals and courses.

Ocean River Sports (☎ 250-381-4233; www.oceanriver.com; 1824 Store St; rental per 2hr/24hr $30/48; ☉ 9:30am-6pm Mon-Wed & Sat, 9:30am-8pm Thu & Fri, 10am-5pm Sun) Rents kayaks and leads tours, including popular 2½-hour sunset tours ($65).

Prince of Whales (☎ 250-383-4884, 888-383-4884; www.princeofwhales.com; 812 Wharf St; adult/child $100/80) Whale-watching tours.

Springtide Charters (☎ 250-384-4444, 800-470-3474; www.springtidecharters.com; 1119 Wharf St; adult/child $99/69) Whale-watching tours.

If you want to time your Victoria visit to take in a festival or two, consider these events:

Dine Around Stay in Town (www.tourismvictoria /dinearound) Three weeks of bargain prix-fixe meals at restaurants around the city; mid-February.

Victoria Day Parade Street fiesta shenanigans with dancers and marching bands; mid-May.

Victoria International Jazzfest (www.jazzvictoria.ca) Nine days of jazz performance; late June.

Victoria Ska Fest (www.victoriaskafest.ca) Held in mid-July, this is Canada's largest ska music event.

Moss Street Paint-In (www.aggv.bc.ca) One hundred artists demonstrate their skills at this popular one-day community event in mid-July.

Victoria Fringe Theatre Festival (www.victoriafringe .com) Two weeks of quirky short plays staged throughout the city from late August.

INFORMATION

Downtown Medical Centre (☎ 250-380-2210; 622 Courtney St; ☉ 8:30am-5pm Mon-Fri) Handy walk-in clinic.

Main Post Office (☎ 250-953-1352; 706 Yates St; ☉ 9am-5pm Mon-Fri) Central post office near the corner of Yates and Douglas Sts.

Stain Internet Café (☎ 250-382-3352; 609 Yates St; per hr $3.50; ☉ 10am-2am) Late-opening internet spot.

Visitor Centre (☎ 250-953-2033, 800-663-3883; www .tourismvictoria.com; 812 Wharf St; ☉ 8:30am-8:30pm Jun-Aug, 9am-5pm Sep-May) Flyer-lined tourist information center overlooking the Inner Harbour.

EATING

Fort Café (742 Fort St; mains $6-10; ☉ 11am-3pm Mon-Fri & 7:30pm-midnight Tue-Sat; ☉) Warm and welcoming subterranean hipster haunt with heaping fresh-made nosh – turkey avocado wraps and hot pepper beef sandwiches recommended – plus Salt Spring Brewing drafts. Check out the Atari game system at the back.

Hernande'z (www.hernandezcocina.com; 750 Yates St; mains $4-7; ☉ 11:30am-9pm) Hidden in a covered passageway between Yates and View Sts, Victoria's best Mexican hole-in-the-wall has a line-up as soon as it opens. Vegetarian options abound but the *huarache de pollo* – thick tortilla with chicken – is legendary. Cash only.

Red Fish Blue Fish (www.redfish-bluefish.com; 1006 Wharf St; mains $6-10; ⊙ 11:30am-7pm) On the waterfront boardwalk at the foot of Broughton St, this freight container take-out shack serves fresh-made sustainable seafood treats like wild-salmon sandwiches, Pacific Rim chowder and excellent scallop *tacones* (cone-shaped tacos).

Camille's (www.camillesrestaurant.com; 45 Bastion Sq; mains $18-26; ⊙ 5:30-10pm Tue-Sat) A charming subterranean dining room with a lively, ever-changing menu reflecting great local ingredients. With its smashing wine list, this spot invites adventurous foodies.

John's Place (www.johnsplace.ca; 723 Pandora Ave; mains $7-16; ⊙ 7am-9pm Mon-Thu, 7am-10pm Fri, 8am-10pm Sat, 8am-9pm Sun) A diner-esque legend with wood floors, high ceilings and funky memorabilia lining the walls. Weekend brunch is an in-stitution, but the heaping comfort-food dinners are also great – don't miss a giant slab o' fruit pie.

Tibetan Kitchen (www.tibetankitchen.ca; 680 Broughton St; mains $7-15; ⊙ 11am-3pm & 5-8:30pm Tue-Fri, noon-3pm & 5-9pm Sat & Sun) Lunch specials are an excellent deal (check the board outside) at this cozy Asian eatery, where fresh-made treats range from noodle to curry dishes. Whatever you end up trying, wash it down with a lip-smacking lychee *lassi* (a yoghurt-based, shake-like drink).

Pig BBQ Joint (www.pigbbqjoint.com; 749 View St; mains $5-6; ⊙ 11am-5pm Mon, 11am-6:30pm Tue-Sat) Hulking hot sandwiches of the melt-in-your-mouth pulled-pork variety (beef brisket and smoked-chicken variations are also offered) dominate the simple menu here, washed down with homemade iced tea.

Brasserie L'Ecole (www.lecole.ca; 1715 Government St; mains $20-24; ⊙ 5:30-11pm Tue-Sat) This country-style French bistro has a warm, casual atmosphere and delectable menu favorites, such as lamb shank served with mustard-creamed root vegetables and braised chard.

DRINKING & NIGHTLIFE

Spinnakers Gastro Brewpub (www.spinnakers.com; 308 Catherine St) Lip-smacking craft brews here include light Honey Blonde Ale and dark Nut Brown. The superior food menu includes excellent seafood.

Big Bad John's (www.strathconahotel.com; 919 Douglas St) Evocative little hillbilly-themed pub where the floor is covered in peanut shells and the ceiling has a few grubby bras hanging from it. Great fun.

Canoe Brewpub (www.canoebrewpub.com; 450 Swift St) The own-brewed beers include hoppy Red Canoe Lager and summer-friendly Siren's Song Pale Ale. It's also good for a meal and there's a great waterfront patio.

Lucky Bar (www.luckybar.ca; 517 Yates St; cover free-$10) This club, a Victoria institution, offers live music from ska and indie to electroclash, plus dance-floor tunes when there's no band performing.

SLEEPING

Prices indicated are for the May to September peak season (sans taxes), when it is difficult to find anything central for less than $100 a night; rooms are reduced by up to 50% off-peak, when the weather is often pleasantly mild. Tourism Victoria's room reservation service (☎ 250-953-2033, 800-663-3883; www.tourismvictoria.com) books B&Bs, hotels and everything else.

Swans Suite Hotel (☎ 250-361-3310, 800-668-7926; www.swanshotel.com; 506 Pandora Ave; d/ste $199/289; 🛜) An old brick warehouse transformed into an art-lined boutique hotel, rooms are decorated with a comfy combination of wood beams, rustic chic furniture and deep leather sofas. The full kitchens are handy, but continental breakfast is included.

DETOUR: TOFINO

Like a waterfront Whistler, lovely Tofino – hugging itself against the crashing surf on the west coast of Vancouver Island – has boomed in recent years, becoming the de facto capital of the rainforested Pacific Rim National Park. You'll find plenty of seaside hotels and resorts and a smattering of good seafood restaurants in and around the town, but it's really all about the outdoors here: the area's tumultuous waves attract surfers and storm watchers in equal measure, while Clayoquot Sound is famed for its idyllic kayaking. There are also plenty of hiking trails and wilderness treks. Check the Tourism Tofino (www.tourismtofino.com) website for ideas.

You can drive here via Hwy 1 and Hwy 4 from Victoria (314km). You can also fly: Orca Airways (www.flyorcaair.com) services arrive at Tofino Airport from Vancouver International Airport's South Terminal ($159, 55 minutes, one to three daily).

Parkside Victoria Resort & Spa (☎ 250-716-2651, 866-941-4175; www.parksidevictoria.com; 810 Humboldt St; ste $269-299; 🛜 🖳) A slick new apartment-style hotel where the rooms are ideal if you want to have a home-style base steps from the city center. Full kitchens, balconies and a gym will make you want to move in permanently.

Fairmont Empress Hotel (☎ 250-348-8111, 866-540-4429; www.fairmont.com/empress; 721 Government St; r from $199; 🔀 🖳 🖳) Rooms at this ivy-covered, century-old landmark are elegant but conservative and some are quite small, but the overall effect is old-school classy.

Oswego Hotel (☎ 250-294-7500, 877-767-9346; www.oswegovictoria.com; 500 Oswego St; d/ste from $159/229) Victoria's swankiest new hotel, this designer lounge spot in a quiet residential location comes complete with granite floors, cedar beams, deep baths and (in most rooms) small balconies.

Hotel Rialto (☎ 250-382-4157, 800-332-9981; www.hotelrialto.ca; 653 Pandora Ave; r $139-249; 🛜) Totally refurbished from the faded old budget hotel it used to be, the new Rialto is a well-located downtown option for mid-price travelers. Each of the 38 mod-decorated rooms has a fridge, microwave and flatscreen TV, and some have tubs as well as showers.

James Bay Inn (☎ 250-384-7151, 800-836-2649; www.jamesbayinn.bc.ca; 270 Government St; r from $129) This well-maintained old charmer has an array of room types, most with busy patterned carpets and furniture that's not quite antique. Some rooms have kitchenettes and there's a downstairs bar serving pub grub.

Abbeymoore Manor B&B Inn (☎ 250-370-1470, 888-801-1811; www.abbeymoore.com; 1470 Rockland Ave; r from $165; 🛜) A romantic 1912 Arts and Crafts mansion, Abbeymoore's handsome colonial exterior hides seven antique-lined rooms furnished with Victorian knickknacks and the kind of beds you have to climb to get into. Some rooms have kitchens and jetted tubs.

Chateau Victoria Hotel & Suites (☎ 250-382-4221, 800-663-5891; www.chateauvictoria.com; 740 Burdett Ave; d/ste/penthouse from $152/202/400; 🔀 🖳 🖳) There's a well-maintained '80s feel at this perfectly located tower-block hotel, and the rooms are clean and many have handy kitchens. The hotel's top-floor restaurant has the city's best views.

Ocean Island Inn (☎ 250-385-1788, 888-888-4180; www.oceanisland.com; 791 Pandora Ave; dm/s/d from $27.50/30/55; 🖳 🛜) A funky, multicolored sleepover option with a labyrinth of dorms and private rooms. There's also a large communal kitchen

and a licensed lounge with quiz nights and open mikes.

WHISTLER

Named for the furry marmots that populate the area and whistle like deflating balloons, this gabled alpine village is one of the world's most popular ski resorts. It was home to many of the outdoor events at the 2010 Olympic and Paralympic Winter Games, so feel free to slip on your skis and aim (if only in your imagination) for a gold medal of your own.

Nestled in the shade of the formidable Whistler and Blackcomb mountains, the wintertime village has a frosted, Christmas-card appeal. But summer is an increasingly popular time to visit, with Vancouverites and international travelers lured to the lakes and crags by a wide array of activities, from mountain biking to scream-triggering zipline runs.

Centered on four main neighborhoods – approaching via Hwy 99 from the south, you'll hit Creekside first – Whistler Village is the key hub for hotels, restaurants and shops. You'll find humbler B&B-type accommodations in the quieter Village North area, while the Upper Village is home to some swanky hotels, clustered around the base of Blackcomb. Don't be surprised if you get lost when you're wandering around on foot – there are plenty of street signs and lots of people around to help with directions.

Comprising 38 lifts and almost 82 sq km of skiable terrain crisscrossed with over 200 runs (more than half aimed at intermediate-level skiers), the sister mountains of Whistler-Blackcomb (www.whistlerblackcomb.com; 1-day lift ticket adult/child/youth $93/46/78) were physically linked for the first time in 2009. The mammoth new 4.4km Peak 2 Peak Gondola includes the world's longest unsupported span and takes 11 minutes to shuttle wide-eyed powder hogs between the two high alpine areas, enabling you to hit the slopes on both mountains on the same day.

The resort's winter season usually starts in late November and runs to April on Whistler and June on Blackcomb – December to February is the peak – but there's also glacier skiing available into July. Be aware that skiing off piste is strongly discouraged here and avalanches are a major risk in these unmarked areas. If you want to emulate your fave Olympic ski heroes – or prepare for the next Games – Whistler Creekside was the

TRANSPORTATION: WHISTLER

Direction 122km north

Travel time 1½ to two hours by vehicle; three hours by train

Bus Services from Greyhound (www.greyhound.ca) arrive at Creekside and Whistler Village from Vancouver (from $25, 2¾ hours, seven daily). SkyLynx buses from Pacific Coach Lines (www.pacificcoach.com) also arrive from Vancouver (from $35, 3½ hours, six daily). Snowbus (www.snowbus.com) also operates a winter-only service from Vancouver (adult/child $30.95/19.05, three hours, two daily). Local Whistler and Valley Express (WAVE; www .busonline.ca; adult/child/one-day pass $2/1.50/5) transit buses are equipped with ski and bike racks. There's a free service in July and August between the village and Lost Lake.

Car Take W Georgia St through Stanley Park and over the Lions Gate Bridge. Exit the bridge on the Marine Dr W turnoff. Take the first right on to Taylor Way. Travel up the hill and turn left on to Hwy 1. Follow the signs and take Exit 2 to Hwy 99, which takes you all the way to Whistler Village.

Train Trundling in from North Vancouver is the Rocky Mountaineer Whistler Sea to Sky Climb (www .rockymountaineer.com; tickets from $129, three hours, May to mid-October).

setting for all the 2010 downhill skiing events.

You can beat the crowds with an early-morning Fresh Tracks ticket (adult/child $17.25/12.60), which must be bought in advance at Whistler Village Gondola Guest Relations. Be at the gondola for a 7:30am start the next day. The price includes a buffet breakfast at the Roundhouse Lodge up top. Weekdays are recommended for this, since tickets sell out quickly on weekends. Night owls might prefer the evening Night Moves (adult/child $18/12) program operated via Blackcomb's Magic Chair lift after 5pm.

Snowboard fans should also check out the freestyle terrain parks mostly located on Blackcomb, including the Snow Cross and the Big Easy Terrain Garden. There's also the Habitat Terrain Park on Whistler.

If you didn't bring you own gear, Mountain Adventure Centres (www.whistlerblackcomb .com /rentals; 1-day ski or snowboard rental adult/child from $46/32; hrs vary) has several equipment rental outlets around town. They offer online reservations – you can choose your favorite gear before you arrive – as well as lessons for ski and snowboard virgins.

If you're craving some five-ring action, Whistler Sliding Centre (www.whistlerslidingcentre.com; 4910 Glacier Lane; adult/child $7/free; 10am-5pm), which hosted Olympic bobsled, luge and skeleton events, is now open to the public. You can wander exhibits and check out video footage from the track or take a general tour (adult/child $15/free) or behind-the-scenes tour (adult/child $69/59).

Colonizing the melted ski slopes in summer and accessed via lifts at the village's south end, Whistler Mountain Bike Park (www.whistlerbike.com; 1-day pass adult/child/youth $53/29/47; 10am-8pm mid-Jun–Aug, 10am-5pm May–mid-Jun, Sep–mid-Oct) offers barreling downhill runs and an orgy of jumps, beams and bridges twisting through 200km of well-maintained forested trails. Luckily, you don't have to be a bike courier to stand the gonad-crunching pace: easier routes are marked in green, while blue intermediate trails and black diamond advanced paths are offered if you want to Crank It Up – the name of one of the park's most popular routes. Outside the park area, regional trails include Comfortably Numb (a tough 26km with steep climbs and bridges); A River Runs Through It (suitable for all skill levels, it has teeter-totters and log obstacles); and the gentle Valley Trail, an easy 14km loop that encircles the village and its lake, meadow and mountain chateau surroundings – this is recommended for first-timers.

Two legs are almost as handy as two wheels here. With more than 40km of flower-and-forest alpine trails, most accessed via the Whistler Village Gondola, this region is ideal for those who like nature of the strollable variety. Favorite routes include the High Note Trail (8km), which traverses pristine meadows and has stunning views of the blue-green waters of Cheakamus Lake. Route maps are available at the Whistler Visitor Centre. Guided treks are also offered by the friendly folk at Whistler Alpine Guides Bureau (☎ 604-938-9242; www.whistlerguides.com; Unit 19, 4314 Main St; guided hikes adult/child from $79/59; 10am-5:30pm), who can also help with rock climbing and rap jumping excursions.

If adrenaline-rush thrills are more your bag, consider a harnessed ziplining swoop through the trees with Ziptrek Ecotours (www.ziptrek.com;

WHISTLER

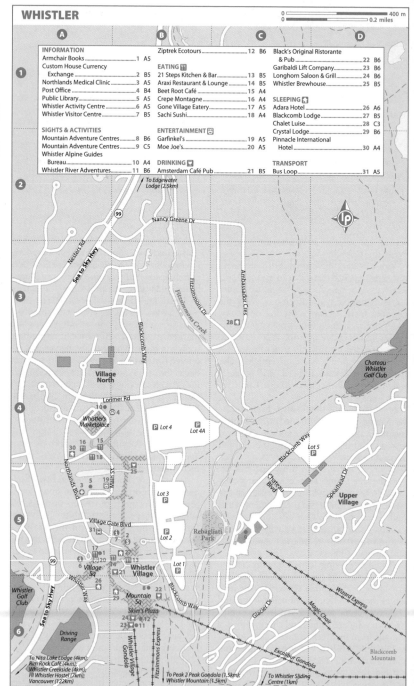

INFORMATION	Ziptrek Ecotours.....................12 B6	Black's Original Ristorante
Armchair Books.......................1 A5		& Pub...22 B6
Custom House Currency	**EATING** 🍴	Garibaldi Lift Company.............23 B6
Exchange.................................2 B5	21 Steps Kitchen & Bar...........13 B5	Longhorn Saloon & Grill...........24 B6
Northlands Medical Clinic.......3 A5	Araxi Restaurant & Lounge.....14 B5	Whistler Brewhouse..................25 B5
Post Office...............................4 B4	Beet Root Café........................15 A4	
Public Library..........................5 A5	Crepe Montagne......................16 A4	**SLEEPING** 🛏
Whistler Activity Centre..........6 A5	Gone Village Eatery.................17 A5	Adara Hotel..............................26 A6
Whistler Visitor Centre............7 B5	Sachi Sushi..............................18 A4	Blackcomb Lodge......................27 B5
		Chalet Luise.............................28 C3
SIGHTS & ACTIVITIES	**ENTERTAINMENT** 🎭	Crystal Lodge............................29 B6
Mountain Adventure Centres...8 B6	Garfinkel's...............................19 A5	Pinnacle International
Mountain Adventure Centres...9 C5	Moe Joe's.................................20 A5	Hotel..30 A4
Whistler Alpine Guides		
Bureau......................................10 A4	**DRINKING** 🍷	**TRANSPORT**
Whistler River Adventures......11 B6	Amsterdam Café Pub...............21 B5	Bus Loop..................................31 A5

Carleton Lodge, Mountain Sq; adult/child $99/79; ☼ 9:30am-6pm, reduced off-season), or have a splashing good time on a white-knuckle rafting trip with Whistler River Adventures (☎ 604-932-3532, 888-932-3532; www.whistlerriver.com; Village Gondola Building; adult/child/youth from $95/59/75; ☼ 10am-6pm, reduced off-season). You'll never have more fun wetting your pants.

Whistler also hosts some great annual events worth timing your visit for, including the following:

WinterPride (www.gaywhistler.com) Gay-themed snow action and late-night partying in early February.

Telus World Ski & Snowboard Festival (www.wssf.com) Nine-day showcase in mid-April of pro ski and snowboard competitions, plus live bands.

Kokanee Crankworx (www.crankworx.com) Bike stunts, speed demons and general two-wheeled shenanigans; mid-August.

Cornucopia (www.whistlercornucopia.com) Bacchanalian food and wine fest held in mid-November.

Whistler Film Festival (www.whistlerfilmfestival.com) Four days in late November of movie screenings and industry glad-handing.

INFORMATION

Armchair Books (☎ 604-932-5557; 4205 Village Sq; ☼ 9am-9pm) Well-located bookstore with good travel section.

Custom House Currency Exchange (☎ 604-938-6658; 4227 Village Stroll; ☼ 8:30am-8:30pm May-Sep, 9am-6pm Oct-Apr) Central exchange.

Northlands Medical Clinic (☎ 604-932-8362; 4359 Main St; ☼ 9am-5:30pm). Walk-in medical center.

Post Office (☎ 604-932-5012; Unit 106, 4360 Lorimer Rd; ☼ 8am-5pm Mon-Fri, 8am-noon Sat)

Public Library (☎ 604-935-8433; 4329 Main St; ☼ 11am-7pm Mon-Sat, 11am-4pm Sun) Register at front desk for free internet access.

Whistler Activity Centre (☎ 604-938-2769, 877-991-9988; 4010 Whistler Way; ☼ 10am-6pm) Bookings for local activities.

Whistler Visitor Centre (☎ 604-935-3357, 800-944-7853; www.whistler.com; 4230 Gateway Dr; ☼ 8am-8pm) Flyer-lined visitor center.

EATING

Beet Root Café (Unit 129, 4340 Lorimer Rd; light mains $6-11; ☼ 7:30am-4:30pm) This is Whistler's best home-style hangout, with bulging breakfast burritos, huge packed sandwiches and a rolling cavalcade of fresh cookies and baked goodies. Pull up a cushion by the window and make yourself at home.

Araxi Restaurant & Lounge (☎ 604-932-4540; www.araxi.com; 4222 Village Sq; mains $30-45; ☼ 11am-11pm) Whistler's best fine-dining option, Araxi offers an exquisite Pacific Northwest menu plus courteous service. Try the Queen Charlotte Islands halibut and drain the 15,000-bottle wine selection. Reservations recommended.

Crepe Montagne (www.crepemontagne.com; 4368 Main St; mains $8-14; ☼ 8am-9:30pm) This small, authentic creperie – hence the French accents percolating among the staff – offers a bewildering array of sweet and savory buckwheat crepes with fillings that include ham, brie, asparagus, banana, strawberries and more. Good breakfast spot – go the waffle route.

Rim Rock Café (www.rimrockwhistler.com; 2117 Whistler Rd; mains $16-22; ☼ 9am-11pm) On the edge of Creekside and accessible just off Hwy 99, this locals' favorite chefs up treats like seared scallops, venison tenderloin and a highly recommended Seafood Trio of grilled prawns, ahi tuna and nut-crusted sablefish.

Gone Village Eatery (www.gonevillageeatery.com; 4205 Village Sq; mains $6-12; ☼ 7am-9pm; ☞) Hidden behind Armchair Books, this wood-floored haunt serves hearty breakfast grub (have the omelet burrito), lunch specials (sandwiches, falafel or the $10 burger and beer deal do the trick) and any-time-of-day baked treats (snag a chewy toffee cookie).

21 Steps Kitchen & Bar (www.21steps.ca; 4320 Sundial Cres; mains $14-22; ☼ 5:30pm-midnight) High-end comfort food such as steak, chops and seafood. Check out the great attic bar, a Whistlerite favorite.

Sachi Sushi (Unit 106, 4359 Main St; mains $8-22; ☼ noon-2:30pm Tue-Fri, 5:30-10pm daily) Serving everything from good sushi to crispy popcorn shrimp to stomach-warming udon noodles, this is a relaxing après-ski hangout – go for a warming hot sake.

DRINKING & NIGHTLIFE

Check The Pique and Whistler Question (both free) for listings.

Whistler Brewhouse (www.markjamesgroup.com; 4355 Blackcomb Way; ☼ 11:30am-midnight Sun-Thu, 11:30am-1am Fri & Sat) A large, lodge-like resto-bar crafting its own beer (try the Lifty Lager), this is also an ideal spot to catch a game on TV and scoff some excellent fish-and-chips.

Amsterdam Café Pub (www.amsterdampub.com; Village Sq; ☼ 11am-1am) This boozy, brick-lined party joint is in the heart of the village. You can treat your hangover the next day by coming back for a late fry-up breakfast.

Garibaldi Lift Company (Whistler Village Gondola; ☼ 11:30am-11pm) The closest bar to the slopes (watch the powder-mad geeks on Whistler Mountain slide to a halt from the patio) the rock-lined GLC is a reliable après-ski hangout for a big burger and a Kootenay Mountain Ale.

Longhorn Saloon & Grill (www.longhornsaloon.ca; 4290 Mountain Sq; ☼ 7am-11pm Sun-Thu, 7am-midnight Fri & Sat) Fanned out at the base of Whistler Mountain with a patio that threatens to take over the town, the Longhorn is a local legend. Food and beer is standard pub grub but the atmosphere here on a hopping winter evening is electric.

Black's Original Ristorante & Pub (www.whistlerpub restaurant.com; 4270 Mountain Sq; ☼ 7am-11pm) Across from the Village Gondola base, this trad resto-bar leans toward pasta and pizza but has a good international bottled-beer menu. Among the BC drafts, the Russell Cream Ale is recommended.

Garfinkel's (www.garfswhistler.com; Unit 1, 4308 Main St; ☼ 9am-2am Tue-Sat) Mixing mainstream dance grooves with a few live bands, Whistler's biggest club is ever-popular. Arrive early on weekends when it's especially packed.

Moe Joe's (www.moejoes.com; 4155 Golfer's Approach; ☼ 9am-2am Tue-Sat) More intimate than Garfinkel's, this is the best place in town if you like dancing yourself into a drooling heap. It's always crowded on Friday nights.

SLEEPING

Winter is the peak for prices here, but last-minute deals can still be had if you're planning an impromptu overnight from Vancouver; check the Tourism Whistler website (www .whistler.com) for room sales and packages. Most hotels extort parking fees (up to $20 daily) and some also slap on resort fees (up to $25 daily) – confirm these before you book.

HI Whistler Hostel (☎ 604-962-0025; www.hihostels .ca; 1035 Legacy Way; dm/r $39/153; 🖳 🛜) Replacing Whistler's former too-small HI, this smashing new hostel repurposes part of the 2010 Olympic athletes village near Function Junction – it's 7km south of town with transit bus access. The large, lodge-like building with its IKEA-esque furnishings

includes 188 beds in small four-bedded dorms as well as 14 sought-after en suite private rooms. There's a well-equipped kitchen plus a barbecue deck and cafe.

Nita Lake Lodge (☎ 604-966-5700, 888-755-6482; www .nitalakelodge.com; 2135 Lake Placid Rd; r from $250; 🛜) Adjoining Creekside train station – handy if you're coming up on the Rocky Mountaineer Sea to Sky Climb – this swanky timber-framed lodge has lakefront views and pampering rooms with rock fireplaces and small kitchenettes. Creekside lifts are just a few minutes away.

Adara Hotel (☎ 604-905-4009, 866-502-3272; www .adarahotel.com; 4122 Village Green; r from $180; 🕸 🛜) Sophisticated and quirky, this top-end joint offers art-lined interiors and dramatic mod rooms where the fireplaces look like TVs and faux-fur throws abound. Despite the ultra-cool aesthetics, service is warm and relaxed.

Edgewater Lodge (☎ 604-932-0688, 888-870-9065; www.edgewater-lodge.com; 8020 Alpine Way; r from $150; 🛜) A few minutes' drive past Whistler on Hwy 99, this 12-room lakeside lodge is a nature-lover's haven and has a great on-site restaurant. Kayaking available on the glassy lake.

Chalet Luise (☎ 604-932-4187, 800-665-1998; www .chaletluise.com; 7461 Ambassador Cres; r from $125; 🛜) A Bavarian-look B&B pension with eight sunny rooms – think pine furnishings and white duvets – plus a flower garden and outdoor hot tub. Free parking; short walk to the village.

Blackcomb Lodge (☎ 604-935-1177, 888-621-1117; www.whistlerpremier.com; 4220 Gateway Dr; r/ste from $109/139; 🕸 🖳 🛒) With an excellent Village Sq location, the top rooms here have deep leather sofas, darkwood furnishings and full kitchens, while the standard rooms without kitchens are almost as comfortable.

Pinnacle International Hotel (☎ 604-938-3218, 888-999-8986; www.whistlerpinnacle.com; 4319 Main St; d from $139; 🛜 🐾) Well-established midrange property where the rooms have gas fireplaces, double Jacuzzi tubs and full kitchens. Ski and snowboard storage available; adult oriented.

Crystal Lodge (☎ 604-932-2221, 800-667-3363; www .crystal-lodge.com; 4154 Village Stroll; d/ste from $130/175; 🕸 🛒 🐾) Combining chic loungey rooms with motel-style rooms, there's something to suit most budgets here. You're also in the heart of the action, less than 100m from the Village Gondola lift.

SQUAMISH

Midway between Vancouver and Whistler on Hwy 99, Squamish enjoys an incredible natural setting at the fingertips of Howe Sound. Once little more than a rough-and-ready logging town, it's undergone an Olympics-triggered boom and is now a popular base for outdoor activities, especially in summer. Pull over at the slick Squamish Adventure Centre (☎ 604-815-4994, 866-333-2010; www.tourismsquamish.com; 38551 Loggers Lane; ☼ 8am-8pm Jun-Sep, 9am-6pm Oct-May) to find out what's on offer in and around the region.

Just before the town on Hwy 99, the Britannia Mine Museum (www.britanniaminemuseum.ca; adult/child $19.75/12.75; ☼ 9am-4:30pm) is a popular stop. Once the British Empire's largest copper mine, it's been preserved with an impressive restoration. Its underground train tour into the pitch-black mine tunnels is a highlight and there are plenty of additional kid-friendly exhibits – including gold panning – plus a large artsy gift shop.

Continuing your drive, you'll soon see a sheer, 652m granite rock face looming ahead. Attracting hardy climbers, it's called 'The Chief' and it's the highlight of Stawamus Chief Provincial Park (www.bcparks.ca). You don't have to be geared-up to experience the summit's breathtaking vistas: there are hiking routes up the back for anyone who wants to have a go. Consider Squamish Rock Guides (☎ 604-892-7816; www.squamishrockguides.com; guided climbs half-/full-day from $75/115) for climbing assistance or lessons.

The 100 or so trails around Squamish draw plenty of mountain-biking enthusiasts. The Cheekeye Fan trail near Brackendale has some easy forested rides, while downhill thrill seekers will prefer the Diamond Head/Power Smart area, where the routes have inviting names like Dope Slope and Icy Hole of Death. Drop in on Corsa Cycles (☎ 604-892-3331; www.corsacycles.com; 830-1200 Hunter Pl; rental per day $45; ☼ 9:30am-5:30pm) for rentals and trail advice. Also check the website of the Squamish Off Road Cycling Association (www.sorca.ca).

Historic-train nuts should continue just past town to the popular West Coast Railway Heritage Park (www.wcra.org; 39645 Government Rd; adult/child $15/10; ☼ 10am-5pm). This large, mostly alfresco museum is the final resting place of BC's legendary *Royal Hudson* steam engine and has around 90 other historic railcars, including 10 working engines and the original prototype SkyTrain car. Check out the new

TRANSPORTATION: SQUAMISH

Direction 64km north

Travel time 55 minutes by vehicle

Bus Services operated by Greyhound (www .greyhound.ca) arrive from Vancouver (1½ hours, $17, seven daily) and Whistler (one hour, $14, eight daily). The more salubrious Pacific Coach Lines (www.pacificcoach.com) buses also arrive here from Vancouver (1½ hours, $39.20, up to eight daily).

Car See the driving directions for Whistler (p215) for instructions on how to reach Hwy 99 from Vancouver. Around 55km along the highway, turn left onto Cleveland Ave to reach downtown Squamish.

Roundhouse building, housing the park's most precious artifacts.

If you prefer to travel under your own steam, Squamish Spit is a popular kiteboarding (and windsurfing) hot spot; the season runs from May to October. The Squamish Windsports Society (www.squamishwindsports.com) is your first point of contact for weather and water conditions and information on access to the spit.

EATING & SLEEPING

Grilled Fromage (www.grilledfromage.com; 38134 Cleveland Ave; mains $4-9; ☼ 11am-6pm Tue, 11am-midnight Wed-Sat, 11am-8pm Sun) If you thought a grilled cheese sandwich was just that, step inside this funkily painted spot and peruse the menu of more than 50 varieties. The Napoleon (camembert and bacon on sourdough) is popular but go for the decadent High Roller (lobster and smoked Gruyère).

Sunflower Bakery Café (www.sunflowerbakerycafe .com; 38086 Cleveland Ave; mains $4-9; ☼ 7:30am-5:30pm Mon-Sat) This bright and breezy spot serves fresh wraps and bagel sandwiches plus an array of chunky cakes and bulging fruit pies that will have you committing to some heavy exercise.

Howe Sound Inn & Brewing Company (www.howesound .com; 37801 Cleveland Ave; r $119; ☎) This sleepover has 20 warm and inviting rooms with plenty of woodsy touches. The on-site brewpub is also worth a visit – try the yam fries and lip-smacking Oatmeal Stout.

Sunwolf Outdoor Centre (☎ 604-898-1537, 877-806-8046; www.sunwolf.net; 70002 Squamish Valley Rd; cabins from $100) Good value, rustic riverside cabins, plus guided eagle viewing and rafting trips.

BUNTZEN LAKE

If you've been fighting the peak-season crowds at Vancouver's main tourist attractions and all you need is a restorative day-long commune with the natural world, this dramatic, sigh-inducing area will remind you just what Mother Nature (and 'Beautiful BC') is supposed to be all about. It's also ideal if you're itching for some calf-stretching hikes away from the shuffling shoppers down on Robson St.

An expansive, naturally occurring reservoir hidden on the fringes of suburban Coquitlam, Buntzen Lake is embraced on three sides by steep, tree-covered mountains and on its fourth side by a shaded, gently curving beach, complete with picnic tables, old-growth trees and those ambling, beady-eyed Canada geese.

Originally named Lake Beautiful – it's not hard to understand why – it was the first hydroelectric power system to serve Vancouver, coming online to supplement an old steam plant in 1903. Renamed after BC Electric Company manager Johannes Buntzen, the lake sends water flowing through penstocks down the steep mountain slope to two power plants located on the banks of Indian Arm. Not that you'd notice any of that when you visit. In fact, it's the all-enveloping quietude that particularly strikes most first-time visitors here as they sit back and drink in the scenery.

If watching the natural world go by only appeals for a minute or two, there are plenty of well-marked, multihour hiking and mountain-bike trails through the forest. Most of the routes are fairly challenging and are not aimed

at first-timers. The Buntzen Lake Trail (8km) is the area's signature hike. It encircles the water, weaves through mature forest and takes you over several bridges, some of them of the swaying suspension variety. An alternative is the Diez Vistas Trail (7km one way), which appeals to fit hikers with its steep climbs that open onto some spectacular views of the mountains and waterways surrounding the entire Vancouver region. Among the area's dedicated biking trails, the Academy Trail (4km one way) is a popular trek.

If you'd prefer to hit the water but can't find that canoe you packed in your suitcase, there's a handy rental store (☎ 604-469-9928; Sunnyside Rd; ☷ 9am-7pm Sun-Thu, 9am-8pm Fri & Sat) near the park entrance. Don't paddle out too far – the lake is bigger than it looks.

Whatever you decide to do here, make sure you bring a picnic. Buntzen is an ideal spot to unfurl a blanket (or grab one of the tables, if they haven't all gone), munch on some sandwiches and let the city disappear from your mind. It'll be one of the most memorable green-hued highlights of your trip.

BOWEN ISLAND

So you want to visit some of the islands winking at you on the horizon, but you just don't have the time? Actually, you do. Bowen is a brief saunter via ferry from West Vancouver's Horseshoe Bay terminal or by water taxi from Granville Island. Known as the 'Happy Isle,' Bowen hit its stride as a picnickers' paradise in the 1920s when the Union Steamship Company arrived, providing a regular service from the mainland. Today, you can stroll the waterfront boardwalks of Snug Cove, the small village where the ferry docks. Most of the village, with its early-20th-century heritage buildings housing restaurants, pubs, galleries and shops, straddles Government Rd, which runs straight up from the ferry terminal. On your right as you depart the ferry, the Visitor Centre (☎ 604-947-9024; www.bowenchamber.com; 432 Cardena Rd; ☷ 10am-5pm Thu-Sun mid-May–early Sep, reduced off-season) has plenty of suggestions for what to do here.

Good swimming beaches are at Mannion Bay, next to Snug Cove, and Bowen Bay, at the west end of the island. There are numerous walking trails, which range from a five-minute stroll toward the picnic tables at Snug Cove to a 45-minute trek from the ferry dock to

---

TRANSPORTATION: BUNTZEN LAKE

Direction 30km east

Travel time One hour

Car From Vancouver, follow Hastings St (Hwy 7A) east through the city to Burnaby and then Coquitlam, where it becomes Barnet Hwy. Take the loco Rd exit and follow loco to the left. Turn right on 1st Ave and continue to Sunnyside Rd. Turn right again and continue to the Buntzen Lake entrance.

TRANSPORTATION: BOWEN ISLAND

Direction 19km northwest

Travel time One hour (including ferry) by vehicle

Bus Island-spanning public transportation is available via the Bowen Island Community Shuttle for $2.50.

Car From Vancouver, follow Hwy 1 west to Horseshoe Bay and take the Bowen Island ferry to Snug Cove.

Ferry Services operated by BC Ferries (www.bcferries.com) from Horseshoe Bay (adult/child/vehicle $9.75/4.90/27.90, 20 minutes, up to 16 daily) arrive at Snug Cove throughout the day between 6am and 9:35pm. English Bay Launch (www.englishbaylaunch.ca) runs a handy boat taxi service to Snug Cove from Granville Island and Coal Harbour (one-way/return $20/30, 35 minutes, up to six daily).

Crippen Regional Park. Inside the park an easy 4km loop around Killarney Lake is favored by bird-watchers; the more difficult 10km Mt Gardner Trail reaches the island's highest point (719m). Many other trails are accessible to cyclists and horseback riders. If you fancy something more adventurous, Bowen Island Sea Kayaking (☎ 604-947-9266; www.bowenislandkayaking.com; Snug Cove ferry dock; rentals per 3hr/day $45/70, tours from $65; ◷ 9am-5pm) offers rentals and short kayaking tours, including a recommended sunset paddle.

EATING & SLEEPING

Artisan Eats (www.artisaneats.ca; mains $5-12; ◷ 9am-6pm Tue-Sat, 9am-4pm Sun) It's worth the uphill hike from Artisan Sq to find this locals' favorite; you can reward yourself with sterling Howe Sound views and a menu of deli tasting plates, gourmet sandwiches and a great Sunday brunch.

Doc Morgan's Restaurant & Pub (www.ussc.ca; mains $8-14; ◷ 11am-11pm) This traditional, old-school resto-bar has a couple of inviting patios overlooking the park and the harbor – a good spot to scoff your fish-and-chips.

Lodge at the Old Dorm (www.lodgeattheolddorm.com; 460 Melmore Rd; r $95-150) A five-minute stroll from the ferry dock, this heritage building has six rooms with art deco accents. Continental breakfast included.

SOUTHERN GULF ISLANDS

When Canadians refer to BC as 'lotusland,' the Gulf Islands are really what they're thinking about. Languidly strung between the mainland and Vancouver Island, Salt Spring, Galiano, Mayne, Saturna and the North and South Penders are the natural retreat of choice for locals and in-the-know visitors. Combining a mild climate, gentle natural beauty and an infectious, laid-back ambience, these small communities seem remote but are generally easy to access from the mainland by ferry. The most popular destination for visitors is Salt Spring, but Galiano is also ideal if you want a rustic retreat without sacrificing too many comforts.

INFORMATION

Galiano Island (www.galianoisland.com)

Mayne Island (www.mayneislandchamber.ca)

North and South Pender Islands (www.penderislandchamber.com)

Salt Spring Island (www.saltspringtourism.com)

Saturna Island Tourism Association (www.saturnatourism.com)

SALT SPRING ISLAND

A former hippie enclave that's now the site of many rich vacation homes, pretty Salt Spring justifiably receives the majority of Gulf Island visitors. The heart of the community is Ganges, also the location of the Visitor Centre (☎ 250-537-5252; www.saltspringtourism.com; 121 Lower Ganges Rd; ◷ 9am-5pm Jul & Aug, reduced off-season).

If you arrive on a summer weekend, the best way to dive into the community is at the thriving Saturday Market (www.saltspringmarket.com; Centennial Park, Ganges; ◷ 8am-4pm Sat Apr-Oct), where you can tuck into luscious island-grown fruit and piquant cheeses and peruse locally produced arts and crafts. You can visit some of these artisans using a free downloadable Studio Tour Map (www.saltspringstudiotour.com). Among the best is the rustic Blue Horse Folk Art Gallery (www.bluehorse.ca; 175 North View Dr; ◷ 10am-5pm Sun-Fri Mar-Dec), complete with some funky carvings of horses. The friendly owners recently opened an on-site B&B (www.bloomorganicbandb.com; d $150).

If you haven't eaten your fill at the market, drop by Salt Spring Island Cheese (www.saltspringcheese

SOUTHERN GULF ISLANDS

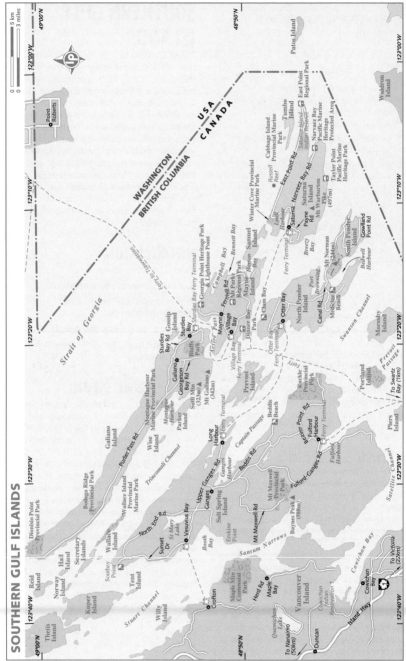

TRANSPORTATION: SOUTHERN GULF ISLANDS

Direction Southwest

Travel time One to three hours by ferry; 20 minutes by plane

Air Services from Salt Spring Air (www.saltspring air.com) arrive throughout the Southern Gulf Islands from downtown Vancouver and Vancouver International Airport. Check its website for the myriad schedules.

Ferry Services from BC Ferries (www.bcferries .com) arrive from Tsawwassen terminal at Galiano, with connections from there to North Pender. There are also direct weekend services to Mayne (Sunday only) and Salt Spring (Friday to Sunday). For more frequent services to these and the other islands, you will need to travel from Tsawwassen to Vancouver Island's Swartz Bay terminal, then board a connecting ferry. Fares from Tsawwassen to the Gulf Islands are adult/child/vehicle $15.70/7.85/50.30.

.com; 285 Reynolds Rd; 🕙 11am-5pm May-Sep, 11am-4pm Oct-Apr), where you can take a self-guided tour of the facilities – be sure to check out the miniature ponies – then sample up to 10 curdy treats in the winery-style tasting room.

Pick a favorite cheese then add to your picnic-in-the-making with a bottle from Salt Spring Vineyards (www.saltspringvineyards.com; 151 Lee Rd; 🕙 11am-5pm mid-Jun–Aug, reduced off-season), where you can sample a few tipples to find the one you like best – the rich blackberry port is dangerously tasty.

Pack up your picnic and head over to Ruckle Provincial Park (www.bcparks.ca), a southeast gem with ragged shorelines, arbutus forests and sun-kissed farmlands. There are trails here for all skill levels, with Yeo Point making an ideal pit stop.

It's not all about hedonism on Salt Spring. If you crave some activity, touch base with Salt Spring Adventure Co (☎ 250-537-2764; www .saltspringadventures.com; 124 Upper Ganges Rd; tours from $50; 🕙 10am-5pm Mon-Sat, 11am-5pm Sun, reduced off-season). It can kit you out for a bobbling kayak tour around Ganges Harbour.

Eating

Tree House Café (www.treehousecafe.ca; 106 Purvis Lane; mains $11-18; 🕙 8am-10pm, reduced off-season) This magical outdoor spot in Ganges, in the shade of a large plum tree, serves comfort pastas, Mexican specialties and gourmet burgers. Make sure you also tuck into a large bottle of Salt Spring Gold Ale, brewed right here on the island.

Raven Street Market Café (www.ravenstreet.ca; 321 Fernwood Rd; mains $8.50-18; 🕙 noon-8pm) On the north part of the island, this neighborhood nook serves gourmet pizzas and an awesome seafood-and-sausage gumbo.

Restaurant House Piccolo (www.housepiccolo.com; 108 Hereford Ave; mains $20-28; 🕙 5-11pm) White-tablecloth dining – the duck is recommended – along with Salt Spring's best wine list make this a longtime Ganges favorite.

Barb's Buns (121 McPhillips Ave; mains $6-9; 🕙 7am-5pm Mon, 7am-10pm Tue-Sat, 10am-2pm Sun) Heaping pizza slices, hearty soups and bulging sandwiches draw the Ganges lunch crowd here, many of them grateful vegetarians.

Sleeping

Love Shack (☎ 250-653-0007, 866-341-0007; www .oceansidecottages.com; 521 Isabella Rd; cabins $135) Near Fulford Harbour, this groovy waterfront nook is lined with kitsch-art flourishes. The private deck here has great sunset views.

Lakeside Gardens (☎ 250-537-5773; www .lakesidegardensresort.com; 1450 North End Rd; cabanas/ cottages $75/135; 🕙 Apr-Oct) This is a tranquil, family-friendly clutch of rustic cottages, some with TVs, en suite bathrooms and kitchens. It's a 10-minute drive from Ganges.

Harbour House Hotel (☎ 250-537-5571, 888-799-5571; www.saltspringharbourhouse.com; 121 Upper Ganges Rd; r from $129; 🛜) In a great Ganges location, this place has a combination of motel-style and superior rooms with Jacuzzis.

Seabreeze Inne (☎ 250-537-4145, 800-434-4112; www .seabreezeinne.com; 101 Bittancourt Rd; r $119-199; 🛜) A short uphill walk from Ganges, this immaculate, family-run motel is a cut above the average – think continental breakfast, barbecues and an outdoor hot tub.

Wisteria Guest House (☎ 250-537-5899, 888-537-5899; www.wisteriaguesthouse.com; 268 Park Dr; r/cottage from $120/180) A 10-minute stroll from the Ganges hubbub, this comfortable, home-style B&B serves truly gourmet breakfasts.

GALIANO ISLAND

The busy ferry end of Galiano is markedly different to the rest of the island, which becomes increasingly forested and tranquil as you continue your drive from the dock.

Supporting the widest ecological diversity of any of the Southern Gulf Islands – and regarded by some as the most beautiful isle in the region – this skinny landmass offers a bounty of activities for visiting marine enthusiasts and landlubbers alike. The main clutch of businesses and services is around the ferry dock at Sturdies Bay and includes a garage, post office, bookstore and Visitor Info Booth (☎ 250-539-2507; www.galianoisland.com; 2590 Sturdies Bay Rd; ☒ Jul & Aug). Check the island's official visitor website for Galiano maps and listings.

Once you've got your bearings – ie driven off the ferry – head for Montague Harbour Marine Provincial Park for trails to beaches, meadows and a cliff carved by glaciers. In contrast, Bodega Ridge Provincial Park is renowned for its eagle, loon and cormorant bird life and has some spectacular drop-off viewpoints.

The protected waters of Trincomali Channel and the more chaotic waters of Active Pass satisfy paddlers of all skill levels. Gulf Island Kayaking (☎ 250-539-2442; www.seakayak.ca; Montague Harbour Marina; 3hr/day rental from $38/75, tours from $55; ☒ 10am-5pm, reduced off-season) can help with rentals and guided tours.

If you're without a car or you just want to stretch your legs, you can explore the island with a bike from Galiano Bicycle (☎ 250-539-9906; www.galianoisland.com/galianobicycle; 36 Burrill Rd; rental per 4hr/day $25/30; ☒ 10am-5pm, reduced off-season).

Eating & Sleeping

Daystar Market Café (96 Georgeson Bay Rd; mains $4-10; ☒ 10am-5pm Mon-Fri, 9am-6pm Sat, 9am-5pm Sun) A 3km drive from the Sturdies Bay ferry dock, this funky locals' hangout serves hearty salads, thick sandwiches and fruit smoothies.

Hummingbird Pub (www.hummingbirdpub.com; 47 Sturdies Bay Rd; mains $8-12; ☒ 11am-midnight Sun-Thu, 11am-1am Fri & Sat) Sup ale with the locals on the patio here or try the bar-grub menu for sustenance. It's 2km from Sturdies Bay.

Bodega Ridge (☎ 250-539-2677, 877-604-2677; www.bodegaridge.com; 120 Manastee Rd; d $200; ☜) A peaceful retreat of seven north island cabins, each with three bedrooms and furnished in a rustic country fashion.

Galiano Inn (☎ 250-539-3388, 877-530-3939; www.galianoinn.com; 134 Madrona Dr; r $249-299; ☜) This immaculate Tuscan-style villa has 10 elegant rooms, each with a fireplace and romantic oceanfront terrace. Adult, sophisticated and soothing, it's close to the Sturdies Bay ferry dock.

TRANSPORTATION

Vancouver is easily accessible from major international destinations, via air or sea, and is also a short drive or train hop from the US border. Cross-Canada rail, bus and flight operations also service the city, which is the main gateway for accessing destinations throughout British Columbia. Within the city, the transit system – bus, light rail and commuter vessels – is extensive, although the downtown core and its environs are highly foot-friendly. Flights, tours and rail tickets can be booked online at www .lonelyplanet.com/travel_services.

AIR

Most visitors fly into the area via Vancouver International Airport. While airline websites frequently offer seat sales, additional sites worth trying include Expedia (www.expedia.com), Kayak (www.kayak.com), Orbitz (www.orbitz.com) and Travelocity (www.travelocity.com). Keep in mind that Seattle's Sea-Tac airport is just across the border – about three hours drive away – and can offer additional savings on international flights to the Pacific Northwest.

Airlines

International, domestic and BC-region airlines serving Vancouver International Airport include the following:

Air Canada & Air Canada Jazz (code AC; ☎ 514-393-3333, 888-247-2262; www.aircanada.com)

Air New Zealand (code NZ; ☎ 800-663-5494; www .airnewzealand.com)

Air North (code 4N; ☎ 800-661-0407; www.flyairnorth .com)

THINGS CHANGE...

The information in this chapter is particularly vulnerable to change. Check directly with the airline or a travel agent to make sure you understand how a fare (and ticket you may buy) works and be aware of the security requirements for international travel. Shop carefully. The details given in this chapter should be regarded as pointers and are not a substitute for your own careful, up-to-date research.

Air Transat (code TS; ☎ 866-847-1112; www.airtransat .com)

Alaska Airlines (code AS; ☎ 800-252-7522; www .alaskaair.com)

American Airlines (code AA; ☎ 800-433-7300; www .aa.com)

British Airways (code BA; ☎ 800-247-9297; www .britishairways.com)

Cathay Pacific (code CX; ☎ 800-268-6868; www .cathaypacific.com)

China Airlines (code CI; ☎ 604-682-6777; www.china -airlines.com)

Continental Airlines (code CO; ☎ 800-523-3273; www .continental.com)

Delta Air Lines (code DL; ☎ 800-221-1212; www.delta .com)

Horizon Air (code QX; ☎ 800-547-9308; www.horizonair .com)

Lufthansa (code LH; ☎ 800-563-5954; www.lufthansa .com)

Pacific Coastal Airlines Ltd (code 8P; ☎ 800-663-2872; www.pacific-coastal.com)

FLOATPLANES & 'COPTERS

Handy floatplane services swoop directly into the Vancouver waterfront area from Vancouver Island and points around BC. These include frequent Harbour Air Seaplanes (www.harbour-air.com) and West Coast Air (www.westcoastair .com) services from Victoria's Inner Harbour ($145, 35 minutes). Merging operations in mid-2010, these airlines form the largest all-floatplane company in the world and will likely increasingly combine their routes and services. Both also fly in and out of Vancouver International Airport (South Terminal).

For a different type of ride, Helijet (www.helijet.com) helicopter services arrive on the waterfront, just east of Canada Place, from Victoria (from $139, 35 minutes). It also offers a limited service from Vancouver International Airport (South Terminal).

See p226 for more information on the location of helicopter and floatplane terminals.

CLIMATE CHANGE & TRAVEL

Climate change is a serious threat to the ecosystems that humans rely upon, and air travel is the fastest-growing contributor to the problem. Lonely Planet regards travel, overall, as a global benefit, but believes we all have a responsibility to limit our personal impact on global warming.

Flying & Climate Change

Pretty much every form of motor transport generates carbon dioxide (the main cause of human-induced climate change) but planes are far and away the worst offenders, not just because of the sheer distances they allow us to travel, but because they release greenhouse gases high into the atmosphere. The statistics are frightening: two people taking a return flight between Europe and the US will contribute as much to climate change as an average household's gas and electricity consumption over a whole year.

Carbon Offset Schemes

Climatecare.org and other websites use 'carbon calculators' that allow travellers to offset the greenhouse gases they are responsible for with contributions to energy-saving projects and other climate-friendly initiatives in the developing world – including projects in India, Honduras, Kazakhstan and Uganda.

Lonely Planet, together with Rough Guides and other concerned partners in the travel industry, supports the carbon offset scheme run by climatecare.org. Lonely Planet offsets all of its staff and author travel.

For more information, check out our website: www.lonelyplanet.com.

Qantas Airways (code QF; ☎ 800-227-4566; www.qantas.com)

United Airlines (code UA; ☎ 800-241-6522; www.united.ca)

WestJet (code WS; ☎ 888-937-8538; www.westjet.com)

Airports

Canada's second-busiest airport, Vancouver International Airport (YVR; Map pp54-5; www.yvr.ca) is about 13km south of the city on Sea Island in Richmond. There are two main terminals – international (including flights to the US) and domestic. An additional South Terminal is for floatplanes and smaller aircraft, and it's linked to the main airport via a free shuttle bus.

Each of the main terminals has food courts, shops, a spa, baggage storage facilities, ATMs, currency exchange booths and tourist information desks. Once you're past security, the international terminal has a fancy new shopping and dining plaza with its own stream, aquarium and First Nations artworks. In addition, the domestic terminal has a medical clinic, a dental clinic and a pharmacy. Baggage carts are free (no deposit required) throughout the airport.

In downtown Vancouver there is a floatplane terminal (Map pp68-9) in Coal Harbour just west of Canada Place, and a helicopter terminal (Map pp58-9) on the east side of Canada Place near Waterfront Station.

BICYCLE

Vancouver is a relatively good cycling city, with more than 300km of designated routes crisscrossing the region. Cyclists can take their bikes for free on SkyTrain and SeaBus services, as well as on bike-rack-fitted buses and some miniferries. Cyclists are required by law to wear helmets here.

Pick up a *Metro Vancouver Cycling Map* ($3.95) from a convenience store or bookshop for details on area routes and bike-friendly contacts. You can also view and download the map for free on the TransLink (www.translink.bc.ca) website. Further bike maps and resources are available via the City of Vancouver (www.vancouver.ca/cycling) website, while the University of British Columbia (UBC) offers a handy cycling route planner at www.cyclevancouver.ubc.ca. For more tips and resources, check in with the Vancouver Area Cycling Coalition (www.vacc.bc.ca) and consider timing your visit for June's annual Velopalooza (www.velopalooza.ca), a multiday, family-friendly bikey love-in of tours, gatherings and pedaling shenanigans.

If you're traveling sans bike, you can rent from businesses around the city (see p182).

BOAT

Vessels large and small sail Vancouver's waterways. Cruise ships, big business here from May to September, dock at downtown's Canada Place (Map pp58-9) or at Ballantyne Pier (Map pp54-5) just to the east.

Ferries

BC Ferries (www.bcferries.com) services arrive at Tsawwassen, an hour south of Vancouver, as well as at Horseshoe Bay, 30 minutes from downtown in West Vancouver. The company operates one of the world's largest ferry networks, including some spectacular routes throughout the province. Visit its waterfront Vancouver store (Map pp58-9; 1010 Canada Place) for information, packages and tickets. In 2010, the company also began introducing free wi-fi on some of its vessels.

Main services to Tsawwassen arrive from Vancouver Island's Swartz Bay, near Victoria (adult/child/vehicle $14/7/46.75, 90 minutes), and Duke Point, near Nanaimo (adult/child/vehicle $14/7/46.75, two hours). Services also arrive from the Southern Gulf Islands (see p223).

Services to Horseshoe Bay arrive from Nanaimo's Departure Bay (adult/child/vehicle $14/7/46.75, 90 minutes). Services also arrive here from Bowen Island (adult/child/vehicle $9.75/4.90/27.90, 20 minutes) and from Langdale (adult/child/vehicle $12.85/6.45/43.20, 40 minutes), the only ferry route to and from the Sunshine Coast.

You can buy passenger-only tickets at the ferry terminals (no reservations required). You can also make vehicle reservations for a $17.50 fee – definitely recommended if you're traveling on weekends or anytime in July or August.

To reach Tsawwassen by transit bus (adult/child $5/3.50, 1¼ hours), take the Canada Line to Richmond-Brighouse and transfer to bus 620.

To reach Horseshoe Bay (adult/child $3.75/2.50, 45 minutes), take bus 257 or 250 from W Georgia St near Granville St in downtown Vancouver.

A pricier but more convenient bus option is the Pacific Coach Lines service (p228), which runs between Victoria and Vancouver via the ferry. You can also buy a ticket for this service once you're on board the ferry for onward bus travel into either city.

Miniferries

Running frequent minivessels (some big enough to carry bikes) between the foot of Hornby St and Granville Island, Aquabus Ferries (www.theaquabus.com; adult/child from $3/1.50) services several spots along the False Creek waterfront as far as Science World. Its rival is False Creek Ferries (www.granvilleislandferries.bc.ca; adult/child from $3/1.50), which operates a similar Granville Island service from the Vancouver Aquatic Centre at Sunset Beach, plus additional ports of call around False Creek. Both operators offer day passes at the same prices (adult/child $14/8) as well as discounted books of tickets for those making multiple runs.

See p230 for information on TransLink's picturesque SeaBus service from Waterfront Station to Lonsdale Quay.

BUS

Most out-of-town buses trundle to a halt at Vancouver's heritage, neon-signed Pacific Central Station (Map p79; 1150 Station St, Chinatown). The station has a ticket office and left-luggage lockers, and is also the city's trans-Canada and

GETTING INTO TOWN

SkyTrain's 16-station Canada Line (www.translink.bc.ca; adult one-way fare to downtown $7.50-8.75) operates a rapid-transit train service from the airport to downtown. Trains run every 8 to 20 minutes and take around 25 minutes to reach downtown's Waterfront Station. The airport train terminus is located just outside, between the domestic and international terminals. Follow the signs and buy your ticket from the platform vending machines. They accept cash, credit and debit cards – look for green-jacketed Canada Line staff if you need assistance after your bleary-eyed long-haul flight.

If you prefer to cab it, budget $30 to $40 for the 30-minute taxi ride from the airport to your downtown hotel. For $10 to $20 more, consider arriving in style in a limo from Aerocar Service (www.aerocar.ca).

Alternatively, all the usual hire-car companies have desks at the airport. Once you're strapped in – seat belts are compulsory here – proceed east after leaving the airport on Grant McConachie Way, and follow the Vancouver signs over the Arthur Laing Bridge. Take the Granville St exit and travel north along Granville St toward the mountains, continuing over the bridge into downtown.

If you're in transit or want to stay at a hotel close to (or in) the airport, check the options in the boxed text on p204. Many airport-area hotels provide free shuttle buses.

cross-border train terminal (see opposite). The Main St-Science World SkyTrain station is just across the street for connections to downtown and the suburbs.

Vancouver-bound bus and coach operators include the following:

Greyhound (www.greyhound.ca) Services arrive from Whistler (from $25, 2¾ hours, seven daily), Kelowna (from $48, six hours, seven daily) and Calgary (from $79, 14 to 17 hours, four daily), among others.

Malaspina Coach Lines (www.malaspinacoach.com) Serving the Sunshine Coast, twice-daily buses arrive from Gibsons ($19, two hours), Sechelt ($29, three hours) and Powell River ($58, five to six hours).

Pacific Coach Lines (www.pacificcoach.com) Traveling via the BC Ferries Swartz Bay–Tsawwassen route, frequent services arrive from downtown Victoria ($28.75 to $42, 3½ hours). The company also operates its SkyLynx service between Whistler, Vancouver and Vancouver International Airport (from $35, from 3½ hours, six daily).

Quick Coach Lines (www.quickcoach.com; 📶) Express shuttle between Seattle and Vancouver, departing from downtown Seattle (US$40.85, four hours, seven daily) and the city's Sea-Tac International Airport (US$54.15, 3½ hours, seven daily).

Snowbus (www.snowbus.com) Popular winter-only ski-bus service to and from Whistler (adult/child $30.95/19.05, three hours, two daily).

See p230 for information on city transit buses.

CAR & MOTORCYCLE

For sightseeing around town, you'll be fine without a car. However, for visits that incorporate the wider region's mountains and suburbs, a car makes life much simpler.

Driving

With a few exceptions, you can legally drive in Canada for up to six months with a valid driver's license issued by your home country. You may be required to show an international driving permit if your license isn't written in English (or French). If you've rented a car in the US and you are driving it into Canada, bring a copy of the rental agreement to save any possible hassle by border officials. Seat belts are mandatory here and there is also a recently introduced ban on using handheld electronic devices while driving.

Vancouver doesn't have any expressways going through its core, which can lead to some major congestion issues. Evening rush-hour traffic can be a nightmare, with enormous lines of cars snaking along W Georgia St waiting to cross the Lions Gate Bridge. Try the Second Narrows Ironworkers Memorial Bridge (known simply as the Second Narrows Bridge to most locals) if you need to get across to the North Shore in a hurry. Other peak-time hot spots to avoid are the George Massey Tunnel and Hwy 1 to Surrey.

For handy driving routes in and around the region, visit www.hellobc.com/drive.

Parking

Parking is at a premium downtown: there are some free spots on residential side streets but many require permits and traffic wardens are predictably predatory. Many downtown streets also have metered parking (from $1 to $5 per hour). Pay-parking lots (typically from $4 per hour in downtown locations) are a better proposition – arrive before 9am at some for early bird, day-rate discounts. For an interactive

---

BRIDGING THE FIRST NARROWS GAP

Among the many spans built over Metro Vancouver's waterways, it's the Lions Gate Bridge that stands out as a Vancouver icon. And not just because it seems to be on every other postcard you see here.

The Guinness family led the charge to build it, keen to give locals a way to access its swanky new British Properties housing estate in West Vancouver. However, it took several years for the bridge to be approved, as the accompanying plan to build a 2.4km causeway through the center of Stanley Park was a contentious issue. Construction finally began in 1936, and the project was completed in 1938 at a cost of $6 million.

As the years passed, the bridge struggled to keep up with the demands of increased traffic loads. Consequently, in the early 1990s, the provincial government examined a variety of plans to resolve the issue: build a tunnel under the inlet, build a new, larger bridge or widen the current bridge's span.

Choosing the least expensive option, the government began a $99.8 million rehabilitation project of the existing structure in 1999. Improvements included seismic upgrading and widened traffic lanes. Many residents complain it's still not enough, and when you spot the giant tailback waiting to cross during rush hour, you'll likely agree with them.

map of parking-lot locations, check EasyPark (www.easypark.ca).

Rental

Major car-rental agencies with reservation desks at Vancouver International Airport, as well as multiple offices around the city, include the following:

Avis (☎ 604-606-2847, 800-230-2498; www.avis.ca)

Budget (☎ 604-668-7000, 800-268-8900; www.budget bc.com)

Enterprise (☎ 604-688-5500, 800-261-7331; www.enterprisecar.ca)

Hertz (☎ 604-606-4711, 800-263-0600; www.hertz.ca)

Thrifty (☎ 604-606-1655, 800-847-4389; www.thrifty.com)

TAXI

Vancouver taxi meters start at $3.05 and add $1.73 per kilometer. Flagging a downtown cab – almost all of which are hybrid-vehicle cars – on main streets shouldn't take too long, but it's easiest to get your hotel to call you one. If you're wandering the streets and can't find a taxi to flag down, head to one of the area's big hotels, where they tend to congregate. A 15% tip is the norm.

Reliable operators around the city include the following:

Black Top & Checker Cabs (☎ 604-731-1111)

Vancouver Taxi (☎ 604-871-1111)

Yellow Cab (☎ 604-681-1111)

TRAIN

Trains arrive from across Canada and the US at Pacific Central Station (Map p79; ☎ 604-661-0325; 1150 Station St, Chinatown). The station has a ticket office and left-luggage lockers and is also the area's main bus terminal (see p227) for out-of-town services. The Main St-Science World SkyTrain station is just across the street for connections to downtown and the suburbs.

Operators and services include the following:

Amtrak (www.amtrak.com) US Cascades services arrive from Eugene (from US$67, up to 13½ hours), Portland (from US$50, eight hours) and Seattle (from US$35, three to four hours). Buses are substituted on some of the services – check Amtrak's website for details. From Seattle, you can connect to the Coast Starlight train to Los Angeles.

Via Rail (www.viarail.ca) Trains on the Canadian service arrive from Kamloops North ($86, 10 hours, three weekly), Jasper ($179, 20 hours, three weekly) and Edmonton ($241, 27 hours, three weekly), among others.

Other city train services:

Rocky Mountaineer (Map pp54–5 www.rockymountaineer .com) From once-in-a-lifetime luxury trundles – they're like cruises on the rails – through BC's spectacular outback, to leisurely three-hour ambles along the coastline via the Whistler Sea to Sky Climb (from $129, three hours), this company offers some of the best ways to sit back and encounter the region's spectacular vistas.

West Coast Express (www.westcoastexpress.com) Commuter service arriving five times daily Monday to Friday at downtown's Waterfront Station from Mission City ($11.25, 70 minutes), Pitt Meadows ($8.25, 45 minutes), Port Coquitlam ($6.75, 35 minutes) and Port Moody ($6.75, 25 minutes), among others.

See p230 for information on Vancouver's SkyTrain system.

TRANSLINK

TransLink (www.translink.bc.ca) oversees public bus, SkyTrain light rail and SeaBus commuter boat services. Its website has a useful trip-planning tool or you can buy the handy *Getting Around* route map ($1.95) from many convenience stores.

A ticket bought on any of these services is valid for up to 90 minutes of travel on the entire network, depending on the

TRUNDLING INTO THE PAST

Rattling along the old rails from a stop next to the Canada Line's Olympic Village station to its terminus near Granville Island, the Downtown Historic Railway (www.trams.bc.ca; adult/child & senior one-way $2/1; ☉ noon-6pm Sat, Sun & holidays, Jun–mid-Oct; ♿) uses antique heritage streetcars from decades past to take passengers on a fun 10-minute jaunt. Staffed by twinkle-eyed volunteers, it's the kind of trip your kids will love and it's also a great way to get from downtown to Granville Island: take the Canada Line to Olympic Village station, then nip around the corner and hop on the shiny streetcar. It's a two-minute walk from the Granville Island station to the island itself. The society that runs the service hopes to ultimately extend it around False Creek, across the downtown core and toward Stanley Park.

number of zones you intend to travel in. One-zone tickets are $2.50/1.75 (adult/child), two-zone tickets are $3.75/2.50 and three-zone tickets are $5/3.50. An all-day, all-zone DayPass costs $9/7. If you're traveling after 6:30pm or on weekends or holidays, all trips are classed as one-zone fares and cost $2.50/1.75. Books of 10 FareSaver tickets for one/two/three zones cost $21/31.50/42 for adults and $17 for children (all zones). They are sold at convenience stores and drugstores throughout the city. Children under five years travel for free on all transit services.

Bus

The bus network is extensive in central areas and many vehicles have bike racks. All are wheelchair accessible. Exact change (or more) is required since all buses use fare machines and change is not given.

The 99B-Line express buses operate between the Commercial-Broadway SkyTrain station and UBC. These buses have their own limited arrival and departure points and do not use the regular bus stops.

There is a handy night-bus system that runs every 30 minutes between 1:30am and 4am across the Lower Mainland. The last bus leaves downtown Vancouver at 3:10am. Look for the night-bus signs at designated stops.

SeaBus

This iconic aquatic shuttle service operates every 15 to 30 minutes throughout the day, taking 12 minutes to cross Burrard Inlet between Waterfront Station and Lonsdale Quay. At Lonsdale there's a bus terminal servicing routes throughout North Vancouver and West Vancouver – this is where transit buses to Capilano Suspension Bridge and Grouse Mountain depart. SeaBus services leave from Waterfront Station between 6:16am and 1:22am Monday to Saturday (8:16am to 11:16pm Sunday). Vessels are wheelchair accessible and bike-friendly. Tickets must be purchased from vending machines on either side of the route before boarding.

SkyTrain

The SkyTrain rapid-transit network consists of three routes and is a great way to move around the region: consider taking a spin on it, even if you don't have anywhere to go.

The original 35-minute Expo Line takes passengers to and from downtown Vancouver and Surrey, via stops throughout Burnaby and New Westminster. The Millennium Line alights near shopping malls and suburban residential districts in Coquitlam and Burnaby. Opened in late 2009, the new Canada Line links the city to the airport and Richmond.

Expo Line trains run every two to eight minutes with services departing Waterfront Station between 5:35am and 1:15am Monday to Friday (6:50am to 1:15am Saturday; 7:15am to 12:15am Sunday). Millennium Line trains run every five to eight minutes with services departing Waterfront Station between 5:54am and 12:31am Monday to Friday (6:54am to 12:31am Saturday; 7:54am to 11:31pm Sunday).

Canada Line trains run every eight to 20 minutes throughout the day. Services run from the airport to downtown between 5:10am and 12:57am and from Waterfront Station to the airport between 4:50am and 1:05am. If you're heading for the airport from the city, make sure you board a YVR-bound train – some are heading to Richmond but not the airport.

Tickets for all services must be purchased from station vending machines (change is given for bills up to $20 but most machines also accept debit and credit cards) prior to boarding. Checks by fare inspectors are frequent and they can issue on-the-spot fines if you don't have the correct ticket. Avoid buying transfers from the 'scalpers' at some stations, since they're usually expired or close to expiration (the transfers, not the scalpers).

While SkyTrain ticket prices mirror the zones used across the TransLink network, there is one notable exception. Passengers departing on Canada Line trains from the airport are charged an extra $5 AddFare when purchasing their ticket from station vending machines. You do not have to pay this extra charge when traveling back to the airport from downtown.

DIRECTORY

BUSINESS HOURS

Standard business hours are 9am to 5pm weekdays. Some postal outlets may stay open later and on weekends. Most banks adhere to standard hours but some branches keep shorter hours and others also open on Saturday mornings. Typical retail shopping hours are 10am to 6pm Monday to Saturday, and noon to 5pm on Sunday (although some shops are closed on Sunday). Shopping malls often stay open later than regular stores. Supermarkets often stay open until 9pm or beyond. Restaurants are usually open for lunch on weekdays from 11:30am until 2:30pm and serve dinner from 5pm until 9pm or 10pm daily, later on weekends. A few serve breakfast, and many serve weekend brunch. If they take a day off, it's usually Monday.

Pubs and bars that also serve lunch open before midday, with some bars waiting it out until 5pm before opening their doors. Clubs may open in the evening around 9pm, but most don't get busy before 11pm. Bars and clubs, especially those downtown, can serve liquor until 3am. Twenty-four-hour supermarkets, pharmacies and convenience stores are dotted around the city, particularly in the West End.

Tourist attractions often keep longer hours in summer and reduced hours during winter.

CHILDREN

Family-friendly Vancouver is stuffed with things to do with vacationing kids. Pick up a copy of the free *Kids' Guide Vancouver* flyer from racks around town and visit www .kidsvancouver.com for tips, resources and family-focused events. See the boxed text on p106 for a list of top children's attractions and activities. If you still haven't wowed them, consider a five-day Knight Camp course (p232) where they'll learn all about the art of chivalry and swordplay. All kid-friendly businesses and operators are marked with the 👶 symbol throughout this book for easy reference.

Children can usually stay with their parents at motels and hotels for no extra charge. Some B&Bs may refuse to accept pint-sized patrons, often preferring to remain adult-oriented –

while others charge full price for tots. Some hostels have family rooms.

Car-hire companies rent car seats, which are legally required for young children, for a few dollars per day, but you'll need to reserve them in advance. If you're traveling around the city without a car, make sure you hop on the SkyTrain or SeaBus transit services or the miniferry to Granville Island: kids love 'em, especially the new SkyTrain cars, where they can sit up front and pretend they're driving. Children under five years travel free on all transit.

Childcare equipment – including strollers, booster seats, cribs, baby monitors and toys – can be rented from the friendly folk at Wee Travel (☎ 604-222-4722; www.weetravel.ca). Your hotel can usually recommend a licensed and bonded babysitting service.

Make sure children coming to Canada from other countries (including the USA) have a passport or birth certificate with them. Divorced parents with a child should also carry a copy of their custody agreement. Children traveling with a nonparent should have a letter of permission from the parent or legal guardian.

For more on holidaying with children, check out Lonely Planet's *Travel with Children*, by Brigitte Barta et al.

CLIMATE

Vancouver's climate is one of the mildest in Canada, averaging 20°C in summer and 2°C in winter. But you don't hear much about that accolade. Instead you hear about the rain. Yes, bucketloads of it fall, especially in winter (January, February and March). In the mountains, a mere 20 minutes away,

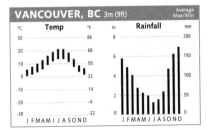

this translates into snow for excellent skiing. July through September are the best bets for sunshine. Check www.weatheroffice .pyr.ec.gc.ca for online forecasts and see p12 for general information on the best times to visit.

COURSES
Arts & Crafts
Vancouver's community centers offer inexpensive classes in everything from life drawing to flower arranging to knitting:

Coal Harbour Community Centre (Map pp68-9; ☎ 604-718-8222; www.coalharbourcc.ca; 480 Broughton St, West End; 🚌 19)

Roundhouse Community Arts & Recreation Centre (Map p72; ☎ 604-713-1800; www.roundhouse.ca; 181 Roundhouse Mews, cnr Davie St & Pacific Blvd, Yaletown; Ⓜ Yaletown-Roundhouse)

West End Community Centre (Map pp68-9; ☎ 604-257-8333; www.westendcc.ca; 870 Denman St, West End; 🚌 5)

Cooking
The city's top chefs and foodie types often teach short classes at the following places:

Barbara-Jo's Books to Cooks (Map pp96-7; ☎ 604-688-6755; www.bookstocooks.com; 1740 W 2nd Ave, Kitsilano; 🚌 4)

Dirty Apron Cooking School (Map pp58-9; ☎ 604-879-8588; www.dirtyapron.com; 540 Beatty St, downtown; Ⓜ Stadium-Chinatown)

Dance
Skip the light fantastic on a fun dance course at these local favorites:

Broadway Ballroom (Map p93; ☎ 604-733-1779; www.broadwayballroom.ca; 1050 W Broadway, Fairview; 🚌 9) Hit the dance floor in style and take a course in waltz, tango, cha-cha and more.

Salsa Vancouver (www.salsavancouver.net) Energetic workshops in Cuban, mambo, tango etc at locations around the city.

Language
ESL schools are rampant, and are especially popular with students from Asia. For other languages, try the following:

Berlitz (Map pp58-9; ☎ 604-685-9331; www.berlitz .ca; 808 W Hastings St, downtown; Ⓜ Waterfront)

Le Centre Culturel Francophone de Vancouver (Map p93; ☎ 604-736-9806; www.lecentreculturel.com; 1551 W 7th Ave, South Granville; 🚌 9)

Outdoors
Canada West Mountain School (Map p83; ☎ 604-878-7007, 888-892-2266; www.themountainschool.com; 47 W Broadway, SoMa; 🚌 9) is a long-established and well-respected institution, offering training and guided-excursion courses in Vancouver's spectacular outdoor backyard. Programs include climbing, mountaineering and winter camping.

Swordplay
Academie Duello Centre for Swordplay (Map pp58-9; ☎ 604-568-9907; www.academieduello.com; 412 W Hastings St, downtown; 🚌 9) is the spot to indulge your inner knight in ye olde Vancouvere. This popular downtown school offers thrilling classes and workshops for kids and adults that show you how to wield everything from rapiers to broadswords. There's also a small on-site museum (entry by donation) covering the history of weapons, armor and heraldry.

CUSTOMS REGULATIONS
Adults aged 19 and older can bring in 1.14L of liquor or wine, 24 cans or bottles of beer, 200 cigarettes, 50 cigars and 200g of tobacco. You can also bring in gifts valued up to $60 plus a 'reasonable amount' of personal effects, including cars, computers and outdoor equipment. Dispose of any perishable items, such as fruit, vegetables or plants, before crossing the border. Mace, pepper spray and many firearms are also prohibited. For the latest regulations, contact the Canada Border Services Agency (☎ 204-983-3500, 800-461-9999; www .cbsa.gc.ca).

DISCOUNT CARDS
Aside from the city's free attractions (see the boxed text, p60), there are other ways to stretch your visitor dollars here. If you're planning to take in lots of sights in a few days, the See Vancouver Card (☎ 877-295-1157; www .seevancouvercard.com; 2/3/5 days adult $125/155/229, child $85/105/155) can be a good idea. It covers entry to dozens of regional attractions and activities and is especially good value if you include big-ticket items like harbor cruises, whale watching and the Capilano Suspension Bridge.

You can save on entry to a triumvirate of Kitsilano (p96) attractions with a combined Vanier Park Explore Pass (adult/youth $30/24) that covers the Museum of Vancouver, Vancouver Maritime Museum and HR MacMillan Space Centre. The pass, which includes one entry to each attraction and has no time restrictions, is available at any of the three attractions and saves you up to $8 on separate admissions. The University of British Columbia (UBC) also recently introduced a combined-entry discount passport (see the boxed text, p101) for some of its campus-based attractions.

It's also a good idea to drop by the city's tourist information centre (p239) for a free Visitor Guide – it has pages of coupons in the back. And don't forget Green Zebra (www .greenzebraguide.ca), a coupon book covering the region's eco-supporting stores, eateries and activities.

ELECTRICITY

Canada, like the USA, operates on 110V, 60Hz AC. Gadgets built for higher voltage and cycles (such as 220/240V, 50-cycle appliances from Europe) will function poorly. North American electrical goods have plugs with two (flat) or three (two flat, one round) pins. Overseas visitors should bring an adapter, or buy one, if they wish to use their own razors, hair dryers or other appliances. Visit www .kropla.com for useful info on electricity and adapters around the world.

EMBASSIES & CONSULATES

Most countries maintain embassies in Ottawa in the province of Ontario. Vancouver consulates are generally open only on weekday mornings, although a few are also open after lunch until 4pm.

Australia (Map pp58-9; ☎ 604-684-1177; Suite 2050, 1075 W Georgia St, downtown; M Burrard)

China (Map p93; ☎ 604-734-0704; www.vancouver .china-consulate.org; 3380 Granville St, South Granville; 🚍 10)

France (Map pp68-9; ☎ 604-637-5300; www .consulfrance-vancouver.org; Suite 1100, 1130 W Pender St, West End; M Burrard)

Germany (Map pp58-9; ☎ 604-684-8377; www .vancouver.diplo.de; Suite 704, 999 Canada Pl, downtown; M Waterfront)

India (Map pp58-9; ☎ 604-662-8811; www .cgivancouver.org; Suite 201, 325 Howe St, downtown; M Waterfront)

Ireland (Map p72; ☎ 604-683-9233; Suite 210, 837 Beatty St, Yaletown; M Stadium-Chinatown)

Italy (Map pp58-9; ☎ 604-684-7288; www .consvancouver.esteri.it; Suite 1100, 510 W Hastings St, downtown; M Waterfront)

Japan (Map pp68-9; ☎ 604-684-5868; www .vancouver.ca.emb-japan.go.jp; Suite 800, 1177 W Hastings St, West End; M Burrard)

Korea (Map pp68-9; ☎ 604-681-9581; Suite 1600, 1090 W Georgia St, West End; M Burrard)

Mexico (Map pp68-9; ☎ 604-684-3547; www .consulmexvan.com; Suite 411, 1177 W Hastings St, West End; M Burrard)

Netherlands (Map pp58-9; ☎ 877-388-2443; www .cgvancouver.org; Suite 883, 595 Burrard St, downtown; M Burrard)

New Zealand (Map pp58-9; ☎ 604-684-7388; Suite 1200, 888 Dunsmuir St, downtown; M Burrard)

UK (Map pp68-9; ☎ 604-683-4421; Suite 800, 1111 Melville St, West End; M Burrard)

USA (Map pp68-9; ☎ 604-685-4311; www.vancouver .usaconsulate.gov; 1095 W Pender St, West End; M Burrard)

EMERGENCY

See p234 for hospital emergency rooms and clinics.

Crisis Centre (☎ 604-872-3311, 800-784-2433; www .crisiscentre.bc.ca; 🕒 24hr) Provides counselors who can help with all types of emotional crises.

Poison Control Centre (☎ 604-682-5050, 800-567-8911)

Police, fire and ambulance (☎ 911)

Police – nonemergency (☎ 604-717-3321)

Rape Crisis Centre (☎ 877-392-7583; www.wavaw.ca; 🕒 24hr)

GAY & LESBIAN TRAVELERS

Vancouver's gay and lesbian scene is part of the city's culture rather than a subsection of it. The legalization of same-sex marriages in British Columbia (BC) has resulted in a huge number of couples using Vancouver as a kind of gay Vegas for their destination nuptials. For more information on tying the knot, visit www.vs.gov.bc.ca/marriage/howto.html.

Vancouver's West End district (p66), complete with its fluttering rainbow flags, pink bus shelters and hand-holding locals, houses western Canada's largest 'gayborhood,' while the city's lesbian contingent is centered more on Commercial Dr (p85).

Pick up a free copy of *Xtra!* for a crash course on the local scene, and check www .gayvancouver.net, www.gayvan.com and www.superdyke.com for pertinent listings and resources. For nightlife options see the boxed text on p163. Don't miss the giant annual Pride Week (p15) in August, which includes the city's biggest street parade.

For support and resources of all kinds, Qmunity (Map pp68-9; ☎ 604-684-5307; www.qmunity .ca; 1170 Bute St, West End; 🖳 6) provides discussion groups, a health clinic and advice for lesbians, gays, bisexuals and the transgendered. These friendly folk also staff the Prideline (☎ 604-684-6869, 800-566-1170; ☻ 7-10pm Mon-Fri), a peer-support service.

Check the online directory of the Gay & Lesbian Business Association of BC (☎ 604-739-4522; www .glba.org) or pick up its glossy free brochure for listings on all manner of local businesses, from dentists to spas and hotels. You can also drop in and tap the local community at the popular Little Sister's Book & Art Emporium (p114).

HOLIDAYS

During national public holidays, all banks, schools and government offices (including post offices) are closed, and transportation, museums and other services are often on a Sunday schedule. Holidays falling on weekends are usually observed the following Monday.

Public Holidays

Major public holidays in Vancouver:

New Year's Day January 1

Good Friday & Easter Monday Late March to mid-April

Victoria Day Third Monday in May

Canada Day July 1

BC Day First Monday in August

Labour Day First Monday in September

Thanksgiving Second Monday in October

Remembrance Day November 11

Christmas Day December 25

Boxing Day December 26

INTERNET ACCESS

Vancouver hotels often provide in-room wi-fi or high-speed cable internet services for guests, although not all include it for free:

check when you book. If you're toting your hardware around town and it's time to update your travel blog, drop into one of the many branches of Blenz (www.blenz.com), Take 5 (www .take5cafe.com) or Waves (www.wavescoffee.ca) coffee shops, where wi-fi is free. Some other free hot spots across the region are listed at www .wififreespot.com/can.html. If you don't have your computer with you, check your email for free at one of the many computers in the Apple Store located in downtown's Pacific Centre mall (p113).

You can also hit the computers and get online at these locations:

Internet Coffee (Map pp68-9; ☎ 604-682-6668; 1104 Davie St, West End; ☻ 9am-1:30am; per hr $3.25; 🖳 6) Busy little storefront with 20 computers, as well as fax, CD burning and printing services.

Vancouver Public Library (Map pp58-9; ☎ 604-331-3603; 350 W Georgia St, downtown; ☻ 10am-9pm Mon-Thu, 10am-6pm Fri & Sat, noon-5pm Sun; Ⓜ Stadium-Chinatown) Free internet access on library computers as well as free wi-fi access with a wi-fi guest card from the information desk.

In this book, the 🖳 icon is used for those places with internet-access computers. In addition, the 📶 icon is used for any establishment offering wi-fi access.

MAPS

The Tourism Vancouver Visitor Centre (p239) provides a handy free map of the city's gridlike downtown core. The more comprehensive *Greater Vancouver Streetwise Map Book* ($5.95) has an easy A-Z format and is available at local bookshops and convenience stores. For online maps of the region, check out the City of Vancouver's free VanMap (www.vancouver.ca/vanmap) system.

MEDICAL SERVICES

There are no reciprocal healthcare arrangements between Canada and other countries. Non-Canadians usually pay cash up front for treatment, so taking out travel insurance with a medical-cover component is strongly advised. Medical treatment in Canada is expensive: hospital beds can cost up to $2500 a day for nonresidents.

Clinics

The following walk-in clinics cater to visitors:

Care Point Medical Centre Commercial Dr (Map p86;
☎ 604-254-5554; 1623 Commercial Dr; 🚌 20);
Downtown (Map pp58-9; ☎ 604-687-4858; 711 W
Pender St; Ⓜ Granville); West End (Map pp68-9;
☎ 604-681-5338; 1175 Denman St; 🚌 5) For additional
locations see www.carepoint.ca.

Stein Medical Clinic (Map pp58-9; ☎ 604-688-5924;
Bentall 5, Suite 188, 550 Burrard St, downtown;
🕒 8am-5:30pm Mon-Fri; Ⓜ Burrard) Appointments
not necessary.

Travel Medicine & Vaccination Centre (Map pp68-9;
☎ 604-681-5656; Suite 314, 1030 W Georgia St, West
End; Ⓜ Burrard) Specializing in travel shots;
appointments necessary.

Ultima Medicentre (Map pp58-9; ☎ 604-683-8138;
Bentall Centre Plaza Level, 1055 Dunsmuir St, downtown;
🕒 8am-5pm Mon-Fri; Ⓜ Burrard) Appointments not
necessary.

Emergency Rooms

Vancouver's emergency rooms include the
following:

BC Children's Hospital (Map p93; ☎ 604-875-2345;
4480 Oak St, Fairview; 🚌 17)

St Paul's Hospital (Map pp58-9; ☎ 604-682-2344;
1081 Burrard St, downtown; 🚌 22) Downtown accident
and emergency hospital.

Vancouver General Hospital (Map p93; ☎ 604-875-
4111; 855 W 12th Ave, Fairview; Ⓜ Broadway-City Hall)

Pharmacies

Vancouver is well stocked with pharmacies,
including the following:

Pharmasave (Map pp58-9; ☎ 604-801-6991; 499
Granville St, downtown; 🕒 7am-8pm Mon-Fri, 9am-
5:30pm Sat, 9am-5pm Sun; Ⓜ Granville)

Shoppers Drug Mart (Map pp68-9; ☎ 604-669-2424;
1125 Davie St, West End; 🕒 24hr; 🚌 6)

MONEY

Prices in this book are given in Canadian
dollars, unless otherwise stated. See p238 for
information on the taxes that may be added
to your bill, p17 for general information on
costs, and the inside front cover for exchange-
rate info.

Paper bills come in $5 (blue), $10 (purple),
$20 (green) and $50 (red) denominations.
Coins include the penny (1¢), nickel (5¢),
dime (10¢), quarter (25¢), 'loonie' ($1) and
'toonie' ($2). Most Canadians do not carry
large amounts of cash for everyday use,

relying instead on electronic transactions:
credit cards, ATMs and direct-debit cards.

ATMs

Interbank ATM exchange rates usually beat
the rates offered for traveler's checks or
foreign currency. Canadian ATM fees are
generally low, but your home bank may charge
another fee on top of that. Some machines
also dispense US currency, if you're planning a trip across the border. ATMs abound
in Vancouver, with bank branches congre-
gating around the business district bordered
by Burrard, Georgia, Pender and Granville
Sts. Drugstores also frequently have ATMs.

Changing Money

You can exchange currency at many bank
branches, which often charge less than the
bureax de change dotted around the city.
Aside from the banks, try Vancouver Bullion &
Currency Exchange (Map pp58-9; ☎ 604-685-1008; 800
W Pender St, downtown; 🕒 9am-5pm Mon-Fri; Ⓜ Granville),
which often has a wider range of currencies
and competitive rates.

Credit Cards

Visa, MasterCard and American Express are
widely accepted in Canada. Credit cards can
get you cash advances at bank ATMs, usually
for an additional surcharge. Be aware that
many US-based credit cards now convert
foreign charges using unfavorable exchange
rates and fees.

NEWSPAPERS & MAGAZINES

24 Hours (www.vancouver.24hrs.ca) Weekday free
commuter paper.

Adbusters (www.adbusters.org) Vancouver is the home of
this globally popular alt-magazine.

Eat Magazine (www.eatmagazine.ca) Regional freebie
food mag.

Georgia Straight (www.straight.com) Alternative weekly
providing Vancouver's best entertainment listings. Free
every Thursday.

Metro (www.metronews.ca/vancouver) Free commuter
daily.

Province (www.theprovince.com) Vancouver's 'tabloid'
daily.

Tyee (www.thetyee.ca) Award-winning online local news
source.

Vancouver Magazine (www.vanmag.com) Upscale lifestyle, dining and entertainment monthly.

Vancouver Review (www.vancouverreview.com) Local literary quarterly for the artsy set.

Vancouver Sun (www.vancouversun.com) Main city daily, with Thursday listings pull-out.

Westender (www.westender.com) Free, quirky downtown listings paper.

Xtra! (www.xtra.ca) Free, gay-oriented, alternative paper, distributed biweekly.

ORGANIZED TOURS

Each of these operators offers at least a couple of tour options, so make sure you check out the full selection before choosing.

Boat Tours

Accent Cruises (Map p89; ☎ 604-688-6625; www .accentcruises.ca; 1698 Duranleau St, Granville Island; dinner cruise $60; ☼ May–mid-Oct; 🚌 50) Popular salmon buffet cruise along the coastlines of English Bay, Stanley Park and Ambleside Beach in West Vancouver. Departures are from Granville Island and it's a relaxing way to spend your evening after a long day spent trawling the sights.

Harbour Cruises (Map pp68-9; ☎ 604-688-7246, 800-663-1500; www.boatcruises.com; north foot of Denman St, West End; adult/child/youth & senior $30/10/25; ☼ May-Oct; 🚌 19) View the city – and some unexpected wildlife – from the water on a 75-minute narrated harbour tour. Tours weave past Stanley Park, Lions Gate Bridge and the North Shore mountains. There's also a 2½-hour sunset dinner cruise (adult/child $75/65), with West Coast cuisine (ie salmon) and live music, plus a long, languid lunch trek to stunning Indian Arm ($65).

Bus Tours

Big Bus (☎ 604-299-0700, 877-299-0701; www.bigbus .ca; adult/child/youth & senior $38/20/35; ☼ year-round) On cold and rainy days, you'll still see passengers huddling together for warmth on the open outer decks of these colorful tour buses – luckily they can also shelter inside if a tempest hits. Stay on for the full 90-minute narrated loop or use your ticket as a hop-on hop-off pass for up to 23 stops around the city. Departures are every 15 to 20 minutes during peak season, and good-value family tickets are $90. A two-day ticket option is also offered for a few dollars more.

Landsea Tours (☎ 604-255-7272, 877-669-2277; www .vancouvertours.com; adult/child from $65/42; ☼ year-round) Landsea's comfortable tours in 24-passenger stretch minibuses attract an older crowd. Treks include a three-hour city highlights tour (adult/child $65/42), departing 9am and 2pm; and a six-hour North Shore and Grouse Mountain tour (adult/child including admission $119/85). Additional guided tours to Victoria or Whistler are offered if you fancy traveling further afield.

Vancouver Eco Tours (☎ 604-290-0145; www .vancouverecotours.com; adult/child/senior $65/55/60; ☼ year-round) Departing from North Van's Lonsdale Quay, this green-themed company takes the emissions out of bus tours with its biofuel vans. Its excellent four-hour trek ambles through the mountain-fringed forests of the North Shore, including highlights such as Deep Cove, Grouse Mountain (entry not included) and Lynn Canyon (with its free suspension bridge). Even better, it also offers a free, shortened version of the tour to introduce its services – see the website for details.

Vancouver Trolley Company (☎ 604-801-5515, 888-451-5581; www.vancouvertrolley.com; adult/child/student & senior $38/20/35; ☼ year-round) This company operates jolly replicas of San Francisco trolley cars (without the tracks), providing a hop-on hop-off service to attractions around the city. The circuit takes 80 minutes and you buy your tickets from the driver – attraction tickets are also sold on board. If you're here in late October, the buses are decorated in spooky Halloween garb, while Christmastime sees a karaoke theme adopted for those who like to ride and sing at the same time. Check the website for discount tickets, especially off-season.

Walking & Cycling Tours

Vancouver offers a good range of guided walking tours, including specific themed treks like the excellent Sins of the City (p74) and the lip-smacking Edible BC market trawl (p88), as well as several intriguing behind-the-scenes tours of everything from breweries to sports stadiums.

Check out these options:

Architectural Institute of British Columbia (☎ 604-683-8588, ext 333; www.aibc.ca; tours $5; ☼ 1pm Tue-Sat Jul & Aug) Local architecture students conduct these excellent one- to two-hour wanders, focusing on the buildings, history and heritage of several key Vancouver neighborhoods. There are six tours in all and areas covered include Gastown, Strathcona, Yaletown, Chinatown and the West End.

Vancouver Food Tour (☎ 778-228-7932; www .vancouverfoodtour.com; tours from $138; ☼ year-round) Led by local food writer Melody Fury, bring your appetite for the 4½-hour Gastown Tasting Tour (from $138), which includes tastings, dinner and a beer in arguably Vancouver's best dining district. An all-day version (from $219), covering additional neighborhoods, is available if you're really hungry. Plans were afoot for Asian, Yaletown and dessert tours during research, so check ahead to see what's on the menu before you arrive.

Vancouver Tour Guys (☎ 604-690-5909; www.tourguys.ca; tours free; ☺ year-round) Travelers on a budget should check in with this friendly operation and its three tours covering Stanley Park, Gastown and Downtown, and the West End and Granville Island. The tours are free but gratuities are highly encouraged ($5 to $10 should cover you). Its schedule is ever-changing, so check the website for the latest itinerary. Booking ahead is also recommended, especially during the summer peak.

Vancouver Urban Adventures (☎ 604-451-1600, 877-451-1777; www.vancouverurbanadventures.com; tours from $25; ☺ year-round) Offering core walking tours of popular Vancouver districts like Gastown, Chinatown and Granville Island, this company also invites you to pedal along on a five-hour city-wide guided cycling trek ($75, including bike) that takes in Stanley Park, the seawall and several must-see neighborhoods – it's the ideal way to spend a sunny day in the city.

Specialty Tours

Harbour Air Seaplanes (☎ 604-274-1277, 800-665-0212; www.harbour-air.com; tours from $99; ☺ year-round) Vancouver is home to the world's largest fleet of floatplane operators and, along with their regular scheduled services (p225), some offer soaring sightseeing tours. Taking off and landing (you'll dive-bomb the water at a rate of knots) is thrilling in itself, but the scenery while you're up there will make you realize just how beautiful this region is. Harbour Air's 20-minute panoramic flight ($99) is great fun and there are additional longer flights depending on your budget.

Sewell's Sea Safari (Map pp54-5; ☎ 604-921-3474; www.sewellsmarina.com; 6409 Bay St, Horseshoe Bay, West Vancouver; adult/child/youth, student & senior $73/43/65; ☺ Apr-Oct; 🚌 250) Head to the marina near Horseshoe Bay to book a seat on a rigid-hulled inflatable for your two-hour, high-speed ride out to sea. With the spray in your face and the wind rattling your sunglasses, keep your eyes open for possible whale-pod sightings – barking seals and soaring eagles are almost guaranteed. It can be a cold and bouncy ride, but visitors are suited up in cushiony red coveralls to absorb some of the bite.

Stanley Park Horse-Drawn Carriages (Map p63; ☎ 604-681-5115, 888-681-5110; www.stanleypark.com; Stanley Park; adult/child/youth & senior $29/16/27; ☺ Mar-Oct; 🚌 19) These narrated, one-hour tours are a leisurely – actually, extremely slow – but informative way to see the park without having to walk. Lumbering Clydesdale and grey shire horses pull the 20-passenger carriages past all the usual park highlights and you'll hear some fascinating tales about the area's history and development. Tours depart from near the information booth, just off the park's W Georgia St entrance.

PASSPORTS & VISAS

Citizens or permanent residents of all countries – including the US – need a passport to enter Canada. Visitors from the US, Scandinavia, European Union and most Commonwealth nations do not need a visa for tourist visits, but citizens of more than 100 other nations do. For further information as well as the latest updated passport and visa rules, see the website of Citizenship & Immigration Canada (www.cic.gc.ca).

A passport and/or visa does not guarantee entry. Proof of sufficient funds or possibly a return ticket out of the country may be required. Visitors with medical conditions may only be refused if they 'might reasonably be expected to cause excessive demands on health and social services' (ie they admit to needing treatment during their stay in Canada).

If you are refused entry but have a visa, you have the right of appeal at the port of entry. If you're arriving by land, the best course is simply to try again later (after a shift change) or at a different border crossing.

POST

Canada Post (www.canadapost.ca) may not be remarkably quick, but it is reliable. The standard (up to 30g) letter and postcard rate to destinations within Canada is 57¢. Postcards and standard letters to the US cost $1. International airmail postcards cost $1.70.

Postal outlets are dotted around the city, many of them at the back of drugstores – look for the blue-and-red window signs. Handy branches:

Canada Post Main Outlet (Map pp58-9; ☎ 604-662-5723; 349 W Georgia St, downtown; ☺ 8:30am-5:30pm Mon-Fri; Ⓜ Stadium-Chinatown)

Howe St Postal Outlet (Map pp58-9; ☎ 604-688-2068; 732 Davie St, downtown; ☺ 9am-7pm Mon-Fri, 10am-5pm Sat; 🚌 6)

Poste restante letters and packages should be addressed as follows:
FAMILY NAME, First Name
c/o General Delivery
349 W Georgia St
Vancouver, BC
V6B 3P7

Poste restante mail will be held for 15 days before being returned. Pick up your mail at downtown's Canada Post Main Outlet. Packages sent to you in Canada will be ruthlessly inspected by customs officials, who will then assess duties payable by you on collection.

RADIO

Around Vancouver, flip the dial to these stations or listen in online before you arrive:

650CISL (650AM; www.am650radio.com) Classic oldies.

Beat (94.5FM; www.thebeat.com) Mainstream pop.

CBC Radio One (690AM, 88.1FM; www.cbc.ca/bc) Canadian Broadcasting Corporation's commercial-free news, talk and music station.

CFRO (102.7FM; www.coopradio.org) Community co-op station where anything goes: storytelling, poetry and contemporary First Nations news.

CITR (101.9FM; www.citr.ca) UBC's station for indie music, news, spoken word and arts.

CKNW (980AM; www.cknw.com) News, traffic, sports and talk.

Fox (99.3FM; www.cfox.com) New rock and chatter.

JACK-FM (96.9FM; www.jackfm.com) Groovy retro rock station.

News 1130 (1130AM; www.news1130.com) News 24/7.

Peak (100.5FM; www.thepeak.fm) Popular mainstream new rock station.

Virgin Radio (95.3FM; www.vancouver.virginradio.ca) Poptastic music station.

SAFETY

Vancouver is relatively safe for visitors. Purse-snatching and pickpocketing do occur, however, so be vigilant with your personal possessions. Theft from unattended cars is not uncommon, so never leave valuables in vehicles where they can be seen.

Persistent street begging is a big issue for many visitors; just say 'Sorry' and pass on if you're not interested and want to be polite. A small group of hardcore scam artists also works the downtown core, preying on tourists by asking for 'help to get back home.' These mostly male reprobates never seem to make it home and the locals roll their eyes when they see them plying their tricks on unsuspecting visitors. Do not engage in conversation with these scammers.

The city's Downtown Eastside area is a depressing ghetto of lives blighted by drugs, prostitution and mental illness. Crime against visitors is rare in this area but you are advised to be vigilant and stick to the main streets, especially at night. You will likely be discreetly offered drugs here by a small-fry pusher or two at some point – just walk on and they won't bother you again.

TAXES & REFUNDS

The former Goods and Services Tax (GST) and Provincial Sales Tax (PST) were merged in BC into the new Harmonized Sales Tax (HST) on July 1, 2010. This means that most items you pay for here will attract an extra charge of 12%, which will be added to your bill when you pay.

Tax rebates for visitors have mostly been discontinued in recent years. However, if you booked your trip as part of a package you may be able to claw back some of the HST paid for your accommodation. Don't hold your breath but check in with the Canada Revenue Agency (☎ 902-432-5608, 800-668-4748; www.ccra.gc.ca /visitors) for the latest information.

TELEPHONE

Local calls cost 50¢ from public pay phones, but it's increasingly difficult to find them in the city – gas stations are usually a good bet if you need one in a hurry. If calling from a private phone, local calls are free – a gratis approach that usually doesn't apply to calls made from hotel rooms.

Most Vancouver-area phone numbers, as well as Whistler and the Sunshine Coast, take the 604 area code, although 778 is increasingly being introduced for new numbers. Dial all 10 digits of a given phone number, including the three-digit area code and seven-digit number, even for local calls. In some instances (eg between Vancouver and Whistler), numbers will have the same area code but will be long-distance; at such times you need to dial 1 before the area code.

Always dial 1 before other domestic long-distance and toll-free (800, 888, 877 etc) numbers. Some toll-free numbers are good anywhere in North America, others within Canada only. International rates apply for calls to the US, even though the dialing code (+1) is the same as for Canadian long-distance calls. Dial 011 followed by the country code for all other overseas direct-dial calls.

Cell Phones

Cell phones use the GSM and CDMA systems, depending on your carrier. Check with your cellular service provider before you leave about using your phone in Canada.

Calls may be routed internationally, and US travelers should beware of roaming surcharges (it can become very expensive for a 'local' call).

Phonecards
Prepaid phonecards for long-distance and international calls can be purchased at convenience stores, gas stations and some post offices. Beware those phonecards that advertise the cheapest per-minute rates, as they may also charge hefty connection fees for each call. Leading local phone company Telus (www.telus.com) offers a range of reliable phonecards available in retail outlets around the city.

TIME
Vancouver is in the Pacific time zone (PST/PDT), the same as the US West Coast. At noon in Vancouver it's the following:

11am in Anchorage

3pm in Toronto

2pm in Chicago

8pm in London

9pm in Paris

6am (the next day) in Sydney

8am (the next day) in Auckland

During Daylight Saving Time (from the second Sunday in March to the first Sunday in November), the clock moves ahead one hour.

TOURIST INFORMATION
The Tourism Vancouver Visitor Centre (Map pp58-9; ☎ 604-683-2000; www.tourismvancouver.com; 200 Burrard St, downtown; ☒ 8:30am-6pm daily Jun-Aug, 8:30am-5pm Mon-Sat Sep-May; Ⓜ Waterfront) is a large repository of resources for visitors, with a staff of helpful advisors ready to assist in planning your trip. Services and info available here include free maps, visitor guides, half-price theater tickets, accommodation and tour bookings, plus a host of glossy brochures on the city and the wider BC region.

TRAVELERS WITH DISABILITIES
Vancouver is an accessible city. On arrival at the airport, vehicle-rental agencies can provide prearranged cars with hand controls,

while accessible cabs are also widely available here and throughout the city, on request.

All TransLink (www.translink.bc.ca) SkyTrain, SeaBus and transit bus services are wheelchair accessible. Check its website for a wide range of information on accessible transport around the region. Also, head to www.accesstotravel .gc.ca for information and resources on accessible travel across Canada.

Guide dogs may legally be brought into restaurants, hotels and other businesses in Vancouver. Many public-service phone numbers and some pay phones are adapted for the hearing impaired. Almost all downtown sidewalks have sloping ramps, and most public buildings and attractions are wheelchair accessible. Check the City of Vancouver's dedicated website (www.vancouver.ca /accessibility) for additional information and resource links.

Other helpful resources:

BC Coalition of People with Disabilities (☎ 604-875-0188, 800-663-1278; www.bccpd.bc.ca) Programs and support for people with disabilities.

Canadian National Institute for the Blind (☎ 604-431-2121; www.cnib.ca) Support and services for the visually impaired.

Western Institute for the Deaf and Hard of Hearing (☎ 604-736-7391; www.widhh.com) Interpreter services and resources for the hearing impaired.

WOMEN TRAVELERS
Vancouver is generally quite safe for women traveling solo, although jogging alone after dark in parks and hanging out late-night in the Downtown Eastside without company is best avoided. See opposite for information on general safety issues for all visitors. Note it is illegal to carry pepper spray or mace in Canada. The Vancouver Women's Health Collective (Map p79; ☎ 604-736-5262; www.womenshealthcollective .ca; 29 W Hastings St, Chinatown; Ⓜ Stadium-Chinatown) provides advice and referrals for health issues as well as free yoga classes. See p233 for a sexual-assault crisis line.

WORK
Non-Canadians generally need a valid work permit to get a job here and obtaining one can be difficult because employment opportunities go to the locals first. However, some jobs are exempt from permit requirements. Also, there is an ongoing shortage of workers in the hotel and hospitality industries in BC

(Whistler is a hot spot for temporary jobs for example), so employers are increasingly looking overseas to fill the gap. Contact potential employers and see if they can help you with the paperwork.

For further information on working in the region – including a list of sought-after professions – visit the website of Citizenship & Immigration Canada (www.cic.gc.ca).

Each year several thousand one- or two-year Working Holiday Program visas are available to New Zealanders and Australians between the ages of 18 and 30 (35 for New Zealand). Competition is stiff, so apply as early as possible. Information and applications for Australians are available at www.whpcanada.org.au; New Zealanders should head to www.dfait-maeci.gc.ca/newzealand.

Run by the Canadian Federation of Students, the popular SWAP Abroad (www.swap.ca) program facilitates working holidays for US and overseas students and people under 30 (sometimes 35). Participants come to Canada from nearly 20 countries, including Australia, France, Germany, New Zealand, the UK and the USA.

Doing Business

Vancouver does brisk business in conventions and trade shows, with the newly expanded Vancouver Convention & Exhibition Centre (Map pp58-9; ☎ 604-689-8232, 866-785-8232; www.vcec.ca; Canada Pl, downtown; Ⓜ Waterfront) hosting hundreds of events annually. Tourism Vancouver (www.tourismvancouver.com) assists business travelers and provides a useful list of suppliers (copying, printing etc) on its website.

Volunteering

If you're interested in volunteering during your visit, contact one of the following local organizations:

Charity Village (www.charityvillage.ca)

Go Volunteer (www.govolunteer.ca)

Volunteer Canada (www.volunteer.ca)

GLOSSARY

Canada Line – new SkyTrain transit line linking the airport to downtown Vancouver

Canucks – usually refers to the Vancouver Canucks National Hockey League team; also a slang term for a Canadian

Downtown Eastside – Vancouver's poorest neighborhood, centered on the intersection of Main and Hastings Sts

First Nations – denotes Canada's Aboriginal peoples; this term is often used instead of Native Indians or Native people

Granville Strip – Granville St nightlife area, located between Robson St and the south end of Granville Bridge

Hollywood North – denoting Vancouver's large film and TV industry

HST – Harmonized Sales Tax on most goods and services; combines the old GST and PST and is currently levied at 12%

Hudson's Bay Company – historic department store chain, referred to as 'the Bay'

loonie – slang term for Canada's one-dollar coin, usually with a loon bird on one side

Lower Mainland – area covering southwestern British Columbia, including Vancouver

Metro Vancouver – new official name for the Greater Vancouver region

North Shore – geographic area encompassing North Vancouver and West Vancouver

SkyTrain – regional rapid-transit train system

toonie – slang term for a Canadian two-dollar coin

BEHIND THE SCENES

THIS BOOK

This 5th edition of *Vancouver* was researched and written by John Lee. John also wrote the 4th edition. The 3rd edition was written by Karla Zimmerman. The guide was commissioned in Lonely Planet's Oakland office, laid out by Cambridge Publishing Management, UK and produced by the following:

Commissioning Editor Jennye Garibaldi

Coordinating Editors Carolyn Boicos, Catherine Burch

Coordinating Cartographer Corey Hutchison

Coordinating Layout Designer Donna Pedley

Managing Editor Melanie Dankel, Bruce Evans

Managing Cartographers David Connolly, Alison Lyall

Managing Layout Designer Celia Wood

Senior Editor Helen Christinis

Assisting Editors Michala Green, Ceinwen Sinclair

Assisting Cartographer Brendan Streager

Cover Research Naomi Parker, lonelyplanetimages.com

Internal Image Research Sabrina Dalbesio, lonelyplanetimages.com

Color Designer Paul Queripel

Indexer Marie Lorimer

Thanks to Jessica Boland, Michelle Glynn, Carol Jackson, Yvonne Kirk, Lisa Knights, Martine Power, Kirsten Rawlings, Averil Robertson

Cover photographs Front top: Plaza of Nations Marina at False Creek Vancouver, Canada, Richard Cummins.
Bottom: Capilano suspension bridge, Vancouver, Canada, Rudy Sulgan

All images are copyright of the photographer unless otherwise indicated. Many of the images in this guide are available for licensing from Lonely Planet Images: www.lonelyplanetimages.com.

THANKS
JOHN LEE

Hearty thanks are due to my friends and family in Vancouver, who likely forgot what I looked like during my beard-growing write-up phase – I almost forgot as well. Thanks also to Jennye at Lonely Planet for this assignment: this is always my favorite title to work on. I'd also like to remember my primary school teacher, Mr Williams, who taught me about the value of working to the best of my ability on all projects. Finally, a tip of the hat to the ever-helpful Tourism Vancouver team…and special thanks to my niece Scarlett, the world's second-best Mousetrap player.

OUR READERS

Many thanks to the travelers who used the last edition and wrote to us with helpful hints, useful advice and interesting anecdotes:

James Attwooll, Stephen Campbell, Jose Ignacio Rojas Gregorio, Colin Guthrie, Philip Hacker, Eryn Lackie, Ashley Longair, Robert Motta, Ami Muranetz, Navida Nuraney, Marisa Reynaldi, Tiffany Soper, Nicole Tebbutt, Sandra Ueltzhoeffer

SEND US YOUR FEEDBACK

We love to hear from travelers – your comments keep us on our toes and help make our books better. Our well-traveled team reads every word on what you loved or loathed about this book. Although we cannot reply individually to postal submissions, we always guarantee that your feedback goes straight to the appropriate authors, in time for the next edition. Each person who sends us information is thanked in the next edition and the most useful submissions are rewarded with a free book.

To send us your updates – and find out about Lonely Planet events, newsletters and travel news – visit our award-winning website: lonelyplanet.com/contact.

Note: We may edit, reproduce and incorporate your comments in Lonely Planet products such as guidebooks, websites and digital products, so let us know if you don't want your comments reproduced or your name acknowledged. For a copy of our privacy policy visit lonelyplanet.com/privacy.

BEHIND THE SCENES

Notes

INDEX

100-Mile Diet 31, 44

A

Abbotsford International
Air Show 15
accommodations 193-204,
see also Sleeping
subindex
airport hotels 204
B&Bs 194
costs 195
Downtown 195-8
Fairview & South
Granville 201-2
Granville Island 201-2
historic sleepovers 196
Kitsilano 202-3
Metro Vancouver 203-4
sustainability 47
taxes 194
tipping 194
University of British
Columbia 202-3
Victoria 213-14
West End 198-200
Whistler 218
Yaletown 200-1
activities 182-8, *see also*
individual activities,
Sports & Activities
subindex
outdoor activity courses
232
air travel
airlines 225
airports 226
climate change 226

floatplanes 225, 237
helicopters 225
scenic tours 237
travel to/from airport
227
Apple Festival 138
aquarium 113
architecture 34-7, *see also*
Sights *subindex*
area codes, *see inside front*
cover
art galleries, *see* Sights
subindex
artists 27
arts 26-34, 169-80, *see also*
Arts *subindex*, cinema,
dance, literature, music,
theater, TV, visual arts
festivals 173
ATMs 235

B

B&Bs 194, *see also* Sleeping
subindex
Bard on the Beach 13-14,
33, 178, 179
Bare Buns Fun Run 15-16
bars, *see also* Drinking
subindex, individual
neighborhoods
bar food 136
baseball 191
BC Place Stadium 192
BC Sports Hall of Fame &
Museum 71
beaches, *see also* Sights
subindex
top 97
beauty salons 189-90, *see*
also Sports & Activities
subindex
beer
microbreweries 152
Vancouver Craft Beer
Week 13
begging 238
bicycling, *see* cycling
bird sanctuary 64
Bishop, John 144
blogs 18, 39
food blogs 140
music blogs 28

shopping & lifestyle
blogs 124
boat travel 226-7
ferries & miniferries
227, **8**
in Vancouver 230
sea safaris 237
SeaBus 230
to/from Vancouver 227
tours 236
books, *see also* literature,
Shopping *subindex*
cookbooks 125, 135
environment 42
history 21
local authors 30
Bowen Island 220-1
breweries, *see also* Drinking
subindex
Granville Island Brewing
88-9
microbreweries 152
bridges, *see* Sights *subindex*
Bright Nights in Stanley
Park 17
Britannia Shipyard 109
Buddhist temple 109-10
Bula, Frances 39
Buntzen Lake 220
Burnaby 106
bus travel
in Vancouver 230
night-bus 230
to/from Vancouver 227-8
tours 236
business hours 231, *see also*
inside front cover
coffeehouses 150
nightlife 162
pubs & bars 150, 231
restaurants 129
shops 112, 231
business travelers 240

C

cafes, *see* Drinking *subindex*
Campbell, Larry 38
campuses, *see* Sights
subindex
Canada Day 14
cannabis legalization
campaign 116

Capilano Suspension Bridge
105
car travel 228-9
parking 228-9
rental 229
Zipcar network 45
Car-Free Vancouver Day
14
carbon offset schemes
226
Caribbean Days Festival
15
Carol Ships Parade of
Lights 17
Carr, Emily 27
castle 212
cathedral 57
Celebration of Light 15
cell phones 238-9
Celticfest Vancouver 13
Cheakamus Lake 215
cheese factory 221, 223
chemists 235
children, travel with 231
attractions 106
Vancouver International
Children's Festival 13
Chinatown 23, 78-81,
79, **5**
drinking 154-6
food 137-8
shopping 118-19
walking tour 80-1
Chinatown Festival 15
Chinatown Night Market
79
Chinese New Year 12
choral music, *see also* Arts
subindex
Choy, Wayson 30
Christ Church Cathedral
57
cinema 31-2, *see also* film
City Farm Boy 46
classical music 170-2, *see*
also Arts *subindex*
climate 231-2
climate change 226
clinics 234-5
clothing, *see also* Shopping
subindex
sizes 117

ARTS

CLASSICAL MUSIC

DANCE

FILM

OPERA & CHORAL

PERFORMING ARTS VENUES

SPOKEN WORD

THEATER

000 **map pages**
000 photographs

GREENDEX

The following businesses and organizations have been selected because they demonstrate active sustainable tourism policies. Some are engaged in conservation or environmental initiatives while others are owned and operated by locals committed to responsible tourism approaches. Sustainable practices garners inclusion in this list for shops and farmers markets, while restaurants listed here are mostly members of the Ocean Wise seafood sustainability drive. Accommodations are only included if they have demonstrated a greater commitment to the environment than simply asking you to reuse your towels. See the Green Vancouver chapter (p41) for more information on making your visit here as ecofriendly as possible.

We want to increasingly develop our sustainable tourism content, so please send us your own on-the-road green discoveries at www.lonelyplanet.com/feedback. In addition, please check out our continuing focus on this subject at www.lonelyplanet.com/responsibletravel.

MAP LEGEND
ROUTES

.... Freeway
.... Primary
.... Secondary
.... Tertiary
.... Lane
.... Unsealed Road
.... One-Way Street

.... Mall/Steps
.... Tunnel
.... Pedestrian Overpass
.... Walking Tour
.... Walking Trail
.... Walking Path
.... Track

TRANSPORT

.... Ferry
.... Metro/SkyTrain

.... Rail
.... Cable Car, Funicular

HYDROGRAPHY

.... River, Creek
.... Swamp

.... Water

AREA FEATURES

.... Airport
.... Beach
.... Building
.... Campus
.... Cemetery
.... Forest

.... Land
.... Mall
.... Market
.... Park
.... Reservation
.... Sports

POPULATION

☼ ... CAPITAL (NATIONAL)
● .... Large City
○ .... Small City

◉ .... CAPITAL (STATE)
● .... Medium City
○ .... Town, Village

SYMBOLS

Information
⑤ .... Bank, ATM
☺ .... Embassy/Consulate
✛ .... Hospital, Medical
ⓘ .... Information
@ .... Internet Facilities
☉ .... Police Station
☉ .... Post Office, GPO

Sights
◳ .... Beach
▣ .... Buddhist
✝ .... Christian
▯ .... Monument
▥ .... Museum, Gallery
● .... Point of Interest

Shopping
▣ .... Shopping

Eating
▥ .... Eating

Drinking
▽ .... Drinking
▭ .... Cafe

Nightlife
▣ .... Nightlife

Arts
▣ .... Arts

Sports & Activities
▣ .... Pool
▣ .... Skiing

Sleeping
▣ .... Sleeping
▲ .... Camping

Transport
▣ .... Airport, Airfield
▣ .... Bus Station
▣ .... Cycling, Bicycle Path
▣ .... Parking Area

Geographic
▣ .... Lighthouse
▣ .... Lookout
▲ .... Mountain, Volcano
▣ .... National Park

Published by Lonely Planet Publications Pty Ltd
ABN 36 005 607 983

Australia (Head Office)
Locked Bag 1, Footscray, Victoria 3011,
☎ 03 8379 8000, fax 03 8379 8111,
talk2us@lonelyplanet.com.au

USA 150 Linden St, Oakland, CA 94607,
☎ 510 250 6400, toll free 800 275 8555,
fax 510 893 8572, info@lonelyplanet.com

UK 2nd fl, 186 City Rd, London, EC1V 2NT,
☎ 020 7106 2100, fax 020 7106 2101,
go@lonelyplanet.co.uk

Printed by Hang Tai Printing Company Ltd,
Printed in China.